A World Trimmed with Fur

A World Trimmed with Fur

WILD THINGS, PRISTINE PLACES,
AND THE NATURAL FRINGES OF QING

Jonathan Schlesinger

STANFORD UNIVERSITY PRESS

STANFORD, CALIFORNIA

Stanford University Press
Stanford, California

Printed in the United States of America on acid-free, archival-quality paper

Library of Congress Cataloging-in-Publication Data

Names: Schlesinger, Jonathan, author.
Title: A world trimmed with fur : wild things, pristine places, and the natural fringes
  of Qing rule / Jonathan Schlesinger.
Description: Stanford, California : Stanford University Press, 2016. | Includes
  bibliographical references and index.
Identifiers: LCCN 2016015575 (print) | LCCN 2016021994 (ebook) |
  ISBN 9780804799966 (cloth : alk. paper) | ISBN 9781503600683 (ebook)
Subjects: LCSH: Luxuries—China—History—18th century. | Luxuries—China—
  History—19th century. | Natural resources—China—Manchuria—History. |
  Natural resources—Mongolia—History. | Restoration ecology—China—
  Manchuria—History. | Restoration ecology—Mongolia—History. | China—Kings
  and rulers—Social life and customs. | China—History—Qing dynasty, 1644–1912.
Classification: LCC DS754.12 .S35 2016 (print) | LCC DS754.12 (ebook) |
  DDC 951/.03—dc23
LC record available at https://lccn.loc.gov/2016015575

Typeset by Thompson Type in 11/14 Adobe Garamond

To Max & Marie

Contents

Acknowledgments

When asked why I wrote this book, and I reflect on what makes this research so vivid and wonderful to me, I come to only one conclusion: I have been fortunate to have learned from great historians and teachers. The sustained, creative, and rigorous support of my mentor Mark Elliott has long stood behind the best in my scholarship, ever since I was his disheveled student. He set the scholarly standard and showed through example how to think, teach, and advise; more than anyone, this book bears his imprint. He once offered a signature lesson on how the tapestry of Qing history was like woven silk: We must study the fringes to understand its construction. The metaphor always stuck.

Others helped enormously along the way as well. Peter Perdue provided inspiration, guidance, and incisive feedback at each stage of the writing process, and my work would not exist without his foundational research. Henrietta Harrison and Michael Szonyi contributed their own careful readings of early drafts and offered honest and provocative feedback as well. Lai Hui-min, too, offered mentorship (and innumerable references and ideas); it was her scholarship that first opened my eyes to the fascinating world of fur, the Uriankhai, and Qing fashion. The late Philip Kuhn provided indispensible vision and support as I was formulating the project.

Generous grants from the American Center for Mongolian Studies Research (ACMS) Fellowship and the Luce Foundation, the Fulbright-Hays Doctoral Dissertation Research Abroad Fellowship, and the Taiwan Fellowship of the Ministry of Foreign Affairs supported three years of research in Mongolia, China, and Taiwan. At Harvard, a Sheldon Fellowship, the Davis Center, the Reischauer Institute, and a Harvard University Presidential Scholarship supported additional research in London, Berlin, St. Petersburg, and Tokyo. A postdoctoral fellowship from the Council on East Asian Studies at Yale supported a generous year in residence in New Haven to complete the manuscript. In Indiana, my work was partially funded by the Office of the Vice Provost of Research at Indiana University Bloomington through the Grant-in-Aid Program and by Indiana University's East Asian Studies Center.

In Ulaanbaatar, Baigalmaa Begzsuren, Enkhee Denkhee, Tuya Myagmardorj, and Brian White at the ACMS provided on-the-ground support and guidance, and Demberelïïn Olziïbaatar and a team of patient archivists made research possible at the National Central Archives. Li Sheng, Ding Yizhuang, and Jia Jianfei provided access, assistance, and invaluable feedback at the Chinese Academy of Social Sciences and the Borderlands Institute in Beijing, and Wu Yuanfeng and Li Baowen helped guide research at the First Historical Archives. In Taipei, Peter Chang, Jane Liau, and Keng Li-chun at the Center for Chinese Studies served as indefatigable sponsors while conducting research at the National Library and Academia Sinica. Chuang Chi-fa was my consummate guide to the Manchu materials at the National Palace Museum. In New Haven, Peter Perdue, Valerie Hansen, and Fabian Drixler made Yale the ideal place to research and write; I never failed to leave a lunch or dinner with them without feeling inspired and invigorated intellectually. Special thanks as well to Kazumi Hasegawa, Seunghan Paek, Abbey Newman, Nicholas Disantis, and Jessica Chin for making the year at the Council for East Asian Studies so fun, productive, and special.

At home in Indiana, Christopher Atwood offered a careful reading of the full manuscript and teased out, as only he could, unnoticed insights, conceptual knots, and unnerving glitches in the transliterated Mongolian. Scott O'Bryan also offered incisive and provocative readings of the text, while pushing me to think anew about environmental history. Lynn Struve too has served as a role model in Bloomington as a historian, teacher, and a member of the community; since my arrival here, she has offered invaluable scholarly and practical advice (while indulging my love of cats). Other colleagues at IU provided inspiration and support as well, including Gardner Bovingdon, Nick Cullather, Peter Guardino, Ke-Chin Hsia, Sarah Knott, Jason Lee, Pedro Machado, Krista Maglen, Michael McGerr, Jason McGraw, Marissa Moorman, Roberta Pergher, Michael Robinson, Kaya Sahin, Eric Sandweiss, Rebecca Spang, Christina Synder, Wang Fei-Hsien, Ellen Wu, and the members of the Eighteenth-Century Studies Group.

Many of the original ideas in the book were tested at the Association for Asian Studies' "Politics of Environment" Workshop in Chicago; special thanks to Michael Paschal, Nancy Peluso, Michael Hathaway, and all other participants for their critical feedback. Early versions of Chapters Two, Three, and Four were presented at the annual meetings of the Association for Asian Studies and the American Society for Environmental History and at talks or seminars at Cambridge University, New York University, University of California–Berkeley, Rutgers, Georgetown, Renmin University, Stanford, Michigan, UBC, and ANU. David Bello, Pär Cassel, Gregory Delaplace, James Delbourgo, Johan Elverskog, Ann Fabian, Hsing You-tien, Caroline Humphrey, John McNeill, Tessa Morris-Suzuki, Tom Mullaney, Micah Muscolino, Oyunbilig, Oyunjargal, Matthew Sommer, Joanna Waley-Cohen, Emily Yeh, and Yeh Wen-hsin all provided fresh perspectives and critical feedback at the forums. While I was still formulating the ultimate direction for the book, Judd Kinzley provided careful readings of the chapters and offered key analytical insights. Other colleagues pushed me forward as well: Brian Baumann, David Brophy, Sakura Christmas, Afton Clarke-Sather, Mette High, Hoong Tak Toh, C. J. Huang, Christopher Leighton, Loretta Kim, Benjamin Levey, Li Ren-yuan, Ellen McGill, Matthew Mosca, Victor Seow, Ying Qing, and Lawrence Zhang all contributed in their own way.

Stanford University Press has been the ideal shepherd for bringing the book to print. Special thanks to Jenny Gavacs, whose feedback added clarity and rigor to the manuscript and who provided encouragement and support at each step of the publishing process. The book also drew enormously from the anonymous reviewers who read the draft manuscript and provided thoughtful, original, and pragmatic comments.

Lastly, I must extend a special heartfelt thank you to Pamela Crossley, my original and longtime mentor, and all the participants in the Dartmouth workshop who helped review this book, especially Peter Perdue, Lillian Li, and Jonathan Lipmann; the book that exists today, to the best of my ability, reflects their provocative readings of the text. Pamela has offered a helping hand and served as an inspiration at every stage of my career. Without her charismatic and committed advising, I would never have discovered my love for Qing history: She still challenges me like no other to think more deeply, globally, and creatively about my research.

If I have learned to experience wonder at all, it is because of my family: my parents, who supported me in all my endeavors (no matter how odd);

my sister, whom I have always looked up to; and my grandparents, who offered perspective with stories, reality checks, and sometimes stiff cocktails. Nikki Marie Skillman helped see the book to completion, too, but her love leaves everything else beautifully inconsequential; she is beyond my acknowledgments. I cannot thank her, my family, and all my advisors, mentors, and colleagues enough for all they have contributed to this book. The shortcomings that remain are entirely my own.

Transcription Conventions

This book uses *pinyin* for all Chinese words and names, the Möllendorff system for Manchu, and the McCune-Reischauer system for Korean. Unfortunately, there is no agreed-upon way of transliterating classical Mongolian. For readability, I have opted to use the new Library of Congress system, except in cases where conventional spellings are more familiar (Chinggis Khan, Kiakhta, and so on); to further enhance readability, I have modified the transcription of a few commonly used Mongolian terms (for example, *aimaġ*, not *aiimaġ*). Intercalary months are marked with an asterisk.

A World Trimmed with Fur

Introduction

In 1886, H. Evan James discovered pristine nature in Manchuria. As he breathlessly reported to the Royal Geographic Society, "The scenery . . . is marvelously beautiful—woods and flowers and grassy glades—and to the lover of nature it is simply a paradise." A glimpse of this world was a glimpse before the Fall: "It was like being transported into the Garden of Eden." Climbing Changbaishan, he recalled,

> We came upon rich, open meadows, bright with flowers of every imaginable colour, where sheets of blue iris, great scarlet tiger-lilies, sweet-scented yellow day-lilies, huge orange buttercups, or purple monkshood delighted the eye. And beyond were bits of park-like country, with groups of spruce and fir beautifully dotted about, the soil covered with short mossy grass, and spangled with great masses of deep blue gentian, columbines of every shade of mauve or buff, orchids white and red, and many other flowers.[1]

The land was a cornucopia of nature. Other European travelers marveled that Manchuria had been "hardly touched by man"; it seemed "uninhabited," having long been "evacuated."[2] A contemporary Russian explorer "encountered such an abundance of fish as he had never before seen in his life. Salmon, trout, carp, sturgeon, husos,[3] shad, sprang out of the water and made a deafening noise; the [Amur] river was like an artificial fish-pond."[4] In the skies, when the salmon and shad made spawning runs, "the swan, the stork, the goose, the duck, [and] the teal" followed them "in numberless flocks."[5] Forests were so thick and untamed one needed a hatchet to cut through them. Gustav Radde, having chopped his way through the Hinggan Mountains, declared after his triumphant assault that "nature in her full virgin strength has produced such a luxuriant vegetation" that it was "penetrated . . . with the greatest trouble."[6] As A. R. Agassiz advertised, "Now that game is rapidly disappearing from most places, except where it is rigidly preserved, few countries offer the sportsman the attractions offered by Manchuria."[7] The forests teemed with wild animals: tigers and bears, elk and boar, foxes and sable. The only order in Manchuria was Nature itself.

Two centuries earlier, in his 1743 *Ode to Mukden*, the Qianlong emperor (r. 1735–1795) celebrated Manchuria's bounty with similar language. Like James, Qianlong was taken by the diversity of native life, the "tigers, leopards, bears, black bears, wild horses, wild asses, [four kinds of] deer, wolves, wild camels, foxes, [and] badgers." He celebrated the lushness of plants (reeds, thatch, water scallion, safflower, knotweed, and so on) and the multitudes of birds (pheasant, grouse, geese, ducks, herons, storks, cranes, pelicans, swallows, and woodpeckers).[8] Yet to Qianlong, Manchuria's generative power did not end with its flora and fauna. Its power touched the human realm: "Established on a grand scale, it promulgates the rule of great kings . . . Such a propitious location will last forever, generation after generation. It surpasses and humbles all [other] places and has united [lands] within and [lands] without."[9] Being himself a "great king" of Manchu descent, Qianlong thus shared something in common with the region's tigers, leopards, and bears. He surrounded himself accordingly with Manchuria's finest things: sable- and otter-fur robes, dishes of steppe mushroom, and hats encrusted with freshwater pearls. There was power in Manchuria's nature.

Both Qianlong and James published their writings because Manchuria seemed unique; its environment and its products stood out in their respective worlds. Both men celebrated the land as a catalogue of resources and a fountain of natural vitality; the land had a creativity unto itself, apparently free from human intervention. And both men understood its nature to be atavistic; the land was uncorrupted by time. Yet where James and his contemporaries saw a land before history, and a landscape divorced from human agency, Qianlong saw Manchuria as a timeless source of sustenance and secular power. For James, Manchuria was another frontier. For Qianlong, it was home: It nurtured civilization like the emperor himself. We may recognize James's vision from similar accounts of Asian, African, and American wilderness. What, though, do we make of Qianlong's vision? Did Manchuria produce kings, or did kings produce Manchuria? What constituted pristine nature in the Qing empire, and how did it come to be?

This book uses Manchu and Mongolian sources to rethink the environmental history of China under Qing rule. China's frontiers, such as Manchuria, occupy an ambiguous position in environmental history: They are a chief topic of research, and yet most sources they produced are utterly ignored. Many have studied frontiers as outlets of agricultural and commercial expansion or as objects of the literary imagination; most have done so from the vantage of the Chinese record and in service of a larger narrative about China. Such approaches miss half the story: The Qing empire's Manchu and Mongolian archives paint an altogether different picture of the frontier from the ones we find in published Chinese accounts. New histories can emerge from a synoptic perspective. We must learn, then, to see both ways across the frontier: There is more to Chinese history than a story about China.

This book reveals the story in particular of the environmental changes Qing Manchuria and Mongolia witnessed in the period from 1760 to 1830, when an unprecedented commercial expansion and rush for natural resources transformed the ecology of China and its borderlands alike. That boom, no less than today's, had profound institutional, ideological, and environmental causes and consequences. Amid the ensuing turmoil, anxieties about the environment and a sense of crisis mounted. Petitions poured into Beijing: Sables, foxes, and squirrels had vanished from forests; ginseng had disappeared from the wild; mushroom pickers had uprooted the steppe; freshwater mussels no longer yielded pearls. The court did everything in its power to revive the land and return it to its original form. It drafted men, erected guard posts, drew maps, registered populations, punished poachers, investigated the corrupt, and streamlined the bureaucracy. It razed ginseng plantations, raided the camps of mushroom pickers, and created territories where no person could enter, kill, or even "spook" wildlife. "Nurture the mussels and let them grow," the emperors ordered. "Purify" the Mongol steppe.

The resulting "purity" of Mongolia and Manchuria was not an original state of nature; it reflected the nature of the state. The empire did not preserve nature in its borderlands; it invented it. The book documents the history of this invention and explores the environmental pressures and institutional frameworks that informed it. To illustrate its unfolding, the book focuses on three events that dominate the archival record: the destruction of Manchurian pearl mussels, the rush for wild mushrooms in Mongolia, and the collapse of fur-bearing animal populations in the borderlands with Russia. Each of these events belonged to a broader spectrum of commodity booms that swept from the Qing borderlands to Southeast Asia and the greater Pacific in the late eighteenth and early nineteenth centuries. By 1800, that is, fur trappers from Mongolia to California were operating in the same world, facing common problems, and meeting a common demand. Such an environmental history becomes evident, however, only with a multilingual and multiarchival approach.

THE CHINA STORY ON THE FRONTIER: FROM EMPIRE TO NATION

In most Chinese history textbooks, the natural world serves as a setting or an original condition; it is a drumbeat of recurring floods, droughts, and plagues, or it is the loess soil from which civilization emerges.[10] In such accounts, China's frontiers are no different. In some cases, frontiers represent, like loess soil, an environment in which Chinese civilization will take root. In this mode of history, frontiers tend to follow a common trajectory, and their distinctiveness progressively vanishes into the past. In other cases, frontiers are perennial; like floods and plagues, they embody timeless limits and perennial threats.

Most scholarship on Manchuria after 1644 treats the region's past like loess soil: It becomes Chinese. Today, Manchuria is a bastion not of nature but of industry; homesteaders cleared its forests long ago for farmland. Most historians no longer even use the word *Manchuria*, and we call the region, more simply, "Northeast China."[11] When and how did Manchuria become Chinese? For most, the answer lies in the historical legitimacy of modern borders: Some argue the Northeast was always Chinese; others that it became so only in modern times. The stakes of the dispute are high— for many they speak to the historical legitimacy of the region's Chinese,

Japanese, Korean, and Russian states—and in studies of the Qing empire's northern borderlands in particular, conflicting claims to territory have left the field fragmented into competing national schools.[12] In terms of China-centered scholarship, scholars make two types of claims. The first is statist: The Qing state, like the Ming and Yuan states before it, *was* China, and thus its boundaries provide a basis for modern claims. The second is nationalist: Modern claims derive not from the presence of the state, but of people. National histories of Manchuria thus have a strong demographic focus.

Such national histories note, for one, that the Qing dynasty's Manchu emperors tried to preserve Manchuria as an imperial enclave and so instituted "policies of closing off" (Ch: *fengjin zhengce*) to restrict Chinese immigration. These policies, however, proved unworkable: Particularly in the eighteenth and nineteenth centuries, land-hungry farmers, pushed by China's enormous demographic and commercial expansion, overwhelmed the imperial infrastructure. In the final decades before its fall, the court recognized a fait accompli: The frontier had become Chinese and thus had to be governed so. The empire collapsed, and the nation-state was born.[13] The story of the Manchurian frontier, in this sense, is similar to that of other frontiers that became part of the modern Chinese nation, including Inner Mongolia, Xinjiang, Tibet, and Taiwan. Its historiography likewise dovetails with accounts of state building in the American West, Australia, the Russian Far East, and other settler frontiers of the same period.[14]

Some of the most productive work on China's environmental history has operated within this "China-centered" paradigm. The framework has allowed us to connect the histories of the interior and borderlands in new ways, while creating common ground for rethinking the global and comparative dimensions of the past.[15] As historians such as Kenneth Pomeranz and Peter Perdue have argued, putting China at the center challenges environmental histories that argue for the stand-alone importance of the Enlightenment, the British economy, or European-centered capitalism in the making of the global environment. We know now, for one, that well before the Opium Wars Qing society was pushing its natural limits.[16] Indeed, a combination of peace, prosperity, and (New World) potatoes allowed for unprecedented commercial and demographic expansion under Qing rule. The changes that ensued were immense. After taking over a millennium to double, between 1700 and 1850 alone the population of the Qing empire nearly tripled. At the same time, the acreage of cultivated land doubled, as settlers from the agricultural heartlands migrated into new wetlands, highlands, and borderlands at the edges of the empire.[17] To what degree did the Qing state align itself with this frontier expansion? For many historians, that has become the question. The answer requires a thesis about the nature of the state: Did the court support pioneering settlers and attempt to integrate the polity through a "civilizing mission," as in European colonial empires, or did it back native claims to land and defend internal pluralism? Did China belong to a larger zeitgeist of "developmentalism" in the early modern world?[18]

Embedded in China-centered histories are key but problematic assumptions that wed national identity to natural environment. Too often, wilderness represents the natural border of the Chinese nation and state; it is the point where the dynamism of the core can no longer support the extension of political control.[19] Agriculture accordingly serves as shorthand for Sinicization, wild forests and the steppe as outposts of native life. Even in critiques of these accounts, the alignment of China with agriculture and development usually remains in place. In some nationalist Mongol scholarship, for example, Chinese merchants and farmers are alien minorities, and Mongols are the majority, grounded in the land and its values: The terms of the debate are the same, but the moral framework is reversed. This "antidevelopmentalist" scholarship has repackaged Mongol and minority folk traditions as a type of historical environmentalism; scholars are mining tradition for solutions to environmental crises in much the same way as some American environmentalists, who idealize the Native Americans' relationship with the land, and prewar German environmentalists, who emphasized the rootedness of the German *volk*.[20] National histories continue to structure environmental ones.

FROM NATION TO EMPIRE: A CLOSER LOOK AT THE QING

Although useful in some contexts and time scales, the "developmentalist" narrative of Chinese environmental history poses critical problems in others. For one, not all frontiers were equal in the Qing period. State policies represented complex imperial hierarchies. "Native officials" (Ch: *tusi*) in the southwest, for example, had a relatively limited stature and significance at court, and the court increasingly pursued civilizing missions in the region.[21] The context was radically different in Mongolia and Manchuria: Mongol

and Manchu bannermen did not need civilization; they defended civilization. Sitting at the apex of the imperial order, their classical ways of life
(pastoralism and hunting) were instead promoted and protected, and assimilation was discouraged.[22] Pluralism, if not equality, was the norm in Qing
Inner Asia: Chinese language and institutions governed the Chinese interior; Mongolian institutions, Mongolia; and Tibetan institutions, Tibet.[23]

Migration and land reclamation are thus important stories, but they are
not the only ones: Each frontier was also a homeland, and each homeland
had its own dynamic history. As in accounts of the American West, when
we frame Chinese settlers as the sole agents of change, Manchus, Mongols,
and other indigenous people of the frontier tend to become undifferenti-
ated. In some accounts, Manchus and Mongols disappear altogether. Their
land becomes a "vacuum," and its environment becomes a wilderness peculiar to settler colonialism: "wilderness in its ideal form . . . free of people," with territories "empty and wild so that anyone can come to use and
claim them."[24] Yet farmers never expanded into a vacuum, and nowhere was
the land unclaimed. The Qing court, moreover, cared about local claims.
When we misconstrue the nature of Chinese frontier, we thus not only
skew aspects of a regional history but also blind ourselves to the nature and
structure of imperial power as a whole.

Recognizing the plurality of Qing rule, and taking the Qing empire seriously as an empire, have been at the heart of much recent Qing history.
Historians have uncovered how efforts to define, delimit, and maintain ethnic groups—such as Manchus, Chinese, and Mongols—were woven into
the ideological and institutional fabric of the empire.[25] Indeed, as Manchus,
the emperors considered the maintenance of ethnic and regional difference
to be central to the imperial project, both to preserve their position as conquest elite and to consolidate expansion. Questions of identity were inseparable from the institutionalization of the imperial hierarchy: The more
privilege lost its distinctive marks, the more the court strove to uphold and
define it. The Qing empire, in this sense, was like other empires: Territorially large states engaged in "self-consciously maintaining the diversity of
people they conquered and incorporated."[26] It was not, however, the same
thing as "China": Neither the nation nor the civilization map onto an entity
ruled by Manchus and simultaneously legitimated with Confucian, Ching-
gisid, and Tibetan Buddhist ideologies.[27]

Manchuria and Mongolia in particular held a special place within the
imperial order. In part their special stature was strategic. They had value,

first, as military buffers between neighboring states, such as Russia and Korea, while also providing seemingly ideal terrain for soldiers to train and hone their skills as warriors and men. For this reason, emperors had cause to maintain a northern "wilderness" (Ma: *bigan*): The denser the forest, the stronger the defensive deterrent.[28] Manchuria and Mongolia also had unique stature as the homelands of the Manchus, the ethnic group to which the emperors belonged, and the Mongols, who had unique historical and personal ties with the court.[29] The emperors took pride in their origins in the Manchu homeland.[30] Ordinary Manchus celebrated the ancestral homeland too in literature, from popular folktales to poetry, and in their material culture, from fur clothing to distinct foods and medicines, such as elk tail and wild ginseng. The court, in turn, codified and promoted Manchu and Mongol identity through segregation, sumptuary laws, mandatory language instruction, and special schooling. It likewise took steps to militarize, monopolize, and conserve the natural frontier in its image. Movement into, or even through, Manchuria or Mongolia was strictly monitored and regulated, and both frontiers ultimately came under the administration of military institutions: the military governors in Manchuria and the Mongol banner system in Mongolia. Reflecting the multiethnic character of the state, there was never a single governing language.

To understand identity and ideology, then, the field is increasingly turning to not only sources in Chinese but also to materials written in the court language, Manchu, and regional languages like Mongolian.[31] Scholars of the Qing empire's northern frontiers in the PRC already have published significant works using the Manchu and Mongol archives since the 1980s, as have scholars in Mongolia, Taiwan, Japan, the United States, and elsewhere. Yet most studies of Qing frontiers continue to rely on published Chinese-language accounts, such as the *Veritable Records*, local gazetteers, and the diaries of exiles.[32] The results of such studies have proved to be limited, as they only can say so much: In both Mongolia and Manchuria, an extreme minority of archival documents were ever written or translated into Chinese until the second half of the nineteenth century. In the case of Outer Mongolia, for example, only trade registers and travel permits for merchants were consistently in Chinese; local officials wrote in Mongolian, and the region's highest officials—the military governor in Uliasutai and imperial representative in Khüree (modern Ulaanbaatar)—used Manchu to communicate with Beijing.

Given the structure of the state, Qing rule is thus indecipherable without a multilingual approach. The court intentionally never translated whole genres of state documents on the frontiers, such as confidential military communications.[33] When Manchu-language memorials were translated, their nuance and tone was often lost. Qing writers and translators elided or transformed the meanings of Manchu words and phrases in Chinese, as Manchu terms and styles could lack easy analogues. Translation, that is, was a fundamental interface through which the Qing empire was integrated; the unity of its disparate realms was structured around such choices of translation.[34] It is only through the study of the extensive non-Chinese materials, however, that the peculiar lens of the Chinese sources is revealed as a historical reflection of empire.[35] By recovering such sources, we might also humanize voices once relegated to the realm of "birds and beasts."

Following this logic, research for this book has relied heavily on Manchu- and Mongolian-language materials held at the Mongolian National Central Archive (MNCA) in Ulaanbaatar, the First Historical Archive (FHA) in Beijing, and the National Palace Museum (NPM) in Taiwan. In Ulaanbaatar, the Manchu and Mongolian records of the office of the imperial representative in Khüree (the "*ambans*") and the military governor in Uliasutai served as central pillars of the research (see Figure I.1).[36] In Beijing, two additional Manchu-language sources proved invaluable: the Accounts of the Imperial Household Department (Ch: *Neiwufu zouxiaodang*) and the Copies of Manchu Palace Memorials of the Grand Council (Ch: *Junjichu Manwen lufu zouzhe*).[37] Taken together, the archival record presents a fuller, more detailed, and more complex picture of the frontiers; allows us to triangulate among texts; and challenges us with perspectives lacking from conventional accounts. It is not too much to say that without these documents it would be impossible to reconstruct the story that is told in these pages.

From the vantage of these documents, and with the insights of a multilingual and multiarchival approach, does the history of Qing frontiers appear different? We have discussed two distinct but productive fields of inquiry: The first delves into commercial expansion in the Chinese interior and the problem of resource depletion; the second investigates how the Qing empire institutionalized ethnic and territorial distinctions. Both processes were simultaneous. How, then, were they related? How do we make sense of the economic, environmental, and political geographies of the Qing empire?

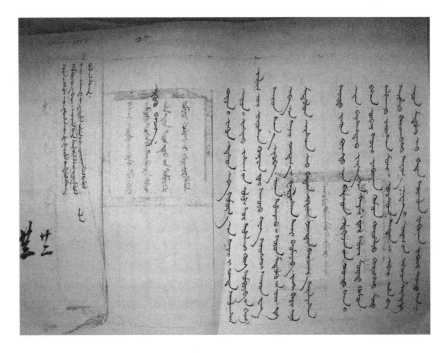

Figure I.I. The Manchu–Mongolian Archive. A typical Mongolian-language document sent to the *amban*'s office in Khüree. On the far left, the document's cover has a clerical synopsis in Manchu, and filing numbers in Chinese by another brush below it.

SOURCE: National Central Archives, Ulaanbaatar.

BETWEEN PEOPLE AND PLACES: AN ENVIRONMENTAL HISTORY OF THINGS

We might begin with the great catalogues of objects and commodities so ubiquitous in Qing poetry, travelogues, and the imperial archives alike: In the Qing world, to know the frontier, or any place, was to know its products. And products were everywhere. In the eighteenth century, China's prodigious commercial expansion and the consolidation of the Qing empire brought an unprecedented volume and diversity of goods to consumers.[38] Even for those who had never traveled, a world of goods was at hand: Scholars studied them in guides, gazetteers, *material medica*, and personal accounts; ordinary consumers inspected them in the marketplace. Material objects mattered in early modern China: People thought, wrote, and cared about commodities more than ever before.[39]

Markets, in turn, helped define places. By the late eighteenth century, merchants from Inner Asia to the Pacific had oriented themselves toward the Chinese interior. Close to the heartland, grains and bulk items dominated trade. Further afield, high-end luxury items were paramount: swallows' nests and gold from Borneo, sea cucumber from Oceania, turtle shells from Sulawesi, sea otters from California, sandalwood from Hawaii, jades from Xinjiang and Burma, sable furs from Russia and the northern borderlands, mushrooms from Mongolia, ginseng and pearls from Manchuria. Facing unprecedented abundance, scholars, consumers, and shop owners found themselves coining new words for once exotic products; the lexicon of earlier times simply could not account for the bounty.

Qing documents accordingly focus not only on people and places but on things. Especially in regions beyond the agricultural core, high-end commodities loomed large in the imperial gaze. From Manchuria to Xinjiang to Yunnan, state finances, legal precedents, and anxieties about crime often centered around high-end commodities such as ginseng, pearls, fur, deer horn, jade, and copper. In some cases, the court claimed a monopoly on such goods through a "tribute" system. In others, commodities provided a logic for Qing rule that transcended territorial and constituent boundaries. Indeed, when we take commodities as our starting point, we discover places and subjects that do not fit easily into any conventional ethnic category or territory at all.

Handlers of commodities included people who identified not only as Mongols, Manchus, or Chinese, but as Uriankhai, Ula, Solon, and Daur. Too many of the latter types of people are ignored in conventional histories; they do fit easily into any popular model of Qing history. Qing writers found them confounding as well, and so reduced them to types of Mongol or Manchu. We should not follow suit. Just as the American frontier was not comprised of "whites" and "Indians" but of a complicated matrix of distinct groups and polities, so too was the world of the Qing.

Unconventional geographies emerge as well when we pursue a history of commodities.[40] Some goods, like fur, traveled on global circuits: Producers like the Uriankhai and Oroncon were enmeshed in networks that extended from Beijing to Lake Khövsgöl, the Amur delta, Sakhalin Island, Siberia, Hokkaido, Alaska, and even Baja California. Others, like mushroom and ginseng pickers, served local and regional markets. Yet whether global or local in scale, high-end commodity trade and production proved central to the business of everyday life and the work of empire: Increasingly, the most intimate contact with the wider world came in the form of a migrant mushroom picker, a fur trader, or a soldier razing your ginseng farm.

Since Owen Lattimore, scholars of the Great Wall frontier have emphasized its material dimensions; above all, Lattimore argued, the frontier was an effect of economic specialization; it was less the point where China met Mongolia than where the sown world met the steppe.[41] Provocatively, William Cronon converged on a similar conclusion for the American frontier, arguing that it too represented a spatial projection of market dynamics.[42] Whether in Beijing or Chicago, the farther one lived from an urban center, the more production favored goods with low transportation costs and high values. In ideal conditions, then, the limits imposed by transportation costs yielded concentric belts of land use around major urban centers: first a belt devoted to agriculture, as the harvest is difficult to transport, then a belt devoted to ranching or pastoralism, and finally a distant belt producing the lightest, most movable goods, such as wild herbs and furs.[43] In this fashion, a predictable sequence from trapping, to herding, to farming, to urban commerce can represent less a teleology of development than a description of synchronous responses to commercial growth.

Such commercial approaches to Inner Asia can overstate the dependence and orientation of the steppe toward China, as Inner Asian political and commercial life was often more autonomous and complex than Chinese sources might suggest.[44] Yet the focus on material exchanges allows us to see how environmental concerns and commodity politics might come to overlap. It also suggests how the expansion of markets had unique consequences in the even most distant peripheries, from the oceans producing whale oil and cod to the mountains yielding musk and wild medicine.[45] No place, no matter how obscure, was left untouched.

ON NATURE

Ultimately, when the markets for high-end commodities boomed, the nature and structure of imperial power shaped the response. Qing observers were anxious about material changes happening before their eyes: the raking away of mussel beds, the uprooting of the steppe, the hunting of animals to near extinction. To the Qing court, it seemed where the world was not being destroyed, it was being perverted: Squirrel fur was made to look like sable; cultivated ginseng was represented as wild; Mongols, Manchus, and

Chinese were "mixed up in chaos." None of these alterations seemed natural; all of them seemed deviations from an original state. Yet recreating ideal subjects, territories, and landscapes was difficult—and often beyond the capacity of the Qing state. It seemed to demand, on one hand, the manipulation of physical environments: creating zones where hunting was illegal, instituting moratoriums on resource exploitation, or destroying artificial ginseng fields. It also called for enhanced discipline: conducting trials, cashiering bureaucrats, punishing poachers, and repatriating undocumented workers back to their (purported) homelands. The Qing court pursued this work on both the environmental and human fronts, and it is through this work that this book finds an increasingly defined, institutionalized, and politically charged world of "nature" in the Qing.

It is impossible to map the English word *nature* onto Qing discourse, and it is not the intention of this book to do so. The word is unusually multifaceted. It can mean the Nature of all of things—that which has been since Creation and always will be—or, more humbly, it can suggest local and contextual states: natural foods, wild places, untamed hearts. As Raymond Williams famously argued, *nature* is "perhaps the most complex word in English language." Yet efforts to distinguish between quintessentially "Western" and Chinese attitudes toward nature have underlain much Western philosophical and historical discourse since at least the sixteenth century.[46] "Nature," according to this view, is a notion peculiar to the West; it is a product of Western Enlightenment, capitalism, science, or Romanticism.[47] In Asian studies, conversely, many agree that modern or Western understandings of "nature" did not exist in Chinese until the late nineteenth century, when they were imported from Europe and Japan. Although China's intellectual history in particular points to fascinating points of comparison with West's, nature as such did not animate minds; diverse and situational concepts of heaven, *qi*, and *fengshui* governed thought instead.[48]

Through a close reading of Qing documents, this book puts these claims to the test and shows that amid the upheaval of the early nineteenth century the Qing world imagined a distinct vision of pristine nature. This Qing invention of "nature" was less metaphysical and lexical than narratological and ideological. Nature often implies a story: To know whether something is natural requires knowing its original state and subsequent history. How was it created? Where did it come from? Has someone modified it, or is it free from human alterations? When we assert that natural landscapes are primordial, or describe a territory as virgin wilderness, we make claims about the past and our power to create anew.[49] Such questions about origins and alterations mattered tremendously in the Qing: They served as arbiters of moral, aesthetic, political, and commercial value.[50] There was no one word for "nature" in Qing China; there were, however, congruent narratives about who we are, where we come from, and how the material world changes about us. The environmental crises of the boom years made these questions of essence and origins pressing and imbued them with new meaning. The demands of the multiethnic empire structured their solution: Those advocating for a strong imperial response promoted the idea that the Manchu and Mongolian homelands were once unspoiled and pristine and acted to restore their natural states; poachers, collaborators, and the corrupt claimed and acted otherwise. In the archives, we can witness this imperial vision of untouched nature at the moment of its creation.

The Qing vision overlaps with a nostalgic sense of "nature" that emerged in English in the late eighteenth century: the sense we use today to describe an unspoiled landscape.[51] This nature resonates with what William Cronon has called the "wrong" nature: an ideal of uncorrupted realms, divorced from human history, that has long animated environmental thought in the United States.[52] Indeed, led by historians such as Cronon, we have come to recognize that this "nature" is itself artificial; on closer inspection no environment lacks a human history, and no dimension of our humanity is divorced from the material and biological sides of life. The natural world informs our own; we are all, in this sense, "hybrids."[53]

At its core, environmental history challenges human–nature dichotomies and finds ways to transcend them: It can show the profound impacts humans have had on past environments; reveal how we are immersed in a larger ecology like other creatures; or explore the ideologies that shape our perceptions of the nonhuman world. By doing so, environmental history allows us to question persisting premises: that humankind progresses to a mastery over nature, that some people are closer to nature than others, that some places are more pristine. Led by scholars such as Mark Elvin, one of the great contributions of "China-centered" historiography has been to demystify Chinese views toward the natural world, challenge Orientalizing scholarship, and find common ground for cross-cultural comparisons.[54] Newer work by scholars such as David Bello has begun to see Chinese "developmentalism," in turn, within a broader matrix of environmental practices across the Qing empire.[55] Ultimately, if we are to transcend entrenched distinctions and build more rigorous frameworks for understanding the environmental history of China, we must more fully account for the contested, plural, and variable dimensions of China's past. This book turns, then, to a wider, more complex world: not to China but to the greater Qing empire.

CHAPTER SUMMARY

The book has four chapters. Chapter One investigates the timing and ideological dimensions of growing consumer demand for frontier resources. Chapters Two, Three, and Four examine production zones transformed by the resource rushes in the late eighteenth and early nineteenth centuries. Manchuria, where the rivers ceased to produce pearls; Mongolia, where mushroom pickers uprooted pastoral life on the steppe; and the borderlands with Russia, where the fur trade destroyed fur-bearing animal populations. In each case, Qing documents reveal how, through congruent processes, all three regions of the Qing empire became at once ethnic homelands, administrative territories, and environmentally "pure." Each chapter analyzes the networks that underlay the great resource rushes, the perceptions of environmental crisis they produced, and the efforts to reestablish the original nature of the effected territories.

Before we visit the mussel beds, the mushroom-picking fields, and the fur-trapping zone, to understand what they shared in common, and to begin to assess the stakes of their environmental ruin, we must start in Beijing. We can appreciate the Qing invention of nature best if we approach it first as an emperor or poet might, in the most intimate of ways: as the pelt on the back, the mushroom on the plate, and the jewel on one's winter hat.

ONE

The View from Beijing

"Ah, it is lamentable! It has been over a hundred years since China fell but, remarkably, the mode of dress is still the same as before the downfall. It has come down through actors in the theater."[1] So mused Pak Chiwŏn (1737–1805), a Korean polymath and satirist, who visited China in 1780 and realized, to his horror, that there were but two types of men dressing in a civilized manner: Koreans and period actors. Everyone else in China dressed rudely, like barbarians, in furs. He had come from Seoul to pay tribute to the Qing emperor, Qianlong (r. 1735–1795). Yet the emperor himself seemed to dress the part of a barbarian ruler: He not only wore furs but mandated others at court do so as well. Indeed, when the diplomacy was concluded, Qianlong sent Pak Chiwŏn home with a signature token of Qing generosity: sable pelts. To be Manchu was to wear fur, and, by the late eighteenth century, not only Manchu elites wore it; Chinese elites did so as well.

Pak Chiwŏn knew something had changed: Prior to the Qing conquest, one could see the difference between Manchus and Chinese. Their bodies were distinct: Chinese men grew out their hair; Manchu men wore the queue.[2] Chinese women bound their feet; Manchu left them natural. Their clothes differed as well. Manchu elites wore fur; Chinese wore silk. Manchus wore riding boots and jackets cut with "horse-hoof" sleeves; Chinese elites dismissed equestrian fashions.[3] By the eighteenth century, 100 years later, the external marks of difference had begun to vanish: One could not so easily tell a Manchu from a Chinese by their looks.[4] In part, this shift in material culture reflected the Manchus' gradual assimilation to life in Beijing; in part, it reflected the fact that, for Chinese elites, furs no longer marked a Manchu sensibility but a broader imperial one.

Indeed, a sea change occurred in eighteenth-century China: Frontier products like fur became markers of elite Chinese fashion. By 1800, visitors to Beijing marveled at what the city had to offer: marten and ermine jackets, steppe mushrooms from Mongolia, freshwater pearls from Manchuria, vendors of game meat, men and women in "horse-hoof" cuffs, and sometimes live elephants, tigers, and bears. In the Ming period (1368–1644), no Chinese word existed for products such as "marten" and "ermine." In the Qing, connoisseurs, pawnshop owners, and the court filled in the blanks: Real knowledge of the marketplace demanded not only a new vocabulary but new stories about the meaning and provenance of such products. Faux furs, farmed ginseng, and imitation steppe mushrooms flooded the streets, but consumers wanted the real thing: undyed, uncultivated products from unvarnished frontiers.

From the mid-eighteenth century, as the following chapters will show, such sensibilities and shifts in consumption helped transform the empire's frontiers. To understand that process, however, we must begin in the imperial center first. Critically, the stories people told about frontier products dovetailed with stories they told about each other: Qing subjects were making sense of their place in the empire, of who should rule, of history, and of untouched nature.

THE MEASURE OF THINGS

It is easy to take for granted how the objects of our lives mark the passing of time. Technology and design are indicative of the age, of course, as are fashion and materiality. It is not only the form of things that marks time, moreover: Their variety and quantity are telling, too. Yet looking back we can only generalize so much: To be without the latest technologies or fashions, or to lack material wealth, is hardly atavistic, and our material legacy, no less than our written one, is neither simple nor one directional. Diversity and inequality have been the norm.

Yet, historiographically, a generalization that seems to hold is that the amount of things in our lives has been growing since the sixteenth century, particularly in centers of commerce and production, such as in China. From the late fifteenth century onward, Ming China had flourished. Consumption surged, markets grew, land use intensified, and industries and agriculture expanded to new frontiers. People in China produced and consumed as many things, or more, as those in Western Europe.[5] Compared to earlier periods in Chinese history, people in the late Ming had more choice and owned more than ever. The luxury consumer had access to products from throughout the Ming empire and from throughout the greater region: wools and felts from the Mongol steppe, musk from Tibet, deerskins from Taiwan, silver from Japan, and ginseng from Korea. After 1571, with the establishment of peace with Altan Khan, who ruled in today's Inner Mongolia, the pace of trade with Inner Asia only increased. That same year, with the founding of Spanish Manila, products from the Americas, too, became accessible via the galleon trade: Silver from Mexico and Potosí came to serve as a new basis for currency and taxation; tobacco smoking went viral; farmers began to plant potatoes, corn, and chili peppers. The global age had begun.[6]

As consumption accelerated, older markers of status grew less important. It became difficult to gauge someone's status simply by looking at him or her: "Nowadays . . . the very servant girls dress in silk gauze, and the singsong girls look down on brocaded silks and embroidered gowns."[7] To maintain their distinction, elites turned to connoisseurship. Guides for cultured living, such as *A Treatise on Superfluous Things* (*Zhangwu zhi*), became bestsellers, offering advice on what the proper gentleman should buy and collect; what made one civilized, such works suggested, was in part a function of what one consumed. As Timothy Brook has shown, maintaining high status required purchasing not just a Ming vase but acquiring the proper Japanese table to place it on and putting the appropriate number of flowers inside ("any more than two stems and your room will end up looking like a tavern").[8]

When the Ming dynasty collapsed in 1644 and the Manchus marched on Beijing, they seemed to belong to a different world. They looked nothing like the people they conquered; rather then dressing like elites, they appeared like "barbarians" (Ch: *hu*). Other differences stood out. They spoke and wrote in a foreign language. Their men shaved their hair in the front and let it grow in the back into a long ponytail (the "queue"). Their women refused to bind their feet and so kept them natural. Their aristocracy rode horses, celebrated warrior culture, and wore furs and freshwater pearls. For all these reasons, European witnesses to the Qing conquest described the Manchus as accessible and natural: "They rejoice to see Strangers; they no way like the grimness and sourness of the Chinese gravity, and therefore in their first abords they appear more human."[9] The Manchus inspired the opposite reaction in Ming loyalists. Some died rather than become their subjects: Wen Zhenheng, the writer of *Superfluous Things*, committed suicide by starvation in 1645 after the Qing conquest of Suzhou.[10]

For their own part, the Manchus intended to look different. The early Qing court worked to win over as many loyalists as possible, and it adopted much of the governing language, institutions, and dress of the Ming court before it. Yet it also attempted to keep Manchus distinct, and although the court embraced classical Chinese political traditions, it simultaneously promoted certain Manchu ones as well. To become Chinese was taboo: The court sponsored organized hunts to encourage proper Manchu values and military élan, and it disciplined Manchus who lacked the required skills in archery, horsemanship, and the Manchu language. In time, as Manchus assimilated, the Qing court under the Qianlong emperor (r.1735–1795) would demand that Manchus compile and submit written genealogies to establish their line of descent. Through such efforts, it was hoped, the Manchus could preserve their unique "Manchu Way." Those who most embodied it were the best at resisting the luxury and decadence of urban commercial life: Like unbound feet, the "Manchu Way" was unadorned, rustic, and "pure" (Ma: *gulu* or *nomhon*; Ch: *chun* or *pu*).[11]

The very fact that the Manchus rose to conquer China reveals, of course, that they were hardly so simple. Manchuria, as much as China, participated in the global moment: like their Chinese neighbors, the people of Manchuria, too, had unprecedented options as consumers by the late sixteenth and early seventeenth centuries, and they too smoked tobacco, traded for silver, and used cannons. The Manchurian economy turned on exports and was similar in this sense to other regions that boomed in the "silver belt" around Ming China, from Mongolia to Taiwan.[12] From as early as the fifteenth century, long-distance fur trade had grown, and Manchuria's southern border regions had become home to merchants and intermediaries that connected

Ming and Chosŏn consumers with trappers in Siberia, Sakhalin, and Outer Manchuria.[13] The ginseng trade was even more lucrative than fur. Nicola Di Cosmo estimates that perhaps one-quarter of all silver imports from Japan and the New World found their way to Manchuria and the early Qing courts through ginseng purchases alone.[14] Trade in high-end commodities, in turn, helped finance the rise of agriculture, which expanded in the sixteenth century to the point, as one historian put it, that "no field was left unplowed" in the south. At the same time, the region witnessed the growth of local markets and, by 1599, the creation of the first iron foundries.[15] The Manchus were neither so simple nor unusually rustic: They were farmers, merchants, trappers, smelters, and soldiers.

The founder of the Qing imperial family, Nurhaci (1559–1626), drew from this economic and cultural diversity in his rise to power. The "Manchuria" of his time was notably diverse: It included myriad clans of Jurchens, who became the foundation of the later Manchu people, as well as Mongols, Chinese, and Koreans. Between 1599 and 1613, Nurhaci successfully incorporated peoples today who are largely forgotten: the Ula, Hada, Hoifa, and Khalkha in the watershed of the Sunggari River; the people known as "Hūrha" and "Warka" farther to the east. By 1616, through military campaigns, marriage alliances, and careful diplomacy, Nurhaci had consolidated control over the border region between the Ming and Chosŏn states. That year, he announced the founding of the "Later Jin" dynasty, in homage to the first Jin dynasty (1115–1234), a medieval Jurchen state from which he claimed descent. In 1635, Nurhaci's son, Hong Taiji (1592–1643), proclaimed that all Jurchens would henceforth be known as "Manchus," and in 1636 he changed the dynasty's name to the Da Qing, literally the Great Purity, from Chinese. The year after his death, the Ming emperor committed suicide, Qing armies crossed the Great Wall, and Qing rule in China began, though it would take almost four decades of further conflict to consolidate control.[16]

RUSTIC ROOTS AND THE QING COURT

We thus can imagine two Manchus. The first, sponsored by the court and central to the Manchu's own sense of identity, draws from the idea of Manchu difference and emphasizes the recovery of a singular and timeless "Manchu Way." The second, reconstructed by later historians, emphasizes the Manchus' place in the larger early modern world, their cosmopolitan connections to greater Northeast Asia, and their adaptability, dynamism, and variability. The Qing court itself reflected the double image, one natural and one historical. The emperors lived as lavish consumers amid incredible opulence, in the center of the largest city in the world, surrounded by dazzling architecture, silks and satins, astrolabes, clocks, and books written in Manchu, Chinese, Tibetan, and Mongolian. Yet amid its opulence, the court also presented itself as the epitome and embodiment of rustic and natural living.[17]

In homage to their Manchu roots, the emperors hunted. The Kangxi emperor (r. 1661–1721) personally shot countless stags and deer, 135 tigers, twenty bears, twenty-five leopards, twenty lynx, ninety-six wolves, and 132 boar; we know about his hunting prowess because literati cited and republished his kill tally throughout the Qing.[18] Kangxi's grandson, the Qianlong emperor, gained fame at age eleven for (supposedly) standing down a charging bear that his grandfather had wounded with a musket.[19] The court established a hunting reserve north of Beijing, in Mulan, and summered in its forests each year. There, they rode on horseback, led sprawling, thousand-man hunts, slept in yurts, and enjoyed the splendors of nature. Although they understood hunting as good training for war and rule, they also appreciated its health and psychological benefits. It was always best to be outside. As Kangxi wrote: "In spring and summer the little ones should play outside in the garden. There's no need to stop them. Don't keep them sitting around on the verandah."[20]

Thus, amid lacquer and silks and others signs of opulence, Nurhaci sat in a throne crafted from stag antlers and used tiger and bearskins as decoration.[21] The emperors likewise reserved a special place on the menu for game meats. The court consumed delicacies from every region of the empire, matching a taste for wild Manchurian honey with an urbane sophistication for Chinese cuisine, Mongol liquors, and Central Asian melons. Yet wild game was best. Before the Qing conquest of Beijing, imperial chefs served tiger, bear, roe deer, elk, mountain goat, boar, wild duck, and pheasant; recipe books record how palace staff cleaned and cut the meat into big hunks, then prepared it in stews of sea salt, soy sauce, green onion, ginger, Sichuan peppers, and star anise.[22] As Wu Zhengge, historian of imperial dining and Manchu foods, explains, "This way of cooking was a little savage, but it expressed the ruggedness, bravery, and straight-forward nature of the Manchu nation's traditional culture."[23] It also reflected ideas about Manchu health. The Kangxi emperor was typically adamant in this regard: "The people of the North are strong; they must not copy the fancy diets of the southerners, who are physically frail, live in a different environment, and have different stomachs and bowels." For elderly Manchus he thus recommended "unrefined milk, pickled deer tongues and tails, dried apples, and cream cheese cakes."[24]

Empresses, concubines, and favored officials received annual allotments of venison that the emperor personally bagged.[25] Whenever the emperor killed a deer, the Imperial Household Department prepared six cuts: tail, breast meat (Ma: *kersen*), croup (Ma: *kargama*), ribs, strips, and scraps (Ma: *farsi*). Though both Manchu and Chinese officials received such cuts, the ethnic background of the food would not have been lost on anyone: The words used for "breast," "croup," and "scraps" lacked Chinese translations altogether, and Chinese archives record only their transliteration: *ke-er-sen*, *ka-er-ha-ma*, and *fa-er-shi*.[26] Game meat, it seems, was served in Manchu. Game birds claimed a similar place on the imperial menu; they, too, embodied the Manchu way.[27] Each pheasant came with a story: The court recorded who killed each bird and how, including whether the hunter had used falconry. The Imperial Household Department often bundled venison and pheasant together as gifts.[28] Court women received regular allotments of each, including an annual gift from the emperor of two catties of pheasant, venison, and fish.[29] The Summer Palace similarly maintained a menagerie of live pheasants and deer for the court's enjoyment.

Certain wild plants and fungi carried a similar charisma. Thus palace chefs often paired game meats with "steppe mushrooms" (Ch: *koumo*, lit. "mushrooms from beyond the [Great Wall] pass"): It only added to the wild flavor of its dishes. Qianlong, along these lines, savored "venison tendon with braised steppe mushroom" (Ch: *lujin shaokoumo*) and "salt-fried meat with steppe mushrooms" (Ch: *koumo yanjianrou*) on his tour of Mukden, the Manchu homeland.[30] His son, the Jiaqing emperor (r. 1795–1820), likewise ate steppe mushrooms while out on hunts.[31] Steppe mushrooms, in fact, never went out of fashion at court. In 1911, on the eve of revolution, the four-year-old emperor Puyi ate steppe mushrooms four times in his final month in power.[32] Palace food, of course, was hardly primitive; though wild in spirit, its production required learning and craft. The recipe for the hearty "venison tendon with steppe mushrooms" was typically cosmopolitan:

Figure 1.1. The Qianlong emperor in court dress, 1735. Painting by Giuseppe Castiglione. Qianlong's outfit was characteristic of Qing emperors: Note the fur trimming on the dragon robe and freshwater pearls atop the fur-lined hat.

SOURCE: Wikicommons. https://en.wikipedia.org/wiki/Qianlong_Emperor#/media/File:Portrait_of_the_Qianlong_Emperor_in_Court_Dress.jpg.

Ingredients: 150 grams ([*ke*]) of tenderized venison tendon; 150 grams tenderized steppe mushrooms; 40 grams soy sauce; 1 gram of salt; 75 grams of hot bean oil; 10 grams white sugar; 15 grams of liquor (*shaojiu*); 4 grams of flavored powder (*weijing*); 150 grams meat broth; 3 grams onion tips; 2 grams ginger; 40 grams starch.

Directions: Soak the venison tendon and (dried) mushrooms in water. When tender, put it on a high flame, pour in the oil, and let it sit until hot. Add the onion and ginger. Add soy sauce, liquor, broth, salt, and sugar. When it comes to a boil, add the tenderized tendon and steppe mushrooms, and let simmer for another 10 minutes. Add flavored powder, bring the fire to high, add starch, sprinkle fragrant oil, and serve.[33]

It was the wild ingredients that made this dish special; venison tendon and "steppe mushroom" said something larger about the Manchus and their rule: They indicated that the emperors were in touch with their roots. Venison, pheasants, and mushrooms, along these lines, formed only part of a larger suite of products associated with Manchu identity; other objects embodied the hunter's tale as well and were prized accordingly as "things hunted" (Ma: *butaha jaka*) by the Qing court.[34]

Fur fashions spoke to this sensibility. Before the conquest, Manchu rulers ordered that the silken dragon robes they received from the Ming court be trimmed with sable—a barbaric choice by Ming standards; after the conquest, they continued to wear Ming-style dragon robes altered to have fur collars and cuffs and sable-fur skirts.[35] The early court celebrated the Manchu character of furs with formal dances at the palace, where groups of attendants dressed in leopard-skin robes and sable-fur hats and sang of the founding of the dynasty.[36] The writer Tan Qian (1593–1657) witnessed the spectacle and described the "Manchu dance" in his diary in detail: Twenty to thirty people dressed in leopard-skin costumes waved fans as four others dressed in sable-fur costumes danced with poles.[37] In winter, Qing emperors wore hats fashioned from black sable pelts, and in the last two months of the lunar year they donned hats of black fox fur. Atop such hats stood a three-tiered finial studded with Manchurian freshwater pearls. Their winter jackets matched: Qing emperors wore black sable in early winter and black fox in the two months before New Year's. In other winter months the emperors wore dragon robes trimmed with sea otter fur (see Figure 1.1). In summer, such furs went into storage, but freshwater Manchurian pearls remained prominent parts of their ensemble, including on hat ornaments and in their prominent 108-bead, Buddhist pearl rosaries.[38] Imperial princes dressed with similar elements: sable, sea otter, and Manchurian pearls.[39]

Gifting practices of the early Qing court reveal the intimate nature of these objects. Through the early eighteenth century, the court gifted furs to those with a close connection to Manchu rulership: members of the inner court, banner elites, Mongol allies, and prominent military men. The Manchu nobility and members of the imperial family in particular received gifts befitting their identity: sable, Manchurian pearls, horses, and engraved saddles.[40] The brides of imperial grandchildren similarly received gifts of sable fur (fit for making either clothing or hats), fox fur (for sitting mats), and sea-otter fur (for trimming). Fathers of the bride, too, received a fox-fur robe, a black sable-fur hat, a robe made of fox-underbelly fur, and six sea-otter fur pelts for trimming and interior lining.[41] Such gifts were typical for members of the inner court. When in 1665 two young women, including the Kangxi emperor's wet nurse, accompanied the emperor on a hunt, he put in a special request to fabricate two preconquest "Jurcen-style sable jackets"[42] for the occasion; such jackets suited them "when going out to the wilderness." The empress dowager advised against his generous gesture, noting that "it was not yet the season for wearing sable jackets." Thus the slave instead received a wool-lined silk gown and sable-lined, black-satin coat and the wet nurse a sable neck warmer, a gown of wool, and "a coat of extra quality sable." The emperor awarded more modest sable hats and coats to two additional young women in this intimate party as well.[43]

Similar gifting practices extended to the Mongols. The founder of the imperial family, Nurhaci, justified alliances between Jurchens and Mongols on grounds of common dress: "Only the speech of our two nations (Ma: *gurun*), Mongol and Jurchen, is different; in the clothes we wear and our way of life, we are alike."[44] Chinese and Koreans, in contrast, wore different clothing and had different ways of life. According to this contrivance of fellowship, the Qing court invited Mongol noblemen to banquet at annual feasts of "wild animals" (Ma: *gurgu*) during the Lantern Festival (the fifteenth of the first month) in Beijing. As part of the festivities, the court served game meat with bread and fermented mare's milk, or *kumiss*,[45] and all Mongol guests received sable coats and coarse woolens for making the trip.[46] The court reinforced the rustic and rural associations of furs by bundling them with gifts of a similar spirit: knives, golden sash rings, and "rump leather" boots.[47] In the Kangxi period, the highest-ranking Mongol aristocrats received the venerable "Jurchen style sable-lined" fur jackets.[48] It was not uncommon, on the other hand, for Mongol nobility to reciprocate with a tribute of hunting falcons and other birds of prey.[49]

Indeed, some of the most prized gifts the court received were the most wild. The emperors sought out such exotic items. Thus in 1760, an envoy dispatched from Ilan Hala to northern Sakhalin purchased live reindeer for the Qianlong emperor, and in 1819, an envoy on tour to the village of Koiman, on the Amur River about 100 miles upstream from the mouth, purchased a set of eighteen live black and arctic foxes.[50] The fiercer and wilder the beast, the more it warranted attention. The Jiaqing emperor (r. 1795–1820) was typical in this regard. In 1804, he received two adult Manchurian tigers from the military governor of Jilin. He was overjoyed; as the emperor enthused, the Manchus of Jilin must truly be "well endowed with manly virtue" to catch such creatures. "I know well that hunting is difficult," he explained, "but you not only captured tiger and bear cubs [as usual], you even got two adult tigers alive—how fierce and manly!" Rewards were in order; he needed details. Who were the hunters, and how had they accomplished the feat?[51] The value of the tigers was inseparable from the hunter's tale: the characters who did the work, the forest setting, and the skill and brawn that led to heroic success.

Pressed for more information, the military governor of Jilin, Siolin, sent a special memorial with the relevant details. Jilin had a terrific amount of snowfall that winter, he explained. One day, hunters had passed cub prints in the snow and began tracking. They knew that "if there was a fully grown tiger, it could not be caught with brute force," so the hunters relied on "cunning" instead. When the time was right, they built wooden cages, dropped piglets inside, and raised a trap door. When the tigers walked in to find food for their cubs, they sprung the trap and had their prize. It had taken "fierce and manly" character as well as inside knowledge of the forest.[52] Three years later, in 1807, Siolin sent another gift of live tigers and bears, and again the emperor demanded a story; this time, however, Siolin admitted the hunters' names "had not been clearly recorded," but an investigation was underway.[53] A month later, the Grand Council's Manchu Affairs Office received word that yet another tiger cub was being transported to Beijing. A patrolman in Jilin's imperial ginseng fields, Sicimboo, was making rounds through the "restricted mountains" when he had spotted its tiny tracks.[54] Again, the Jiaqing emperor was overjoyed: Live tigers embodied the ideal life of the Manchu homeland and the skill and fortitude of the best Manchu bannermen.

Wild things in this way suggested a subjectivity: a tough, intimate, honest, virile, and rustic way of interacting with the world; ostensibly, they represented a man in touch with his original nature. Likewise, the value of the object was inextricable from its provenance and the story of its production. "Steppe mushrooms" had to come from north of the Great Wall. Venison required hunting. Tigers required trapping. To taste a wild mushroom, dine on game meat, or visit the menagerie was to travel in time: to touch something uncorrupted, unaltered, and pristinely Manchu. They invoked a consistent constellation of objects associated with the Manchu Way and Qing rule: manliness (Ma: *haha erdemu*), martial vigor, unadorned "plainness" (Ma: *gulu*), and "purity" (Ma: *nomhon*). All of these values implied a vision of history; to wear pearls and fur was to allude to Manchu origins and an older age.[55]

Of course, the Manchus' origins were not so simple, and their lifestyle was never so rustic. Nurhaci's court depended less on the hunting of furs than on their trafficking.[56] A Japanese sailor shipwrecked off the Pacific coast of Manchuria in 1644 described the ubiquity of fur hats among the Manchus but noted that commoners wore wool, whereas only noblemen dressed in the fine furs unavailable in Japan.[57] Not surprisingly, fine furs—the product of conquest—belonged to the conquest elite, not the common Manchu. The fur they wore came from neighboring communities to the north and east, such as the Hūrha, Warka, and Ula.

The products of the Qing court, that is, were emblematic of the structure of the imperial hierarchy. Many wore furs, but color, species, and cut defined one's place in the empire. In Nurhaci's time, the highest-ranking elites wore Manchurian pearls, sable, and lynx, and lower noblemen dressed in squirrel and weasel.[58] Among the highest-ranking noblemen, still finer grades of distinction differentiated rank: The top ranks wore plaited sable jackets, black sable robes, "Chinese"-style raccoon-dog robes (Ma: *nikan elbihe dahū*), or lynx robes; men of the second rank wore plain raccoon-dog robes or coats lined with sable; and men of the third rank wore dragon robes lined with sable in the "Jurchen" style.[59] As it consolidated rule in the Northeast, the early Manchu court institutionalized these social and political hierarchies through sumptuary laws. In 1637, the court ordered all Manchu noblemen and women to wear freshwater Manchurian pearls in their hats and hairpieces; the higher one's rank, the larger and more numerous the pearls one wore.[60] After 1644, when the court revised sumptuary laws again, first-rank princes henceforth wore ten Manchurian pearls atop their head, second-rank princes eight, third-rank princes seven, and so on down to the lowest-ranking aristocrats, who wore one.[61]

Even after the Qing conquest of China, the project of standardizing Manchu attire continued unabated. In the early days, there were still some in Beijing from the "forests" (Ma: *woji*) of the Northeast who wore fish skins in their capacity as officials; the empire made these men, too, wear proper clothing at court, not the skins.[62] We should be careful, then, in labeling fur a "Manchu" fashion. It was. Yet it was also the projection of an ambition, an image of the ideal Manchu Way, and—particularly for the people of the Northeast—a homogenizing project. Fur and silk befitted the court; fish skin did not.

CAN CHINESE WEAR FUR?

In the Qing empire, clothing and material culture were inseparable from personal identity; one could not separate the fur from the man.[63] Clothing represented one's person as much as the color of one's skin or the pockmarks on one's face; standard "name-age-appearance" bulletins for escaped slaves, runaway wives, and military deserters mixed physical and sartorial descriptions, as if one's outfit never changed.[64] By law, fugitives were "captured and investigated according to their physical appearance and clothing."[65] It was illegal to knock off someone's hat (or tug on his tassels) during a fight.[66] When a foreign man died in Qing Mongolia, his body and clothing alike were returned to his home jurisdiction.[67]

It was because clothing represented identity, and because furs represented Manchu identity in particular and frontiers more broadly, that the fashion aroused such strong reactions. Even today, wearing fur is a loaded practice: Is it civilized or brutal? In our world, we debate fur in terms of enlightened liberalism: The value of fur hinges on questions of rights and abuse. In imperial China, fur commanded a similar position as a civilizational flashpoint; as with the Romans, Byzantines, and Umayyads, pelts in China represented barbarity, with the politics of fur refracted through the politics of foreignness and the frontier.[68] It is a reminder that there is nothing inherently precious about furs or any other material object: Functionality does not determine value; furs do not simply give warmth in winter or resilience in rain.[69] When the frontier epitomized war and exile, and furs represented hardship, loneliness, and brutality, they could lose their value altogether; furs became "skins" or "hides."

Tropes of the fur-clad barbarian abound in the classical Chinese literary canon, and as Antonia Finnane has documented, the barbarian in furs was a recurring element in frontier literature throughout the imperial period.[70] From Sima Qian (135?–86 BCE), who described the Xiongnu "dressed in skins" and sleeping on "fur quilts" to the most celebrated Tang poets, who commemorated the wars with the Turks, the Inner Asian frontier proved inseparable from its material culture. The Tang poet Liu Shang (fl. eighth century) captured the spirit of the metaphor in his *Eighteen Songs of a Nomad Flute* (Ch: *Hujia shiba pai*), which recounted the tragic fate of Lady Wenji, a Han noblewoman forced into a Xiongnu marriage. As the lady laments:

> I clean my hair with mutton fat, but it is seldom combed
> The collar of my lambskin robe is buttoned on the left;
> The fox lapels and badger sleeves are rank-smelling
> By day I wear these clothes, by night I sleep in them.[71]

Literati of the Southern Song (1127–1279), writing after the rival Jurchen-led Jin state conquered northern China, similarly associated fur with Jurchens and barbarity. Xu Mengxin (1126–1207) painted a typically vivid—and absurd—picture of Jurchen life; in his words, "Even if they catch one single mouse they strip off its skin and keep it."[72] After the Mongols conquered the Jin and Song states, literati associated Mongols, too, with furs. Xiongnu, Khitan, Jurchen, Mongol, and Manchu were all alike: They all trafficked in the product.

To be sure, Chinese elites wore fur as well, and historians could write a parallel history of Chinese fur fashion to match the Inner Asian. In the Warring States period (475–221 BCE), for example, two headpieces for officials incorporated elements of sable fur: the *diaochan* (lit. sable "cicada"-style hat) and the *erdiao* (lit. "sable earring"), two hats that featured a sable tail dangling from the cap. Literary tradition held that King Wuling of Zhao (r. 325–299 BCE) invented the *diaochan* as part of an effort to build esprit de corps: "Dress as a barbarian, fight as a cavalryman" was the axiom of his day.[73] The *diaochan* remained fashionable in the Tang empire (618–907 CE) as well; Edward Schafer noted how the headpieces were for "daring youths who went out to the Tatar frontier, or returned to their native soil for hawking and hunting."[74]

Likewise, from the Han dynasty onward, the dynastic histories faithfully record the submission of tribute from people of the Northeast, showing how fur could represent Chinese imperial power too. Furs also had a certain popular appeal, especially after the Mongol conquest. Mongol influences on Chinese fashion proved strong into early Ming times, including in Ming fashions such as the *bijia* (a type of long vest), the *zhisun* (a single-colored court robe, from the Mongol *jisün*), and the so-called *humao*, or barbarian hat.[75] In 1430, the Chosŏn court in Korea noted that "the people of China treasure above all leopard and sable furs"; the Chosŏn court itself soon required sable-fur ear-warmer hats for its highest-ranking nobility and squirrel fur hats for the rest.[76] Fashion and material culture crossed political and ethnic boundaries; dressing like a barbarian did not necessarily entail being one.

Thus in the late fifteenth and early sixteenth centuries, fur fashions endured in Ming China and Chosŏn Korea alike. Through tribute and trade with Mongols and Jurchens, with a commercial network that extended to Siberia and Sakhalin Island, new volumes of furs began to reach the two courts and, Northeast Asian elites.[77] The far Northeast increasingly specialized in fur: Beginning in the 1460s, for example, the *Veritable Records* of the Ming court cease to record Jurchen deliveries of horses and other "local products" (like pearls) and instead document the delivery of sable pelts (Ch: *diaopi*).[78]

Consumers came to know fur more intimately. Li Shizhen (1518–1593), in his *Bencao gangmu* (*Compendium of Materia Medica*), described sable fur as if he had inspected it himself: "The fur is used for coats, hats, and neck-warmers during the winter months. One can stay warm in the wind and dry when it is wet. If there is snow, [the fur] will dissolve it like a flame brushing across ones face."[79] As a doctor, he recommended using the sleeve of a sable-fur coat to brush dust from one's eyes.[80] Other fur-bearing animals make an appearance in his work as well, including sea otters, of which he noted: "Today they are used for neck-warmers, but they are second-rate compared to sable."[81] Fur was popular enough in Ming Beijing to create a backlash. In 1506 the Ming court issued a new sumptuary law that prohibited servants, courtesans, and people of low status from wearing sable-fur coats (Ch: *diaoqiu*).[82] A century later, strategists at the the Ming court warned that fur was funding the rise of Nurhaci and Hong Taiji.[83]

To other thinkers, the primary threat of fur was that it debased Chinese culture. In one striking document, dated March 6, 1491, a Ming censor warned ominously of "foreign dress and language" among the men and women of Beijing and of Chinese men wearing sable- and fox-fur hats like "nomad barbarians" (Ch: *hu*). Demanding the "restoration of pure Chinese culture" (Ch: *fu huaxia zhi chunfeng*), he urged the Ming court to "sweep away the mean customs of the barbarian Yuan" and "make customs and practices pure and correct" (Ch: *xisu chunzheng*).[84] Chinese people were wearing fur, but wearing fur was not Chinese. To purge China of foreign influences and reestablish its original culture, all foreign clothing, particularly fur, would have to go. Thus if Manchu fur fashion was a political project, so too was the Chinese aversion to it. Both projects, in their own ways imagined a timeless and original purity.[85]

For this reason, fur remained a flashpoint well after the Qing conquest. Tan Qian, writing in his *Record of Travels North* (*Beiyou lu*) a decade after the Manchus' arrival in Beijing, found himself in a new and frightening world. In a journal entry from March 15, 1654—the Shunzhi emperor's birthday—he recorded how officials at the Board of Rites honored the occasion by spending a week dressed in either sable- or fox-fur coats. To Tan Qian, it was enough to drive a poor bureaucrat to ruin. "I heard the emperor dressed in a black fox-fur robe, valued upwards of 3000 *jin*, and that all the various ministers wore black robes worth no less than a 1000 *jin*."[86] Yet nothing could be done about such waste: Fur was the new order.

Although Tan Qian critiqued fur as wasteful, others emphasized that ethnic or civilizational pride was at stake. The Jesuit Father Pierre Joseph D'Orléans (1641–1698) noted the indignity of Chinese having "to cut off their hair and adopt the Tartar dress."[87] Korean travelers, who continued to abide by Ming sumptuary standards, lampooned the rise of fur in China. After sneaking into the palace's New Year's ceremony, the Chosŏn emissary Kim Ch'angŏp (1658–1721) was struck above all by the small carpets Qing officials used to bow and kneel: "The rug for the highest rank was a tiger skin with the head and claws on it. The next rank down had a tiger skin without head and claws, the next had a wolf skin, the next a badger skin, the next a raccoon-dog skin, the next a wild sheepskin, then a dog skin and lowest of all a mat of white felt."[88] Kim had disguised himself as a servant, but the plan backfired: He misguidedly had adorned himself in "a leopard fur that attracted the attention of some of the barbarians," and, as he later wrote in his diary, "I had to take it off in the end to get rid of them."[89]

Chinese voices that would have been censored in the Qing ring out in such Korean travelogues. An official at the Board of Rites, Pan Deyu, wrote to Kim Ch'angŏp, for example, of the Kangxi emperor's favoritism toward "Tatars," using the character *ta*, or "otter," for "Tatar." Accusing the emperor of being frugal in word but not in deed, he derided the court for wasting money on Mongol "Otters" who lived "somewhere beyond Ningguta" to receive nothing but fur and ginseng in return.[90] Manchu ritual life was impenetrable; riffing on puns and mistranslations, Kim found himself wondering about the difference between "otters" and "Tatars":

> The Korean interpreter asked who was the General Deng [Ch: Deng *jiangjun*] in whose shrine the Emperor prayed at the beginning of each year. The Chinese explained that Deng *jiangjun* did not mean "General Deng," but was the name of a cap that had belonged to Nurhaci's father, the ancestor of the Manchu Emperors. It was kept in this shrine and the Emperor went to burn incense to it at the beginning of every year. The Koreans thought it must be precious, but the Chinese said that on the contrary it was nothing but a moth-eaten piece of otter-skin. And they all laughed about it.[91]

Travelers like Kim Ch'angŏp were quick to draw conclusions about the Manchus based on their dress, just as later Chosŏn emissaries generally focused on clothing as well.[92] In his descriptions of various ethnic groups and foreigners living in Beijing, the envoy Hong Taeyong (1731–1783) recorded the color, cut, and fabric of everyone's gowns and hats. Ambassadors from the Ryukyu Islands pleased his eye with their long, flowing satin robes. Manchus and Mongols produced the opposite effect. At best absurd, they otherwise appeared terrifying and "fierce."[93]

THE QING INTEGRATION

It is difficult to imagine how exotic, novel, and beastly these fashions would have seemed to Chinese, Korean, and others steeped in the classical tradition; they had no language to describe some of the more nuanced aspects of Manchu fur culture that the Qing conquest had introduced. Neologisms proliferated. As with game meats, where new words emerged for certain cuts of venison, so too did the Chinese lexicon expand to describe furs and other exotic objects from the far north. Lynx, for example, lacked a Chinese character, and a new word for the animal was coined only after 1644: *shelisun*, from the Mongolian *silügüsün*.[94] The same held for Manchurian freshwater pearls (Ma: *tana*), which became known as "eastern pearls" in Chinese (Ch: *dongzhu*). "Steppe mushroom," or *koumo*, was another neologism of the Qing; no references to the product exist before the late seventeenth century.

Translation proved to be a constant problem, and in the generation after the Qing conquest, literati struggled to bridge the gap between Manchu and Chinese words and to standardize terminology. Shen Qiliang (fl. 1645–1693) tackled the problem most directly in his *Da Qing quanshu* (1683), the first Manchu–Chinese dictionary.[95] He compiled the dictionary for practical reasons; the ruling elite spoke and wrote in Manchu, whereas their subjects lived and worked in mostly Chinese or Mongolian. Yet the lexical differences between these languages proved formidable. Pointedly, Shen Qiliang included in his dictionary roughly 300 Manchu words that lacked known Chinese translations; in his dictionary, he left the space for these translations blank. Many of these untranslated words, in turn, were flora and fauna common to the far north, including corsac fox (Ma: *kirsa*), marten (Ma: *harsa*), and saltbush (Ma: *ule*). Animal anatomy and behavior proved similarly obscure. There was no Chinese equivalent for the Manchu words for "hair on a sable's chin" (Ma: *baltaha*) or "deer brushing against trees during mating season" (Ma: *gūyambi*). Other untranslatable terms encompassed objects familiar to Manchurian households: willow-reed baskets for holding sewing materials (Ma: *kaipi*), millstones (Ma: *niyeleku*), and sleighs (Ma: *huncu*).[96]

Other bilingual texts of the early Qing similarly lacked one-to-one translations for Chinese and Manchu words that described the natural or built environments. In his *Record of a Mission to the Distant Border* (*Lakcaha jecen de takūraha babe ejehe bithe/Yiyulu*, published 1723), Tulišen provided more detail and clarity on the things he encountered on his journey to Russia in his Manchu text than in his Chinese: He left some Manchu words in Chinese transliteration; he translated other words inconsistently or omitted altogether. Thus, while traveling through far northern Manchuria, Tulišen noted in Manchu seven different types of fish found in the rivers: salmon trout (*jelu*), salmon (*niomošon*), golden carp (*onggošon*), "yellow fish" (*mušurhu*), tench (*takū*), dragon liver fish (*can nimaha*), and sturgeon (*kirfu nimaha*). His Chinese version, however, lists only five fish, and they were different: *lu*, carp, crucian carp, eel, and (Yangzi) sturgeon.[97] Flora similarly proved a problem: Japanese larch (Ma: *isi*) became a fir in Chinese.[98] Still other exotics included salmon trout (Ma: *jelu*), dragon liver fish, reindeer (Ma: *oron buhū*),[99] and moose (Ma: *kandahan*), all of which Tulišen left in transliteration.[100]

In contrast, a contemporary Manchu–Mongol dictionary, the *Han-i araha Manju Monggo gisuni buleku bithe* (Mo: *Qaġan-u bicigsen Manju Mongġol ügen-ü toil bicig*) (1717), included sentence- or paragraph-length definitions for all of the terms missing from texts like the *Da Qing quanshu*.[101] It identified the corsac fox (Ma: *kirsa*; Mo: *kirsa*), for example, as "similar to the fox, [but] with a whitish hue." The text provided comparable detail for the marten (Ma: *harsa*; Mo: *suusar*): "Its length is like the sable. It has a foul odor and a thick black tail, and it catches and eats honey by dipping its tail in it." Other animals, such as the moose (Ma: *kandahan*; Mo: *qandaġai*), which lacked Manchu and Chinese entries alike in the *Da Qing quanshu*, also receive extensive treatment. Moose, for example, "belong to the deer family. Their body is big with a hump on the back. There is a skin under its throat like a bridle decoration [Ma: *kandaraha*], the neck is short, and the antlers flat and wide. The females are called *eniyen*." The dictionary includes further entries for adult moose (Ma: *toho*; Mo: *toqi*), the moose's young (Ma: *niyarhoca*; Mo: *qotul*), and abnormally large moose (Ma: *anami*; Mo: *manji*).

Manchus and Chinese, it would seem, lived in different worlds, populated by different creatures and things: Manchus knew of moose and martens; Chinese did not. Ultimately, it was the imperial encounter that led these two worlds to overlap more fully and for new translations to arise, as fur and other wild objects became part of a larger, shared, and peculiarly Qing material culture.

We can chart this imperial integration through shifting sumptuary laws and gifting practices. The nascent Qing empire faced formidable challenges in integrating its disparate realms; it is easy to forget, nearly 400 years later, the dislocation, violence, and anguish that the Ming–Qing transition produced. Yet we cannot understand the seemingly trivial focus on fur in politics without invoking it. Looking back, the stakes for combatants were no less than those of Western religious and colonial wars of the same period; for those who fought through them, civilization itself was on the line. Looking back from the twentieth century, many scholars have portrayed the Ming–Qing conflict as a national war between Manchus and Chinese. Many oversimplified: The battle lines of the seventeenth-century crisis never aligned cleanly with any national blocs. Different localities experienced different traumas and were moved by different political dynamics; elites and the poor did not always agree on why they fought. Survivors often depicted their struggles in terms more personal than national; one chose not just between Manchu and Chinese but between loyalty and expediency, right and wrong.

The Manchu identity of the conquest elite mattered nonetheless, and in the immediate aftermath of the conquest, the perception that the Manchus were "barbarians" (Ch: *hu*) lingered in many minds.[102] There were those, like the influential writer Wang Fuzhi (1619–1692), who argued on principle that Manchus were barbarian from birth, and thus perpetually rooted in alien lands and customs.[103] For others, their problem with Manchus stemmed from specific policies or experiences: Some witnessed the massacres in the towns of Qian'an, Yongping, and Yangzhou; others were the victims of "Manchu apartheid" and displaced from their homes in cities like Beijing and Hangzhou in the creation of banner neighborhoods. Still others objected to the edict of 1645 ordering all Chinese men to wear their hair like Manchus, in a queue, on pain of death.[104] It was this last policy, a sumptuary law, that aroused the greatest resistance among civilians. In Jiangnan in particular, the edict united scholars and peasants alike against Qing rule.[105] As one scholar remembered, "We young men cherished our hair, and when we saw people with shaven heads, they didn't seem human."[106] In practice, material culture focalized the question "Who am I?" like nothing else; the queue represented an affront to the body and so served as the ultimate symbol of barbarism. Indeed, it is no accident that the Qing court put so much weight on sumptuary laws: Rooting out resistance was in part the point.

In 1644, a year before the queue proclamation, the Qing court issued new sumptuary laws for proper dress at court, ordering all aristocrats to wear both Manchurian pearls and furs according to rank.[107] In 1651, it further mandated that all visitors to the palace use fur floor mats in winter. Fur would symbolize rank: princes of the first rank would use mats of sable, princes of the second degree sable-trimmed lynx, princes of the third degree unadorned lynx, and so on down to the lowest-ranking visitors, who would sit on goat pelts and deerskin mats (see Table 1.1).[108] The regulations held until 1765, when the Qianlong emperor slightly modified the law and

TABLE I.I.
Winter sumptuary laws for fur mats at court, 1651.

Rank (English)	Type of fur mat
Prince of the first rank	Sable
Prince of the second degree	Lynx with sable trim
Prince of the third degree	Lynx
Prince of the fourth degree	Snow leopard
Prince of the fifth degree	Red leopard
Prince of the sixth degree	Leopard (minus head and tail)
Lesser aristocratic ranks	Tiger (minus head and tail)
First rank (bureaucratic)	Wolf
Second rank	Badger
Third rank	Raccoon-dog
Fourth rank	Goat
Fifth rank and below	Deer

ordered princes of the first rank to use lynx fur trimmed with sable and princes of the second degree to use sable trimmed with lynx.[109]

At the same time, the Qing court began gifting fur pelts, robes, and jackets to favored Chinese officials, particularly those involved in successful military campaigns. Ming military defectors were the first to receive such gifts. Kong Youde (d. 1652), Chi Zhongming (1604–1649), and Shang Kexi (1604–1676)—the great Chinese "feudatories" of the preconquest generation—received twenty sable pelts each in 1637 on the occasion of Emperor Hong Taiji's birthday; they further received ten pelts in 1638 and eighty pelts in 1642.[110] In the final stages of the Qing conquest, in 1654, both Kong Youde and Geng Jimao accepted dyed sable-fur hats and fox-belly and sable-lined robes.[111] In a similar spirit, the Kangxi emperor began awarding sable pelts to exceptional soldiers he inspected during his imperial tour of 1704, as did the Yongzheng (r. 1722–1735) and Qianlong emperors on their own tours of 1728 and 1739.[112] Indeed, most decorated military men received comparable gifts until the end of the dynasty. From the Dzungar campaigns and expansionary wars of the eighteenth century to the civil wars and rebellions of the nineteenth, honored soldiers received precious furs: otter-fur "war-skirts," black fox-fur hats, and sable riding gowns and floor mats.[113]

At the same time, the number and type of civilians receiving gifts of fur expanded. The Yongzheng emperor began a new tradition of gifting furs to Qing subjects who lacked any association to the military or the inner court whatsoever.[114] He signaled a shift in this regard in 1724, when he awarded sable pelts to the living descendants of Confucius. No longer bundled with horses or armor, the pelts came instead with fine tea and ink—objects befitting literati.[115] The palace's New Year's celebrations similarly became more mixed and eclectic in their material culture. In 1726, with his highest Chinese and Manchu officials assembled, the Yongzheng emperor ordered that all attendees receive sable pelts, silk, and copies of the Kangxi edition of the *Essentials of the Comprehensive Mirror in Aid of Government (Tongjian gangmu)*.[116] Yongzheng's son, the Qianlong emperor (r. 1735–1795) followed this precedent, and at the New Year's celebration of 1738 again awarded the assembled officials sable, silk, and the book.[117] In 1754 (QL19), the Qianlong emperor further mandated that for the two and a half months surrounding New Year's, from the first of the eleventh month to the sixteenth of the first, all those participating in court sacrifices wear sable-trimmed court clothing.[118] That same year, he bestowed sable furs on the descendants of the Song scholar Fan Zhongyan.[119]

At court, that is, while furs continued to resonate as Manchu and military garb, they also became symbols of imperial prestige more broadly. From the Yongzheng reign onward the court gifted pelts to Manchus and Chinese, military generals and civilians, men and women alike. The National Palace Museum in Taiwan holds fifty-six palace memorials from the Yongzheng reign in which officials in the field thanked the emperor for gifts of sable. Of these, the emperor sent seventeen pelts to officials serving in northern China and thirty-nine to officials serving in the south: Fourteen pelts found their way to tropical Yunnan and Guizhou, eight to Guangdong, six to Fujian or Taiwan, and four to Guangxi. Of the fifty-six memorialists, twenty-two were officials serving in a military capacity; the rest were mostly civil governors or governors-general.[120] Sable fashion was no longer confined to the northern frontiers, the inner court, or the military; it transcended old dichotomies and belonged to all the empire's elites.

Fur in time became a favored symbol of filial piety. The Yongzheng emperor set yet another precedent when he gifted four sable pelts to an elderly matriarch on her one hundredth birthday.[121] Thereafter, the Qianlong emperor took up the practice with gusto and similarly awarded such pelts to prominent moms: One governor's mother received four pelts, another ninety-one-year-old mother received ten, and many more received pelts on the occasion of their hundredth birthdays.[122] The practice crossed conventional boundary lines: In 1781, news of a 108-year-old Muslim woman in Xinjiang receied a gift of sable and satin; in 1787 a 106-year-old Kyrgyz woman received the same.[123] And although venerable mothers were the most common beneficiaries, after 1751 the occasional elderly father also received a package of sable and silk, bundled up in the wrapping and seal of the Qing court.[124]

Fur thus became a symbol of the emperor's grace, power and largesse. Just as tribute bearers to Beijing were expected to carry characteristic gifts (rhinoceros horn from the Lao, horses from Kazaks, and so on), the Qing court represented itself with telling gifts in return: a mix of sable and silk. Korean tribute missions received fur at every lunar New Year's, on the emperor's birthday, at imperial weddings, and at other holidays and special events.[125] In 1743, when the Qianlong emperor met with Korean emissaries on his imperial tour of Mukden (Shenyang), in explicit homage to his heritage he presented the Koreans with 100 sable pelts together with bows and arrows and saddled horses.[126] Into the eighteenth and nineteenth centuries, participants in the tribute system returned home with gifts of fur, and tribute missions from Chosŏn Korea, the Lao Court of Lan Xang, the Ryukyu Islands, and Annam (Vietnam) all received pelts of sable or fox.[127]

THE NEW NORMAL

By the late eighteenth century, the material distinctions between Manchu and Chinese was collapsing; by and large, one could not tell a Manchu from a Chinese by looking (see Figure 1.2).[128] Manchus continued to take pride in their imagined history and identity; to receive stipends as bannermen; to speak, read, and write Manchu; and to wear the queue and dress in furs. Yet in Beijing by the late eighteenth century every man wore the queue; almost everyone spoke Mandarin Chinese; and everyone marked high status with once exotic products, such as furs, freshwater pearls, and steppe mushrooms. For the right price, one could simply buy all the wild emblems the imperial imagination conjured: jet-black Uriankhai sable; wild ginseng from Manchuria; mushrooms from Xanadu. For less, one could own dyed or cultivated fakes that resembled the original.

Fur moved from the court to the streets. The Jesuit missionary Jean Baptiste du Halde tantalized European readers of the mid-eighteenth century with descriptions of fur treasuries, where there "are kept many Habits lined with various Furrs of Foxes, Ermine, or Zibeline [sable], which the Emperor sometimes bestow on his Servants." Outside the palace, too, he saw "a vast Quantity of the finest Sort of Skinest."[129] Describing the city in

Figure 1.2. Detail from "Twenty-Seven Old Ones" (*Ershiqi lao*), by Jia Quan. Qianlong period (1735–1795). Under Qianlong, it was often impossible to tell who was Manchu simply by looking: Everyone who could wore furs.

SOURCE: Feng Ming-chu, *Qianlong huangdi de wenhua daye*, 93. The Collection of the National Palace Museum.

the years 1711–1723, the Italian priest Matteo Ripa similarly wrote of how elite urbanites "adopt the furs of ermine, sable, and fox, in the same gradation. In the depth of winter, besides having both the ppow-zoo [*paozi*] and why-ttao [*waitao*] lined with foxes' skin, they wear an under waistcoat of lambs' skin, and the loose gown over it wadded; and when it snows they put on a long cloak covered over with seal-skin."[130] He also marveled at the abundance of wild game in Beijing markets:

> During the period of frost, that is, from October till March, Northern Tartary sends to the capital an enormous quantity of game, consisting chiefly of stags, hares, wild-boars, pheasants and partridges; whilst Southern Tartary furnishes a great abundance of excellent sturgeon and other fish, all of which being frozen, can easily be kept during the whole winter.

At the close of the old year, and the beginning of the new, huge heaps of game and fish are exposed for sale in the streets, and it is surprising to see how cheap they are sold. For seven or eight silver tchens, which are equivalent to four shillings, one may buy a stag; for trifle more a wild-boar; for five half-pence, a pheasant; and so on in the same proportion.[131]

Local residents, too, enjoyed the spectacle at Beijing's game markets. Casually, one eleven-year-old child recorded in a Manchu schoolbook, which most likely dates to the mid-eighteenth century, that "there is lots of stuff coming from Mukden this year. On the streets are piled up roe deer, four-year-old wild boar, deer, pheasant, hare, geese, and ducks, and other such things." He was not overly impressed: "While there are lots of people looking, few people are buying. I don't value these kinds of things too much. But I am very fond of eating sturgeon and crane."[132] Wild animals were at your fingertips—whether you desired them or not.

Beijing became particularly famous for its fur markets. By the early nineteenth century, the biggest markets had emerged just outside Qianmen gate, on the south side of the inner city wall where the Manchu and Chinese cities converged.[133] The most active market, the Beijing Pearl Market, specialized in not only pearls, but furs and wild ginseng. A travelers' manual, the *Guide to the Capital* (*Dumen jilue*, published 1845) detailed the locations of each of the main markets for new tourists and sojourners. For newcomers, the book explained: "The wealthy of the capital—including those famous for finishing first in the exams—regularly wear sable-fur robes and palace pearls."[134] The guidebook promised a bustling scene at the Pearl Market: "Pedestrians crowd and squeeze, people laugh and rub shoulders, and everywhere merchants are calling out to sell something. One cannot help but smile."[135] Notable shops specializing in fur hats and neck warmers were located nearby; so too were specialty ginseng shops.[136]

Pawnshops, so ubiquitous in the Qing world, thrived on the used fur market.[137] A seasonal rhythm dictated their business in Beijing: In the spring, bannermen pawned fur coats and hats; in the winter, they redeemed them. Later, the pawned fur coat became a metaphor for the old guard; the writer Lao She (1899–1966) thus lampooned an opium-addled magistrate in his story "Also a Triangle," in which the bedridden man is too weak to even pawn a lowly lamb-fur gown and so pleads for understanding: "Sure would save me from making a fool of myself running all over town trying to get rid of a lamb-fur jacket. No one's wearing lamb now, or even fox leg!"[138]

(Lao She himself once claimed "with tears in his eyes" to have sold his own fur coat to provide food and clothes for his mother in winter.[139])

One sign of this fashion shift appears in the language and spirit of late-eighteenth-century sumptuary laws: The court no longer worried about Chinese officials dressing like Manchu elites but common subjects dressing the part, too. From its inception, the Qing court proved sensitive to complaints of overindulgence in luxury. Kangxi and Yongzheng in particular prided themselves on frugality; fur was regal, but only in moderation. In 1664, the Kangxi emperor decreed that new gray fox-fur hats, often awarded to favored officials of the inner court, be given only to officials who truly needed them: "Cancel [the new order] if [their existing hat] is a good one. Replace it with a new one only if it is worn-out."[140] The emperor similarly halted the annual gifting of sable pelts to favored officials during the Three Feudatories Rebellion (1673–1681), as sable's decadence "portended trouble from within Yunnan." No virtuous generals or officials received pelts until victory was in sight, in 1680, when victory was in hand.[141] It was easy to overstep one's bounds. In one instance, Kangxi tut-tutted to a coterie of lavishly dressed officials after a policy discussion:

> Now about your clothing and headgear. Your fondness for expensive things made of sable and silk is a minor detail, but it is a matter of being economical. Don't you know how many fox-fur hats one sable hat could buy? Or how many sheepskin coats one silk garment is worth? Why do you wear such costly items?[142]

Despite such injunctions, many Manchus ignored sumptuary laws and dressed beyond their rank. To Yongzheng, it was a sign of profligacy: Buying furs was beyond the means of ordinary Manchus, and overspending would ruin them. The debates at court on what to do revealed the degree to which fur fashion was outpacing courtly norms. As one official protested:

> Laws must be enforceable for prohibitions to work. If the laws are clearly known but unable to be successfully applied, then prohibitions cannot work. If former prohibitions have been failures, how can they be reissued?[143]

The Yongzheng emperor dismissed such arguments: "High ministers and officials can buy [satins and furs] when the price is low and after their households have earned money and become rich," he explained. Common soldiers, in contrast, could not afford to be "profligate." To protect their livelihood, the emperor argued, the court had a moral duty to admonish "those who overstep their bounds," to teach and to guide them, so that they may "come to their senses." He recognized it might take generations: Eventually, "years in future, people will reform themselves on their own accord" and be frugal.[144] Thus, in 1725, he reissued the sumptuary laws for bannermen that prohibited the wearing of satin, sable, and lynx robes.

Yet extravagance could not be contained. One measure of fur's newfound popularity was its increased stature in popular literature. The charged symbolism surrounding sable made it fit for caricature and absurdity in ways almost difficult to imagine outside the Qing context. Li Lüyuan's novel *Lantern at the Road Fork* (*Qiludeng*, published c.1777) includes a character that is nothing less than a walking, talking sable pelt.[145] Not surprisingly, characters with strong connections to the court typically wear furs. *A Romance to Awaken the World* (*Xingshi yinyuan chuan*), a novel popularly attributed to Pu Songling (1640–1715), thus opens with a prince hunting in sable fur and shifts to a discussion of ambitious officials worried about their need to wear fine furs.[146] It was not easy to dress the part in this world: The novel provided the outrageous figure of fifty-five silver taels to buy a single sable-fur hat.[147]

Fur in Cao Xueqin's *Dream of the Red Chamber* (*Hongloumeng*)—published almost a century after *A Romance to Awaken the World*—is even more ubiquitous.[148] By day characters slip into fur to entertain guests and by night to ward off cold. They gift fur to friends and relatives and discuss the quality, warmth, and upkeep of their jackets and robes. The text delights in the variety and style of fur fashions: Lady Xifeng has a sable overcoat, squirrel jacket, and ermine skirt; Baoyu dresses in a fox-fur–lined archer's vest and a dark sable robe.[149] The identity-bending possibility of dress was always at play: In one scene, Baoyu pushes Fangguan to experiment with her hair style and try on a sable-fur hat—then whimsically imagines she is a frontiersman named Yelü Xiongnu: a Khitan Hun.[150] At its height, Baoyu's family keeps a treasure box filled with gold, silver, jade, ivory, and nine strings of Manchurian pearls. Their savings also included a bewildering embarrassment of fur:

Eighteen black fox pelts, six dark fox belts; thirty-six sable pelts, thirty yellow fox pelts, twelve lynx pelts, three *maye* pelts, sixty imported squirrel pelts, forty pelts of squirrel and fox legs, twenty reddish-brown sheep pelts, two *huli* fox pelts, two yellow fox leg-fur pelts, twenty pieces of small arctic fox pelts, thirty pieces of foreign wool . . . ten mountain weasel tubes, four pieces of *doushu* pelts . . . one piece of *meilu* fur, two cloud-fox tubes, one role of badger cub fur . . . 160 grey squirrel pelts, eight badger pelts, six tiger pelts, three fur seal pelts, sixteen sea otter pelts . . . ten black fox-fur hats, twelve *wodao* hats, two sable hats, sixteen small fox pelts, two aquatic raccoon dog pelts, two otter pelts, [and] thirty-five cat pelts.[151]

Yet another measure of the popularity and marketability of furs was the proliferation of counterfeits.[152] In *A Romance to Awaken the World*, Pu Songling imagines a hatter named Luo Jiacai who makes his fortune peddling fakes:

> He was a sable-fur artisan. For years sable was extremely expensive. He would construct hats by taking the most pretty part of the sable's spine, stretching it out as big and wide as possible and piling a great many together. Then, to cobble together the hat, he stitched the insides together with a string of dark ramie. People see only that the fur is plush and the color is black; nobody knows that myriad strips of shoddy pelts compose the interior and fringes. He made twenty to thirty taels silver selling each and so gradually built up the family business.[153]

As we shall see in the coming chapter, counterfeit ginseng proliferated as well, as did fake steppe mushrooms. Around Beijing, as one late nineteenth-century gazetteer recorded, everyone knew that real steppe mushrooms (Ch: *koumo*) "grew on the bones of cattle and sheep," but that "these days local people call all of our local products 'steppe mushrooms.'"[154] If customers knew the origins of these *koumo*, they would plummet in value. Origins mattered.

If wild frontier objects thus had once been reviled for their provenance, they were now celebrated for it: Their value continued to derive from stories of their origins and alterations. Where did they come from? How were they created, and how had they been changed? It took a considerable amount of knowledge about the nature of pelts to appraise them; those without any market knowledge were likely to get duped. The problem was acute enough to inspire a new subgenre: appraisal manuals for pawnbrokers. Given the dominance of fur in the pawn market, guidebooks proliferated for pawnshop owners to help with appraisal. At least one manual, the *Rules for Fine Furs* (*Lun piyi cuxi maofa*), published in 1843, specialized entirely in fur appraisal.[155] The text lists dozens of types of furs, divided into animal types (marmot, fox, steppe fox, Solon gray squirrel, imported squirrel, and so on) and parts of the animal (whole pelts, underbelly fur, leg fur), then provides information on the number of units necessary for producing a robe (Ch: *pao*), gown (Ch: *tao*), jacket (Ch: *magua*), coat (Ch: *dahu*), or overcoat (Ch: *waitao*). Vivid details of fashion and craft emerge from the text. We learn that most animal pelts figured exclusively in robes, gowns, and jackets, but some, such as western fox, steppe wolf, and black fox, were used mostly in jackets and overcoats. We learn that gowns and overcoats were relatively lavish: It generally required twice as many pelts to make a gown or overcoat than a jacket. Full-length robes (see Figure 1.2), however, usually required 30 percent more pelts than a gown or overcoat. The results could be extravagant: 180 fox-heads, 180 Solon squirrels, or 160 leopard pelts per robe.[156]

Although larger animals, in turn, tended to command higher prices than smaller ones, such as squirrels, a pelt's value was only in part a function of its material qualities. Size and other physical properties, such as waterproofing, weight, and wear, mattered as well: Furs were winter wear, meant to keep one warm and dry, and certain pelt types, such as sea otter, were more dense with hairs and so at once more waterproof and sensuous.[157] Yet value reflected a discourse of provenance more than materiality; stories as much as sensuality structured the Qing valuation of furs. According to the *Rules for Fine Furs*, for example, "top-grade" furs invariably derived from "east of the [Great Wall] pass," in Manchuria. The finest sables came from "Solon" lands and the worst from Korea (Koryo). The best squirrels came from Solon lands as well, as did the most luxurious river otters and lynx, though Russian varieties of the latter two species were of comparable value. Steppe foxes were best if from "beyond the Great Wall"; black fox, black wolf, fire fox, *chuanwo*, dark fox, *saoshu*, badger, ermine, wolf, river otter, and marmot were all most valuable when from "East of the Pass," in Manchuria. In a catalogue of fifty types of animal pelts, only two were top grade if from China proper: yellow foxes from Hubei and Hunan and flying squirrels from Shaanxi and Gansu.[158]

Where the provenance and history of products was unclear, or when a product seemed to lack a pedigree, scholars and connoisseurs invented one for it. Some people had intimate firsthand knowledge of where products like fur came from. In his *Talks with Guests over Tea* (*Chayu kehua*), for example, the former President of the Board of Punishments Ruan Kuisheng (1727–1789) devoted an entry in his notes to "[animal] types such as sable and fox."[159] As a participant in the Four Treasuries project and a compiler of the official history of the Dzungar campaigns, Ruan could write about fur with unique authority. As a wealthy consumer, he also knew the luxury markets. Thus in discussing the marten (Ch: *saoxue*)—an animal that lacked a Chinese translation altogether in the *Da Qing quanshu*—Ruan easily explained, "It is bigger than the sable. Its fur is white and the hairs are long, and its luster is inferior to them. The price is also lower." In his discussion of martens (Ch: *diaoshu*), he drew inspiration from more scholarly sources, including the *Guangzhi*, a Jin dynasty (265–420) encyclopedia by Guo Yigong, who associated sable with ancient Fuyu (a contemporary Manchurian kingdom of the far northeast), and the *Shengjing tongzhi*, an imperial gazetteer of Mukden produced during Kangxi's reign. He cites both texts, while adding new information of his own:

> [Martens] prefer eating pine-seeds and [so are found] in pine forests. One type is called the "pine dog," of which there are yellow and black varieties. The jet-black ones [have fur that is] luxuriant but not shiny, and are especially difficult to procure. Its den is either dug into the earth or hollowed from a tree. Trappers rig a net at the entrance to the den, then smoke [the animal] out. It fears the smoke and flees into the net. There are also dogs that hunt martens. The dogs sniff out the location of its tracks, guard [its den] without leaving, [then] wait for [the marten] to come out to catch it in its mouth. Some people also use slings or snares. The *Shengjing tongzhi* names one marten the "pinecone dog," as it prefers to eat pinecones and bark. There are many of these throughout the mountains of Ula. Their pelt is light and warm, and can be made into coats or hats. The *Guangzhi* [states that] martens come from Fuyu.[160]

In establishing a deeper genealogical connection between the animals of the present and those referenced in China's deeper literary tradition, Ruan Kuisheng was not alone: In this same era the Qing court was writing histories of the origins of the Manchus, which connected the Manchus themselves to the ancient Fuyu, and scholars were recovering a Han dynasty past for the newly conquered cities of Xinjiang.[161] When, in this spirit, scholars sought Qing exotics in older texts, many found precedents in the Liao (907–1125), Jin (1115–1234), and Yuan (1271–1368) periods, when the conquest dynasties of the Khitan, Jurchen, and Mongols ruled. As interest in precedents grew, publishers reprinted the poetry of the Liao, Jin, and Yuan courts that celebrated hunting, wearing fur, and luxurious sable-fur yurts.[162] The retrospective Yuan poetry compilation, *Yuanshixuan* (1798), was particularly rich with literary references to sable coats in the era of the Mongol empire.[163] Fur remained indelibly linked with the frontier, the court, and the north—but now it was celebrated as such.

Other products, including the Manchurian freshwater pearl and the steppe mushroom, received similar treatment, as scholars turned to classical texts for precedents. Prior to the conquest, for example, Manchurian freshwater pearls (Ma: *tana*) were so exotic that scholars and consumers had difficulty locating them in earlier texts; the Chinese term "eastern pearl" (Ch: *dongzhu*), in fact, was a seventeenth-century neologism. They did, however, find "northern pearls" (Ch: *beizhu*), which were distinct from "true pearls" (Ch: *zhenzhu*) and which Song literati associated with the Khitan Liao (907–1125) and Jurchen Jin courts (1115–1234). Unlike "true pearls," "northern pearls" had an air of exoticism.[164] Song-period accounts describe how, in the early twelfth century, during the final days of the Liao court, "Extravagance was unbridled, and the imperial palace vied only for northern pearls."[165] The marvel of the pearls, as always, lay in their origins. As one such account recorded:

> Northern pearls all come from due north, from the frontier-market trade. . . . [They] are beautiful. Big ones are like marbles, and small ones are like tung nuts. All come from Liaodong's rivers and coastline. On the fifteenth of every eighth month, there is a bright full moon, and thus a great ripening, and in the tenth month one can collect the pearl oysters. However the north is freezing cold, and by the ninth or tenth month the ice is already a *chi* [approx. ¼ meter] thick. [So] they bore a hole through the ice, descend into the water, and hunt them, which causes the [pearlers] to become sick. There are also swans that can eat the oysters and gobble down the treasure, as well as great birds of prey called "gyrfalcons" (Ch: *haidongqing*) that can attack the swans. People thus use the birds of prey to catch swans, and so they [obtain] the pearls sucked up inside them.[166]

Medieval precedents and similarly fantastical stories dominated descriptions of steppe mushrooms as well, as they too earned a historical pedigree. Like "eastern pearls," the Qing "steppe mushrooms" was a neologism, and scholars had no luck finding them in earlier texts. There were, however, mushrooms called "sand fungi" (Ch: *shajun*), and in the 1780s scholars, poets, and gourmands began to equate the two. The first text to define and elaborate on the *koumo*'s pedigree at length was the *Imperially Commissioned Rehe Gazetteer* (*Qinding Rehe zhi*), the gazetteer for the jurisdiction encompassing the court's hunting grounds. Completed in 1781 under the guidance of two of the closest associates of the aging Qianlong emperor—the Grand Councilors Liang Guozhi (1723–1786) and Heshen

(1746–1799)—the text featured, like all gazetteers, descriptions of local flora and fauna, which in this case included steppe mushrooms. The entry required a bit of explanation. What was a steppe mushroom? It was a "fungus" (Ch: *jun*) similar to *Hericium erinaceus* (Ch: *houtou*, lit. "monkey head" mushroom). The text elaborated that "the best ones are the most valued in China proper [Ch: *zhongtu*,] and are called 'steppe mushrooms'" (Ch: *koumo*). It claimed further that the enormous manure heaps outside a military camp produce "especially delicious" ones, and for this reason steppe mushrooms had the nickname "encampment mushrooms" (Ch: *yingpan mogu*). It then explained that "steppe mushrooms" were also known as "sand fungi" (Ch: *shajun*).[167]

It was an important claim: Sand fungi had a particularly close association with the rustic summer palaces of the Liao court, at Shangjing, and the Mongol Yuan court, at Shangdu—the "Xanadu" of Marco Polo's *Travels*. The *Rehe Gazetteer* thus cites two poems celebrating "sand fungi" in connection to these Yuan retreats, the antecedents to the Qing complex at Rehe. The first poem, by Zhou Boqi (1298–1369), a compiler at the Yuan Hanlin Academy, derived from his "Miscellaneous Poems of the Upper Capital" (*Shangjing zashi*), his celebration of Shangdu's own literary predecessor: Shangjing, the Liao dynasty's summer retreat. In one verse, Zhou wrote concisely that "fungi that emerge from sand are delicious" (Ch: *jun chu shazhong mei*). A second cited poem belonged to Xu Youren (1287–1364), an assistant grand councilor in the Yuan secretariat and husband to Zhaoluan, the famed Mongol calligrapher and musician. His verse, like Zhou Boqi's, derived from another commemoration of the Liao retreat, Xu's "Ten Songs of Shangjing" (*Shangjing shiyong*). He titled his poem "Sand Mushrooms":

> Moisture by the hooves of cattle and sheep,
> The product of the land is flowering.
> At the foot of the tent, on ground stamped by horses,
> "Nail-heads" are gaily capped with sand.
> The kitchen offers golden delicacies,
> Fur ropes unfold from the felt cart,
> No one can but drool thinking about it,
> No one in the family will be late.[168]

In a personal annotation to the poem, Xu Youren explained the allusions to hooves and horses: Mushrooms grew in rings in the stomping ground around tents.

In time, Qing scholars collected more verses on sand fungi. An updated version of the Rehe gazetteer, the *Chengde Prefecture Gazetteer* (*Chengde fuzhi*, published 1826), added two extra lines on sand fungi by Yuan-period literati. The first, by the scholar-official Liu Guan (1270–1342), derived from his *Houluanshui qiufeng shi* ("Poems on Autumn Wind on the Lower Luan River") a third collection honoring summer retreats. The second belonged to Yang Yunfu (fl. fourteenth century), a Yuan poet who praised mushrooms in his own "Mixed Songs of Shangdu" (*Luanjing zayong*).[169] The Chengde gazetteer included a final line of verse from the early Qing period, from a poem by Zha Shenxing (1650–1727, *jinshi* 1703), who served as tutor to the Manchu Grand Councilor Mingju's children.

Such literary references helped connect the Qing "steppe mushroom," which lacked a clear precedent, to China's past, Inner Asian courts, and imperial hunting grounds, from Liao Shangjing to Yuan Shangdu to Qing Chengde. Through their imagery, they also connected the mushrooms to the wider world of the steppe and the outdoors, with allusions to the frontier, livestock, and military life. Whether Qianlong and Khubilai tasted the same thing we will never know; we may even doubt whether "steppe mushroom" itself was a singular, material entity. What is certain is that Qing writers took the historical and contemporary mushrooms to be identical, and they established a textual genealogy that linked the steppe mushrooms of the present with those of an imperial and Inner Asian past.

The gazetteers had an impact: Through the course of the eighteenth century, the language and imagery found in them began to resonate in other genres of writing, from poetry and *biji* to cookbooks. Literati elaborated on the newly invented tradition, emphasizing its Inner Asian aspects, its imperial antiquity, and the mushrooms' rustic origins amid dung heaps and trodden grass. The Hangzhou poet Wu Xiqi (1746–1818, *jinshi* 1775) celebrated *koumo* "like nails in the ground" in his "Mixed Songs of Rehe" (1808), which included a typical annotation that identified steppe mushrooms with sand mushrooms and encampment mushrooms, citing Zhou Boqi ("fungi that emerge from sand are delicious").[170] Bin-liang (1771–1847), a Manchu poet with personal administrative experience in Mukden and Rehe, wrote of *koumo* in his own nostalgic take on Mongol Shangdu. In one annotation, he elaborated in detail: "Local people say that mushrooms produced beyond the Great Wall grow when a drip of milk falls from a horse or a cow to the grass, then is infused with the steamy mist after a summer rain. The especially sweet and crisp sprouts of the ones that grow by a planted tent are famously called 'encampment mushrooms.'"[171]

Although associated with the frontier, by the late eighteenth century steppe mushrooms had become one of the most famous and coveted delicacies in the empire, particularly in the North. To Bin-liang, the steppe mushroom was every bit as good as other delicacies; he described it as the "companion" of elm oyster, water chestnut, and tender bamboo shoots.[172] By 1800, others enthused that the steppe mushroom was a product whose "name rang out above all."[173] Into the late Qing and early Republican periods, steppe mushroom would continue to serve as a symbol of excellence in north and northeast China, one which local gazetteers measured all other mushrooms against.[174] Although associated with China's Inner Asian past, they had earned a reputation as products desirable to everyone, not just Manchus or Mongols.

A WORLD BOUND BY SUPERFLUOUS THINGS

If Qing consumers reimagined the provenance and antiquity of frontier exotics, we should not follow suit: There is no evidence that medieval "sand fungi" or "northern pearls" were the same as the Qing period's "steppe mushrooms" or "eastern pearls." At the very least, their very ubiquity in the Qing marketplace suggests differences between their value in the eighteenth-century world and previous eras. Even in the Qing, of course, these products remained luxury goods, and only a tiny fraction of the Qing populace had access to them. Yet even if they were discussed more than consumed, demand for them by the late eighteenth century rose high enough to create unprecedented ripple effects throughout the empire and, ultimately, across the wider world. Donald Worster once powerfully argued that environmental history in its first iteration should be a history of food: Humanity shares no more profound connection to the land than the work we do to produce our daily bread.[175] The history of staple goods, to be sure, matters tremendously. Yet people have died for and found meaning in far less existential pursuits. Mushrooms and fur may have been luxuries, but their existence in material culture provides a powerful standard for the historian: They too can serve as measures of an age. Ultimately, they also provide the vital material links between local, Qing, and global histories.

As demand for natural resources in the Qing world surged between 1700 and 1850, new commercial networks emerged that transformed relationships across the empire and between China and seemingly disparate realms. As commerce intensified, the empire's population roughly tripled and the amount of land under cultivation doubled.[176] Some agricultural expansion occurred in forested uplands; some through diking and reclaiming land by lakes, rivers, and the coast; and some in external frontiers, as in the empire's Southwest, western Taiwan, and the plains of Mukden in southern Manchuria (from the seventeenth century), and in Xinjiang and parts of Inner Mongolia (from the the mid-eighteenth). Homesteading proceeded at a relatively steady pace: In 200 years, from roughly 1650 to 1850, the amount of land under cultivation within the Qing empire rose from about 100 million to 200 million acres, or a rate of 500,000 acres per year. The modern expansion of agriculture, by comparison, proved significantly faster: in the sixty-four years between 1893 and 1957 alone, China's total farmland grew to 280 million acres, with average growth at 1.2 million acres per year, or 250 percent faster.[177] In some regions, including Outer Mongolia and the territories of Heilongjiang and Jilin, homesteading remained negligible until the late nineteenth and early twentieth centuries or never took hold at all.

In many regions it was instead the rushes for luxury commodities such as fur and mushrooms that dominated local economies, especially from the last quarter of the eighteenth century.[178] International trade with China boomed in this period. At the Russo–Qing border town of Kiakhta, trade had stalled for much of the 1700s, the result, in part, of disputes that had led the Qing court to embargo the trade through the years 1764–1768, 1779–1780, and 1785–1792. After 1792, the Kiakhta trade took off, and trade thereafter grew exponentially; its value quadrupled in the years 1775–1805 alone.[179] Overland trade with Burma followed a similar trajectory. As in the North, a series of conflicts in the Southwest between the Qing and Konbaung courts, which had culminated in the Sino–Burmese War of 1765–1769, led the Qianlong court to embargo this cross-border trade as well, and commerce plummeted as a result.[180] When the Qing court finally lifted the ban in 1790, imports of jade, bird nests, rhinoceros tusk, deer horn, and shark fin grew rapidly. Overland trade with Luang Prabang, in modern Laos, likewise accelerated in this period, buoyed by demand for a similar array of products: ivory, peacock feathers, rhino tusk, and deer horn.[181] On the coast, the Chinese junk trade with the Sulu Sultanate, in the modern Philippines, doubled between 1760 and 1814, and, between 1750 and 1820, seaborne trade with Cochinchina (southern Vietnam) quadrupled.[182] Amid the boom, the port city of Canton, spurred in part by the massive growth of the Pacific sea otter and Hawaiin sandalwood trades, witnessed a dramatic rise in American and British shipping.[183]

Natural resources, such as furs, minerals, ocean life, and forest products were at the heart of this new trade, which arose only as the wars of the eighteenth century came to their conclusion. The "jade rush" for nephrite in Xinjiang peaked between 1776 and 1821.[184] The jadeite trade with Burma followed a similar timeline: Its "booming period" lasted from 1760 to 1812, as the value of Burmese jade "soared."[185] In Xinjiang and Mongolia, authorities fought to control the growth of new Chinese gold mining camps in the 1770s and 1780s.[186] Copper production on the Southwestern frontier began notably earlier, starting in the first quarter of the eighteenth century. Yet the golden age of copper production in the Southwest began only after 1760, when production reached unprecedented peaks; production there, too, remained high until roughly 1820.[187] Chinese-run mines moved across the border into northern Vietnam in this era, and by the early nineteenth century, Chinese mines dominated the economy of the Vietnamese highlands.[188] At the same time, in maritime Southeast Asia, new Chinese mining operations for gold and tin began to dot the landscapes of Borneo, Phuket, Kelantan, Perak, Selangor, and Bangka.[189]

Rushes for pearls, sea turtle shells, and sea cucumber (also called *trepang* or *beche-de-mer*) likewise defined the period. Chinese merchants on the Tumen and Yalu rivers had long bought sea cucumber at the Korean border market towns of Kyŏng'wŏn and Hoeryŏng, and Koreans brought sea cucumber to Beijing as tribute throughout the eighteenth century.[190] Sea cucumber poaching, however, became a recognized issue on the Pacific coast of Manchuria only in the period from 1785 to 1818, when beachcombing took off.[191] In the South China Sea, sea cucumber harvesting grew from the 1760s in the Sulu Sultanate and from the 1780s in Sulawesi, in the Dutch East Indies. In both locations, trade peaked in the early nineteenth century: By the 1820s, sea cucumbers rivaled pepper in the Dutch East Indies as the most valuable export.[192] Sea cucumber production for the China market expanded in these years to the coast of northern Australia, and, by the 1820s and 1830s, the industry had moved to distant Fiji and other islands in Oceania.[193]

Much of Southeast Asia and the Pacific as a whole experienced resource rushes. Between 1760 and 1835, mother-of-pearl exports to China from the Sulu zone increased sixfold, from 2,000 to 12,000 piculs a year. The sea turtle trade out of Sulawesi similarly boomed from the 1780s, despite repeated attempts to curtail and control it by the Dutch.[194] The bird's nest trade with China boomed too, particularly on the east coast of Borneo, where, until the trade devastated its swallow populations, the birds roosted in prodigious numbers.[195] The better-known sandalwood trade with China followed a similar trajectory from the 1790s, as Europeans and Americans entered the business. Sandalwood harvesting shifted first from Malabar and Timor to Fiji in the early 1800s and to the Marquesas and Hawaiian Islands in the 1810s and 1820s. Under the leadership of King Kamehameha I, who established a royal monopoly over the product, a quarter to a third of all Hawaiians were participating in the trade by the late 1820s.[196]

Though some of these trades would endure, in diminished form, into the modern period, overexploitation had doomed most of these booms to bust by 1840. Swallows were "plundered ad libitum" and disappeared from Borneo; Sulu's pearl oyster beds were picked bare; Hawaiian sandalwood stands were logged away.[197] Indeed, as we shall see, freshwater pearl mussels, wild ginseng, sea otters, and sables would suffer a similar fate in these same years. Some of these commodities were hunted, others mined or logged. Some came by the hands of European or American shippers, others by way of Chinese merchants. Some came from Inner Asia, others from Southeast Asia, Oceania, or the Americas. Yet similar patterns and challenges emerged from the booms and busts in their production. Of course, China's economic peripheries were hardly untouched before the late eighteenth century. Yet the "ecological shadow" of the era's rushes was unprecedented.[198] There was no extensive sea cucumber trade in 1700; no Pacific fur trade; no sandalwood trade beyond Southeast Asia; no large-scale jade mines in Xinjiang or Burma, tin mines on the Malay peninsula, or significant gold mining in Mongolia, Ili, or Borneo; and no Chinese copper mines to dominate northern Vietnam. Pearl oysters abounded on the shores of Borneo and the Philippine Islands; turtles and sea cucumber thrived throughout the seas of Southeast Asia. Fueled by the Qing demand for natural resources in the late eighteenth and early nineteenth centuries, Inner Asia, Southeast Asia, and the greater Pacific began to face similar challenges.[199]

CONCLUSION

A history of this wider region lies beyond the scope of this book. The following chapters focus instead on the story of the fur, freshwater pearl, and mushroom trades of this period. They were different from other products: All of them shared a close association with the court, and the court maintained special controls over their production. They were valued, in large part, because of this imperial connection: Consumers appreciated their special origins in nature and in Qing frontiers. Like the Jiaqing emperor, who treasured live tigers for the method of their capture, or the pawnshop owner, who priced pelts by their provenance, consumers made sense of objects in terms of the people and places that produced them. The nexus that bound products to places and people was not lost, for example, on Jean-Baptiste Du Halde, writing of Beijing in 1735. As he explained to his European audience, the Manchus were "lately come from the midst of Woods and Forests."[200] Their love of furs, to him, was thus only natural. Yet the history of the Manchus and their possessions is hardly so simple. The very ubiquity of products like fur, pearls, and mushrooms suggests a less innocent reality: They were, after all, produced en masse.

We imagine the early modern period as a time when nature and culture became distinct; when science, statecraft, or rationalization created a civilization unto itself. Everywhere modern people were draining swamps, cutting down forests, and reclaiming land. Cities were rising, the wild frontier receding, and humanity for the first time dreamed of a distant and unspoiled nature. Yet the stuff of nature was more part of our lives than it would ever be again: pelts around our necks; horses and camels on the streets; sturgeon, venison, mushrooms, and pearls. The period did not witness just a romance of nature but an economy of it: wild things circulating from hand to hand, from imperial frontiers to the centers of empire. The domains of neither nature nor culture were entirely pure; the world was trimmed with fur.

Pearl Thieves and Perfect Order

Something strange happened in Manchuria between 1785 and 1810: Its precious freshwater pearls disappeared. Perhaps stranger still, the Qing empire did everything in its power to preserve them: It erected guard posts and customs barriers, kept registers and tallies, punished poachers and pearl thieves, disciplined the corrupt, and empowered the military to take charge. A new concern about nature emerged. "Nurture the mussels and let them grow," the emperor ordered; let Manchuria have pearl mussels.[1] What had happened, and what could be done?

We often tell the environmental history of early modern China as a frontier story, in which commercial growth pushed Chinese society past the artificial bounds of empire. In Manchuria in particular, we read, Chinese homesteaders transformed the land from a wilderness to an agricultural breadbasket, prefiguring national revolution and empire's end. The story is simple, clear, and progressive: Manchu emperors vainly preserved the old order; Chinese settlers ushered in the new.[2]

Based on Manchu-language archives, this chapter pursues a different type of story. Pearl mussels fit uneasily into the progressive narrative;

they are not the champions of Chinese history. Yet if mussels seem mute and powerless, history does not belong to the audible and strong.[3] In their multitudes, freshwater mussels upheld river ecosystems, and, through their production of pearls, they underpinned a network of exchange that bound Manchuria to the wider world. Notably, moreover, those who harvested pearls were neither entirely Manchu nor Chinese: They had their own institutional hierarchy; they had special access to riverbeds across conventional boundaries, and, at least until the mid-eighteenth century, they stood apart from the region's territorial administration. Thus until the late eighteenth century, mussels and their harvesters are more visible in the archives than Manchuria itself: In the empire's "Three Eastern Territories" (Ma: *dergi ilan golo*; Ch: *Dongsansheng*), Manchuria became a rallying cry only as its mussels disappeared.

This chapter explores the history told in the archives, from the establishment of the Qing freshwater pearl fishery in the Northeast, to the collapse of the mussel populations, to the resulting efforts of the court to, in its own words, "nurture the mussels and let them grow." The history of ginseng management followed a connected path: As the court worked to protect pearl mussels, it also was conserving wild ginseng and attempting to stop the spread of the plant's domestication. On both fronts, the Qing court drew increasingly sharp distinctions between human and natural products, positioned itself as protector of the natural, and empowered territorial authorities to defend its vision on the ground. All of these changes, I argue, dovetailed with the rise of a new discourse of the Three Eastern Territories as the original Manchu homeland. The territory of Manchuria and the bounds of nature, then, were twins of a sort: The boundaries of both emerged from a common dynamic.

MANCHURIA AS A PRODUCTIVE SPACE

At court, Manchurian pearls were part of the suite of products that represented the Qing court and its Northeast roots; like game meats and furs, they represented the Manchus, their ways, and their homeland. Perhaps no text from the era captures the court's celebration of Manchu roots better than the Qianlong emperor's *Ode to Mukden* (Ma: *Mukden-i fujurun bithe*), published with fanfare in 1743.[4] After a trip to his ancestral tombs, outside the modern city of Shenyang, Qianlong grew enchanted with Mukden as a natural wonderland. The poem catalogued all the creatures Qianlong imagined in the homeland: tigers, leopards, bears, wild asses, and so on.

The *Ode* was, in part, a response to the troubles of the time, as the mideighteenth century was a trying moment for the Qing court. Commerce was thriving, and the population was growing fast, but perhaps too fast, and statesmen were anxious that farmland might be insufficient to feed everyone. To promote homesteading, the Qianlong court forgave the land tax on newly opened farms. In 1741, the court further endorsed a plan to relocate unemployed Manchu bannermen from Beijing to Manchuria to produce their own food. In the 1750s, the Qianlong emperor justified the conquest of Xinjiang, in part, in a similar spirit: It was as a way to secure new farmland for the unemployed.[5] Idle Manchu bannermen particularly unsettled the court. Ideologically, Manchu bannermen were the "root" (Ch: *genben*; Ma: *da*) of the empire, but in Beijing and in the garrisoned cities, it seemed that the Manchus had lost their "old way" (Ma: *fe doro*). They seemed to be assimilating: The children of the conquest generation spoke Chinese and favored Chinese fashions and entertainment; they lived in cities and knew little of horses or hunting or war.[6] Thus when Qianlong celebrated the natural wonders of Manchuria, he was also pushing a political agenda. It should be no surprise, in this context, that Manchuria was everything China was not. If the Manchus had lost the "old way" after settling in Chinese cities, the homeland had been left unchanged. If China was corrupting, Mukden had remained pure. As such, the Manchu homeland was not like any other frontier: It was special, timeless, and unaltered.

To a degree, Manchuria stood apart because it was so far from the empire's political and commercial centers. Simply to get there required contending with preindustrial travel: impossibly long distances over mountains, mud, and overflowing streams; banditry; suffering animals; insects; and disease. Weight more than anything was king: Before mechanized travel, the price of a bag of grain rose by 3 percent for every mile traveled by land; after twenty-five miles, accordingly, the bag doubled in price.[7] For long-distance trade, merchants could afford to work only with high-value, low-weight items. In the waterways of southern China and on the coast, trade in heavier and bulkier items was possible, and items like porcelain and sandalwood found markets. In the far north, furs, pearls, ginseng, mushrooms, and tea dominated long-distance trade.

Under Qing rule, Manchuria conformed largely to the model predicted by economic geography for market-oriented peripheries: The southern coast

shipped grain to Chinese markets, whereas the northern interior specialized in exporting expensive, light-weight natural resources, like furs, pearls,
ginseng, and medicinal deer horn. Today, farmland stretches from the
coastal crescent around Liaodong Bay northeast for roughly 600 miles to
the Russian border, then, following contours formed by mountains and
rain shadows, loops to the west and curls back down to the south; aerial
imagery reveals this zone of agriculture to be roughly the shape of a pirate's
hand hook. To the east of this zone, mountains that rise above 500 meters
have made farming impractical; to the arid west, where rain totals less than
twenty inches per year, sustainable agriculture has proved impossible.[8]

In 1800, however, and almost until 1900, the region's farmland remained
confined to the coastal crescent; beyond this core lay a mere patchwork of
small farms interspersed amid an enormous expanse of steppe to the northwest and thickly forested mountains to the northeast. If we imagine ourselves gazing down from a hot-air balloon in the summer of 1800, the land
would look radically different from the hook shape so apparent today. What
would we see? In 1800, as today, the climate followed the monsoon: Each
winter, dry and cold winds blew down from Siberia, and each summer, wet
winds blew up from the sea. If we drifted north with the summer winds, we
would see farmland along the southern plains of the Liaodong peninsula as
today: a light-green quilt of rectangular strips, broken only by gray villages
arrayed every half a mile from each other, with bigger villages interspersed
every five to ten miles and small towns thirty to forty miles apart.[9] Although
at times parts of the coastal zone had been given to pasture, some form of
agriculture had been practiced there throughout recorded history and even
deep into the Neolithic past.[10] Though devastated in the Ming–Qing transition, the Qing reconstruction encouraged immigration into this region,
spurring a rapid recovery of agriculture in the late seventeenth and early
eighteenth centuries. Supported by Qing policies, the population grew by
57 percent between 1681 and 1734 , and the amount of registered farmland
grew eightfold, from roughly 313 thousand *mu* of land in 1681 (about eighty
square miles) to 2,622 in 1734 (about 680 square miles). Of this growth,
96 percent of the population and 95 percent of the new lands registered were
on or adjacent to the coast; a mere 5 percent of new farmland—a total of
113 thousand *mu*, or thirty square miles—was northeast of Shenyang (Ma:
Mukden).[11]

Beyond the coastal plain, agriculture in 1800 remained scattered and
relatively small in scale, with most farms centered around military garri-

Map 2.1. The Northeast and the Three Eastern Territories.

sons along the great rivers: Jilin on the Sunggari, Ningguta on the Mudan, Bedune and Mergen on the Nen, and Sahaliyan Ula (Heilongjiang) on the Amur (see Map 2.1).[12] There one found a wide mix of farmers: Manchu and Chinese bannermen managed banner farms to help supply the garrisons; Daur Mongols, after being relocated from the Amur, practiced agriculture in the Nen River valley; unemployed bannermen from Beijing, transplanted by order of the court in 1741, held farms in Bedune; and immigrant Chinese peasants, who worked much of the land for bannermen, struck off on a small scale as homesteaders from the mid-eighteenth century onward, prompting edicts against the practice in Jilin in 1762 and in both Jilin and Sahaliyan Ula (Heilongjiang) in 1776.[13] Beyond the garrisons, along the middle and lower reaches of the Amur, on the Ussuri, and out to the Pacific coast, light agriculture (in combination with fishing, hunting, and trapping) supported myriad villages along the river valleys. Homesteading between modern Changchun and Shuangcheng accelerated after 1800, and throughout the region from the late nineteenth century onward, but we should not imagine Manchuria becoming a breadbasket before then; outside the fertile coastal crescent, homesteading dominated neither the land nor the time of most inhabitants.

If our balloon carried us inland to the northwest, we would see not the quilted farmlands of the southern plains but the brown-green steppe, which stretched out for roughly 150 miles east of the Greater Khinggan mountains, the mountain range that divided the region from the high Mongolian plain. If our balloon drifted east toward the Pacific coast, farmland would give way to a quilted green blanket of mountains, crisscrossed by myriad small creeks and rivers. These waterways collected in one of the largest river systems in the world, the greater Amur watershed, which was fed from the south by the Sunggari, Mudan, and Ussuri Rivers in the vast lowlands north of the Korean Peninsula before emptying into the Pacific Ocean near Sakhalin Island. Like the mouth of the Hudson River and early New York City, the mouth of the Amur served as a trade hub linking riverine, coastal, and island trades. All of the region's rivers supported freshwater pearl mussels.[14]

The Northeast was productive well before the Qing conquest. Pearls were an important trade item from at least the Liao period (907–1125), and there are records of fur tribute exchanges from as early as the Han (206 BCE–220 CE). The recorded volume of trade grew from the fifteenth century onward, spurred by demand for fur and ginseng in the Ming and Chosŏn states. By the late Ming, these trades channeled goods and people from as far away as the Amur River to Kaiyuan, Liaodong's great marketplace along the Ming border. Under the leadership of the Hada, the Hūlun confederation (identified as "Haixi" Jurchens in Ming sources), used trade patents issued by the Ming court to dominate the trade in the early sixteenth century, much as Nurhaci fought to dominate it in the late sixteenth and early seventeenth centuries.[15] No one language, political system, ethnic identity, or environment held the Northeast together. In this time period what brought people together, more than anything, was trade.

Long-distance trade was particularly vital to the Manchurian economy. Commerce was driven by consumers in the Qing, Chosŏn, and Tokugawa worlds, facilitated by Chinese, Manchu, Russian, Daur, Ewenki, and Ainu merchants and underpinned by trappers, diggers, and pearlers in the forested uplands around the Amur River basin. Han Chinese merchants grew increasingly active in the region in the seventeenth century, but they were not alone: Daur and Ewenki kept ties to the caravan trade with Khalkha Mongolia and to fur trappers throughout the Greater Khinggan, and they used a system of "sworn brotherhood" (Ma: *anda*) relationships to prosper in the commercial world of the Nen River valley. Ewenkis too traded across the border with Russia throughout the Qing period, long after the Treaty of Nerchinsk forbade it.[16] Others, based in the Amur delta and Sakhalin Island, as Matsuura Shigeru has documented, held special marriage and tributary ties to the Qing court as *hojihon* (lit. a "son-in-law" in Manchu), which they used to build their own fur trade operations.[17] Many remember "Manchuria" as the colonial periphery it became in the late nineteenth and twentieth centuries. We should not let its modern fate blind us: Into the eighteenth and early nineteenth centuries, the region was a commercial center in its own right, responding to its own internal markets as well as those of Siberia, China, Hokkaido, and Korea on its periphery.[18]

All Manchurian states depended on this commerce, but it fueled the rise of the nascent Qing state in particular. The estimates for the value of high-end Manchurian exports in the preconquest period are eye popping: As much as one-quarter of the silver imported into Ming China in the early seventeenth century made its way to Manchuria to pay for ginseng purchases alone.[19] Jurchens and Manchus were not primitive nomads from Manchuria's forests; rather, spurred by the commercial boom of the sixteenth century, Jurchen leaders like Nurhaci thrived more as "commercial capitalists" than as simple hunters. Silver was as central to the life of Nurhaci's state as it was to other regimes of the era: the "pirate" Zheng state in the South China Sea, the mixed agrarian-nomadic state of Altan Khan in Hohhot, and the mercenary regimes of Ming generals like Mao Wenlong, who competed with Nurhaci for ascendancy in the Northeast. The Qing state was born of the "silver belt" wrung about the late Ming empire; it was a product of the early modern age.[20]

BEYOND THE MANCHU HOMELAND: IMPERIAL
INSTITUTIONS AND CATEGORIES

"Manchuria," then, was more than just the homeland of the Manchus, though the Manchus would make it their own through the course of time. In the opening decades of the seventeenth century, the early Qing court—dubbed the "golden" state (Ma: *Aisin*; Ch: *Jin*) in the years 1616–1636—expanded out to the Ussuri, the upper Amur, and the Pacific coast.[21] A generation later, in the 1650s and the 1680s, the empire expanded north and east again in a mobilization against Russian troops, culminating in the Treaty of Nerchinsk in 1689. Thereafter, as the Dzungar Wars began (1690s–1730s), the Qing pivoted west to create new garrisons in the Nen River valley. The first wave of militarization saw the creation of the Eight Banners and the establishment of tribute systems; the second witnessed the creation of the military governors and the garrison system; the third culminated in the creation of new banners and the expansion of tribute networks on the Lower Amur and Sakhalin Island.

Once established, the garrisons served as administrative and commercial hubs for the region. After 1683, all members of the Eight Banners stationed in the Northeast fell under the command of one of three "military governors" (Ma: *jiyanggiyūn*; Ch: *jiangjun*), each of whom ruled one of the Three Eastern Territories: Mukden (Ch: Fengtian or Shengjing), Jilin (called Ningguta before 1676), and Sahaliyan Ula (Ch: Heilongjiang).[22] Beneath the three military governors stood "lieutenant governors" (Ma: *meiren i janggin*; Ch: *fudutong*), who oversaw smaller districts nested around the garrisons. As early as the Kangxi period, the Chinese presence around the garrisons was large, with Han bannermen, exiles, and licensed merchants establishing "trade districts" (Ma: *puseli giya*, lit. a "shop street") just outside them (usually by the southern gate); these communities grew steadily throughout the eighteenth century.[23] The region, however, was not administered by the same institutions governing the Chinese interior: Although today we divide the Northeast into three Chinese "provinces" (Ch: *sheng*), until the final decades of the empire, the state governed them in Manchu and not as "provinces" but as "territories" (Ma: *golo*).[24]

Yet there was not always a single governing logic that united the region as a whole. The vast region was not, for one, governed as the homeland of the Manchus. Significantly, the early Qing court made a distinction between the three territories and its homeland, called "Mukden," which included Mukden territory and a "Greater Mukden" in adjacent parts of Jilin.[25] The court governed Mukden according to special rules and with elevated language; in Chinese, for example, the territory became the land of the "Flourishing Capital" (Ch: Shengjing) or of the "Reception of Heaven" (Ch: Fengtian). Sahaliyan Ula and Jilin were different. Given their location on the Russian border, these later territories held a high strategic value to the court and thus were governed as special military zones. Yet they were not perceived as territories from which the court or the Manchus arose, and they earned no special monikers. Rather, the Kangxi emperor characteristically described Sahaliyan Ula and Ningguta as important for being "close" to Mukden, the imperial family's true homeland, not for being part of it.[26] Later, during the rule of the Qianlong emperor, the court began to impose greater unity on the greater region: In 1736 the court stopped the practice of exiling Chinese convicts to the territories; in 1740 it banned all Chinese immigration to them; and in 1751, it mandated that all their top authorities be Manchu.[27]

Thus in their entirety the three territories were no more the Manchu "homeland" than Siberia the Russian or America the English: Manchuria itself, like China as a whole, was a thinly garrisoned imperial colony. Indeed, within the three territories, Manchus and other members of the Eight Banners were never in the majority.[28] In Sahaliyan Ula, for example, Eight Bannermen represented only one-tenth of the population, according to one estimate from 1806.[29] Nor did the court administer the region by the logic that it was fundamentally Manchu. Unlike the Chinese interior where the "county-prefecture" system (Ch: *junxian*) was universal, the Northeast had no administrative homogeneity: Some people belonged to the Eight Banners; others were free of them; and still others belonged to banners unique to the Northeast. Each group, moreover, had ad hoc rules applying to them: Some had fixed territorial domains; others had access to multiple territories. No one administrative system unified the idiosyncratic arrangements between court and community at the local level.

Though complex, commodities such as fur and pearls help make sense of the confusing institutional matrix. The court, for example, claimed special rights over Manchurian freshwater pearls, and all exchanges of pearls were illegal except as a form of tribute. In general, *tribute* (Ch: *gong*; Ma: *jafara jaka* or *alban*; Mo: *alban*) denoted a special obligation to the court, though it never entailed universal norms, rituals, or institutions; the practice varied according to the product, place, and people in question.[30] Yet, in the

Northeast at least, there was one rule of thumb that usually applied: Tribute obligations ceased as soon as one enrolled in the Manchu Eight Banners. Though there were exceptions, the court only rarely required Eight Bannermen to submit furs, pearls, or (after 1730) ginseng as tribute.

The local distinction between fur providers and bannermen was as old as the state itself. The earliest recorded example of fur tribute dates to 1599, when a group of 100 "Hūrha" households presented a tribute of fox and sable to Nurhaci.[31] In 1607, Nurhaci forced the submission of additional tribute from the "Warka," who had been living in the Mudan and Ussuri river valleys near the Pacific Coast.[32] A group of roughly 500 of such Warka (called the "Kuyala" in Chinese sources) that submitted to the Qing court in 1641 was typical in this regard. Both the "Hūrha" and "Warka" were catchall terms for various fur-trapping communities; the terms applied to people who lived in villages (Ma: *gašan*) of roughly 300 to 3,000 people.[33] In the early 1600s, in fear of Nurhaci's wars of expansion, the residents of one such village, not far from the Pacific Coast, fled and relocated to Lefu Island, or modern-day Askold Island, in Posyet Bay. Their autonomy, however, proved short lived. In 1641, the Qing court sent a special division armed with cannons against them, forcing their quick surrender. The village was thereafter resettled to a village near Hunchun at the mouth of the Tumen River where they were ordered to submit an annual tribute of sea otter pelts.[34] Later, in 1714, the court established a garrison in Hunchun and enrolled them into the Eight Banners. As soon as they enrolled, they were freed from their former tribute obligation.[35] Similar patterns played out throughout the region. Into the 1730s, when villagers in the middle reaches of the Amur were brought into the Eight Banners as the "New Manchu" or "Kuyar" banners, their enrollment required entering a garrison and beginning life as farmers: They were provisioned with land, given equipment and (in some cases) slaves, and ordered to support the community through agriculture.[36]

When we follow commodities like furs and pearls to their source in Sahaliyan Ula and Jilin, then, we do not find Manchus at all; instead, we find a wide range of people outside the regular Eight Banner system: autonomous villages in the Amur delta and Sakhalin Island, poachers and black market merchants, and members of institutions unique to the Northeast, such as the so-called "hunter" banners. Some, like those in distant Sakhalin Island, maintained only nominal ties to the court, as we shall see in Chapter Four. Others, including those in "hunter" (Ma: *butha*) banners, maintained uniquely close ties to the court and proved to be some of the empire's most loyal subjects.

The largest group of "hunter" banners were the Butha Eight Banners, based in the Nen River valley and the Upper Amur, in western Sahaliyan Ula. Their name elided two fictions: They were neither simple "hunters" nor normal members of the regular Eight Banners.[37] Unlike regular Eight Bannermen, who received a monthly salary from the state, members of the *butha* banners received no salary at all until 1760 and only half pay thereafter. The *butha* banners were also notably diverse, featuring companies of Solon, Daur, Oroncon, Old Barga, and Birar drawn from the Northeast, as well as Telenggut, Ker Sakal, Uriankhai, and others repatriated from the Northwest during the Dzungar wars.[38] The Eight Banners proper, in contrast, were divided more simply into Manchu, Chinese, and Mongol divisions. Further, unlike members of the Eight Banners, who were free of any tribute obligations, each able-bodied male over five feet in the *butha* banners had to submit an annual tribute of one sable pelt per head.[39] To facilitate submissions, the court organized an annual "gathering" (Ma: *culgan*) in Qiqihar for submitting tribute, a formal institution peculiar to the Northeast.

Yet, though responsible for submitting fur, these men were hardly all "hunters" by trade. The Daur (also called "Sawalça") were mostly farmers, growing millet, buckwheat, and barley; many were also active merchants in the caravan trade. The Daur maintained a close relationship with the Solon (people also identified as Ewenki), who were mainly nomadic pastoralists but who practiced farming, fishing, hunting, and trapping as well. Other members of the Butha Eight Banners included Old Barga Mongols, who had been subject to a Daur-Ewenki "Solon" confederation before the Qing conquest, as well as other Mongolian groups, including Öölöds, who surrendered to the Qing in Western Mongolia during the Dzungar Wars before being deported to Hulun Buir.[40] Only the Oroncon, divided into "Horse" and "Pedestrian" groups in Qing documents, were devoted hunters and trappers.[41] The designation "hunter," then, reflected a role in the tribute system as providers of fur, not a way of life.

Others that provided tribute stood outside banner systems altogether, including most of the people who lived in the Amur River basin, along the Pacific Coast, and on Sakhalin Island. Matsuura Shigeru's recent study, the first to make extensive use of the Manchu archives from the Northeast, has provided an unprecedentedly detailed look at the history of these regions, which long served as production centers of fur.[42] The villages dotting the major rivers of the far Northeast supported, in the late seventeenth century, a bewildering constellation of people, most of whom are largely forgotten today: the Merjele, Tokoro, and Heye on the middle Amur; the Ujala and Bayar on the lower Sunggari; the Nuyele, Geikere, and Husikari on the Amur below the Sunggari; and the people called "Fishskin Tartars" or "Fiyaka" by Chinese exiles and Jesuit travelers in the early Qing: the Kiyakara, Urgengkere, Horfoko, Namdulu, Muliyaliyan, Gufatin, and Sinulhū, who resided mostly at the confluence of the Amur and the Ussuri. Each of these groups had its own idiosyncratic relationship to the Qing court; they were not all alike, nor did they all see themselves as natural allies of the Qing. Some, like the Merjele, Tokoro, Heye, and Ujala, were enrolled into "New Manchu" banners in 1674 and were relocated to the military colony at Ningguta. Others resisted, fled their colony, and escaped enrollment altogether.[43] Some of those who remained outside the banner system submitted an annual tribute in furs either in the town of Ningguta or, after 1779, further north in Ilan Hala (Ch: Sanxing), where the court hoped to better attract and control the fur trade. From both of these towns, the court also dispatched special envoys downstream to the lower Amur to collect tribute from communities based on the Pacific Coast and Sakhalin Island. There, as control was limited, the Qing court worked not through banners but through local hierarchies of "clan heads" (Ma: *hala i da*), "village heads" (Ma: *gašan i da*), "young brothers" (Ma: *deote jusa*), and "locals" or "commoners" (Ma: *ba i niyalma*).[44]

Parallel to the recognized clans and villages stood special *hojihon* (lit. "son-in-law" in Manchu) and their wives (Ma: *sargan jui*), who operated within yet another tribute system. *Hojihon* belonged to the world of the Amur delta, but they did not present furs in Ningguta or Ilan Hala: They came in person to Beijing to do so at court. In return, they received a special allotment of imperial gifts (Ma: *ulin*) and entered into arranged marriages with Manchu bannerwomen from the capital.[45] Their trips to Beijing were notoriously long and difficult, and they were not only fraught with logistical challenges but with the threat of disease. Many died of smallpox. Yet, through the eighteenth century, various *hojihon* braved the journey to Beijing multiple times, with one recorded to have made the trip as many as six times in his lifetime. The rewards for making the trip were high. Like others, *hojihon* did not personally trap the furs they presented but traded for them from more distant forests to the north of the Amur or in the mountainous interior of Sakhalin Island. Indeed, *hojihon* often ventured personally to Sakhalin Island to procure the rarest and most valuable furs, including black and arctic foxes. Leveraging their connections to the court, they dominated a commercial network that extended from the Pacific Coast to Sakhalin Island to even as far as northern Hokkaido. They were their own political center.[46]

We must be careful, then, in how we imagine the Qing Northeast. Today, most historians remember Manchuria as a special frontier that the court protected through a "policy of closing off" (Ch: *fengjin zhengce*), which excluded Chinese from entering the protected homeland. We can read Manchuria's history, according to this view, as a function of what it was not: open to Chinese development. Yet when we call the Northeast "Manchuria" or imagine it as ethnically coherent, we not only do violence to the complexity of its past, we ignore the people and categories that were meaningful in Qing times. "Manchuria" as a category, as we shall see, was meaningful. The history of Manchuria, however, is not one of simply Manchus and Chinese; its environmental history is illegible without taking seriously categories like Solon, *hojihon*, and *butha*.

In the abstract, then, Qianlong was right about Mukden: The Manchus' homeland *was* different from the Chinese interior, both in the imperial and consumer imagination and in the resources of its natural environment. Mukden, however, was not the same thing as the Three Eastern Territories, as even in the imperial imagination, it covered only part of the expanse. In practice, the region stood out less as a singular, Manchu ethnic space than as a land of institutional and ethnic diversity. There were the territories, run by Eight Banner military governors through a network of garrisons. There were Chinese farmers along the southern coast, who belonged to their own county system, and Mongol herders on the steppe, who lived within the Mongol banner system. There were villagers on the Amur and Sakhalin Island who generally submitted an annual tribute but who were otherwise autonomous. And there were ad hoc institutions, unique to the Northeast, such as the Butha Eight Banners, in which people lived within a "banner" system but who remained separate from the standard Eight Banners and paid an annual tribute in furs as designated "hunters." We are left, then, with a core irony: the "hunters" and others who produced Manchu products for the court were not Manchus at all.

ULA, PEARLS, AND THE QING COURT

Manchurian pearls came from yet another "hunter" group based on the Up-per Sunggari: the Hunter Ula (Ma: *butha ula*; Ch: *buteha wula*). Like the "Butha Eight Banners," the Butha Ula were separate from the regular Eight Banners, were of diverse origins, and earned their moniker for their contin-ued participation in the tribute system. Unlike the other "hunter banners" of the Nen River, however, the Ula were not required to present furs: Their primary responsibility was to harvest mostly Manchurian freshwater pearls. Through the Ula, the Qing court claimed a monopoly over freshwater pearl production from the Tumen watershed on the Korean border to the rivers that fed the Amur in the far north.[47] The rules governing pearls, though, transcended the bounds of territory: It was illegal for anyone, anywhere, to buy, sell, or traffic in Manchurian freshwater pearls. They could enter Beijing only as "tributary" gifts to the emperor from the Ula.

Known in Ming sources as "River Savages" (Ch: *jiangyi*), the Ula had risen to ascendancy in the freshwater pearl trade during the sixteenth cen-tury, and in the early seventeenth century, as Nurhaci's state grew, they were among the first to resist.[48] After a series of failed marriage alliances—which collapsed in 1603 when Nurhaci married a daughter to the Ula headman Bujantai, and Bujantai "shot whistling arrows at her"—Nurhaci personally led a successful expedition to subjugate the Ula in 1613.[49] Thereafter, the Ula became personal bondservants of either the emperor or the conquer-ing Manchu nobility. In time, Ula bondservants became responsible for providing an annual tribute of ginseng, honey, and freshwater pearls to the court.[50] Later, during the early eighteenth-century military campaigns, ad-ditional subjects entered the Ula banners, including Solon and Daur *butha* bannermen in 1742 and 1792.[51] Thereafter, some Ula belonged to bondser-vant banners, but others belonged to the Eight Banners. What bound them together as Ula were their tribute obligations and their unique status in the empire. They maintained their own separate governing office, or *yamen*, in the territory of Jilin, just north of Jilin garrison, but, administratively, they fell outside the jurisdiction of Jilin's military governor. The highest official among the Ula was a "supervising commandant" (Ma: *uheri da*; Ch: *zong-guan*), who reported until 1748 to the Office of the Hunt (Ch: *Duyusi*), a branch of the Imperial Household Department (see Figure 2.1).[52] In a nod to their special status, the court further granted the Ula rights to mountains

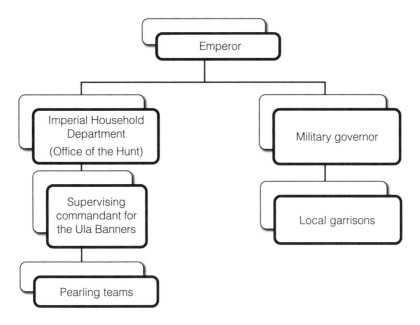

Figure 2.1. Administration of the Ula banners (pre-reform).
SOURCE: DQHDSL 12:1081a.

and mussel beds in Mukden, Jilin, and Sahaliyan Ula to support the collection of the required pearls, ginseng, and honey.

Although the Ula thus remained outside the Eight Banner system, the court nonetheless subjected them to military discipline. Each pearler worked in a "pearling team" (Ma: *tana butara meyen*; Ch: *zhuxuan*) staffed by a commanding brigadier (Ma: *galai da*; Ch: *zongguan yichang*), lieutenants (Ma: *funde bošokū*; Ch: *xiaoqixiao*), and corporals (Ma: *bošokū*; Ch: *lingcui*); on average, there was an officer for every twenty pearlers.[53] There was a seasonal rhythm to official life. Reaching some mussel beds required a 1,000-mile round trip, and it was not uncommon to spend three months traveling for every month pearling.[54] If traveling by rivers, they rowed in three-person canoes; on the road, everyone marched as officers paced them on horseback. At each step of the process, the supervising commandant kept records on the pearling teams: the names and ranks of the officers, the names of the pearlers, the amount of allotted grain, and the number of horses, muskets, and canoes supplied to each unit. Once a season, the commandant personally toured the mussel beds himself to oversee production at selected sites.[55]

Pearl mussels grew extensively throughout the Amur River's catch basin, including on the Sunggari (Ch: *Songhua*) and Ussuri River systems, as well as on the rivers that fed the Tumen, on the border with Korea. Pinpointing the particular species they targeted is difficult: There were at least fourteen different pearl-producing freshwater mussel species in the region, from ten different genera, including the Chinese pond mussel (*Sinanodonta woodiana*), cockscomb pearl mussel (*Cristaria plicata*), the thick-shelled river mussel (*Unio crassus*), and two varieties of freshwater pearl mussel, *Margaritifera middendorffi* and *Margaritifera dahurica*.[56] And although this last variety, the freshwater pearl mussel *Margaritifera dahurica*, is most likely the species that produced Qing pearls, it is impossible to say for certain; today, no less than in the Qing, the classification of freshwater pearl mussels remains contentious, as twentieth-century natural histories of local mussels have proved particularly difficult to square with modern genetics-based studies. [57]

The problems of identification are compounded when we try to align Qing categories with the evolving modern ones. Manchu and Chinese language texts distinguish between "Manchurian pearls" (Ma: *tana*; Ch: *dongzhu*, lit. "eastern pearls") and "standard pearls" (Ma: *nicuhe*; Ch: *zhengzhu*) but not between types of "mussels" (Ma: *tahūra*).[58] The *Shengjing tongzhi*, an imperial commissioned gazetteer for Mukden from the early eighteenth century, differentiates between varieties of elongated "mussels" and "oysters" (Ch: *bang*) and rounded "clams" (Ch: *ge*) and between their saltwater and freshwater varieties, and it notes that long and narrow freshwater types made the most lustrous pearls.[59] A later gazetteer, the *Heilongjiang zhigao* (1887), described Manchurian pearls as the product of Sunggari River mussels, which cluster on the river bed in deep waters and whose protective shells made opening them dangerous when careless. The reward for those who found such a mussel was nonetheless immense: "The pearls are light blue in color. Big ones are half a *cun* in length [approximately 1.67 cm] and small ones are pea-sized."[60]

We in fact know far more about the pearling process than about the pearl mussels themselves. The work required patience, expertise, and grit: Finding "big ones" was not easy. When a team located a mussel bed, rowers used poles to spear the mussels and gather them from the river bottoms. On shore, they roasted the mussels over an open fire until their shells popped open and their insides were revealed. Perhaps one in a thousand mussels contained pearls. Of these, infinitesimally fewer contained tribute-quality jewels. As the court kept records of the weight of each tribute pearl, with a grading system that measured down to half a *fen* (roughly twenty grams), we likewise know that even among tribute-grade pearls, the harvest yielded exponentially more small pearls than large ones. The harvest in 1797, for example, yielded 935 pearls, but only three were over ten *fen* (0.38 kilogram or 1.9 carats), while 91 percent weighed four *fen* or less (0.15 kilogram), and 41 percent of the pearls weighed less than a single *fen* (0.038 kilogram). Similar ratios held in 1798.[61]

Multiple offices recorded the pearlers' progress at each step of the process. Every month while they were out, the supervising commandant forwarded a register and summary report to Beijing. Within days of each team's returning, the supervising commandant tallied all types and sizes of all pearls collected and sent it to the throne.[62] He further recorded the total number Manchurian pearls (Ma: *tana*) and regular pearls (Ma: *nicuhe*) harvested and appraised the quality of the *tana* pearls using five grades: "poor quality," "low brightness," "one-sided," "two-sided," or "high quality," with only the last fit for the emperor.[63] He then wrapped and packaged the pearls, placed them in a box, and sent them under armed guard to the Imperial Household Department in Beijing. There, the Board of Revenue (Ch: *Hubu*) and the Office of the Hunt checked and weighed them before releasing them back to the Imperial Household Department.

To encourage production and discipline, the court not only paid the pearlers a monthly salary but awarded prizes for any catch above quota and punishments for any haul below it. In 1701, the Kangxi emperor set the quota level for each team at sixteen first- or second-class Manchurian pearls.[64] For every pearl over quota, the commanding brigadier received two bolts of blue cotton cloth. For every thirty pearls over quota, the court offered an additional two bolts of cloth, and the brigadier received an extra bolt of satin, the lieutenants received silk, and corporals earned a reward in accordance with their team's production. If they submitted a thousand pearls beyond the quota, the brigadier received a full promotion. If they were under quota by a single pearl, however, the brigadier was whipped ten times; if they were ten pearls under quota, he was docked a month's pay and the corporal was whipped; and if they were twenty pearls under quota, the brigadier was docked a year's salary and demoted in rank and the corporal whipped 100 times.[65] Expectations were high.

To meet demand and ease the burden on pearlers, the court gradually offered higher salaries and expanded the number of participants in the system to lower individual quotas. The number of pearling teams thus tripled through the course of the eighteenth century, from thirty-three teams in 1701 to seventy-six in 1733 to ninety-four by 1799. To facilitate this expansion, the court forgave the Ula their other tributary obligations, such as honey collection. As more men entered pearling units, the expectations for each individual eased. In 1754, for example, each hunter was responsible for an average 0.67 pearl per person; after 1767, the quota dipped to 0.5 pearl per person. That year, despite the diminished expectations, everyone also got a raise.[66]

The court lowered quotas and raised rewards, in part, because the burden of pearling was immense. In 1796, the Ula commandant, Gilu, asked for leniency for his men because the distance between mussel beds was "vast" (Ma: *onco leli*), and they were "ranging widely between several hundred *li* and two or three thousand *li*," or up to a thousand miles to reach productive beds. Flooding could make rivers impassable and rainstorms could turn roads into quagmires. In some cases, because it took months for a team to arrive at the mussel beds, the men started their work exhausted.[67] The difficulty of the labor and the isolation of the sites led some to desert. In 1798, for example, a thirty-six-year-old named Ajingga—described in his missing-person-report as dark-skinned, pockmarked, wearing blue pants, a felt hat, and sheepskin boots—disappeared just four days into his tour, prompting a provincewide manhunt.[68]

Deaths occurred on the job. In a disaster in 1809, a man died when a canoe capsized in the Arcin river, near Aihūn. That year, the team led by a corporal named Bayamboo had managed to collect six Manchurian *tana* pearls between 0.8 and 2.0 *fen* (0.3 to 0.76 kilogram, or 1.5 to 3.8 carats) as well as two standard *nicuhe* pearls. Having packed the pearls away, they had just started up the Jan River, when Bayamboo's canoe crashed into a rock: Bayamboo, three pearlers, and the box containing the tribute—as well as all the remaining food and supplies—sank into the water. One man drowned, and the pearls were lost. For failing to avert the accident, the court charged Corporal Bayamboo with recklessness: "Manchurian pearls are the emperor's tribute. . . . [He] should have been cautious." The deceased bannerman's family was awarded 12 taels of silver as compensation.[69]

Local archival records from the garrison of Hunchun, only recently made public, provide an especially textured picture of the hunt. Ula teams passed through the Hunchun district each spring in the third lunar month. Most kept relatively close to the garrison, heading west to the Burhatu,

Gahari, and Hailan Rivers—which feed into the Tumen River—or northeast to the Suifun (Ru: Razdalnaya) and its tributaries, which flowed into Amur Bay and the Pacific. Other teams sometimes traveled to Ningguta to work the Mudan, Fulgiyaha, and other rivers further to the northeast.[70]

Throughout the Jiaqing reign (r. 1795–1820), Hunchun garrison recorded the entry of every pearling team active in the area. From these records, we know that, on average, each pearler received 0.6 bushel (Ma: *hule*) of grain and a pack horse. Teams were generally armed, most traveling with two muskets, lead balls, and gunpowder.[71] Notably, moreover, the documents reveal that the number of men working the Hunchun area declined in this era, from 112 men in 1798 to eighty-five men after 1818.

Most strikingly, however, Hunchun's records suggest the degree to which the system as a whole unraveled in these years, with pearl production falling precipitously after 1786. Declines were particularly dramatic over the five-year span between 1786 and 1790: On the Burhatu River, *tana* pearl production fell from eighty-seven pearls per year to eighteen; on the Gahari, it fell from seventy-eight to seventeen; on the Hailan River, it fell from seventy-five to zero. All three rivers experienced a brief and modest recovery in the early nineteenth century but declined once again and remained stagnant thereafter. In 1786, the Hunchun area produced 240 tributary pearls; in 1819 it produced thirty-six, or 15 percent of the original haul.[72]

Indeed, Manchu archival records kept in Beijing tell a similar story for Jilin territory as a whole: a rapid decline in the final years of the eighteenth century, a brief recovery in the 1810s, then another decline (see Table 2.1).[73] Between 1795 and 1815, the pearl yield within the territory dropped threefold, from a high of 2,890 pearls in 1750 to fewer than a

TABLE 2.1.

Pearl harvest tallies from Jilin, 1795–1815.

Year	Total pearls
1795	2,890
1796	2,753
1797	2,042
1798	1,975
1801	369
1813	1,158
1814	642
1815	895

thousand thereafter. We are thus left to wonder, as the emperors increasingly did themselves: What was happening in Manchuria? What had gone wrong, and what could be done?

MUSSELS, MEN, AND PROBLEMS OF ORDER

It takes significant pressure to undercut freshwater mussel populations. Pearl mussels are resilient and adaptable, having survived since the upper Paleozoic.[74] Their reproductive strategy is suitably complex: Fertilized females emit glochidia that latch on to a fish's gills, where they grow in the oxygen-rich environment and travel to new streams and rivers. When old enough, the glochidia metamorphose into mussels and drop down to a new riverbed.[75] Though they reproduce sexually, under severe pressure hermaphrodism and single-sex reproduction can occur. This adaptation helps explain why population density does not effect mussel fecundity: The fewer the mussels, the more females simply reproduce on their own. Because freshwater mussels never stop reproducing and can also live for a hundred years or longer—they are the longest-living invertebrates known to gerontology—female mussels can produce hundreds of millions of larvae in a single lifetime.

Given the nature of the sources, it is difficult—and perhaps ultimately impossible—to disentangle the environmental, bureaucratic, social causes of the reported mussel scarcity after the eighteenth century. Mussels' gills are sensitive to sedimentation, and one can imagine that homesteading or some other agent of siltation could have been the culprit.[76] The documents, however, consistently point in different directions. Because the Ula were the only ones harvesting pearls and the only ones policing and monitoring the process, the court at first suspected the Ula themselves of various crimes: pilfering, poaching, smuggling, and lying. Well before the crisis of the late eighteenth century, then, the court attempted to enhance discipline. As early as 1682 (KX20), the Kangxi emperor ordered that any "Ula men" in Ningguta found guilty of independently collecting clams (Ch: *eli*), honey, river otters, or Manchurian pearls would be punished according to the rules for poaching ginseng: death by strangulation to the ringleaders, two months in the cangue and 100 lashes for their followers. In addition, he ordered that anyone found guilty of buying or selling government permits granting access to restricted zones would likewise receive 100 lashes and two months in the cangue.[77]

The court likewise attempted in 1724 to crack down on smuggling by enhancing border controls at the Great Wall. To inspire zeal, it rewarded guardsmen that captured more than 400 *fen* of pearls a cash payment worth five times the weight of the seized pearls; if they oversaw the capture of more than 1,600 *fen* of pearls, the commanding officer received a full promotion.[78] If, on the other hand, pearl smugglers successfully crossed into China, the commanding officers would be demoted three ranks, and the patrolmen struck eighty times with a heavy rod. If collaboration and corruption came to light, the commanding officer would be removed from office, and the patrolman would be caned 100 times and serve a month in the cangue.[79] Yet these efforts had no long-term effect: New reports of mussel "scarcity" arrived in Beijing in 1733.[80]

As more problems in pearl production emerged, the court increasingly moved to empower the territories' military governors to strengthen controls over mobility within their territories and provide enhanced oversight over the Ula. Thus in 1741 the Qianlong emperor endorsed a plan of the lieutenant governor of Fengtian, Jakuna, to step up policing on the roads and waterways that led to Jilin's ginseng-producing mountains and pearl-producing rivers.[81] Despite the costs, guard stations, called *karun* (Ma: *karun*; Mo: *qaraġul*; Ch: *kalun*), were established around the mussel beds of the Muleng and Suifun Rivers. Not long after, in 1748, the court endorsed a still more dramatic proposal: It ordered the military governor of Jilin to oversee all pearling operations (see Figure 2.2).[82] The Ula commandant thus became a secondary figure: All registers, tallies, and communications to the court thereafter went through the Jilin military governor's office, and when the pearls arrived in Beijing, they were affixed with the governor's seal. Though Ula Hunters continued to do the work, they had lost their autonomy. Pearling had become a territorial concern.

The reforms of 1748 had consequences on the ground; it was not simply a case of administrative reshuffling at the top. Most important, the territories immediately began to enhance policing and border controls. New *karun* guard posts went up in 1751, and the court added officers to the Ula corps in 1759 and again in 1762.[83] Territorial authorities took charge of other tasks that had formerly been the responsibility of the Ula commandant, including the compiling of household registers, which determined the pearlers' salaries and compensation.[84] At the same time, the Ula began

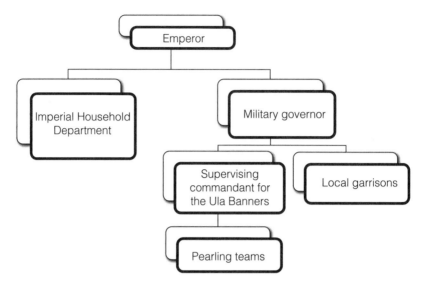

Figure 2.2. Administration of the Ula banners (post-reform).
SOURCE: DQHDSL 12:1081a.

doing double-duty as both pearlers and guardsmen. While on their journey to the mussel beds, they were made to sweep through and inspect villages and strategic choke points (Ma; *oyonggo kamni bade*) along the way. If they found any smugglers or poachers, they had to arrest them, seize their contraband, and report the matter to the military governor's office. After their return, they took posts at choke points and *karun* scattered throughout Sahaliyan Ula, Ningguta, Bedune, Ilan Hala, and Alcuka. At each step, they alerted garrison officials of their movements.

Yet these reforms, too, proved incapable of stopping mussel tribute from periodically declining or, after the 1780s, from plummeting. The court thus switched strategies. Now, beyond calling for more guard posts, border checks, and men, the court also enacted moratoriums on pearling altogether. In 1781 the Qianlong emperor ordered his first moratorium on tribute collecting: Nobody, not even Ula bannermen, could visit the mussel beds for five years. A decade after the moratorium ended, the emperor ordered yet another. As he explained in the summer of 1795:

> During the Shunzhi, Kangxi, and Yongzheng reign periods [1644–1735], the *tana* pearls in storage were all high quality, and the harvest of high-quality *tana* pearls was plentiful. Yet for years the pearls hunted have not

been high-quality at all. It will not do if the pearl beds in the Sunggari River area do not produce pearls anywhere. If we rest [the pearl beds] for several years, we will get high-quality pearls [again].[85]

The problem lay in the easy "lootability" of pearls:[86]

The territory is vast and there are many rivers and creeks, so it cannot be guarded in its entirety, and it is impossible to quash poaching. . . . [High-quality *tana* pearls] are most certainly sold to the rich merchants in this territory [Ma: *golo*] [Jilin] and other merchants who buy ginseng, and they are smuggled into the interior. There must be no allowance for crossing the border and conducting such sales.[87]

The moratorium in this way demanded more stringent control over territorial boundaries and markets. Qianlong thus ordered the military governor of Jilin, Siolin, to crack down on the smugglers; Siolin sent the orders down to the garrisons; and the garrisons enacted the plan through the *karun* network.[88] In 1796, in line with the new imperial orders, Siolin confirmed that they were "resting the rivers where mussels have grown scarce from previous harvests" and "strictly investigating illegal pearl-harvesting." In the meantime, to ensure continued production, the court allowed Ula bannermen to expand pearling operations to the Ercuke River, where mussels still remained "large, plentiful, and of good quality."[89] That year eighty canoes departed for the expedition, and the following year, seventy made the voyage.[90] Production did not stop: It shifted outward.

Yet the mussel beds continued to wither. In 1799, the Qianlong emperor's successor, Jiaqing, ordered another moratorium on pearl harvesting, this time for three years. He justified the policy on three grounds: It granted a reprieve to downtrodden pearlers; it allowed the mussels to recuperate; and it reflected the emperor's empathy for all forms of life. As he explained, "I have a tenderness toward all living things; it is not that I treasure the pearls."[91] In 1802, the court added more lieutenants for oversight at the *karuns*.[92] Yet, throughout the early nineteenth century, mussels grew increasingly "scarce" on the Hūlan and Neme Rivers near the garrison of Sahaliyan Ula and around the Suifun and Muren Rivers near Ningguta. Once again, the emperor ordered that mussel beds be rested for "several years" to allow the mussels to be better "cultivated and nurtured" (Ma: *fesumbure ujime*). Yet the mussels failed to recover.[93]

Achieving even minimal output eventually became impossible. In 1821, Jiaqing's successor, the Daoguang emperor (r. 1820–1850), reinstated yet another three-year ban. As in the years 1800–1805, it was necessary to "restore the mussels." To enforce the edict and curb poaching, he ordered more *karun* established at river mouths and mountain passes. In the summer of 1822, the first year of the three-year moratorium, troops surveyed the area, and authorities in Sahaliyan Ula and Jilin hashed out jurisdictional boundaries and responsibilities. The court divided Hunchun into six policing zones, each with its own *karun*, to be manned through the summer pearling season.[94] The court also granted more powers to the territories: In 1824 the Jilin military governor's office, for example, received the right to appoint all Ula clerks responsible for the paperwork on pearling operations.[95]

At least in terms of the harvest, the accumulating reforms had little effect. When, in 1825, the pearl harvest resumed, it proved a major disappointment, and in 1827, the military governor of Jilin, Luceng, reported the region's tribute pearls "small and utterly useless."[96] The emperor concluded that "if we hunt [for pearls] annually, then the mussels will be ravished," and the effort and suffering of the pearl harvesters would mount further. He thus proposed resting the pearl beds again for three years to "nurture the mussels and let them grow," and he ordered that the military governors of Sahaliyan Ula and Jilin reinforce *karun* along the roads and waterways leading to the pearl beds. Troops were dispatched to new guard posts that summer.[97] The emperor ordered another moratorium in 1827, and the pearl beds "rested" thereafter; the court ordered another three-year moratorium in 1830–1832 and another in 1833–1835.[98] Every three years, requests were put in to open up the pearl beds, and each time the emperor declined, ordering: "Stop the hunt for these upcoming years!"[99] No one was to touch the remaining mussels; no one was to even enter their territory. The land was to remain, permanently, in an untouched state of nature.

The Qing state went to extraordinary lengths, if ultimately failed ones, to protect the pearl fishery. How should we understand its striking attempts to "nurture the mussels"? If pearl mussels disappeared, why did it matter? A few answers seem reasonable. Given the history of the region and the pragmatism of the court, we might guess that the court's efforts to save pearl mussels reflected a fiscal interest. Commercial logic was neither novel nor foreign to the Northeast. *The Old Manchu Chronicles*, the dynasty's in-house records, emphasized Nurhaci's rectitude, generosity, and cosmic purpose, but Ming sources described the man in ways not unlike how the *New York Times* might describe Vladimir Putin: a despot whose power

derived from control over natural resources, not a moral authority.[100] The
Chosŏn court produced similar accounts of other Jurchen leaders, who likewise seemed to derive power from fur exports.[101] After 1644, and through
the eighteenth century, the Qing court continued to profit immensely from
exports such as fur and ginseng. With so much at stake, is there evidence
that the Qing court thought in terms of profit and power when it came
to pearls?

The answer, in short, is not quite: Like *The Old Manchu Chronicles*,
which emphasized moral rectitude, the archival sources point in other directions. The Daoguang emperor justified the 1821 moratorium in terms of
two ambitions: to "conserve the energy of hunters" and to "lovingly care for
the lives of mussels." The first ambition—grace toward hunters—was a cor-
nerstone of Qing ideology. The work of the hunters was indeed dangerous
and hard, and, even as it encouraged more production, the court positioned
itself as the protector of the Ula's well-being. Even when the court clearly
had ulterior motives, it kept on message: In 1732, for example, when draft-
ing Ula soldiers into active military service, the Yongzheng emperor justified the policy in terms of helping relieve the hunters of their hardships.[102]

The second justification for the moratorium—"to lovingly care for the
lives of mussels"—is more curious and demands attention. Was the court
participating in something akin to an environmentalist discourse? Or should
we dismiss the ambition as imperial bluster masking hard-nosed calcula-
tions? When we turn to the most lucrative regional trade of all, ginseng,
there is evidence that something more than a fiscal logic was at work.

THE CASE OF GINSENG

Qing rule over ginseng production provides a helpful counterpoint to the
case of pearls and sheds light on broader dynamics that informed both the
pearl crisis and the empire's response to it. Given the strong parallels between their histories, their overlapping legal and institutional regimes, and
the congruent discourse surrounding their conservation, we cannot fully
understand the story of pearls without at least touching on ginseng first.
Scholars have studied the ginseng monopoly in depth, and it has received
multiple book-length (and even multivolume) treatments.[103] Here, with the
aid of Manchu-language documents, we can highlight certain aspects of
ginseng's environmental history in Manchuria. Ginseng picking shared

crucial similarities with pearl production: The geography overlapped, a troubling decline in production occurred around 1800, and the Qing state responded with a series of reforms that included the empowerment of territorial authorities to curtail poaching, smuggling, and corruption. Unlike pearls, however, when wild ginseng ultimately became scarce in the wild, diggers responded by domesticating the plant and starting ginseng plantations. The court refused, however, to embrace the horticultural revolution. It burned down farms instead: No ginseng, it seems, at all was better than farmed ginseng.

Although both pearls and ginseng shared an association with the Northeast in the Qing period, ginseng did not signify "Manchus" in the same way as pearls. In part, ginseng's distinct branding reflected the plant's shifting range over time. Ginseng prefers shade and tends to grow on the dark north side of hills and mountains, particularly in pine forests. Unlike pearl mussels, which emit thousands of glochidia each year, ginseng can go years without flowering. The plant is robust, but it grows and reproduces slowly. In China, its history accordingly has been tied to the progressive deforestation of the central plain and the surrounding mountains, which once flourished with pine.[104] In early imperial times, when forests remained relatively uncut, ginseng grew in a largely uninterrupted swath from the Taihang Mountains to Liaodong and the Korean Peninsula. The most famed ginseng, called *dangshen*, came from Shangdang, in modern Shanxi; an early imperial *material medica*, the *Bencao jingji zhu* by Tao Hongjing (456–536), for example, noted that ginseng from Liaodong was inferior to *dangshen*. In the Song period, ginseng pickers worked the Hedong and Mount Tai regions in Shandong, as ginseng was already in short supply in Shanxi; we find in this period, for example, skepticism about the authenticity of *dangshen* in the marketplace.[105] By the late sixteenth century, at least by the account of Li Shizhen (1518–1593), people still valued Shanxi ginseng as the best, but it was already gone from the wild: "The people of [old Shangdang] ravaged the land for ginseng [*min yi renshen wei difang hai*], so that it could no longer be gathered, and today all [non-Korean] ginseng we use comes from Liaodong."[106] Thus consumers of the Ming and Qing periods turned to the Northeast and Chosŏn Korea for supplies. The destruction of wild ginseng in North China, together with the expansion of the pharmaceutical market in China in the sixteenth century, created an unparalleled convergence in Manchurian history: It forged a bottleneck that made Manchuria unusually important in regional commerce, enabling those who cornered the ginseng trade, like Nurhaci, to get rich.

Unlike the management of pearls, which relied solely on the Ula banners, Qing rule over ginseng was always more complex. In the earliest years of Qing rule, nobility between the ranks of *gong* ("duke") and *wang* ("prince") could dispatch men to the Northeast and collect ginseng without the approval of the court. The court reined in their powers only in stages: After 1649, aristocrats had to register their collection teams or face punishment, and after 1684 the court restricted these teams to no more than fifteen to 140 men, depending on the rank of noblemen dispatching them. Thereafter, each picker in a collection team had to carry a special "ginseng license" (Ch: *shenpiao*), which was subject to inspection by territorial authorities while in transit and in the mountains. Collectors also had to pay a tax. In 1694, the court issued a total of 5,000 permits through this system; the rest of the ginseng it monopolized for itself. To collect it, the court used Ula bannermen, a group of 150 bondservants under the Mukden Imperial Household Department, and a separate team of Eight Bannermen, which the court dispatched to 147 designated sites that it prohibited other outsiders from entering.[107]

Licensed ginseng collection proved a failure: The court issued 5,000 permits in 1694, but authorities later estimated that 30,000 undocumented pickers were secretly active as well, leading the ginseng yield to decline.[108] In response, in 1723, the Yongzheng court opened ginseng picking to anyone who could afford it, not just privileged teams. Each person who applied for a ginseng license had to meet a quota, which was assessed on a sliding scale based on their picking zone's productivity. If they met their quota, they were free to sell any surplus on the market. As the court opened up the territory to merchants, it simultaneously doubled down on the number of troops in Mukden and Ningguta and established new *karun* posts. From 1724 onward, the court also expected territorial authorities to memorialize on the number of poachers arrested and all contraband seized. To ensure reliability, the emperor also dispatched censors (Ch: *fuduyushi*) and other metropolitan officials to act as independent observers.[109]

This system, too, proved a failure, and so in 1730 the Yongzheng court reformed the ginseng monopoly once again. That year, Nasutu, the military governor of Mukden, had warned of inefficiencies in the permit system: Licensed ginseng pickers had trouble meeting their quotas in regions where productivity had declined, while quotas were too low in regions that still offered high yields. Nasutu thus proposed that the court issue 10,000 permits to merchants in Mukden to help recruit 10,000 ginseng pickers. For every sixteen ounces (Ch: *liang*) of ginseng each picker collected, the court would earmark ten ounces for itself and leave six ounces for the merchants to sell as they wished. The emperor eagerly endorsed the proposal. Yet the annual target of 10,000 permits proved too optimistic: In 1732 the Mukden military governor's office was able to issue only 5,915 permits, and, in 1737, the court issued fewer than half that number. Too few people wanted to participate in the system: Pickers felt squeezed by the merchants, and they profited more from the black market than from legal trade.[110]

Undocumented ginseng picking thus continued unabated. In 1731 alone, patrolmen in Ningguta arrested 105 poachers and seized forty kilos (1066.3 ounces) of ginseng root and 6.5 kilos (170.95 ounces) of ancillary parts of the root (Ma: *se solo*, lit. "the upper root near the stem" [*se*] and "the root's hairs" [*solo*]); the same bust also turned up sixty-two undocumented sable pelts. Sentries at the Willow Palisades were on guard for contraband as well. In 1732, they arrested seventy-two men coming from Elmin and Halmin and impounded another 57.72 ounces of ginseng root, 1.22 ounces of ancillary parts, 190 stems of "raw" (Ma: *eshun*) ginseng, eighty-four sable pelts, twenty-seven raccoon-dog skins, and five muskets.[111]

Finally, in 1744, in response to the failure to attract merchants or stem poaching, the Qianlong emperor instituted a final, more lasting set of reforms: He empowered territorial officials to oversee ginseng collection.[112] To aid them, the court established a new Ginseng Bureau (Ch: *Guanshenju*) under the military governor of Mukden and mandated that licenses be issued to pickers, not merchants. The pickers themselves thus became responsible for meeting quotas. Under the new system, the authorities divided ginseng into three types: "tribute ginseng" (Ma: *alban orhoda*), "public-use ginseng" (Ma: *siden de baitalara orhoda*), and "surplus ginseng" (Ma: *funcehe orhoda*). Following the harvest, no matter how much surplus ginseng they collected, permit holders had to return two ounces of ginseng root back to their local garrisons. The garrisons then submitted five-sixths of this share to the Imperial Household Department in Beijing as tribute and kept one-sixth locally for "public use" in the garrisons.[113]

Under the military governors, a more organized and bureaucratic management system fell into place, and paperwork proliferated. The garrisons gave out permits for entering the ginseng-producing mountains (Ma: *temgetu bithe*; Ch: *jinshan zhaopiao*), which one obtained prior to departure.

They issued travel permits, good for areas in southern and eastern Mukden. They issued permits for traveling by boat from Ula to the Ussuri and the Suifun.[114] They issued "return passes" (Ma: *alin ci bederere temgetu bithe*; Ch: *xiashan zhaopiao*) presented after the harvest; licenses for bodyguards (Ma: *fiyanjilara temgetu bithe*; Ch: *yapiao*); engraved wooden plaques used for identification that one wore around one's belt (Ma: *ashara šusihe*; Ch: *yaopai*); and special licenses for resellers ("red permits," Ma: *fulgiyan temgetu bithe*; Ch: *hongpiao*). Merchants who dealt in surplus ginseng, when crossing through the Great Wall gate at Shanhaiguan, had still other licenses stating the quality, grade, and quantity of their ginseng.[115]

Communications between territorial authorities and the court were regularized. Just before the Lunar New Year, the military governors sent a memorial to Beijing requesting the release of the coming year's ginseng licenses.[116] When the temperature warmed between the fourth and fifth months and the picking season began, the military governor reported a tally of all permits issued. In early autumn (usually in the seventh month), his office memorialized again with notices of all pickers' debts incurred through the summer. When the season ended in the early winter, the office issued a final accounting statement. Garrisons at Alcuka, Bedune, Jilin, Ilan Hala, and Ningguta all compiled separate digests of all permits issued. These reports required, at minimum, a record of the number and types of permits granted to Chinese pickers, the number of nonstandard "stamped forms" (Ma: *doron gidaha bithe*) issued, a comparison with the previous year's output, and the quantity of unused licenses left remaining. In the military departments of Ningguta and Jilin, where ginseng picking was more extensive and the management infrastructure was more elaborate, the garrisons kept tallies of the number of licenses for "brewer-guarantors" (Ma: *arki bureku temgetu bithe*) and merchants (Ma: *hūda salibuha temgetu bithe*). They forwarded these statistics to the military governor's office twice: once in the middle of the season and once at the end.[117] If an official failed to make any of the reports, he was censured.[118] The court expected to receive regular reports on contraband seizures and arrests as well, and so local authorities had to navigate between the Scylla of arresting too few men and so appearing corrupt and the Charybdis of arresting too many and seeming to have allowed poaching to proliferate; the documents reflect the tension accordingly.

As with pearl production, which came under territorial oversight in 1748, the ginseng reforms of 1744 streamlined the administrative structure while empowering territorial authorities. Yet as with pearl production, territorial authorities nonetheless failed to stem poaching and declining yields. Indeed, even through the fog of bureaucratic obfuscation, it is clear that the amount of wild ginseng passing through licensed channels declined dramatically from the late eighteenth century onward. Financial stress on the system provides one measure of this decline. Pickers were financially liable if they fell below quota; an extremely poor harvest might mean bankruptcy for pickers and major losses for the state. To manage the problem, the court mandated that all license holders have a backer, who became liable in case the quota could not be met; in the gritty world of the Northeast, the pickers turned to local *kaoliang* brewers for help, and the court thus called the permits for guarantors "brewers' licenses." Yet brewers could not fully subsidize the failing ginseng monopoly. Finally, after 1800, the garrisons began to accept subsidies generated from customs on grain exports to the Chinese interior to maintain business.[119]

The tallies generated by the monopoly tell the story of plummeting returns. In 1744, the court issued 9,000 permits to ginseng pickers. By 1789, the number had fallen to 2,330 permits, a decline of 75 percent. By 1852, the number of issued licenses shrunk again by 68 percent to a mere 753 per year.[120] The crash in production came at different moments in different locations. A drought that started in 1789 sparked two large-scale wildfires in 1791 and 1792. When the fires swept through the ginseng-producing areas in Jilin and destroyed the crop, pickers and brewers alike went bankrupt.[121] In the garrison districts of Jilin and Ningguta, which accounted for almost 90 percent of the territory's total harvest, dramatic declines occurred again between 1797 and 1801. In both districts, the number of permits dropped in half in these five years alone, from a combined 718 permits to a mere 320.[122]

What was happening? Climate and other natural causes mattered: They certainly were a factor, for example, in the proliferation of the forest fires of the early 1790s. The archives offer more information, however, on human failings: corruption, moral lapses, and lack of discipline. As with the pearl crisis, the Qing court blamed poachers, black market merchants, and corrupt or negligent officials for the collapsing system.[123] Bannermen were acting in ways unbecoming of Manchus; Chinese migrants were out of line.

Each decade seemed to reveal a new and spectacular case of negligence or corruption. In 1777, the military governor of Jilin submitted his resignation after failing to stop widespread poaching.[124] In 1785, another military governor of Jilin, Dorjya, was implicated in yet another scandal.[125] Corruption at the Ginseng Bureau was rampant.[126] In one case, the court brought down two regiment colonels (Ch: *xieling*) at the Ginseng Bureau in 1794 in a scandal that precipitated the special dispatch of three of the most trusted officials in Beijing—Fuk'anggan, Sungyūn, and Lin Ning—to conduct an investigation.[127] In anticipation of their arrival, Siolin reported, authorities had already begun to cook the books.[128] Corruption extended down to local bannermen themselves. In 1783, the court discovered that sixty-seven guards from Kaiyuan had built homes within the restricted ginseng-producing mountains and were now farming the product, while seventy-eight patrolmen in neighboring Fuzhou, who were charged with patrolling the area, had failed to report them. The court passed down severe sentences for both groups: It exiled the sixty-seven farmers to Ili and the seventy-eight patrolmen to Uliasutai.[129]

New types of surveillance emerged. Between 1748 and 1792 in the Ussuri and Suifun regions, for example, troops had been making regular patrols, departing in spring and returning in autumn with the rhythm of the picking season. Because these patrols seemed too predictable, in 1793 the military governor of Jilin, Hengsio, memorialized that the troops dispatched to these regions should not only establish new *karun* but begin making sudden, irregular raids into the mountains to catch undocumented ginseng pickers. These patrolmen, led by two colonels (Ma: *gūsai da*) from Ilan Hala, served on yearlong tours of duty.[130] They left for the restricted hunting grounds in the seventh month, in the late summer, when the ginseng harvest was at its peak. The main targets of their inspections were the diggers' camps where they "nested" (Ma: *tomobure*). When the patrols reached designated high grounds, they made winter camp and commenced their "thorough roving inspections of the mountains and valleys." The following autumn, when ginseng pickers returned from the mountains, the troops followed behind them in a rear-guard action and began their raids. Each year they reported on successful busts and seizures, and for their work they received an extra half year's salary.[131] Other troops, called up for summer tours, received three months' worth of bonus salary.[132] By rule, all had to be specially selected "capable soldiers and guards."[133]

Reports of arrests and seizures thus continuously poured into Beijing.[134] To add extra incentive, the court rewarded all officers who made arrests with the captured loot. The court reserved some of the most valuable, including sable and ginseng, for itself; local authorities put all captured sable, ginseng, and pearls into a local treasury and, at the end of the year, dispatched it under guard to the Imperial Household Department. Other items were deemed too incendiary and so were destroyed on site, including all cultivated ginseng and the pickers' huts.[135] The guards kept everything else that they seized: muskets, horses, tents, and cookware. They also could keep any second-rate furs, such as raccoon-dog pelts (Ma: *elbihe*).

Their work, though, was only so effective, as, it seems, the only thing that curtailed poaching was poaching itself. Too scarce in the wild to support large-scale trade, wild ginseng disappeared from the black market as fast as it did from the tribute system. Legitimate and undocumented poachers alike responded by traveling to ever more distant regions for the product. As early as 1684, reports had surfaced that overharvesting in the Elmin and Halmin areas had made ginseng collection untenable there, prompting the Kangxi court to open the coastal Ussuri region to pickers. Yet wild ginseng grew scarce there as well. By the early nineteenth century, no matter what the location, a fortunate picker might find three to five shoots in a single day. Most would search for days without seeing a single plant.[136]

The undocumented responded with a radically sustainable solution: They stopped poaching wild ginseng altogether and began to cultivate it instead. Indeed, while there is evidence of ginseng farming on a modest scale from the sixteenth century, only in the late eighteenth did ginseng domestication become widespread.[137] As the market for ginseng boomed in the late eighteenth century, drawing in merchants from Korea, Japan, and North America, the Manchurian product kept pace—only now as the new cultivated variety, not the wild one, that dominated the trade. The ginseng market in the Northeast transformed itself in a generation: By one estimate, by 1810 up to 90 percent of the ginseng in Jilin was farmed.[138] That year, a corruption scandal likewise revealed most of the ginseng entering the tribute system was no longer wild but farmed.[139]

In retrospect, the court's reaction to the phenomenon is almost unbelievable: It threw its full weight behind a campaign to eradicate cultivation, doubling the number of *karun* in the Northeast and ordered all ginseng farms to be destroyed.[140] Even before 1810, the Jiaqing court was staunchly anticultivation. Roving patrols had standing orders to destroy any ginseng farm they discovered: Huts were razed; crops were uprooted. In 1800, for example, 320 troops on a thirteen-month tour discovered illegal ginseng fields in the mountains of Nentun, Fantun, and Sikada, and so razed the farmers' huts and dug up their fields. The emperor was displeased: Following a precedent from 1789, he demanded an investigation into corruption and negligence, as none of the arrests had happened in the backcountry; the patrolmen had found them too close to established patrol routes.[141] Thus in 1801 the court put patrolmen under renewed pressure to step up seizures and arrests and so fully "purge" (Ma: *geterembume*) the area of all farms and poachers; in the language of the documents, they had to ensure "the interior of the mountains was thoroughly searched and purged and no illegals were wintering [there]." The garrisons at Ningguta and Ilan Hala drafted new men to the cause. This time, the tours went far to the east, from the Dekdenggi Mountains, clear to the Pacific coast. Throughout the region, they razed farmers' huts, destroyed ginseng fields, and hung fresh placards on trees to mark the territory as restricted and warn trespassers of the law.[142]

If the court was fully driven by profits and fiscal interests, perhaps it might have established its own farms or decriminalized and taxed the existing ones. In 1881, the struggling Qing state did just that: It began to promote cultivation, and a legal Manchurian ginseng trade grew exponentially thereafter.[143] The Qing court of the early nineteenth century, however, adhered to a different agenda. As the Jiaqing emperor proclaimed with indignation, the only true ginseng was the natural variety, not the stuff made by men:

> Ginseng is a delicate product of a numinous land [Ch: *diling zhong-chan*] . . . using the power of people to cultivate it is like forgery! The power of ginseng produced by the mountains is naturally vast [Ch: *qili zihou*]. If one plants ginseng, then it will be without its power when used.[144]

In other edicts, the Jiaqing emperor expressed similar sentiments: Farmed ginseng was "incomparable to the true ginseng"; or, more grandiloquently, "Mukden, Jilin, Ningguta, and such places give birth to ginseng, a divine and auspicious product of the land. How can we let that which is true descend into the chaos of falsity?"[145] The emperor was hardly alone in distrusting the value of cultivated ginseng. As the pharmacist Wu Qirui (1789–1847) wrote, although ginseng from "Liaodong" was better than all other varieties, the planted product was not: "Transplanted ginseng shoots, and ginseng planted from seeds are all weak in strength."[146] The market made the distinction between the farmed and the wild, and consumers wanted the wild variety. The Jiaqing emperor made the distinction as well, seeing the defense of wild ginseng as a defense of authenticity, for the essence of ginseng lay in its origins and the story of its creation. Consumers agreed that the best ginseng was a special and natural product of Manchuria.[147]

The tools used to enforce this distinction between the cultivated and the natural, in practice, were territorial administration, stepped-up patrolling, bureaucratic oversight, permits, and tallies—the same technologies of control used in the freshwater pearl monopoly. In both cases, the court empowered the territories' military governors through the course of the eighteenth century to deal with endemic and growing problems of control. In 1744, the Qing court empowered the territories to manage ginseng production; in 1748 it did the same with pearls. Thereafter, even as the territories proved ineffective in managing the problem, their presence on the ground expanded. The number of *karun* posts grew and with them the number of guards. The complexity of Qing rule diminished accordingly, as groups like the Ula were brought under the unified command of the territories. Strikingly, amid both the ginseng and the pearl crises, the court used similar rhetoric: Mussels and ginseng were valuable in themselves, not just as objects of consumption. Ginseng was a product of the land, not human labor; the emperor loved mussels, not just men. The court imagined a similar history of the two: Wild ginseng and Manchurian pearls were originally abundant, but corruption, poaching, and illegal trade had brought about a decline. They belonged, in all these ways, to a new history of a transformed entity: Manchuria.

REIMAGINING MANCHURIA

Efforts to protect ginseng and pearls in the wild helped transform both the administration and, over time, the logic of Qing rule. Indeed, the slow drive toward territorialization and bureaucratization created the framework for a new identification between Manchuria on the one hand and the "Three Eastern Territories" on the other. We take for granted that Manchuria, and what became Northeast China today, overlap with the Three Eastern Provinces; like the national boundaries that emerged from empires, we have naturalized and reimagined them as permanent in the modern age.[148] Yet the idea, at least in the Qing, that the Manchu homeland equaled the "Three Eastern Provinces" has roots only in the late eighteenth century, and it became a touchstone refrain only in the early nineteenth amid the region's rapid transformation.

With the major institutional changes of the era, that is, there came a quiet discursive one: Increasingly, people began to think in terms of the territories. Until the mid-eighteenth century, neither Jilin nor Sahaliyan Ula territories held special importance to the court as either dynastic or Manchu homelands.[149] Only two places carried this significance: "greater Mukden," which included both Mukden and adjacent parts of Jilin, and Changbaishan, to which the Manchus traced their mythical origins.[150] Throughout Qing rule, one finds multiple references to Mukden and Changbaishan as the "homeland" (Ch: *genben zhi di*, lit. "foundation land") and Changbaishan specifically as the "dynastic homeland" (Ch: *faxiang zhi di*, lit. "land where [the dynasty] arose"). It was common to raise the word "Mukden" up a notch in texts as a sign of respect, just as one would do for an imperial decree. Jilin and Sahaliyan Ula, in contrast, received no such honor. Rather, these regions were important for being "close" to the homeland or for serving as the "screen" (Ch: *fanli*) of Mukden. In 1729, the Yongzheng emperor thus justified policies in Sahaliyan Ula and Jilin on grounds that they were "adjacent to Mukden," the unique "land from which our dynasty arose."[151] Through the mid-eighteenth century, the Qing court likewise justified policies in Sahaliyan Ula, including land reclamation initiatives in Lalin, on grounds that it was *not* "important homeland" (Ch: *genben zhongdi*).[152]

This language began to change only with the empowerment of the territories. The shift happened only in stages. In 1741, for example, Military-Governor Jakuna called for stepped-up policing of poachers as a means of protecting "Manchu roots," which he now identified with the entire territory of Jilin. The prime threat to the Manchu's land of origins, he also suggested, was an undocumented "floating population" (Ch: *liumin*) of Chinese.[153] In 1762, with reports that ginseng poaching was endemic throughout the Three Eastern Territories, the Qianlong emperor first described the region as a whole as compromised; all three territories, he argued, were originally spaces where "customs were simple and pure" (Ch: *fengsu chunpu*).[154] Yet changes seemed underfoot: The original character of Manchuria was under duress.

After 1800, equating the "Three Eastern Territories" with the Manchu homeland became much more common, particularly as a jurisdiction for imperial policy. In 1803, the Jiaqing emperor proclaimed the "Three Eastern

Territories" to be the dynastic homeland, and, at the same time, he explicitly described the Ula as "belonging to the Manchus" (Ch: *jie xi manzhou*); he thus ordered that they practice hunting to preserve their old ways.[155] He identified the homeland with the three territories multiple times during his rule, as did the Daoguang emperor after him.[156] In many cases, the emperors were simply aping the language of the territories' governors themselves. Fugiyūn, who served as the military governor of Jilin, leveraged the idea of Jilin as the "dynastic homeland" to justify policies multiple times.[157] He called Mukden and Jilin the "Manchu homeland" in 1816, for example, noting that they were distinctive for their "pure customs" (Ch: *chunfeng*).[158] In 1821, he described Jilin as "our homeland where the dynasty arose" and Mukden and Ningguta as the same.[159] Such claims circulated widely. The oft-cited statecraft writer Wei Yuan (1794–1857) would equate the Three Eastern Territories as "the cherished Manchu homeland" (Ch: *Manzhou genben zhongdi*) as well, a claim he reiterated in his touchstone history of the early Qing, the *Shengwu ji* (1842).[160] From texts like the *Shengwu ji*, such imperial and scholarly claims circulated widely in the late nineteenth century, finding a place in official compendia, gazetteers, travelogues, and histories.[161]

In some ways, the expansion of this new discourse in the nineteenth century ran parallel to the mussel and ginseng crises and reflected growing concerns about Chinese homesteading, anxieties about Manchu assimilation, and Russian expansionism. The first reference in *Veritable Records* to the "Three Eastern Provinces" as the "Manchu homeland," dates to 1777, and it came in reference to the problem of Han Chinese migrants in the region. Indeed, after 1800 the refrain became common to justify policies for controlling Chinese refugee flow into the region after natural disasters.[162]

Yet in other ways, the discourse proved inseparable from problems of resource management. The first calls for protecting the "pure" Manchu customs of Jilin were tied to anxieties about ginseng poaching in particular. Anxieties about the Manchu homeland and its natural products were connected; the empire managed both with the same instruments. These anxieties spoke to common concerns: corrupt officials, uninspired bannermen, and undocumented poachers. They also invoked a certain understanding of the past: that the Manchus had emerged from Manchuria, not conquered it; that poaching was different and new; that Manchuria had once been "pure." Both Manchuria the territory and Manchuria the realm of uncorrupted nature, in short, emerged from common mechanisms amid the boom years, when pearls and ginseng first disappeared from the land.

CONCLUSION

From the mussels' perspective, this period in their history was disastrous. Today, freshwater pearl mussels have become endangered in the wild, and to sustain today's industries, freshwater pearls no longer come from nature, but from farms, much as ginseng and furs do. Yet in their demise, they shared much in common with the other species in this same time period: sandalwood in Hawaii, sea turtles in Southeast Asia, and fur-bearing animals throughout the greater Pacific. All witnessed spectacular population declines in the first half of the nineteenth century.

For Qing subjects, the era was transformative as well. The court understood the sustainability of pearl production as a measure of its rule; it read the mussels' demise as a sign of lax discipline, moral failing, and insufficient control. It empowered military governors, strengthening the policing apparatus, and created new border controls. It used the crisis to discipline native Manchurians on one hand and to create a more coherent and definable Manchuria on the other. In the process, it fostered a new convergence of territorial, ethnic, and natural space. The imaginary of "Mukden" and the jurisdiction of the "Three Eastern Territories" came to overlap, and it is this territory that we still call "Manchuria."

THREE

The Mushroom Crisis

In the 1820s, booming demand for steppe mushrooms inspired a rush to the steppes of Mongolia. Each summer, hundreds and ultimately thousands of undocumented Chinese workers crossed the border into the territory for the summer harvest. Complaints began to surface: The Chinese had no license to trade, yet they acted as "lords" of the land; they threatened the Mongol way of life. They littered the steppe with open pits, stripped it of wild mushrooms, cleared it of trees, and killed marmots and fish. In a few cases, when local authorities attempted to evict them, the mushroom pickers resisted with axes and hoes. Ultimately, as local and regional authorities lost control, the Qing court threw its weight behind a plan for total "purification," a drive to repatriate undocumented Chinese, investigate Mongol collaborators, and restore the steppe to an original, timeless form. It is to the history of this rush, and the dramatic response it triggered, that we now turn.

There are no histories of the great mushroom rush; the event is utterly forgotten. In part, the lack of scholarly attention reflects a peculiar silence in the Chinese sources: Generally, the steppe mushroom was a consumer or literary object, not the object of a booming business. There are, however, a few notable exceptions in the sources. The *Xuanzong Veritable Records*, the in-house annals of the Daoguang court (r. 1820–1850), include a single entry on the rush. It dates from the tenth month of the ninth year of Daoguang's reign, November 1829:

> Another edict. Lunbudorji and others sent a palace memorial to the throne:
>
> Chinese civilian Liu Deshan and company colluded with Chen Wu, a clerk at the military lieutenant-governor's yamen in Rehe to procure a forged permit and illicitly collect steppe mushrooms from the pasture territory [Ch: *youmu*] of prince *gong* Sonomdarjya. They have been arrested and investigated.
>
> [The] Chinese civilian Liu Deshan bribed a clerk, Chen Wu, to gain possession of a forged permit. [Liu Deshan] collected more than one hundred men, set up makeshift shelters on Mongol land, and poached mushrooms. He further inspired men to resist arrest. What a loathsome affair! Lunbudorji, etc. arrested Liu Deshan and company as criminal leaders and transferred them to the Board of Punishments. They also arrested the clerk Chen Wu and according to precedent transferred them to the Board. [We] ordered the Board of Punishments to investigate the case, settle on a punishment, and report back to the throne. Lunbudorji expelled all the Chinese mushroom poachers back across the border, and when the [Board] made its decision, all the officials who neglected their duty were impeached. If we are to prevent further disturbances, Mongol leaders cannot be lax. Henceforth, if any person poaches mushrooms or is illegally logging Mongol lands, let Lunbudorji, etc. handle the case.[1]

The Board of Punishments was the top judicial organ under the court, and, by law, it handled cases without clear precedents; it handled the Liu Deshan case because it was novel. For this same reason, two jurists at the Board, Bao Shuyun and Zhu Qingqi, included the Board's decision as a "leading case" (Ch: *cheng'an*) in their *Addendum to the Conspectus of Legal Cases* (*Xuzeng xing'an huilan*), a widely circulated compendium of Board decisions, published in 1840. One finds a short abstract of the Liu Deshan decision under cases of "stealing rice and grain from fields" (Ch: *dao tianye gumai*). Other crimes in the chapter include those of poaching sable and ginseng, illegal mining, stealing water from irrigation canals, and hunting in game parks, holy mountains, or the borderlands of Manchuria and Mongolia.[2]

How, we may wonder, was mushroom picking analogous to these other crimes? Why did the court care about mushroom picking? And why, in 1829,

did it suddenly become an issue of imperial interest? Without further information, the *Veritable Records* and the *Conspectus* are impossible to interpret:
Like short abstracts from any high court, they present a particularly thorny
issue, strip it of context, and boil it down to the legal resolution. As with so
many other phenomena outside China proper, the sources simply fail us.

Answers lie only in the archives. In Beijing, at the First Historical Archives, and in Ulaanbaatar, at the National Central Archives of Mongolia,
there is a staggering volume of material on the Liu Deshan case and similar incidents of mushroom picking extending back to 1818. One finds memorials to the throne, complaints from local authorities, confessions from
mushroom pickers, and registers of known offenders, complete with their
names, aliases, home jurisdictions, and camp locations. A scattering of
these materials, including Liu Deshan's confession, are in Chinese. The
bulk, however, are in Manchu or Mongolian, and the picture they paint is
richly detailed and alive with nuance. We cannot reconstruct the environmental history of Mongolia, or understand the meaning of the published
record, without them.

Historians of the Qing Mongolian frontier, like those of Manchuria,
generally frame their story in terms of the "policy of closing off." Yet in
Mongolia, too, we must be wary of such narratives. Like Manchuria, Mongolia was institutionally mixed: Some subjects fell under Mongol banners,
others belonged to Buddhist monastic land, and still others maintained
idiosyncratic, ad hoc relationships with the court. The rules governing access to their lands were accordingly diverse. In some territories, the court
required documentation to enter or work within them. In others, the court
prohibited entry altogether, including in holy mountains, game parks, and
the borderlands with Russia, which the court designated "restricted land"
(Mo: *caġajilaġsan ġajar*; Ch: *jindi*). How, then, did all of Mongolia, amid
the mushroom rush, become analogous to "restricted" territory? This chapter finds an answer in the pleas and confessions that emerged from the Liu
Deshan affair and other thorny cases: Taken together, they reveal the story
of a commodity, a crisis, and a new politics of nature in Mongolia.

THE FIRST CRIME: BEING UNDOCUMENTED

We begin with the administrative context: We cannot understand the
state response or the nature of the crime without it. Mushroom picking in

Map 3.1. Outer Mongolia in 1800.

Mongolia was not in itself a crime; unlicensed travel to Mongolia, however, was, and men like Liu Deshan knew it: He feared being caught without paperwork, and as the *Veritable Records* recorded, he went to extraordinary lengths to forge his own. By 1829, in response to booming trade and rushes for products such as timber and medicinal deer horn, the Qing court had already elaborated a complex set of rules for movement into and out of Outer Mongolia, where Liu Deshan was ultimately arrested.

For almost the entirety of the Qing period, the court supported various travel restrictions along the Great Wall boundary. These rules governed not only Chinese subjects but Mongols as well: Chinese civilians could not cross into Mongolia; Mongols could not cross out.[3] Most Mongols could not even leave their local jurisdiction, the Mongol "banner" (Ma: *gūsa*; Mo: *qosiġun*; Ch: *qi*), without paperwork.[4] Subjects of a Mongol banner were not only prohibited from entering Chinese territories, that is, but from freely traveling within Mongolia itself. These travel restrictions, in turn, reflected social norms, as rigid boundaries defined both one's place in the social hierarchy and one's access to pastures, even during periods of peace and prosperity.[5] Noblemen had more freedom of movement; their subjects and slaves had less.

In practice, the noblemen formed the backbone of the Qing state in Mongolia, and Manchus and other officials sent from Beijing had a relatively small presence on the ground. Each banner, for example, was the domain of a *jasaġ*, a titled aristocrat who inherited the position; all *jasaġs* were descendants of Chinggis Khan, and, in Outer Mongolia, all of their genealogies ran through a specific branch in the family tree, named the Khalkha.[6] Enforcing the rule of *jasaġs* required regular cooperation between the banners, but only in cases of exceptional significance or complexity did authorities in Beijing intervene. More commonly, banner *jasaġs* notified another, higher-ranking aristocrat, called a "league chief" (Mo: *ciġulġan u daruġa*; Ma: *culgan i da*; Ch: *mengchang*), who managed a provincial-level unit, called an *aimaġ*, to which the banners belonged. After 1725 there were four such *aimaġ* in Outer Mongolia: Secen Qan, Tüsiyetü Qan, Sain Noyan, and Jasaġtu Qan (see Map 3.1). Above the *aimaġ* league chiefs stood a handful of authorities appointed from Beijing, who were based in the towns of Khüree, Kiakhta, Uliasutai, and Khobdo. The highest authority in the west was a military governor (Ma: *jiyanggiyūn*; Ch: *jiangjun*) in Uliasutai; the highest in the east was the imperial representative in Khüree, or *amban* (Ma: *hesei takūraha Kuren de tefi baita icihiyara amban*; Mo: *jarliġ-iyar jaruġsan Küriyen-dur saġuju kereg sidkegci saiid*; Ch: **kulun banshi dachen**; lit. "official dispatched by imperial decree to Khüree to manage affairs"). Both of these officials belonged to the Eight Banners and served a three-year term. In Khüree, the *amban* further served alongside a Mongol counterpart, also called an *amban*, who inherited the position. There were thus two high *ambans* in Khüree: a member of the Eight Banners sent from Beijing, and a member of the Mongol banners drawn from the local aristocracy.

In times of peace, generals and *ambans* rarely intervened in banner affairs. Instead, the Mongolian aristocracy—the patrilineal descendants of Chinggis Qan—ruled over the banners and *aimaġs* with little interference. Inside the banner, *jasaġs* collected taxes, maintained the criminal court, and communicated with higher powers. Higher authorities, in contrast, mainly oversaw interjurisdictional matters. After its establishment in 1762, for example, the *ambans*' office assumed responsibility for managing frontier relations and trade with Russia, maintaining postal roads, coordinating with the Buddhist ecclesiastical authorities, overseeing the Chinese merchant community, and adjudicating interethnic disputes.

Territorial and jurisdictional boundaries were thus a central concern of the court. It accordingly supported efforts to draw maps and erect physical boundary markers on the ground, including cairns (Mo: *obuġa*) and placards.[7] It also supported enforcement: As early as 1629, the court prohibited commoners from crossing banner boundaries; in 1662 it further criminalized hunting beyond banner lines. In part, the enforcement of territorial rule reflected a concession to local Mongol social dynamics: To migrate to another banner was to undermine the authority (and tax base) of one's *jasaġ*. Yet, to a degree, restrictions on mobility transcended class as well: By the eighteenth century, if a nobleman left his banner or wished to marry beyond its bounds, he too had to obtain a special permit from a representative of the court.[8] Banners became fundamental to how the Qing saw Mongol subjects and how Mongols saw themselves: Just as Qing documents and texts identified Chinese subjects by their home county in this period, Mongol texts used banner affiliation to do the same.[9] Nonetheless, like all borders, banner boundaries were often porous, contested, and difficult to maintain, and they represented an ambition for social stability as much as a lived reality.

To control the borders, and so ensure a lasting order, the court gradually moved to a system of passports and licenses. After 1720, for example, Chinese merchants could travel to Khüree only with a special license.[10] To further ensure oversight, in 1727 the court established five inspection points to monitor Sino–Mongolian and Sino–Russian trade, including at Kalgan (Zhangjiakou) and Hohhot (Guihua).[11] Thereafter, though undocumented travel continued unabated, trespassers often went great lengths to avoid being caught without proper paperwork—a testament to the peculiar but limited power of the state. New crimes emerged: passport forgery, permit repurposing, people literally covering their tracks at the border.[12]

Judging by the archival record, the court seemed to care about some forms of border crossing more than others. As a rule, travel into sensitive jurisdictions, including the border with Russia, hunting grounds, and holy mountains, caused more concern. Large groups of travelers similarly attracted more attention than lone wolves. Provoked by the growing numbers of pilgrims in the late eighteenth century, for example, the Qianlong court mandated in 1793 that pilgrim parties of more than ten carry special licenses; if smaller groups or individuals requested one, authorities should grant them, but they were not to be harassed.[13] Pilgrims' licenses were good only one way: When travelers reached their point of destination, they had to register with their local jurisdiction's office and, before leaving, apply for a permit for the return trip.[14] The *ambans'* records thus contain registers of the names, ranks, size, and weapons in each pilgrim caravan.[15]

As the new rules of the 1720s suggest, Chinese merchants were another special concern. Anxiety about Chinese merchants grew deeper in the late eighteenth and early nineteenth centuries, as commerce in and through Mongol banners boomed, and the number of merchants and other travelers plying the main trade routes grew.[16] Trade dovetailed with institutional changes mandated by the court. The Jiaqing emperor (r. 1796–1820), in particular, oversaw major reforms of the rules of trade. In 1797, almost immediately after assuming the throne, his court eased restrictions on Chinese merchants heading to the countryside, giving merchants new access to the banners. Three years later, in 1800, the Jiaqing court endorsed a series of reforms to streamline oversight and better manage the trade. In essence, the reforms divided Outer Mongolia into two: the *ambans* assumed oversight over the two eastern *aimaġ* (Secen Qan and Tüsiyetü Qan), and the military governors took responsibility for the two western ones (Sain Noyan and Jasaġtu Qan). Their jurisdictions thus became territorially defined.

The year 1800 ultimately witnessed an overhaul of the rules of trade. The reforms called for clearer, more standardized paperwork to identify and monitor all caravans that entered Outer Mongolia. As the edict establishing the new system read:

> People going to trade in Khüree, Kiakhta, Uliasutai, and the four Khalkha *aimaġ* should be permanently organized according to established rules and regulations. Henceforth the names, amounts of merchandise, and dates of departure will be clearly written on government permits obtained through the various *yamens* by the merchants. Having attached the government permit and affixed it with a seal, the officials' *yamen* at the trade-destination will be notified. [For all these activities] records will be kept.[17]

The reforms thus entailed regular cooperation between merchants and imperial officials. In an ideal situation, six months prior to issuing trade licenses for travel from Khüree to Uliasutai the *ambans'* office in Khüree received a request for a number of blank permits affixed with the *ambans'* seal; these permits were then transferred to the trade supervisor's office, where clerks issued them to merchants.[18] For merchants traveling from Shanxi or Beijing, the application process usually began in Hohhot or Kalgan (Zhangjiakou), where the caravan leader registered his name, merchant house, destination, number of camels or oxcarts, types and quantities of goods, and the names, home jurisdictions, and sometimes physical descriptions of the Chinese and Mongol caravan members. The *yamen* then issued a permit with a designated length of stay on it—either 100 days, 200 days, or a year, depending on the destination.[19]

If the licenses facilitated trade, they also served to identify merchants to the state and enhance supervision. The license itself was a form letter, in block print, with Mongol text on the left and Chinese on the right. At the top was printed "TEMPORARY PASSPORT" (Mo: *quġucaġ-a temdegtü bicig*; Ch: *xianpiao*). Below were written the rules of conduct in Mongolia, including prohibitions against entering restricted areas, and a message granting the caravan safe passage. The document was standardized: Only the dates and names of the recipients were left blank for clerks to fill in.[20] To further ensure the timeliness of each departure, merchants had twenty days to leave town or the permit would become invalid.[21] Later, when they arrived at their destination, caravans had to report to authorities again; finally, when they returned home, they reported yet again and submitted the used permit to the clerk's office.[22] Throughout their trip, the various offices alerted one another to the caravans' movements. Those who failed to show at their expected destination, reported to the wrong office, arrived with the wrong people or merchandise, or lacked a license altogether, were arrested.

If properly licensed, the Qing state assured merchants a dependable, albeit segregated, place within Mongolia. In each of the main trade hubs—Uliasutai, Kiakhta, and Khüree—Chinese merchants had to restrict themselves to special districts, which were separate from the Mongol neighborhoods around them. In Khüree, Chinese merchants had a "trade quarter" (Ma: *hūdai hashan*); in Uliasutai, they kept to a smaller "trade street" (Ma: *hūdai giya*).[23] These neighborhoods were ideally both segregated and temporary; after the establishment of the merchant quarter in Kiakhta, for example, the court prohibited any women from residing within. It is clear, though, that although most merchant and caravan workers came without their families as single men, and some were between the ages of ten and twelve, many Chinese merchants took Mongol wives.[24]

Similar principles of segregation and temporary residence guided Qing policies in the Mongolian countryside. An overriding concern with identifying and segregating undocumented migrants, for example, marked oversight over firewood collection near the trade hubs. From the 1820s, as trade boomed and trade quarters expanded, so too did the demand for firewood in Kiakhta and Khüree, and new rules emerged to deal with improper collection of the fuel: Chinese caught poaching wood in particular were subject to stiff punishments, including corporal punishment and repatriation under guard back to the Chinese interior.[25] Yet forests continued to attract migrants, and endemic poaching presented a dilemma for authorities: Should wood collectors be arrested or licensed?

In many cases the Qing state settled on licensing as the answer, as the sheer number of wood poachers made mass arrests impractical. In 1828, for example, after reports of extensive wood cutting around Kiakhta surfaced, the *amban* ordered the trade supervisor in Kiakhta to inspect the identities of all "vagrant" Chinese and Mongols logging in the Logar Hiya area, just to the south of town, where migrants had formed a community of wood collectors.[26] Later reports revealed that Chinese entrepreneurs were funding them and that they had erected private enclosures. The *amban* initially ordered everyone arrested, their enclosures razed, and the area made "pure" (Ma: *bolgo*; Mo: *arigun*)—a stringent call for social and environmental order, as we shall see.[27] Yet many migrants to the area had brought their families, and some were so poor that they lacked even the oxcarts to leave.[28] When troops proved incapable of removing them—or unwilling—the local *jasaġ*, Namjildorji, agreed to allow the woodcutters to stay camped in his banner through the winter.[29] In the meantime, he demanded a register of all implicated "Mongol men and women," including their names, ages, household sizes, and home jurisdictions. Policing had to step up: No further outsiders were to be allowed in, neither "lamas nor laymen, men nor women, [Mongol] people nor Chinese."[30] Namjildorji then forwarded the census to the *ambans'* office, which forwarded it to the emperor in Beijing.

In other cases, authorities proved less flexible. Not far from Logar Hiya, a community of fourteen woodcutters was active southwest of Kiakhta, at Bayanbulaġ, on the southern bank of the Buur River. The poachers this time were Chinese men known to be "mixed up living with Mongol women." Especially given the location's proximity to the Russian border, the *amban* explained, it was entirely "improper to have a profusion . . . of Mongol and Chinese firewood and charcoal sellers in the area." After an investigation, the court deemed their encampment too destabilizing, and the wood they provided too inessential as fuel was already available from other sources. Authorities thus tracked down and arrested every household in the community, removing them permanently from the jurisdiction.[31]

The state treated woodcutters in the game parks outside Khüree with a similar level of inflexibility; there, too, logging remained fully prohibited.[32] By rule, all wood entering Khüree had to be certified that it had not come from the restricted grounds. Yet wood poaching intensified in the 1820s nonetheless. In one scandal, a midlevel official at the *ambans'* office, Pungcukdorji, took matters into his own hands and, to drum up local revenue, began issuing permits to loggers in certain designated zones; after a year and a half, he planned to remove all loggers from the park and "purify the land."[33] Thus it happened in the spring of 1830 that loggers "chopped down and ravaged" (Ma: *sacime gasihiyabuha*) 2,300 carts worth of wood within the game park. When the scheme came to light, the court punished Pungcukdorji and subjected all complicit guardsmen to forty lashes each for corruption: Protecting game in this case trumped any other concern.[34]

In other jurisdictions, and with other commodities, authorities were more open minded. As trade in velvety deer horn surged in the early nineteenth century, for example, the Qing state began requiring paperwork for all deer-horn transactions in Khüree. The product, a pharmaceutical used in Chinese medicine, was by weight the most valuable commodity traded in Mongolia; in 1841, one large pair of deer horns cost 180 bricks of tea—enough tea to load down a caravan of thirty-five oxcarts.[35] As hunters rushed to capitalize on the deer-horn trade, cases of deer poaching surfaced in restricted game parks and religious sites. Thus, as early as 1820, the state mandated that all deer-horn deals be registered with authorities in Khüree.[36] As the edict read:

> For all Mongol people, when coming to the market in Khüree to engage in trade, if there is a person selling deer horns, that person must be brought to the trade supervisor's office by the relevant Chinese [buyer] for registration. Every month a report shall be prepared for the *ambans*. This is a strict mandate for all merchant houses.[37]

Thereafter authorities made "all Mongol people coming to Khüree to trade" aware of the new regulation and made both banner authorities and the trade supervisor's office responsible for enforcement.[38]

The profusion of paperwork that emerged from these initiatives provides a strikingly vivid picture of commercial life in this era, while offering an equally powerful sense of the limitations of paperwork. The language of the documents presumes, for example, that the market would have only "Mongol sellers" (Ma: *uncaha monggoso*) and "Chinese buyers" (Ma: *udaha irgese*).[39] It is clear from the archives, however, that marketplace and ethnic identities did not overlap so neatly. The registers, kept in either Manchu or Chinese, listed the names of buyers, buyers' merchant houses, sellers, sellers' home banner or *otoġ* (if they lived on ecclesiastical estates), the date of the transaction, the number of racks sold, price (tallied in bricks of tea), location of the kill, and the name of a guarantor who vouched for all the information.[40] Yet despite the profusion of data, the commodity chain was often obscure. Memorializing on the problem in 1826, the *ambans*' office conceded that those who hunted for deer horn were not always those who sold the product in Khüree; instead, middlemen sold it without any verifiable knowledge of where the deer horns actually came from. The *ambans* could not guarantee, then, that the registers effectively guarded against poaching.[41]

Its limitations not withstanding, by the early nineteenth century the Qing court had taken an increased interest in monitoring and controlling cross-border trade, migration, and commerce in high-value commodities in Outer Mongolia. It remained committed to the principles of border maintenance and segregation, especially in "restricted areas" such as the borderland with Russia, holy mountains, and military game parks, and it attempted to enforce its rule through a range of techniques, from total prohibitions on poaching and trespassing to, increasingly, licensing schemes.[42] If it was to be legal at all, cross-border commerce and travel in Mongolia had to be documented.

THE MUSHROOM BUSINESS

It was into this world of growing trade, new forms of state involvement, and ever ubiquitous paperwork that Liu Deshan, the mushroom picker, entered in the early 1820s. He knew that traveling without a license was illegal, and, as the *Veritable Records* noted, he traveled with a forged counterfeit to avoid detection. His confession and other documents held in the National Central Archives of Mongolia provide a fuller account of his criminal life and the black-market mushroom business that ultimately brought him to ruin.

Liu Deshan was born in Zhaoyuan county, Shandong, but when his marriage prospects fizzled out, he left Shandong, migrated north, and eventually settled in Chifeng, Zhili, a hardscrabble country on the southern rim of the steppe, just south of the Greater Khinggan Mountains (Ch: *Da Xing'an ling*).[43] For decades, the region had drawn unattached, immigrant men like Liu Deshan from Zhili, Shanxi, Henan, and Shandong into the mushroom trade.[44] In 1824, after a few years laboring as a mushroom picker, Liu Deshan reached out to a man named Chen Wu, a clerk from Shandong at the nearby Chaoyang county *yamen*, in a bid to organize his own picking teams. For his part, Chen Wu would later confess (under torture) that finances were tight in Chaoyang, and his office had run without funds for a year. So for the price of one silver tael per page, he agreed to furnish Liu Deshan with blank paper, presealed with the magistrate's chop. With opportunity knocking, Liu Deshan brought in a partner and pooled together enough funds to buy seventeen slips of official paper; he wanted to purchase as much letterhead as possible. They then forged onto each slip an imperial decree, written in the emperor's vermillion-colored ink:

> Give these men safe passage to the Left-Wing, Front Banner of Secen Qan *aimaḡ*. They collect a tribute of mushrooms.

Finally, Liu hired a Mongol lama to translate the Chinese into Mongol, giving the document a proper veneer.[45] For the next four years, he made the trip into Mongolia undetected. The Qing state, it seems, had the power to inspire forgery and to create a market in government letterhead but lacked the power to stop men like Liu Deshan from entering Mongolia in the first place.

And Liu Deshan was hardly alone: The mushroom trade was booming in Chifeng. Each year, after the early summer rains, pickers set off for the foothills of the Greater Khinggan to collect mushrooms. Fantastic stories swirled of getting rich quick: Pickers told of men who stumbled into giant rings formed of dozens of white mushrooms, with every stalk capped by four- to five-inch heads the size of "plates." Those who stumbled into such a ring got rich; it was like winning a gritty lottery. A picker usually collected three or four catties of fresh mushroom from an average "fairy ring" (as we call them in English), but fortunate ones might harvest six or seven catties' worth of mushrooms, or five pounds of mushrooms in a single haul. When dried, the mushrooms lost as much as three-quarters of their weight, but the reward for selling even a small amount could be high: A mere pound of the right kind of mushrooms meant a fortune.[46]

More dangerous than mushrooming in the wooded mountains, and more profitable, was the trade in steppe mushrooms. Which species pickers actually harvested can only be guessed at. In Qing documents they were called simply "mushrooms" in Mongolian and Manchu (Mo: *mögü*; Ma: *sence*), though Chinese records sometimes translated them more specifically as "steppe mushroom," or *koumo*. The "steppe mushroom," in turn, does not equate with any modern species, despite some recent attempts by mycological enthusiasts and online dealers in that direction. From the documents, we can surmise that the mushrooms pickers targeted thrived in late summer and fall; that they were edible and white; and that they thrived north of the Khinggan mountains, particularly in zones where streams fed into the grasslands. Two mushroom species fit the description best, and mushrooms pickers may have marketed both as *koumo*: *Tricholoma mongolicum* Imai and *Agaricus campestris*.

The species share much in common. Both are white and edible, both thrive on the steppe at the end of the Mongolian summer, and both have circular-shaped root structures that cause the mushrooms to bloom in fairy rings ten meters in diameter—the size of a large yurt. To the trained eye, they are distinct: *Tricholoma* is fat and bulbous, whereas *Agaricus* is skinnier at the waist but with a wide-brimmed, sombrero-like cap; most of the other edible mushrooms in the region would have looked significantly different.[47] Today *tricholoma* is endangered and protected in Mongolia.[48] It is a relative of *Tricholoma matsutake*, the matsutake mushroom, and its taste is fleshy, fine textured, and pungent. Rural families near Ulaanbaatar put these mushrooms out to dry for two or three days and eat them roasted with butter or steeped in mutton soup, using them medicinally as a febrifuge.[49] The species is rare and not well studied, and it was not even identified until 1937, when Imai Sanshi, a mycologist at Hokkaido Imperial University and a consultant for the Agricultural Experiment Station of the South Manchuria Railway Company, first isolated a local "white mushroom" (Ch: *bai mogu*).[50] *Agaricus campestris*, by comparison, is common throughout the world and thrives wherever there is horse manure, from steppe pastures to preindustrial city streets. It is a close relative of the button mushroom, *Agaricus bisporus*, and, until *bisporus* farming became widespread after the 1920s, it dominated the European and North American mushroom trade.

Both mushrooms thrived on the grasslands northwest of the Greater Khinggan mountain range. There, on its gentle western slopes, in the eastern tip of modern Mongolia, an usual ecosystem of mixed forests and grassland thrived. Crisscrossed by a patchwork of creeks and rivers, it supported a raucous diversity of plants, animals, and fungi, including millions of Mongolian gazelle (the *zeren*), which still migrate in great herds across the steppe, and rare species of moose, falcon, crane, oriole, and bustard unique to the region.[51] In summer, it was easy to survive: Even without livestock, there was an abundance of wildlife. The region's streams and rivers teamed with Siberian salmon and Manchurian trout, which could weigh up to ninety pounds. Willows lined the rivers and streams, and pine and birch capped the ridgelines, making fuel easy to gather: With strong oxen, one could cart wood back to the Chinese interior. Travel to the region, though, posed difficulties. For one, mosquitoes plagued pack animals and people, making travel unpleasant even today.[52] Mushroom pickers, moreover, had to traverse enormous distances on only animal power: Chifeng lay roughly 325 miles south of the banner. On foot and by oxcart, the trip across the mountains took a month. The winters, moreover, were usually vicious, with temperatures dropping to as low as −47° Celsius.[53] Few mushroom pickers were prepared to stay through the year; most came for the summer and early fall, setting off from Chifeng in June, in July, and departed before the autumn freeze.

Once in Mongolia, the mushroom pickers split into small teams of eight to twelve men, chose their locations, and established camps with thatch and wood huts, centered on a shared "pit house" (Mo: *nüken ger*) for keeping fires going.[54] According to a register of 772 mushroom pickers who made the trip in 1827, the men were divided into eighty-one such camps, most with a leader and pit house, though some had two. That year they targeted thirty-one locations within the Left-Wing Front Banner. Although most locations had only one or two active teams, three—the Delger River, Qadantai, and the source of the Buyan River—shared twenty-eight camps between them; in the Delger River alone, there were 146 men in a thirty-mile strip, or one man every fifth of a mile.[55]

The men (and they were invariably men) who formed these camps were a ragtag group.[56] All were first-generation immigrants to the borderlands; they hailed from Shanxi, Shandong, southern Zhili, and Henan. They were also poor: The documents describe them having "no property." To finance the trip to Mongolia, which required at minimum a three-month commitment, they took loans in the form of rice and other provisions from a local creditor, another fellow migrant. As many lacked experience and needed help, they hired seasoned experts: men who had worked the trade for years, knew the area well, and could speak Mongolian. The guides, in turn, accepted fixed payments in mushrooms in exchange for smoothing over possible disputes with local Mongols. Most of the guides tended to be older men: Some were in their forties, others in their sixties or seventies, and all had lived or worked in Mongolia for decades.

Zhang Zhenglun, a guide arrested in 1828, was typical in this regard: He was seventy-three years old and had worked as a mushroom picker for forty years when authorities captured him. Before starting as a mushroom picker, he had worked for a decade as a laborer in the caravan trade. He thus was long immersed in local banner life. As an interrogator recorded him saying, "Because all of us had for many years lived in the duke *jasaĝ*'s banner, I was familiar with many people, knew the roads well, and I also understood the Mongolian language."[57] Few actually knew him there as Zhang Zhenglun; locally, he went by a Mongol name "Haisandai." After 1826, when he had grown too old to pick mushrooms, he still made the trip and profited by tending to oxen in the pickers' camps at a rate of one pot of rice per ox.

More important, if a quarrel arose with Mongols, he would "talk it out on [the pickers'] behalf and settle the matter" (Ma: *ceni funde gisurceme waciyaha*). For that service, he received a fixed rate of three ounces (Ma: *duka*) of mushrooms per picker per harvest. It was a stiff fee: Depending on the year, it could total between 10 and 30 percent of an individual picker's haul. Though expensive, his service was indispensible, as "quarrels" with local Mongols proved common. Authorities suspected local herders, especially poor ones, of accepting payments as hush money. Without mediators to grease the wheels, it seemed the system could fall apart.

The pickers, for their part, were just one cog in a complex commodity chain that connected the steppe to buyers in Beijing. By Zhang Zhenglun's estimate, a mushroom picker gathered between 5,000 and 6,000 catties of mushrooms in a poor year and 7,000 to 8,000 catties in a fruitful one. Another guide, Hui Wanzong ("Hui Lama") estimated that each individual in his camp collected from between ten and twenty to as much as thirty catties of mushrooms each. After the picking season, and after paying off their guides and debts, they sold their remaining mushrooms to a wholesaler, based in the village of Niulanshan, and the wholesaler sold the mushrooms to four specialty shops in Beijing, all located in bustling districts where the Manchu and Chinese cities met: the Great Jiehuizhen shop, outside the Zhengyang gate; and the Deyu, Xitai, and Longsheng shops, outside Chongwen gate.[58] From these shops, Mongolia's steppe mushrooms entered the consumer world of Beijing. Mushrooms thus changed hands at least four times: Pickers returned their mushrooms to camp leaders and investors, who sold them to a wholesaler, who brought them to the shops in Beijing, who sold them to customers.

At the shops, one could buy steppe mushrooms whole, in both large and small varieties, or one could buy them in pieces.[59] They found their way into dishes such as "roasted chicken pieces with steppe mushrooms" (Ch: *koumo shaorou kuai*), "braised chicken bites with steppe mushrooms" (Ch: *koumo huijiding*), and "flying dragon soup with steppe mushrooms" (Ch: *koumo feilong tang*).[60] They were cut into slices or bites, depending on size and shape of the cap; they were roasted, braised, or boiled.[61] By the late eighteenth century, elites from across China were seeking them out. The most esteemed endorsement for the product came from Yuan Mei (1716–1797), perhaps the most influential poet and literary critic of his time. His guide to fine dining, the *Suiyuan shidan* (1792)—a work that did for food what *Superfluous Things* did for objects in general—endorsed only a precious few ingredients as befitting a gentleman. Of these, Yuan Mei recommended steppe mushrooms, the sand treasure, above all: They tasted excellent in soups and in stir-fry, and they paired well with chicken legs.[62] Others agreed, and the market boomed.

The mushroom trade was thus big business. For their work, an individual picker earned between 0.7 and 1.2 taels per catty of mushrooms (approximately 0.609 kilogram) per season. If the annual haul reached 8,000 catties of mushrooms, the revenue generated from the wholesaler's purchase alone could total 9,000 taels, a king's ransom for a single year: The monthly salary of a low-ranking capital bannerman was four taels per month, and ordinary people often earned a meager ten to fourteen taels per year.[63] As the price for mushrooms was at least 1.2 taels per catty, we can assume that only the wealthiest customers, like Yuan Mei, could afford steppe mushrooms; few would have had the means to purchase or eat them regularly.[64] Indeed, in the late eighteenth century, the customs office in Beijing appraised a catty of steppe mushrooms as equal in taxable value to a newly made sable-fur coat.[65] Yet the incentive for selling the mushrooms had to have been enormous: The trade was illegal, and, after 1818, as the environmental consequences of mushroom picking became a top concern at court, engaging in the trade was becoming increasingly dangerous.

CONTROLLING THE MUSHROOM RUSH: 1818−1829

Perhaps the most dangerous jurisdiction for mushroom pickers, and by far the most popular, was the Left-Wing Front Banner of Mongolia (see Map 3.1). As the testimony of the guide Zhang Zhenglun suggests, mushroom pickers had deep roots in the area, and there is evidence that Chinese pickers were active in the banner as early as 1759, when they were noted to have accidentally started a prairie fire that scorched through the neighboring imperial hunting grounds.[66] We know of these mushroom pickers only because of the fire; there was no reason mushroom picking in itself would have come to the attention of higher authorities. In the Left-Wing Front Banner, the *jasaġ* seemed neither overly concerned nor eager to involve his superiors, and in Mongolia *jasaġ*s ruled. It took extreme circumstances for the court to get involved.[67]

Only in 1818 did mushroom picking become like a prairie fire. That year the banner *jasaġ*, Dasigeleng, reported to his immediate superior, the league chief Artasida, that a torrent of undocumented mushroom pickers had made his territory unmanageable.[68] They disrupted life on the steppe: They "self-indulgently dug holes, cut down trees, pitched tents, planted vegetables, caught fish, and drove off the sheep, goats, horses and cattle Mongols live on." The result was that mushroom pickers were "living as rulers" (Ma: *ejeleme tefi*) over banner pastures.[69] The alert sent the Qing government in Mongolia into motion: Artasida forwarded the report to the *ambans'* office in Khüree, and the *ambans* alerted Beijing. All agreed to draft Mongol banner militiamen throughout the *aimaġ* into active service, and so, in the late summer, cavalry teams moved in on the migrants. Under the joint command of league and banner authorities, they rounded up mushroom pickers, razed their camps, and entered each offender into a register: 442 men from Chifeng, twenty-eight men from Dolon Nuur, and forty-two men from Rehe. They forwarded the register to Khüree, which forwarded it to the Board for Governing Outer Dependencies in Beijing, and the court, which alerted the governor-general of Zhili and the magistrates in the mushroom pickers' home counties.[70] When the dust settled, authorities arrested the pickers' ringleaders, found Dasigeleng guilty of negligence, and began an investigation into whether Mongol herders were secretly harboring migrant Chinese. None were discovered, and for the next three years, no further reports surfaced of mushroom picking in the area.[71]

In 1820, however, Dasigeleng died, and a new successor, Sonomdarjya, inherited the title of *jasaġ* in 1822.[72] His first summer in office, Sonomdarjya reported that over 1,200 unlicensed mushroom pickers had arrived in the banner, and he refused to ignore the problem: "Quarrels and arguments" had started between Mongols and Chinese migrants, and the migrants were acting "on their own accord" (Mo: *joriġ-iyar*), not according to the law:

> Over 1,200 Chinese have come. They have built 130 small camps [Mo: *maiiqan*], dug pits, and erected homes. They plant vegetables, hunt marmots, and pick mushrooms, and so lord over the Mongols' pasture territory and drive away [our] livestock.[73]

None of the migrants had proper paperwork for entering the banner. They were drifters and vagrants: people "without property" who lived in the northern frontier of Zhili, though "not one was [originally] from the province." The report implied that the previous *jasaġ* had covered up the problem, making the matter worse. Now the sheer number of mushroom pickers had taken a toll on the land and its inhabitants, and the banner needed help. Dasigeleng emphasized that the mushroom pickers were undocumented and cited verbatim a stern memorial, dated 1805, by the former military governor of Uliasutai: "The four Khalkha *aimaġ* originally did not have Chinese going [around] on their own whims, and no law sanctioned vagrancy." Mushroom picking, he argued, simply was "making excuses for vagrancy" and thus "in extreme violation of the law"; Mongols could grant "not one" mushroom picker shelter. Thus in 1822 riders took Sonomdarjya's report to Artasida's league office and the *amban*s in Khüree, who forwarded the message with opprobrium to Beijing.[74] The court once again endorsed a plan to call up troops, and by autumn they had razed camps, drawn up registers, and repatriated men.

Still, the *amban*s and the court received reports of illegal mushroom picking in the area every year thereafter until 1829, when Liu Deshan was arrested. Each summer, mushroom pickers simply came back again, in equal or greater numbers, completely undeterred by the state's response. The bureaucracy was not acting as it should: Were the troops incompetent? Were authorities hiding the truth? Or were all tacitly corrupt? In the early summer of 1825, as reports arrived that over 700 mushroom pickers had already entered Sonomdarjya's banner, Artasida felt compelled to get answers. He thus sent a special deputy, the *beile* Sonomdobcin (described as a "capable, moderately high-ranking official who understands this matter") to call up extra reserves, coordinate troop movements, and provide a second pair of eyes on the ground. Thereafter, on-the-spot reports reached Khüree and Beijing from both banner and league sources, which the *amban* cross-checked against one another.[75]

Yet the bungling continued. In the summer of 1825, for example, the deputy Sonomdobcin issued a compromise to the mushroom pickers: If they allowed themselves to be registered by authorities, they could finish their work; they only had to leave by the start of the eighth lunar month (September 12) or face immediate arrest.[76] The plan seemed to work: When the appointed day arrived, only two teams of mushroom pickers, comprised of thirteen men, remained behind. No leniency was shown toward these men; they had used mushroom picking as a "pretext" for "settling down as vagrants and thieves," and they had induced Mongols to "harbor them" and collaborate.[77] League and banner authorities, according to the instructions of the *amban*, had to "purify the banner."[78] Yet as the thirteen stragglers were being rounded up, a much larger group of 393 pickers being escorted across banner lines staged a small revolt, drove off their Mongol guard, and pitched camp for the winter in the southern hills of the banner.[79] Sonomdobcin advised waiting them out, predicting they would not survive the winter; the migrants were confined to the rugged Buyan River area, a "steppe wilderness" on the fringe of the Greater Khinggan range that "Mongols do not use as pastures."[80]

Yet nothing was solved. The following spring, more mushroom pickers "swarmed" into the area, leading the *amban*s to send a new special deputy to the scene from Khüree, the Manchu second-in-command, Weisengge. In coordination with banner and league authorities, he led a team of sixty men into the pickers' camps, destroyed their pits and huts, and escorted the undocumented migrants back from banner territory. The events of 1826 played out as they had in 1825: In July (the sixth lunar month), the mushroom pickers arrived, but by the ninth month, the authorities had registered and removed almost all them. Amid the roundups, mushroom pickers protested. At one camp, Zhang Zhenglun, the guide known as "Haisandai," negotiated for leniency, but a tussle broke out, and in the chaos "men punched an official and caused [him] a small injury."[81]

In 1828, when Sonomdarjya reported the arrival of another "swarm" of mushroom pickers from Chifeng, the league chief Artasida personally arrived on the scene.[82] Yet the mushroom pickers again proved difficult to control. The migrants first came in a wave of 300 men. When confronted, two foremen, Hui Wanzong and Ding Weilian, refused to leave and demanded they be allowed to finish the season's work.[83] When banner authorities stood firm, violence broke out. In the testimony of one guardsman, the mushroom pickers began "speaking altogether in Chinese," then lunged forward with hatchets and hoes. Overwhelmed, the troops retreated, managing to lose four of their horses in the chaos. Yet for the mushroom pickers the victory proved short lived. In short time, troops arrived on the scene with enforcements, and, amid a rain of falling cudgels, they stormed the camp and dispersed the men. As the pickers fled south into the forested hills, banner horsemen went hut to hut, razed their camps, and so "purified the Mongols' pasture land."[84]

The manhunt extended into autumn. Of the two most wanted foremen, the cavalry tracked down Hui Wanzong's team first and, after another bout of violence, managed to subdue him; Ding Weilian and his men were cap-

TABLE 3.1.
Arrested ringleaders of mushroom pickers, 1829.

Foreman	Age	Men led	Province of birth
Li Dengkui	46	13	Henan
Li Dengli	49	7	Henan
Feng Xiang	45	7	Shanxi
Shen Chenglin	49	6	Henan
Dai Han	n/a	4	Henan
Fu Wan	n/a	9	Henan
Zhai Laosan	n/a	11	Shanxi
He Laosan	n/a	11	Shanxi
Xing Wan	n/a	7	Zhili
Song Duan	n/a	3	Zhili
Xing Menger	n/a	7	Zhili

tured soon after.[85] Hui Wanzong was sentenced to three months in the cangue and 100 strokes with a cane as punishment, and he was repatriated back to his home jurisdiction in Chifeng.[86] Stunningly, however, while being transferred he escaped once again, and both Hui Wanzong and Ding Weilian returned to pick mushrooms in Mongolia again in 1829.[87] Liu Deshan, too, was on the scene in 1828, though he learned of the initial raids and managed to cross the borderline before violence erupted.[88] The following summer he too braved arrest and returned once again. He later testified that he was desperate for work and that mushrooms were his only hope: "There was no other trade" in town.

Primed by the violence, troops greeted the mushroom pickers almost immediately in 1829. Again, though, the mushroom pickers proved tenacious, and Liu Deshan and others beat back the Mongol guards with rocks, kitchen knives, hoes, and clubs. Still, after two months of raids and roundups, banner authorities reported that nearly all the mushroom pickers had been registered and repatriated by September 19.[89] They recorded the location of each bust, the name of each worker, and their home jurisdictions. If they were simple laborers, not leaders, they were repatriated back to Chifeng without further punishment.[90] Leaders, including Liu Deshan, became scapegoats. In 1829, eleven such leaders were thus escorted to Beijing, under guard, to be tried by the Board of Punishments (see Table 3.1). Within the imperial city, under torture, all of them confessed to crimes.

That December, the Daoguang emperor condemned illegal mushroom picking as "extremely detestable" (Ma: *jaci ubiyada*; Ch: *qingshu kewu*), issuing the decree that the *Veritable Records* chronicled for posterity. The responsible officials were cashiered for negligence and incompetence. Chen Wu was ordered to repay the seventeen taels he had accepted in bribes, was caned 100 times, and sentenced to be a bondservant in the military garrison in Shuntian prefecture, a "somewhat close frontier." Hui Wanzong was caned seventy times and sent into exile for half a year.[91] Liu Deshan was caned 100 times and exiled for three years. On February 14, 1830, the emperor confirmed their sentences, and the punishments were carried out.[92]

Adjudicating the case had taken months. In part, the delay reflected the strangeness of it all: Though undocumented travel was illegal, in 1830 there was still no legal precedent against mushroom picking in particular. By law, all cases that required sentencing by "analogy" (Ch: *bizhao*) were reviewed by the Board of Punishments.[93] Although no law existed against mushroom picking, the board found a precedent in a prohibition against "leading hired laborers across the Great Wall to pick rhubarb." If the rhubarb pickers numbered fewer than ten, then their leader's punishment was 100 blows with a cane and a year in exile; if they led more than ten men, the punishment was made one notch more severe: a caning followed by three years exile in Ili. It was by the logic of this precedent that the court handed down a relatively light punishment for Hui Wanzong: His picking team had fewer than ten men. The board used a second "analogy" to sentence Liu Deshan: a prohibition on poaching in imperial "game parks" (Ma: *aba hoihan*; Ch: *weichang*). In such cases, first-time offenders wore the cangue for a month, and second-time offenders wore it for two months.[94] As repeat offenders, all the arrested mushroom pickers were thus ordered to wear the cangue.[95] A new precedent was set: Undocumented mushroom picking in Mongolia was criminalized, and a graded set of punishments were established for both organizers and recidivists.

Perhaps, on reflection, we can see rhubarb and mushrooms as analogous things. Yet how was Mongolia, in all its immensity and complexity, analogous to an imperial game park? Before answering that question, it is perhaps worth asking a still more basic question: What was wrong with mushroom picking in the first place? One of the most striking tensions in the Liu Deshan case is between its novelty and its commonness. Although the events of 1829 were unprecedented, and the crime seemed novel, mushroom picking itself was nothing new. Liu Deshan himself had been in Mongolia the year before during the violent summer of 1828, and he had been working there since at least 1824, when he first collaborated with the clerk Chen Wu. Indeed, the emperor and the Lifanyuan had received reports of mushroom picking in this same banner for a over a decade when Liu Deshan was sentenced to exile, and reports had existed of mushroom pickers in the location since at least 1759, when pickers started a prairie fire. How, then, did mushroom picking become an imperial crime?

THE NATURE OF THE IMPERIAL RESPONSE

Interest in mushroom picking swelled slowly, only as the conflict in Sonomdarjya's banner grew intractable and increasingly violent. At first mushroom picking was a local phenomenon; until 1818 the banner *jasaġ* Dasigeleng had kept it quiet. From 1822 league authorities, through special deputies, had taken control. In 1825, the league chief, Artasida, dispatched the *beile* Sonomdobcin, a "capable, moderately high-ranking official"; in 1826, he sent his second-in-command, Coijunjab. After 1826, the *amban*s took the initiative and sent their own deputy, the Manchu second-in-command Weisengge. In 1828 and 1829, Artasida himself went to the banner. In 1829, the Board of Punishments and the court took charge and established a precedent, and it was at this stage that the affair ripples into the official Chinese record via the *Veritable Records* and the *Addendum to the Conspectus of Legal Cases*. In eleven years, the phenomenon had scaled from an entirely local problem, to a regional problem of moderate importance, to a regional problem of top importance, to an imperial-level crisis.

As the degree of state involvement ramped up, so too did the rhetoric in the documents. The documents anticipated the framework of the Board's decision by putting increased emphasis on mushroom picking as a crime distinct from trespassing. The Qing court, after all, did not need a special precedent to arrest the men; the undocumented were already guilty of breaking the law. In 1822 the *jasaġ* Sonomdarjya's complaint listed the mens' "mushroom picking" alongside hunting marmots, fishing, planting vegetables, building shelters, and woodcutting; there is no indication that mushroom picking was the cause of, or even worse than, these other activities. In the grammar of the Manchu and Mongol Qing documents, the phrase "picking mushrooms" always modified the primary problems: "lording" (Ma: *ejelembi*) over the Mongols' steppe and pastures, driving off livestock, and coming to Mongolia without a proper license. The first was a threat to the political order, the second a threat to prosperity, and the third grounds for arrest and expulsion. In 1822, Sonomdarjya accordingly cited the 1805 memorial on unlicensed travel in Mongolia as the key precedent: "The four Khalkha *aimaġ* originally did not have Chinese going [around] on their own whims, and no law sanctioned vagrancy."[96] In 1825 and 1826, officials cited the same precedent. Trespassing, in short, was crime enough.

Yet, beginning in 1825, the documents increasingly describe mushroom picking as a problem in itself. As one communication put it, "Mushroom picking and woodcutting are in special violation of the law" (Ma: *ele kooli de acanarakū*). Along these lines, "mushroom picking" was no longer listed alongside hunting and fishing as equal problems that led to Chinese "lording" over the steppe; mushrooming became a cause and overhunted marmots and fish the effect. By 1826, when the *amban*s dispatched a special deputy from Khüree, mushroom picking became an "important matter" of state (Ma: *oyonggo baita*).[97] Similarly, when clerks at the *amban*s office wrote their one-sentence Manchu-language abstracts on each document's cover, they described the problem simply as "Chinese mushroom pickers" (Ma: *sence tunggiyeme jihe irgese*; lit. "Chinese who have come to pick mushrooms"). After 1827, as resistance grew violent, the documents consistently modified "Chinese mushroom pickers" with the phrase "for which there is no analog" (Ma: *dursuki akū*), and authorities mandated that "mushroom picking, cutting wood, and lording over the land in Mongol territory are permanently and strictly forbidden."[98] Three years before the emperor's decree, that is, mushroom picking was already a special crime.

What was wrong with mushroom picking? The answer changed as the state intervention intensified. In Dasigeleng's report of 1818, he emphasized that Chinese were "lording over Mongol pastures." The *amban*s for their part were anxious about "quarrels and arguments starting," corrupt and incompetent banner authorities, the livelihood of Mongols, the improper "mixing" of Chinese and Mongols, and the possibility of Mongol subjects sheltering criminals. The *amban*s also warned that Mongolia was close to a sensitive border with Russia, suggesting a special strategic interest in the region.[99] When state involvement rose to the highest levels, though, the stakes grew accordingly to include the Mongols' relationship to the court. As Sonomdarjya argued, "If it reaches the point where poor Chinese gradually come to lord over [Ma: *ejeleme*] the Mongol steppe and overthrow the Mongols' way of life, it will not be accordance with the lofty aim of His

Majesty [Ma: *enduringge ejen*, lit. "sacred lord"] to love his humble Mongol servants."[100] Action was justified not only because Sonomdarjya had a special connection to the land, or because the Mongols did, but because it was a foundational responsibility of the emperor.

As "mushroom picking" became a crime and the stakes of the conflict heightened, the imperial still response continued to focus on controlling people; there is no evidence that the state cared about plants, animals, and fungi in and of themselves. Borders had to be tightened; Khalkha "pasture territory" (Mo: *nutuġ*) and the banner's "territorial borders" (Mo: *nutuġ un jiqa*) were to remain inviolable. The state's ambition was total. As the documents frequently enjoined, "Not one person may come across the territorial border" (Mo: *nutuġ-un jiq-a-yi nigecu kümü-i dabuġulju oroġulqu ügei bolaġ-a*).[101] Policing focused on the picking season and targeted the routes mushroom pickers frequented, not the borderline, but the court expected the cavalry to be "constantly on guard and conducting inspections" (Mo: *caġ ügei caġdan baicaġaju*) and the work to be "extremely thorough" (Mo: *masi kinan naribcilan*).[102] After a raid, there was to be "not a single remnant" (Mo: *nigcu üldegdel ügei*) left of the mushroom pickers.[103] They repatriated all men; they razed all huts.

By doing so, the Qing state was working to protect the Mongol character of the banner and its subjects. As the Daoguang emperor expressed in his final pronouncement on the Liu Deshan affair; mushroom pickers were "detestable." The enterprise brought out the worst in people and attracted scoundrels. The character of the migrant pickers grew increasingly suspicious. Early documents describe them acting "on their own accord" (Mo: *joriġ-iyar*, cf. Chinese *si*). Later documents use stronger language: The Chinese were "utterly reckless" (Mo: *oġtu ajiraqu ügei*) (common from 1826), "audacious" and "blind" (common from 1828), or "evil and crafty" (from the 1830s).[104] Though officials "repeatedly made understood" the laws of the land, mushroom pickers ignored them.[105] Every action was marked by a reckless subjectivity—thus the Chinese were "of their own accord" coming to Mongolia, "of their own accord" picking mushrooms, and so on.[106]

Yet Mongols, too, were increasingly "acting of their own accord" as well. Artasida thus expressed concern that Mongols were secretly "harboring" or "sheltering" (Mo: *qorġudaqu*) Chinese.[107] In his first complaint of 1822, Sonomdarjya similarly warned that the "way of life" of his "subject Mongols" was under duress: Some Mongols profited from the arrangement by quietly helping the migrants.[108] Good Mongols lived the honest life of herders; these Mongols acted "blindly" and "impulsively" and, like the Chinese, knew only the "chase for profit."[109] "Poor" Mongols were most at risk; they had the most to gain from the business.[110] The solution was heightened "discipline" (Mo: *cingdalaqu*).[111] Officials were under suspicion as well: The *jasaġ* Dasigeleg had covered up the problem, his successor Sonomdarjya was seemingly incompetent, and the league officials could not be trusted. Only with greater bureaucratic discipline would Mongol subjects come into line.

In this way, state interventions during the mushroom crisis conformed to imperial ideology. Ideologically, the Mongol subject was meant to be a simple herder. One could not act "blindly" or "impulsively"; the welfare of Mongolia depended on temperance. The Mongols in this way were no different from Manchus, for whom austerity was a defining virtue as well: Frugality sustained the banners. As the Yongzheng emperor declared in 1727, in response to the Manchu's indulgence in the marketplace, "The ordinary disposition of us Manchus is to be pure [Ma: *gulu*] and plain."[112] Like Manchus, a Daoguang-era text explained, Mongols were "endowed with a pure and honest nature" (Ch: *Menggu fuxing chunpu*).[113] Emperors had long warned, however, that their original virtue was corruptible; in the Kangxi emperor's words, "It is the Mongols' nature to be easily deceived."[114]

Corruptibility in turn, invariably implied a sense of change over time. In the case of mushroom-picking, if Mongols were corrupted, we gather, they were originally pure; and if mushroom picking was a problem, the phenomenon had to be new. Mongol authorities thus consistently represented the Chinese in Sonomdarjya's banner as both novel and foreign. They identified mushroom pickers by their "home jurisdiction" (Ma: *da susu*) or "place of origin" (Ma: *da bade*), which in practice was not the county in which they were born but the county in which they resided—or, more precisely, where they resided when not living and working in a Mongol banner. In line with the rules on undocumented border crossing, the authorities always investigated and registered "from where [the Chinese] swarmed."[115] Origins determined policy.

In this way, to levy proper punishments, the Qing government had to understand the history of mushroom picking. Sonomdarja's predecessors had failed to properly report the first problems, so the situation "from the start" (Ma: *daci*) was obscure; the *amban*s could trace it back only to the negligence or corruption of the former *jasaġ*, Dasigeleng.[116] Yet they constructed a basic narrative from what they knew. As one document put it succinctly, mushroom pickers "originally came each year in a fragmentary fashion [Ma: *son son i*], and the *jasaġ* and league chiefs did not investigate the matter and expel them at that time. [Mushroom pickers] steadily increased each year to the point that several hundred people were arriving." The problem had a limited pedigree; the mushroom pickers had been coming "for these last few years [Ma: *ere udu aniya dolo*]," but not for more. It was never imagined that mushroom picking was an old practice; rather, the problem had begun only in "recent years" (Ma: *hanciki udu aniya*).[117] By removing Chinese, reinforcing the boundaries of Mongolia and Mongolness, and stopping the rush for mushrooms, the state was not only establishing order but re-reestablishing, in its view, an original one. Once reestablished, this order was to remain "permanent" (Ma: *enteheme*). Indeed, from 1827 onward, the statement that Chinese mushroom pickers were to be "permanently forbidden" became boilerplate.[118]

In short, as the imperial presence expanded on the ground, imperial rhetoric not only drew sharper distinctions and became more extreme, it also began to conjure a type of nature: an original, ahistorical, unaltered state. In an ideal world, in the eyes of the court, there would be complete segregation, total discipline, and a return to original values, and in turn there would be mushrooms, marmots, trees, fish, and pastureland. On other frontiers, Qing policies shifted periodically between making and erasing distinctions between colonizer and colonized. Mongolia was different: The unique imperial status of Mongols (and Mongol aristocrats in particular) made the distinctions between Mongol and Chinese particularly important to the court. The maintenance of Mongol privilege, like the Manchu privilege, was a pillar of Qing rule.[119] Yet order not only depended on segregation and self-discipline, it required a healthy natural environment. Indeed, in the documents the object of "purity" was always material: "the land" (Ma: *ba na*), "Khalkha territory," "the Mongol steppe," or the "Mongols' territorial land" (Ma: *monggoso i nuktei ba*).[120]

We are thus left with a world of sharp contrasts: Mongol and Chinese, pure and corrupted, timeless and modified states. To be sure, the situation on the ground was never so black and white. Arrested mushroom pickers in particular always contested the state's claims. In the spring of 1826, for example, scouts discovered 200 mushroom pickers erecting houses and cutting hay along the Khalkha River. When troops arrived on the scene, and pickers remained behind (claiming their oxen were too weak for the trip south), their leaders pleaded for leniency. As recorded by officers at the scene, they conceded that they had come annually to pick mushrooms and that they had fished, chopped down trees, and hunted marmots. Yet they did so only because they were poor. They also admitted that they came without permits. Yet, each year, they emphasized, they returned home without any intention of permanently settling in the area.[121] They insisted, further, that they had been coming to the banner for generations, through the rule of three consecutive *jasaġs*. They never mixed with "Mongol herder families." Only in recent times, under the rule of Sonomdarjya, they claimed, were they under attack. They even claimed that all of these facts "local Mongols know well."[122] Yet their pleas fell on deaf ears. On August 14, the special deputy and Sonomdarjya issued a Chinese-language proclamation announcing their banishment, and the mushroom pickers were removed.[123] Later, in 1827, the guide Zhang Zhenglun challenged the case against them with a similar defense.[124] As he fluently argued in Mongolian: "We had come to an understanding and returned as usual." Seasonal mushroom picking was ingrained in local life: "We pick mushrooms, cut down trees, fish, and hunt marmots then return back [home] in the eighth lunar month."[125]

Sonomdarjya himself conceded that that mushroom pickers had "been coming for years" (Mo: *jil jil ireğü*), just as Artasida spoke of a "season when they [mushroom pickers] regularly come" (Mo: *teden-ü iredeg caġ*).[126] Of course, not all mushroom pickers were seasoned veterans like Zhang Zhenglun. Most were like Liu Deshan: They arrived in the area only in the 1810s and 1820s, as the mushroom business was booming. Others had participated in woodcutting and mushroom picking in nearby territories, like Hailar, in Inner Mongolia. The camp leader Wei Bing, aged sixty-seven, had been a merchant in Hailar, for example, before becoming a mushroom picker; he entered the trade only after meeting a man named Du He, who had "for many years picked mushrooms, and also understood Mongolian." After obtaining credit and supplies for a mushroom-picking trip, they led seven men into Hailar but were arrested and turned back. Rather than returning home, they instead went to Sonomdarjya's banner, where, again, they were confronted by troops and captured after a "tussle."[127] Still others had connections to both Inner and Outer Mongolia. "Hui Lama" (also known as Hui Wanzong), aged forty-three, testified that he led a small group of mushroom pickers into Sonomdarjya's banner in the summer, then moved to the Qandaġai Mountain area in Hailar territory to buy wood, build carts, and conduct trade in the fall.[128] People's biographies were complex.

The categories of "Mongol" and Chinese," by extension, were often unclear. Just as Mongols were acculturating to the ways of mushroom pickers, the Chinese seemed to be learning the ways of Mongols.[129] Some guides had Mongol names and spoke Mongol fluently; some had Mongol wives or lived in Mongol style *gers*, the traditional nomad's yurt.[130] Mongol names were in fact common in the pickers' registers; one register from 1827 recorded the names of eighty-one team leaders, in which twenty-two of the men had Mongol names: Eleven had both a Chinese and a Mongol name, nine had a Mongol name but no known Chinese one, and two had mixed names like "Hui Lama" and "Baga Yan" (lit. "Little Yan").[131] Many Mongols, on the other hand, married Chinese, participated in the trade, and sheltered mushroom pickers, just as the state feared. Mushroom pickers may have hunted marmots, but they also bought marmot skins and other products from their Mongols in a "petty trade" (Mo: *baġ-a saġa qudalduġ-a*) connected to the camps and travel routes; an arrest from 1828, for example, described a man named "Xiu Lama" who had bought twelve marmot skins and nine sheepskins.[132] Temptation was everywhere: Leave your herds behind, join a caravan, collude with the Chinese.

In the 1820s, then, the life of the banner was not so simple. Some, like "Haisandai" had been part of the fabric of local life for decades, others were relatively new to the scene, and still others, like Hui Lama, were new to mushroom picking but had extensive experience in Mongolia more broadly. None of these distinctions mattered in Qing documents. When the Qing state moved against the mushroom pickers, their names or language abilities were irrelevant: Only their nonnative identity, established by their home jurisdiction, was germane. It is fair then to wonder: Was the Mongol steppe ever "pure"?

PURE PLACES AND RESTRICTED SPACES

In Qing documents, the word that encapsulated best the imperial vision of an original, timeless, and perfect order was *purity* (Mo: *ariġun;* Ma: *bolgo*). The term appears again and again with regards to Sonomdarjya's afflicted banner. In his report to the throne in 1825, the *amban* wrote twice of the need for league officials to "purify the banner" and bring benefit to local

Mongols.[133] Every year thereafter, the call for "purification" (Ma: *bolgo obumbi, bolgo be obumbi,* or *bolgomimbi*) became standard, particularly at the end of documents, when summarizing the mandate. The word distilled the imperial project in Sonomdarjya's chaotic banner to its core: Discipline the bureaucracy, investigate suspicious Mongols, repatriate the mushroom pickers, purify the land.

What did it mean for the land to be "pure"? No one English word captures fully the Manchu or Mongolian; both *bolgo* and *ariğun* had wide semantic fields, having material, moral, and aesthetic dimensions. The early Manchu–Mongolian dictionary, the *Han-i araha Manju Monggo gisun-i buleku bithe,* published in 1717, identified the Manchu and Mongol terms with each other and offered three definitions:[134]

1. Having incorrupt actions and unselfish motives;
2. Everything being without a blemish and extremely beautiful;
3. Clear (for water).

The Manchu–Chinese *Da Qing quanshu* (first published 1683) defined *bolgo* in Chinese with four characters: *qing* ("pure"), *jing* ("clean"), *jie* ("clean"), and *xiu* ("beautiful").[135] Two later court-sponsored dictionaries, the trilingual *Yuzhi Manzhu Menggu Hanzi sanhe qieyin Qingwen jian,* published in 1780, and the *Pentaglot Dictionary* (Ch: *Yuzhi wuti Qingwen jian*), published in 1791, defined the Manchu *bolgo* in terms of household rites ("to make clean," Ch: *ganjing*; Mo: *ariğun*); military feats ("cleaning out," Ch: *jiejing*; Mo: *ceber*) and a moral virtue of being honest and loyal (being "clean," Ch: *qing*; Mo: *ariğun*). Significantly, though, only the ritual and moral meanings of *bolgo* equated with the Mongolian *ariğun,* the word used in the documents; the dictionaries use a different Mongolian word, *ceber,* for military usages.[136] To "purify," in the language of the documents, was not simply a matter of moving people; it was inherently political and moral.

In other contexts, the Manchu phrase "to purify," if translated at all, was usually given as *qingjing* or *suqing* in Chinese; the former carried strong Buddhist and religious overtones (as in "pure land," *qingtu*), whereas the latter had a military meaning, in the sense of "mopping up" an area and pacifying it.[137] Generally, however, the concept almost always referred to actions, people, or places with close connections to the Qing court. The rim of Changbaishan's "Heavenly Lake," as the mythological birthplace of the Manchus, was chief among the empire's "pure" locations; thus, in 1677, on the first Qing mission to scout the mountain and reach the summit, the team reported back that they did not dare linger on the summit because it was a "pure scenic spot" (Ch: *qingjing shengdi*).[138]

Indeed, there were spaces in Mongolia that the court had treated as both special and "pure" prior to the 1820s, including imperial hunting grounds, holy mountains, the borderland with Russia, the monastic center of Khüree, and other "important" or "strategic" (Ma: *oyonggo*; Ch: *yao*) spaces. They all shared common attributes: They had a close connection to imperial rule, they were territories with firm boundaries, and they all implied the need for limiting outside intervention. In Mongolian legalese, these spaces generally overlapped with "restricted land" (Mo: *caġajilaġsan ġajar*).[139]

Holy mountains were typical in this regard. As the "lands of the spirit palace on high" (Ma: *enduri i dergi urdu i bade*),[140] they held strong associations with both heavenly and state authority, and many such mountains took the honorary title khan (Mo: *qan*). The ceremonies that took place on holy mountains, which often involved wrestling and shooting, reinforced the male, martial, and Mongol quality of the space. At Mount Qan (Mo: Qan Aġula; Ma: Han Alin), located just to the south of Khüree, the *ambans* oversaw a grand, multiday ceremony each spring and autumn. All of the league's aristocracy was expected to participate. The *ambans* began preparations months in advance to procure the horses, livestock, and provisions used to support the massive event; the court mandated that "everything for the ceremonies [be] respectfully purified and prepared."[141] On the first day of the ceremony, the *ambans* and the league chief honored the mountain spirit, then they presided over three days of wrestling, archery, and horse racing, the Mongol sports that "cultivated the propitious way of manly virtue."[142] After three days of festivities, they pitched a yellow tent at the archery site, and lamas read sutras and prayed for good fortune. The ceremonies concluded with a sacrifice of oxen and sheep that had been "well purified" (Ma: *saikan bolgomime*), and cloth was tied to the tails of other animals who were released to graze in peace.[143] Similar events were held on other holy mountains, including on Mount Kentei Qan, in Secen Qan *aimaġ*. Both mountains were associated with the authority of the *aimaġ* and league chiefs.[144]

Imperial hunting grounds, too, had similar ideological dimensions, and like holy mountains, they represented martial values, masculinity, heaven, and the state.[145] There were two types of protected parks in Outer Mongolia:

those for catching tribute animals (such as wild boar) and those for military training.[146] Hunting was valued: It cultivated "soldierly virtue"[147] and served as "a way of manifesting power in the frontier."[148] Given their strategic benefits, participating in hunts was an "important obligation to the state"[149] and "incomparable with standard affairs."[150] Qing documents signaled the parks' close association with the court by commonly raising the words *game park* (Ma: *aba hoihan*; Mo: *aba qomorġ-a*; Ch: *weichang*) a notch above ordinary text.[151] Top Mongol authorities participated in the official hunt, including *aimaġ* league chiefs and assistant commanders. As in holy mountains, moreover, public offerings to heaven, earth, and spirits accompanied the hunt.[152] Leading officials oversaw the sacrifice of twenty-one sheep, each "purified, prepared and dispersed to the various banners with the strictest [care]."[153] At hunt's end, the participants honored the court, and the *amban*s assured the emperor that "all [your] Mongol servants kowtowed to the Imperial Palace."[154]

Like holy mountains and game parks, the interior of Khüree was "restricted" and "pure" as well. The Qing government prohibited sojourning Chinese from residing in the monastic interior of the city, where the Jibzundamba Khutugtu's palace lay. In 1763, to protect its sanctity, the Qianlong emperor prohibited women from living in specific quarters or with men "in a mixed up manner," and women thereafter were prohibited from "gathering" in the city.[155] The heart of the city was to be male, monastic, and Mongol; women, laymen, and Chinese were excluded.

In the first half of the nineteenth century, however, booming trade with Russia and increased traffic in domestic products like deer horn, timber, and steppe mushrooms swelled the city with unlicensed peddlers, seasonal laborers, beggars, street performers, and other "vagrants." Segregation laws were ignored: The Mongol and Chinese quarters bled into one another, and women walked the same streets as monks. Memorials began to stream into Beijing: Remove women from the city, banish the Chinese, clean out all "filth, manure, bones, and ashes." Let Khüree, and all of Mongolia, be "pure."[156] The head of the Jibzundamba Khutugtu's secular order, the Šangjudba, issued pleas to the court in 1801, 1806, and 1825, but problems continued.[157] In 1836, the emperor received perhaps the most dire complaint from the *amban* in Khüree: "Mongols and Chinese, lamas and laymen, men and women . . . are mixed up in chaos." That year, the top secular and ecclesiastical authorities in Khüree endorsed a joint petition: Let the emperor "bestow grace" and unite behind their "plan for purifying the interior of Khüree"; the state had to repatriate undocumented Chinese migrants and arrest Mongols who sheltered them. "Now is the time," they wrote, "to purify Khüree."[158]

Holy mountains, game parks, and the interior of Khüree all shared properties of what Caroline Humphrey identified as Mongolia's "chiefly landscapes": an association with heaven (Mo: *tngri*), state power, men, and spiritual "rulers" or "masters" (Mo: *ejen*).[159] Such spaces were all holy, male, Mongol, and imperial. In the Qing period, moreover, all were physically and administratively separated from common banner lands; no people or livestock were permitted within their jurisdiction. They were ideally free from any normal human intervention: Commoners could neither hunt, log, nor fish in them. In hunting grounds, even "spooking" animals was against the law. No trespassing, no change to the environment, no alteration whatsoever was acceptable in the months leading up to the hunt; like moral order itself, the nature of the holy mountain or game park was meant to be timeless. They were at once expressions of pure nature and of total control.[160]

Maintaining the purity of holy mountains and game parks required constant work, ever-vigilant guards, complex bureaucratic oversight, and regular outlays of silver. When "by an edict of grace," the Qianlong emperor deemed Mount Kentei Qan and Mount Qan "state mountains of good fortune," he decreed that henceforth their "wildlife and trees be neither frightened nor defiled." Unique rules for the territory were necessary; therefore it was only "proper that precedents and laws be established suitable for the circumstances of the locality." In all cases the court ordered patrolmen to be on "constant" vigil for signs of poaching, woodcutting, or haymaking within the restricted grounds; in some cases, a network of *karun*s protected parks.[161] "Purifying" Mongolia's parks, in turn, entailed more than preserving the life of game: It meant protecting "game and trees" from being "ravaged" or "spooked."[162] Yet special edicts criminalized "poaching game" and "woodgathering, tea-picking, and trespassing." To enforce them, the state evacuated herders from neighboring jurisdictions before hunts in game parks, pressing them into service as guardsmen instead. Nobody could remain within: "Not one bannerman or temple serf can herd or settle [there]."[163] Making the area "pure" also meant putting out human-made fires and punishing hunters found guilty of smoking badgers from their dens, which often sparked conflagrations.[164] When a fire began, guardsmen had to rush to the scene, organize fire brigades, and attempt to beat it out. Although wildfires were not considered destructive in and of themselves—herders commonly set prairie fires and allowed them to burn intentionally—the restricted hunting grounds were different; protecting "restricted territories" from damaging fires, in fact, was a guardsman's basic duty.[165]

The tools for creating this environmental purity were no different from those used for making proper Qing subjects: training, policing, segregation, discipline, and oversight. Punishments for poaching in restricted territories were harsh. On holy mountains, aristocrats found guilty of poaching were stripped of rank, and commoners were tattooed with the word "criminal" and forced to wear the cangue.[166] Recidivists were exiled to another *aimaġ*, while noblemen found guilty twice were punished as commoners. In the late eighteenth and early nineteenth centuries, as new pressures on resources mounted, the legal framework grew more elaborate and specific. New precedents were set: Merchants who bought deer horns obtained from restricted grounds received special punishments; so did anyone who cut down a living tree on the mountain. In the imperial hunting grounds, those caught poaching flora or fauna, or found to have started a wildfire, were likewise "dealt with severely."[167] As "matters related to game parks" were "extremely important," first-time offenders wore the cangue a month; second-time offenders wore it two months; and third-time offenders were whipped 100 times.[168] The punishments had not always been so strict. In 1773, however, a new precedent was set when the military governor of Mukden, Hong-šang, memorialized that putting first- and second-time offenders in the cangue for one or two months was "an insufficient warning" to poachers in his own jurisdiction. Men like mushroom pickers and woodcutters, he explained, needed new deterrents.[169] Both, that is, were already causing a stir by 1773.

Despite the strict laws and elaborate policing apparatus, the "restricted areas" suffered during the resource boom, and acutely so between roughly 1820 and 1840, when poaching and corruption became endemic, and deer poaching for medicinal deer horn and illegal logging surged. As early as 1805, hunters were complaining that animals were "scarce" in the game parks around Khüree as "many bannermen and monastery serfs [*šabi*] in said hunting grounds herd livestock, scare away animals, and destroy the forests." Locals were surviving through illegal commerce: "Many" Chinese merchants had invested in their enterprises and so induced them to "pitch tents along mountain streams, cut down trees, and reap hay."[170] The official charged with cleaning up the park, Pungcuk, put special emphasis on putting a stop to merchants. An early draft memorial of his on the case described the ravages of "local people"; the final draft crossed out the term and entered *nikasa*, the "Han Chinese," instead.[171] Ultimately, both a new discourse of Mongol values and emphasis on "purity" were emerging as the restricted spaces came under duress: "Mongols and Chinese, lamas and laymen, men and women" were "mixed up in chaos"; animals were spooked and disappearing; and the landscapes that embodied imperial ideals were being undermined. In all of these ways, game parks seemed no different from the Left-Wing Front Banner, where mushroom picking was having the same effect.

CONCLUSION: PURE ENVIRONMENTS AND PLACES

In the period from 1820 to 1840, the Qing state thus mobilized language and institutions used to govern "restricted land" and applied them to the Mongol banners as a whole. In practice, the imperial project was limited. Campaigns for "purification" were confined to locations on the most lucrative trade routes or containing the most valuable resources: the caravan highway linking Beijing to Kiakhta, the mushroom fields of the far east, the holy mountain near Khüree, and, as we shall see in Chapter Four, the borderland with Russia, which yielded fur. From the inception of Qing rule in Mongol territories, flexible institutions, such as licensing, had supported trade and migration, and the empire had found space for Mongols and Chinese to live together. The specter of undocumented migrants, poaching, and environmental decline provoked a more radical vision: "pure" Mongolia.

Undocumented travel upset the imperial order: Boundaries made subjects legible, simplified governance, and helped enforce the social hierarchy.[172] Yet at production sites like the mushroom fields, it was not only unlicensed travel but its perceived environmental consequences that set the gears of empire into motion; *purity*, accordingly, was this motion's administrative and ideological expression. We cannot understand the construction of the multiethnic empire without taking the environmental dimensions into account. Environmental change and protection were not tangential to the multiethnic construction of the Qing empire: They were central to it.

In the case of Manchuria and its pearls, we can question the capacity of the state to achieve its aims. In Outer Mongolia, where the Mongol aristocracy set the tone and initiated action, the empire proved more successful in preserving its restricted spaces as "pure." Today, most remark-ably, the holy mountains and hunting grounds have survived as national parks; the Left-Wing Front Banner, too, now is a park: Nömrög Strictly Protected Area, a Mongolian natural heritage site. Nineteenth-century visi-tors sensed that what Qing documents called "pure" or "restricted" grounds was somehow more natural. In 1821, for example, a Russian traveler was struck by Mount Qan, the only place in sight that was forested. His first explanation was spiritual: "The forests which cover it are held sacred by the Mongols."[173] His second was political: "In the clefts of the Qanola [that is, Mount Qan] there are tents, where sentinels are stationed to hinder people from ascending the mountain."[174] If the mountain was holy, then, it was not so holy as to intimidate all intruders; it required state power to preserve it. As in the banners, it seemed, its untouched nature was nothing less than an artifact of empire: Its boundaries reflected the administrative limits and ideological ambitions of the Qing state.

FOUR

Nature in the Land of Fur

Fur, like mussels and mushrooms, would force itself onto the imperial agenda in this same period. Like a trickle in the late eighteenth century, and like a drumbeat in the early nineteenth, complaints arrived in Beijing: Corruption was rampant, hunting was difficult, and animals were scarce. Unlike mussels and mushrooms, however, the land of fur encompassed an almost impossibly immense swath of territory. Indeed, it stretched beyond the confines of the empire: The Qing fur crisis, it turns out, was part of a larger, global dynamic.

It is one reason why a history of fur in the Qing empire demands a border-crossing history: A full account would entail work in Russian, American, and Spanish archives, to name but a few.[1] A second reason lies in the Qing archives themselves. Take the problem posed by the Tannu Uriankhai, who hunted furs in the northwestern reaches of Outer Mongolia. The Tannu Uriankhai today do not figure in much Chinese history; their descendants, the Tannu Tuvans, are relatively few in number, and they live in Mongolia and Russia, not the Peoples Republic of China, and are accordingly obscure to the field.[2] Their history was obscure in Qing

China as well: The few frontier experts who wrote about them, when not describing their administrative history, usually returned to simplistic and circular tropes: The Tannu Uriankhai were "hunters," they produced furs, they lived in the forest, and they always had.[3]

The archives offer a more challenging account. According to the terms of their incorporation into the empire, each year the Tannu Uriankhai presented nine types of fur to the court: sable, river otter, lynx, wolf, marten, fox, corsac fox, snow leopard, and squirrel. The regularity of their tribute was remarkable: Every winter between 1758 and 1910, Uriankhai hunting parties set off for the forests, flintlocks in hand; every spring, they offered a portion of their captured pelts to the Qing court. As part of this routine process, the bureaucracy produced two types of documents: The military governor in Uliasutai wrote a Manchu-language memorial that recorded all furs sent from Mongolia; the Imperial Household Department in Beijing wrote a memorial in Chinese on all furs received. Although produced in different languages and by different institutions, the two memorials were supposed to be identical.

Yet inconsistencies abound. The Manchu and Chinese records could go years without tallying: One might record a specific number of sable pelts sent, but the other would give a different number of pelts received. Gallingly, if one document recorded more sable pelts than we might expect, it also offset the surplus by recording a deficit in squirrel pelts. As a result, both documents add up to the designated tribute quota, rendering the discrepancy invisible. Put simply, that is, the Manchu and Chinese records tell different stories. How, then, should we interpret the signal from the archives?

We cannot write the environmental history of the Qing empire's fur frontier without answering the question: The archives are too rich and the world of Qing frontiers too complicated without doing so. Only when we take the mixed signals from the archives seriously does a new history emerge. Regional and global dimensions to the Qing past in particular can come into focus: The documents shed light on a synchronicity of scarcity not only across Qing territory but also in lands from Siberia to California. Other patterns more distinctive of the Qing experience become clearer as well. When animals vanished in Uriankhai lands, the court worked to return the land and its people to an unaltered state; the borderland, like Mongolia and Manchuria, was newly defined, defended, and made "pure."

This final chapter explores this history using the Tannu Uriankhai as a case study. It begins with the global dimensions of the fur crisis, shifts to its unfolding in Qing lands, and concludes with the court's efforts to demarcate and preserve Uriankhai territory as the fur-bearing animals disappeared.

THE GLOBAL FUR TRADE

The fur trade was among the first trades to go global. There is evidence of continent-sized fur-trade networks from at least late antiquity, when Viking traders began shipping furs from Scandinavia and Rus' to Byzantine and Abbasid' markets, and the Mohe of Northeast Asia began shipping furs to the Xiong-nu and Han empires.[4] Precious furs circulated widely in medieval Europe, the bustling world of Song China, and throughout the Mongol empire.[5] The product was high value, low weight, easy to carry, and durable and so remarkably well suited for long-distance trade in preindustrial economies; long before the age of cargo ships and railroads, networks of fur, like those of precious metals, silk, and spices, bound Scandinavia to Persia and Sakhalin to Jiangnan.

In the fifteenth and sixteenth centuries, during Eurasia's early modern expansion, fur markets were likewise at the vanguard of commercial and imperial integration. One great network, centered on the Baltic, supplied furs from Muscovy to consumers in the Baltic and Mediterranean.[6] Later, in the sixteenth and early seventeenth centuries, the market grew to include eastern Eurasia, the Great Lakes, and the Atlantic, as the Russian, French, and British empires expanded into modern Canada and Siberia; fur drove the Cossack and the coureur de bois alike.[7] By 1650, Russian trappers had reached the Pacific, and French ones the Gulf of Mexico, and in the process they enlisted myriad communities across Siberia and North America into the network. In 1200, an English prince obtained furs from Scotland or Ireland; by 1500 his furs came from Siberia; by 1600 they came from Hudson Bay or beyond.[8]

Fur markets expanded in the fifteenth and sixteenth centuries in eastern Eurasia as well along a "northern silk road" that bound consumers in Ming China, Chosŏn Korea, and Japan to producers of the Sunggari, Amur, and islands of the northwestern Pacific.[9] This eastern network expanded too in the sixteenth and seventeenth centuries, particularly as the Qing empire consolidated its rule. After the treaties of Nerchinsk and Kiakhta, Russian merchants joined the trade, and the network accordingly spread into eastern Siberia. With the third voyage of Captain Cook (1776–1779) and the establishment of the Russian-American Company (1799), the people of coastal Alaska, the Pacific Northwest, and California entered the trade as well. In 1200, an emperor might wear furs trapped on the Amur; by 1700, his furs might come from Sakhalin or Sitka; by 1830 they might come from Baja California. By the early nineteenth century, the two networks encompassed the entire world: Half of all North American exports went to London, half to the China market via Canton or Kiakhta.[10]

The market was omnivorous; people wore almost anything, from pricey sables and sea otters to the common squirrel. The ecological effects of fur trapping were accordingly complex. Some of the hunted animals were so-cial, like sea otters; they lived mostly arm-in-arm in "rafts" off the coasts of Hokkaido, Siberia, Alaska, and California. Others led a more solitary existence, like the sable: They fought tooth and nail to defend their territory and so were dispersed thin and wide. In the early eighteenth century— before their global population reduced from over a quarter million to less than 2,000—sea otters favored the kelp canopies that grew along coastal shorelines, hunting sea urchins, Dungeness crabs, mussels, and fish.[11] Sables preferred the coniferous forests of Siberia, Mongolia, and Qing Northeast, where they fed on almost anything: pine nuts; shrews, moles, and other small rodents; small birds; berries; and—if hungry—squirrels.[12] Sables thus were but a link in a larger food chain; they themselves were prey for a num-ber of large mammals (tigers, wolves, foxes, bears, and lynxes) and birds (hawks, eagles, and owls). In total, they ultimately shared a direct link in the food chain to thirty-six mammals, 220 birds, twenty-one plants, and two species-specific types of flea.[13]

Neither sables nor sea otters, of course, lived in worlds without people; humans in fact were the foremost predator of both species. Despite the vast differences between them, then, the populations of both tended to move to a common rhythm from the late eighteenth century onward as markets integrated and expanded. The last quarter of the eighteenth century in par-ticular marked a turning point in this regard: From then onwards, and over the next fifty years, both species were driven to the edge of extinction.

Multiple factors converged between 1775 and 1800: Qing demand for furs grew ever stronger; the Kiakhta trade became more reliable; Rus-sian trade expanded eastward with the end of the Chuchki Wars; Hok-kaido became more fully integrated into the Nagasaki trade with China; the American Revolution unleashed new competition in the Pacific; and

Captain Cook, on his third voyage, discovered that sea otter pelts fetched 120 Spanish dollars apiece in Canton—eighteen times their value on the North American coast—spurring a rush to the North Pacific.[14] Beginning in the 1780s, and particularly in the 1790s, merchants made unprecedented inroads in Alaska, the Pacific Northwest, California, and the Hawaiian Islands.[15]

The fur trades at Canton and Kiakhta boomed thereafter, if not always reliably. Border disputes, including over trade in Uriankhai territory, led the Qing court to embargo trade with Russia three times: in 1764–1768, 1779–1780, and 1785–1792. It was not until 1792 that the Kiakhta trade became at all dependable.[16] Commerce flourished again until the French invasion of Russia and the Napoleonic Wars, which dampened trade across the Pacific; the War of 1812 and the Mexican War of Independence (1810–1821) had similar effect on fur trade off the California coast. Only with peace in Russia and the Americas did the fur trade at Kiakhta revive.[17]

The greatest constraint on trade, however, was not political but ecological: Ecosystems could not keep up with consumer demand. The number of fur-bearing animals in the wild plummeted accordingly as the hunt intensified; as the market grew, the population and distribution of animals shrank. Thus, from the mid-eighteenth to the mid-nineteenth centuries, sea otters became scarce in Russian Siberia, then Alaska, then the Pacific Northwest, California, Hokkaido, and Mexico.[18] Sables were overhunted in Siberia by the seventeenth century, and by the nineteenth century, as we shall see, they would largely disappear from Qing Mongolia, Manchuria, and Sakhalin Island as well.[19]

The numbers on this front are revealing. By 1830, fur trade with China was a fraction of what it once was; by then, there were simply not enough animals left to catch. The fur trade at Canton went bust: In 1806, Canton imported 17,446 sea otter pelts; in 1816 it imported 4,300; in 1831 it imported 329. As supply failed to meet demand, prices rose, and the average price per pelt quadrupled between 1806 and 1831.[20] Trade in other species' pelts did not fair much better. After 1830, as hunters replaced sea otter with other furs, North America witnessed cascading declines in fur seal, beaver, fox, river otter, and sable populations.[21] The Kiakhta trade followed a similar trajectory: In 1810, at least 10 million squirrel pelts passed through Kiakhta; by roughly 1850, fewer than 1.5 million pelts did so. The number of sable pelts on the market plummeted as well, from 16,000 in 1800 to virtually none by 1850. Despite rising prices, their relative value in the

Kiakhta trade shrank from about 45 percent of total trade in the early 1830s to 18 percent by the 1850s.[22] Too few wild animals were left to support the trade.

Again, Kiakhta and Canton were connected; as market signals from both hubs informed decision making throughout the Pacific. Russian merchants, for example, frequently circumvented the costs of the overland Kiakhta trade by using American merchants plying the Canton route as middlemen; they likewise tried, and failed, to have the Qing court allow Russians to trade directly in the port.[23] Unsurprisingly, whenever the Qing court shut down the Kiakhta trade, the Canton fur trade boomed; when Kiakhta was closed between 1788 and 1792, fur prices in Canton rose by 20 percent, and, when it reopened, prices in Canton plummeted.[24]

As furs from Hokkaido and Nagasaki entered the market, exports from Tokugawa Japan followed the same signals. Dutch statistics on Chinese junk-boat trade between Nagasaki and the Chinese coast are suggestive in this regard.[25] Chinese merchants imported only a small number of sea otter pelts from Japan before 1785: a total of seventy pelts between 1763 and 1765 and none for the next twenty years. In 1785—the first year of the last Qing embargo on Russian trade—Japanese exports of sea otter grew markedly and remained strong for the next two decades, with an average of 275 pelts exported to China per year. Between 1810 and 1821, during the decade of conflict in Russia and the Pacific, the size of Japan's sea-otter trade almost tripled, growing to an average of 725 pelts per year, with a peak in 1812 of 1,400 pelts exported to Qing China during the Napoleonic invasion of Russia.[26] From Siberia to Hokkaido to California, all roads led to China.

THE BUST IN THE NORTHEAST

Closer to home, too, history was in tune with regional and global patterns. On the basis of Manchu documents, recent research by Shigeru Matsuura has documented how fur trade and tribute on the Lower Amur, the Pacific coast, and Sakhalin Island grew then declined through the course of the eighteenth century.[27] The fate of fur tribute in particular provides a striking measure of the downturn: All of the empire's fur-tribute systems nearly collapsed between the 1830s and 1850s, as the number of people and pelts cycling through them disappeared. The collapses are all the more striking given the differences in how tribute worked. In the Northeast, the Qing court had institutionalized three tribute systems for collecting furs: a clan- and village-based system, operated through Ningguta and Ilan Hala; the *hojihon* system, in which clan or village heads in the Lower Amur main-tained special tribute and marriage relations with the court in Beijing; and the *culgan* system at Qiqihar, used for the Hunter Eight Banners based in the Upper Amur and the Manchurian highlands (see Chapter Two). All three systems experienced major strain after 1800, as scarcity became en-demic, and survived only in radically modified forms after 1830.

The first system, based on collecting tribute from individual clans and villages, drew from communities in the Lower Amur, the Pacific coast, and Sakhalin Island. In this region, and particularly on the lower Amur and on Sakhalin Island, the number of tribute-payers expanded between 1678 and 1750 from 1,209 to 2,250 households. With the exception of 148 households based on southern Sakhalin Island (called the "Kuye Fiyaka"), who paid tribute through Ilan Hala, all submitted their tribute through Ningguta. Some delivered their furs in person; the rest offered their furs to special envoys sent to sites on the lower Amur and the mouth of the Ussuri; the envoys traveled in armed flotillas, using canoes that fit roughly nineteen men per boat. Each year, then, either tribute bearers came to a Qing gar-rison or the garrison came to them.[28] In 1750, to control mounting costs of overseeing collection and sending return gifts (Ma: *ulin*), the court fixed the number of households enrolled in the Ningguta tribute system at 2,250. In 1779, to further manage costs, the Qing court moved the collection and dispatch center to Ilan Hala from Ningguta. Thereafter 2,398 households, comprised of fifty-six clans, submitted fur tribute via Ilan Hala. Each com-moner household offered one sable pelt per year, and households of rank offered two. If they missed a year, the system was flexible: They still could make up the difference the following year and receive gifts in return.[29]

Private trade flourished alongside this tribute system. To better control the high-end market, in 1672 authorities in Ningguta began to purchase all the surplus, top-grade furs that tribute bearers brought with them; from the Yongzheng period onward, moreover, authorities began to supplement their hauls with direct purchases from merchants. Merchants flooded into Ningguta, and from a military outpost and place of exile for political pris-oners, it emerged in the early eighteenth century also as a major hub for the fur trade. The scale of the legal fur trade was enormous: Upward of

10,000 pelts reached Mukden each year from the Ningguta area. To capitalize on the trade, in 1735 the Qing court began to collect special customs on furs at the Great Wall and in Beijing. In 1779, it further began to levy a tax on sables at a rate of 0.03 tael per pelt at Mukden. Sales peaked in 1791; that year, a single group of seven merchants led by one Lin Zichuan petitioned to carry 16,567 "yellow" sable pelts from Ilan Hala to Mukden and Kalgan.[30]

Well before 1791 there were problems in the system. Qianlong, for one, noted the declining quality of furs passing through Ningguta as early as 1750; in 1765, the court complained again that pelts from Ningguta were too small and no longer the proper color, a complaint Qianlong reiterated again in 1772. In each case, the court suspected Chinese merchants were to blame, and, as with pearls, ginseng, and mushrooms, it empowered territorial authorities to act; the period thus witnessed the erection of new *karun* just downstream from Ningguta and Ilan Hala and the establishment of new customs checks at Mukden and Beijing. At the new posts (named Ice Karun at Ningguta and Waliya Karun at Ilan Hala), guardsmen inspected tribute bearers' boats and registered the types and quantities of furs they carried.[31] If illegal trade was diminishing the quality of furs, the court reasoned, then enhanced surveillance and discipline were the solution.

Yet, as Matsuura Shigeru has documented, other issues emerged in this period; the market was not the only factor undermining the system. Many avoided tribute collection, for example, to avoid catching infectious diseases. Smallpox in particular was a problem, with major outbreaks tearing through the Amur in 1747, 1770, 1771, 1776, and 1824. Recurring smallpox epidemics led the court to move the tribute collection center from Ningguta to Ilan Hala in 1779: Authorities thought it might help tribute bearers avoid the summer outbreaks. As the population of the Northeast thinned, fewer people made the trip to Ningguta and fewer appeared when the envoy flotillas arrived. Even in years of health, people sometimes avoided tribute collectors for political reasons. When a debt dispute culminated in the murder of a Sakhalin Islander by a *hojihon* in 1742 and the court issued only a wrist slap, the case became a local cause célèbre, and communities from throughout eastern Sakhalin island stopped submitting tribute altogether, damaging the envoy system and *hojihon* trade alike. One index of the difficulty of procuring tribute in the incident's wake was the growing number of soldiers on tribute flotillas. Another was the unwillingness of the envoys to venture too far down the Amur. Over time, they collected furs ever closer to home: In the early eighteenth century, they went to villages in the mouth of the Amur; at century's end, they went no further than the village of Derin, more than 200 miles upstream.[32]

After 1800, in fact, tribute collection often proved impossible. In 1805, declining yields from the envoys' missions prompted the court to authorize voyages downriver twice a year; after 1821, facing even greater declines, the court ordered envoys to make the trip three times a year. Tribute collectors made up for losses with purchases on the open market, a practice that began during smallpox years but became common from the 1820s. We know, for example, that following the smallpox outbreak in 1824, the lieutenant governor in Ilan Hala purchased 750 sable pelts for 1,500 taels to meet his tribute quota. In the following years, it is unclear who or how, exactly, the authorities met their obligations. Indeed, though the garrison at Ilan Hala kept detailed tribute records, a close look at the records reveals that those after 1825 were fabrications: The names of the tribute payers, and the amount of sable they submitted, remained the same for almost a century. Furs were coming in, but from whom, or through what mechanism, remains unclear. Provocatively, we know that by the late nineteenth century, authorities purchased furs in Khabarovsk to meet quotas. Yet finding furs anywhere was difficult by midcentury. Sable, at the very least, were scarce in Sakhalin Island by the late eighteenth century and throughout the continent by the early nineteenth.[33]

The *culgan* system of the Upper Amur and the Manchurian highlands faced major difficulties for the same reason, and as Cong Peiyuan has shown, it too boomed and busted in this same period; although the system operated according to different rules, it, too, proved unsustainable. Every year, in either the fourth or fifth month, the lieutenant governor (Ma: *meiren-i janggin*; Ch: *fudutong*) of Qiqihar oversaw an annual "gathering" (Ma: *culgan*) in the garrison-town at which members of the Hunter Eight Banners submitted furs. The *culgan* began with a welcoming of the tribute bearers on the road outside the town gates, followed by a festival that featured sports competitions, including an archery contest. Each participant had to bring at least one pelt per household as tribute; many, however, brought extra furs to sell on the side. At the *yamen*, authorities ranked all pelts according to four categories—"top class," "second class," "high-quality third class," and "regular third class"—then selected the very best as tribute.[34] After the submission ceremony, which involved a kowtow, authorities reciprocated with a gift of silks and fine linens.[35] Officers at the garrisons then marked the remaining sable pelts (Ma: *maktaha seke*) by removing a leg, and they were freed to be traded on the open market. A monthlong trading fair ensued. At least in the early Qing period, it was the biggest market event of the year; witnesses reported seeing piles of pelts, stacked thousands high, outside the lieutenant governor's *yamen*; the court granted permission to build a special treasury in Qiqihar to accommodate the enormous volume of pelts that accumulated. The market was the only legal one; any sable trade outside the confines of the *culgan* was prohibited.[36]

Major problems emerged in the system in the late eighteenth century. A corruption scandal in Qiqihar came to light in 1795, for example, when the court discovered that the lieutenant governor was overassessing tribute and keeping the added returns for himself. To better control tribute assessment, the court established a more public presentation ceremony and revamped the reporting requirements for tribute tallies; thereafter, the lieutenant governor and military governor of Sahaliyan Ula reported the quantities and qualities of all sable pelts brought to the *culgan*, including those rejected for being below tribute grade.[37] The First Historical Archives in Beijing, for this reason, have records from 1796 to 1899 of not only the types of sable collected (divided into first-, second-, and high third-class sables), but the number of tribute bearers, the number of sables they brought, and the number of pelts accepted as tribute. Territorial authorities registered tallies, moreover, for three different groups: Solon and Daur (assessed together), Mounted (Moringga) Oroncon, and Pedestrian (Yafahan) Oroncon. In their reports, the military governors of Sahaliyan Ula included the final tallies in Manchu-language palace memorials until 1823, after which they continued to write in Manchu but compiled the attached tallies in Chinese.[38]

Taken cumulatively, these documents provide a rough measure of the *culgan*'s changing character. The number of participants in the event and the number of sables they brought with them both peaked in the 1810s and early 1820s, before declining markedly after 1830 and again, with the outbreak of the Taiping Rebellion, after 1850 (see Figure 4.1). From 1815 to 1829 an average of over 5,000 participants brought at least 10,000 and 12,000 sable pelts to the fair. In 1830, despite a high turnout, the number of sables brought to the *culgan* shrank by 25 percent, from 11,694 in to 8,829 pelts. The numbers never recovered: After 1850, total pelts at the *culgan* would average only 4,100 per year, a third of what it had been at its peak. Unsurprisingly, the number of participants shrank as trade declined:

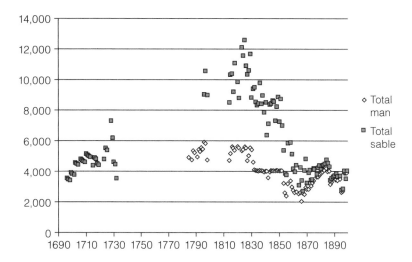

Figure 4.1. Registered participants and sable pelts at the Qiqihar *culgan*, 1696–1899.

SOURCE: *Qingdai Elunchuzu Man-Hanwen dang'an huibian*, MWLF, and NPM-JJCD. See Appendix.

Participation declined by 25 percent between 1831 and 1832 and again by 35 percent between 1852 to 1854, during the Taiping Rebellion. Although the reported number of people at the *culgan* would eventually recover by 1881, it never achieved levels of participation comparable with those of the early nineteenth century.

Yet the documents reveal other dynamics at work. Some communities experienced declines, for example, while others did not. The lieutenant governor of Qiqihar reported that the Yafahan and Birar Oroncon submitted, with little variation, roughly 600 pelts per year through the first half of the nineteenth century. The Solon, Daur, and Moringga Oroncon, in contrast, submitted significantly fewer pelts over time: The Solon and Daur brought over 10,000 pelts to the *culgan* in the early 1820s but only 6,000 pelts by 1850; submissions by the Moringga Oroncon declined from 600 to 400 pelts in the same period. The documents further reveal that the Solon, Daur, and Moringga Oroncon had less choice over what they hunted, sold, and submitted as tribute after 1830. Before that year, for example, there is but a faint correlation between the total number of participants at the *culgan* and the quantity of sables they brought: Some years, hunters brought an average of between two or three pelts per person; other years, they brought just one or two. After 1830, and with almost ironclad certainty after 1850, the tallies show almost no variation: the years of bounty disappeared, and people brought the legal minimum of furs.[39] Likewise, though total submissions declined in the late 1820s, the percentage of high-grade furs actually rose. The lieutenant governor graded over 90 percent of the furs accepted as tribute as "ordinary third class" throughout the 1820s; 5 percent of the remaining sables were usually "quality third class," 2.5 percent "second class," and 0.75 percent "first class." From the 1830s, however, the court accepted twice the number of high-grade sable pelts as before and quadruple the number from the 1850s.

Over time, that is, the *culgan* became a different event. It was no longer a great trade fair: Participants, if they came at all, brought a single pelt, and kept fewer quality pelts for themselves. Trade dwindled, and options disappeared. The years of plenty were over.

THE CASE OF THE URIANKHAI

Similar patterns marked tribute relations far to the west, in the Qing empire's second major fur-producing region: the so-called Uriankhai territory of northwestern Mongolia. Administratively, the region belonged to three "Uriankhai" groups: the Altai Uriankhai, the Altan Nuur Uriankhai, and the Tannu Uriankhai (look back to Map 3.1). Today, most people that trace their descent to the Uriankhai live in Russia or Mongolia: They include the Altai people in Russia, who trace their descent to the Altan Nuur Uriankhai; the Uriankhai of Mongolia, who trace back to the Altai Uriankhai; and the Tannu Tuvans (Russia) and the Darkhat (Mongolia), who trace back to the Tannu Uriankhai.[40] Under Qing rule, all three groups lived within special "Uriankhai banners," and the court levied on each an annual tribute in furs.

Though associated with forests, only a small portion of their vast territory was fit for fur trapping. Three ecological zones could be found in the region: a dry and grassy steppe in the central and western regions, a forested taiga in the mountainous north and east, and a mixed zone in the hills between them, where steppe and taiga ran together in a quilted mix. The land was bound to the north by the Sayan mountains and to the south by the Tannu Ola range, and as a general rule, the northeast was wetter and more densely forested than the southwest. Between the ridges, and in the lowlands between the great mountain ranges, lay grassy valleys where herders pastured animals, and wildlife common to the Mongolian steppe thrived, including steppe foxes, wolves, marmots, ground squirrels, Mongolian gazelle, bustards, partridges, and other creatures. As one moved up the slopes, grasses gave way to birch stands and evergreens: Siberian larch, cedar, and fir. Animals less common to the steppe thrived in these forests: sables, otters, squirrels, snow leopards, elk, maral, and roe deer. Still higher, along the alpine ridgelines, grew a lush carpet of lichen that supported herds of domesticated reindeer. Throughout, moreover, in the region's myriad rivers and streams, swam prodigious quantities of fish: grayling, salmon trout, pike, perch, and gwyniad.[41]

As Sevyan Vainshtein has documented, the vast majority of people living in the region lived in the grassy valleys or in the west, where, like other steppe nomads, they herded cattle, sheep, goats, horses, and camels and lived in lattice-framed felt tents. Although nomadic pastoralism predominated, many wealthier households also owned small farms, growing millet and barley along gravity-fed irrigation systems—a practice that, despite popular myths to the contrary, predated Russian and Qing colonialism in the eighteenth and nineteenth centuries. Only a fraction of the population lived in the rugged forests of the eastern highlands; in the early twentieth century, at least, one in twenty made homes there. Unlike pastoral nomads, most lived by herding reindeer and hunting wildlife; they shot ungulates for food and, in winter, hunted fur-bearing animals for taxes and trade. Their material culture was distinct as well: They mostly lived in teepees crafted from birch bark or animal skins, not the felt tents of Inner Asia. Many, though, did; on the fringe of the forest, a wide mix of households alternated between herding livestock in the summer and hunting furs in winter, shifting strategies depending on the circumstances.[42]

Most Uriankhai, who lived in ways similar to the Mongols around them, were essentially invisible to Beijing; in Qing China, if one knew of Uriankhai territory at all, it was solely as a land of forests, hunters, and furs, and one understood the Uriankhai primarily through their participation in the tribute system. The association, at the same time, predated Qing rule, as long before the conquest other powers had demanded a fur tribute of the Uriankhai.

Indeed, many Qing institutions governing their relationship to the court were inherited. The Uriankhai became Qing subjects through the course of the Dzungar wars and the failed rebellion of a Khotgoid Mongol general, Chinggünjab, in 1756.[43] Before their incorporation into the Qing empire, the Uriankhai organized themselves into units called *döcin* (literally "forties"), each headed by a *demci* and nested within a larger unit, called an *otog̈*, which was headed by *jaisang*. Before Qing rule, the so-called Tannu Uriankhai consisted of sixteen *otog̈*, which belonged to four administrative groups: the Tes, Kem, Toji, and Sarkiten. These governing structures remained intact after the Qing conquest: Uriankhai *döcin* became Qing "companies" (Ma: *niru*), *otog̈* became "banners," *demci* assumed the rank of company captains (Ma: *nirui janggin*), and *jaisang* assumed the rank of supervising commandants (Ma: *uheri da*).[44] The Qing court thus recognized and empowered the local hereditary nobility while establishing lines of authority that bound households to banners, and banners to imperial authorities in Uliasutai and Beijing.

The fur tribute system, too, derived from older arrangements. Before 1756, the various Uriankhai groups paid a tribute in furs to either the Dzungar or Khotgoid Mongol states, and some paid tribute to the Russian empire as well. The Altan Nuur Uriankhai, for example, submitted a tribute of either four or five sable pelts per household to a Dzungar nobleman, named Galsangdorj, and one sable pelt per year to the Russians.[45] Initially, the only modification to the precedent was that the Qing court became the sole recipient of Altan Nuur tribute, and the Qianlong emperor "bestowed grace" and lowered their annual requirement to two pelts from four.[46] Thereafter the annual obligation totaled three sables for every Tannu Uriankhai household and two for every Altan Nuur and Altai Uriankhai.

As the language of imperial "grace" suggests, ideologically, at least, tribute was ideally both personal and hierarchical, framed in terms of each household's "official obligations" (Ma: *alban*) to a "lord" (Ma: *ejen*).[47] Before the Qing conquest, the "lords" of the Tannu Uriankhai were the Khotgoid Mongols; after the Qing incorporation of the Khotgoids, their "lord" became the "divine lord" (Ma: *enduringge ejen*; Mo: *bog̈da ejen*), the Qing emperor.[48] Thereafter, they became *albatu*: people that performed *alban* obligations. Their sole obligation, however, was the annual submission of furs: By imperial decree, the Tannu Uriankhai were to be "without any other kind of onerous obligation." They had little choice in the matter. When the Altan Nuur Uriankhai banners first formed, for example, Qianlong decreed that paying tribute was expected of all Uriankhai, no matter their differences: "The newly submitted Uriankhai all have 'presented tribute' [Ma: *alban jafaha*]. If [the new banners] . . . do not present any tribute, it will not be fair [to others]."[49]

Even if their way of life was similar to Mongols, then, their place within the empire remained; they belonged to "banners" and were supervised by the military governor's office in Uliasutai, but their identity, stature, and governing institutions were distinct.[50] In part for these reasons, the Uriankhai seemed different from the Mongols around them, though perhaps not fully. Indeed, there was ambivalence about their identity. Qing officials, for example, often described the Uriankhai as "Mongol." In justifying policies toward them, the court similarly invoked the trope that "the emperor's people of the *aimaġs*, near and far, are all like one."[51] Acting harshly toward Uriankhai was thus "not in accordance with the loving intention of the emperor towards Mongols."[52] On ideological grounds, the court thus made few attempts to civilize the Uriankhai or intervene in their affairs; it embraced instead an imperial responsibility to protect the Uriankhai way of life, just as it did for Mongols.

Unlike Mongols, however, the court understood the Uriankhai to be hunters by nature, not herders—even if the vast majority were actually pastoralists.[53] The stereotype endured all the same. Qing texts often describe Mongols as a simple people, but compared to the Uriankhai they seemed savvy. In 1758, the military governor of Uliasutai, Cenggunjab, represented the Tannu Uriankhai as barbaric: Their poor were living "like birds and beasts" and were ravaged by war.[54] They lacked proper rulership; for two years since the end of hostilities, Cenggunjab reported, they had been "without a person to rule over and bring them together." Unable to survive, "It seemed the *otoġs* had all dispersed and gone into the mountains and valleys in search of fish and game."[55] To Cenggunjab, then, hunting and fishing was an emergency measure for desperate times. Later writers disagreed. The *Draft Gazetteer of Uliasutai* (*Wuliyasutai zhilue*), an early nineteenth-century manual for incoming officials, explained that Mongols did not need to depend on hunting because they "herd [livestock] for a living."[56] Herding served them well: The rich had camels, horses, and "tens of thousands" of cattle and sheep, and the poor had "dozens" of sheep. Mongols could thus be self-sufficient: They ate meat in the winter and dairy in the summer, made spirits from milk, used dung for fuel, and cut utensils and furniture from wood.[57] The Uriankhai, in contrast, lived a poorer life, as they "hunted wild animals and fished for a living."[58] When two Uriankhai companies, whom the Qing court had relocated for illegal trade across the Russian border, asked to be transferred back north to their former pastures, an investigation revealed they would suffer anywhere:

> They depend on reindeer for riding and pack animals, and, their custom [Ma: *taciha*] is to fish Lake Khövsgöl for food or search for the snakeweed [Ma: *meker*] and bulbous roots [Ma: *tumusu*] growing around the lake. They know nothing at all of the way of raising livestock or seeking good pastures.[59]

Uriankhai and Mongols not only had different ways (Ma: *doro*) of living, they also had differing relationships to the market. Mongols, the state recognized, relied on networks of exchange. Mongol households smoked tobacco and drank tea, and the wealthy wore silk; to obtain what they needed, they traded livestock, hides, felt, and furs.[60] Special rules attended trade among Mongols, but it was legal. The Urianhkai, in contrast, seemed vulnerable to the pitfalls of even regulated commerce, and when they fell under its spell, the consequences seemed more severe. Accordingly, the court prohibited merchants from entering Uriankhai territory altogether.

Anxieties about the Russian border drove these policies. The Uriankhai that the court relocated south, for example, had been secretly conducting trade with merchants from Russia, violating the negotiated terms of border trade, and so prompted Qianlong to have them removed. To better control them, the court moved them south of a string of *karun* stations, which served as the first line of defense against Russia. Later, in 1783, armed Russians and Uriankhai robbed a Chinese caravan on the banks of the Eg, prompting another draconian decree prohibiting merchants from not only crossing into Uriankhai territory, but to even the neighboring "strip of land" (Ma: *girin i ba*) extending to the Eg, Selengge, Onon, and Kherlen rivers. Trade between Uriankhai groups was common, as was a quieter black market trade with Mongols, Russians, and Chinese merchants.[61] The court, however, abided none of it.

The Uriankhai, however, seemed to prefer life with merchants than without them, and they petitioned the court to allow them back into their territory. In 1796, after Qianlong's death, the new Jiaqing emperor relented: If merchants obtained the proper permits, they could journey to the territory of the Uriankhai living south of the defensive *karun* line, but to no others. Yet strategic concerns lingered. In 1804, the military governor of Uliasutai, Fugiyūn, warned that Uriankhai within the boundary were collaborating with those beyond it to smuggle goods across the *karun* line. They could not be ruled like ordinary Mongols: "The Tannu Uriankhai are newly subjugated and rebellious Mongols, and their situation is incomparable with that of Khalkha Mongols." The Qing, two generations after the conquest, lacked control: "There are no higher officials [Ma: *ambakan hafan*] besides a lieutenant colonel (Ma: *jalan-i janggin*) and a company commander in the territory of the three Uriankhai companies [living south of the *karun* line], and so it is difficult to round up the Chinese merchants travelling there." These merchants, he argued, were bound to "entrap" the Uriankhai into unmanageable debts and stir up trouble. Thus stopping trade was in their own interest; trade was a "great hindrance to the Uriankhai way of life." He proposed, then, that all merchants be once again prohibited from the area; only when the Uriankhai presented tribute in Uliasutai should they be allowed to conduct trade.[62] The emperor agreed: Uriankhai could not be trusted.[63]

Yet it was not only strategic anxieties about their vulnerable location near Russia, or their dangerous relationship to trade, that made the Uriankhai distinct in the imperial imagination: Their environment, too, seemed a world apart. The *Draft Gazetteer of Uliasutai* captured this spirit well. The author juxtaposed local products from Uriankhai land with those from Mongolia.[64] Some products, such as moose, existed in multiple jurisdictions; most, however, seemed to derive from a single type of jurisdiction. Mongolia was known for livestock and mushrooms (Ch: *mogu*); Uriankhai territory was known for furs: sable, squirrel, river otter, lynx, corsac fox, marten (Ch: *saoxue*), pine marten (Ch: *aiye diao*), fox, wolf, and badger.[65] Imperial jurisdictions overlapped with "ways of life" and natural products— and if Mongolia was for pastoral nomads and lifestock, Uriankhai territory was for hunters and furs.

This narrow vision of the Uriankhai, of course, was in part a reflection of reality (some Uriankhai did hunt for a living) and in part a reflection of imperial ideology. Though diverse, the court understood Uriankhai in the singular. Though pastoralists, the court identified them as hunters. Though active traders, the court demanded they be austere. It banned cross-border movement and trade; it barred merchants from visiting the region; it required only an annual tribute in furs. We should be weary then, for all of these reasons, of any notion that Qing policies suited the Uriankhai's essential nature. Rather, Uriankhai policy makes sense only as part of the larger, strategic project: the purification of the borderland.

THE PURITY IMPERATIVE

Before turning to Uriankhai tribute and the looming fur crisis, then, we might first ask the basic question: What was the significance of the border, and what was the Uriankhai's relationship to it? In many ways, the defense of the border trumped all other concerns; in this part of the empire, at least, territorial defense was paramount. Like the boundaries of a game park, the border with Russia had to be inviolable, unaltered, permanent, and pure.

The Qing court went to extraordinary lengths to fix, delineate, map, and secure the border with Russia.[66] The treaties of Nerchinsk (1689) and Kiakhta (1727), which fixed the border between the Qing and Russian states and established terms of trade, outlined the basic principles.[67] The treaties' logic, in turn, accorded with how the Qing state managed its internal boundaries between Manchus, Mongols, and Chinese: They clarified jurisdictions, promoted order through segregation, enforced new oversight over trade, and mandated the use of passports.[68] Residential segregation was the norm: The states agreed that Russian subjects must live north of the border, Qing subjects to its south, and all "escapees" (Ma: *ukanju*) on the wrong side of the line must be removed and punished. The Treaty of the Nerchinsk further mandated that all travelers to the border region carry a special "passport" (Ma: *jugūn yabure temgetu bithe*; lit. "permit for traveling on roads"). Later the Treaty of Kiakhta forbade all border trade except at two designated sites: Kiakhta, about 250 miles east of Lake Khövsgöl, and Tsurukhaitu, 500 miles to Kiakhta's east.

The court enforced these rules with the same methods it used to police other "restricted space" in Mongolia, like hunting grounds, and the productive spaces of the Northeast. It relied above all on a string of *karun* posts. Karun, by law, were to be "wherever borders or restricted areas exist."[69] Like all "restricted spaces," the Qing court also attempted to secure Russian border area by emptying it of people. Thus south of the "border" (Ma: *jecen*), the court maintained an additional "boundary" (Ma: *ujan*), where *karun*, each roughly thirty miles from one another, ran the length of the Russian border in Mongolia. Between the border and the *karun* boundary, in the "borderland" (Ma: *jecen i ba*), a special administrative zone emerged that was distinct from regular "Mongol land" (Ma: *monggo i ba*).[70] The size of this borderland varied: Depending on the location, it could be a short day's ride on horseback from north to south, or it could be as many as five or six days' ride, as near Lake Khövsgöl.[71] Ideally, its only permanent residents were to be border guards (Ma: *karun i urse* or *cakda i hafan cooha*). Thus not only Russians but Mongols and Chinese were prohibited from either entering this space or making claims on the land (Ma: *nuktere babe ejelefi*, lit. "ruling over the territory's pastures").[72] All trespassers were to be arrested. If someone built a home, it was to be razed. "Haphazard mixing" (Ma: *suwali-yaganjame*) was criminalized: Migrants and vagrants caught there were to be repatriated to their "native place" (Ma: *da ba*; Mo: *uġ ġajar*); no licensed travel was allowed. As at holy mountains and hunting grounds, guardsmen had standing orders to "purify the borderland" (Ma: *jecen be bolgo obu*; Mo: *kijiġar i ariġun bolġa*; Ch: *suqing bianjie*).[73]

Legally, then, the zone was distinct. In Mongolia, guard duty was a type of corvée service, and guardsmen were drafted from the ranks of local banners on a rotating basis.[74] Once enlisted, however, they became part of a separate chain of command. Depending on their location, *karun* guardsmen reported either to the *amban*s in Khüree or the military governor in Uliasutai, not to their banner *jasaġ*; in the Northwest, for example, there were twenty-three *karun* in the Uliasutai jurisdiction alone, staffed by a rotating group of 850 soldiers (each *karun* with thirty to fifty men) and twenty-three commanding officers of the rank *taiji* (each *karun* with one).[75] In line with their administrative division and separate chains of command, Qing documents invariably contrasted "border guards" with "bannermen" (Ma: *gūsai urse*) and "Mongols" (Ma: *monggoso*): They were different types of imperial subjects, with differing claims to their territories' resources. The *Draft Gazetteer of Uliasutai* accordingly describes "*karun* land" as categorically different from Mongol territory: Its administration, norms, and resources were distinct.[76]

Defending the inviolability of the zone required discipline. The guardsmen's basic job was to sweep the border on regular "patrol routes" (Ma: *karun i jugūn*) in search of trespassers. Each spring and autumn, top officials, including all newly appointed military governors in Uliasutai, audited their work with two additional inspection tours of the forty-seven *karun* on the border.[77] After each inspection—and whether or not any border violations were discovered—they submitted a memorial to the emperor confirming that inspections had, indeed, taken place. In Mongolia's far northwest, in the Ketun River region, for example, a team of 120 Durbet, Uriankhai, and Khalkha soldiers annually assembled for the job. If there were no irregularities, they reported that having "thoroughly investigated every lo-cation," they found "no people residing in or using pastures."[78] Patrolling involved "keeping look-out over the land" (Ma: *baran karara*) and "track-ing" (Ma: *songko faitara*).[79] If locals entered the zone, then, it only made this work more difficult. As the *amban* explained in 1826, when Mongols haphazardly used the borderlands, their activities destroyed tracks, making it impossible to find signs of Russian incursions.[80]

Strategically, a no-man's-land was simply easier to defend. The tactic of evacuating spaces was well tested in the Qing. The Kangxi emperor, who endorsed the Treaty of Nerchinsk, pursued the strategy along the border with Korea and, more famously, along the southwest coast during the war with Zheng Chenggong.[81] By removing supplies and potential collabora-tors, empty spaces made military attacks more difficult.[82] If the wilderness zone were rugged, moreover, it was even stronger. The strategic value of wooded areas as "strong positions" (Ma: *akdun ba*) was well understood.[83] Thus when Kangxi dispatched the emissary Tulišen to Russia in 1712, he ordered him, if ever asked by the Russians, to report that the route between the two countries had "a great many mountains, forests, and steep and nar-row places."[84] Unsurprisingly, the Treaties of Nerchinsk and Kiakhta thus called for the use of natural barriers to demarcate the border:

> If in the vicinity of places ruled by Russian subjects there are mountains, rivers, or taiga, use the mountains, rivers, or taiga as the border.[85] If in the vicinity of Mongol guard-posts and cairns [Ma: *obo*; Mo: *obuġa*] there are mountains, rivers, or taiga, make the mountains, rivers, or taiga the border. If there are no mountains or rivers but there is an open plain [Ma: *šehun necin ba*; Mo: *jildam tübsin ġajar*], divide [the plain] exactly in the middle, erect cairns, and establish the border.[86]

Natural monuments were defensive bulwarks: Any eighteenth-century army would have found formidable such treacherous terrain.[87] As such, the space was different entirely from the Mongol "steppe" (Ma: *tala*; Mo: *tala*) to its south. The *Han-i araha Manju Monggo gisun-i bileku bithe*, the Manchu-Mongol dictionary compiled in 1708, defined the "steppe" as "backcountry with roads" (Ma: *bigan de jugūn bisirengge*; Mo: *keker-e dür jam bui*). The "backcountry" (Ma: *bigan*; Mo: *keger-e*)—defined simply as "open plains" (Ma: *onco šehun ba*; Mo: *aġuu saraġul ġajar*)—thus de-noted a land through which no roads passed. Accessibility, then, defined the steppe: It was a world of vital linkages with the outside, not isolation.

The borderland, in contrast, was backcountry wilderness: Impenetrability defined it.[88]

Of course, it was not pure backcountry; guardsmen, at the very least, made it their home. It was not uncommon, moreover, for disputes to arise between guards and herders to their south over boundary lines. Russians regularly stole across the border, and the archives abound with prosaic reports of their repatriation.[89] Yet incursions by Mongols from the south often drew as much attention from the border guards, particularly in the early nineteenth century, when concern over access rights peaked. The year 1826, for example, witnessed a flurry of such conflicts between border guards and the herders living to their south. In one case, the southern boundary of the borderland near Asinggū *karun*, located about 200 miles east of Kiakhta, seemed "extremely close" to the regular summer pastures of Mongol bannermen. Guards had raised the matter the previous fall, and the *amban*s had endorsed a plan to place new cairns on the southern perimeter, but land management still proved "lax" (Ma: *sulfakan*), and animals from the two jurisdictions had gotten "mixed up" (Ma: *suwaliyaganjame*). To protect the border, the court thus ordered all Mongol herders relocated south to avoid further conflict.[90]

A more complex dispute arose along the boundary line with the *jasaġ* Mingjurdorji's banner, which abutted thirteen *karun* to the east of Asinggū, near the upper reaches of the Onon River. In 1826, winter weather stranded Mongol herders and four caravans who had illegally trespassed on the nearby borderlands.[91] Though the border guards ordered them to leave, their condition was pathetic: The snow had decimated their horses, and gathering fuel was becoming impossible. Leniency would normally be out of the question: They were living in "extreme violation of rules and principles" because of their "haphazardly mixing in *karun* land on the Russian border." Yet the league chief, Artasida, and Mingjurdorji decided to allow the trespassers to stay the winter and repatriate them in the spring and thus peacefully "renewing what has been established and living segregated." The following spring, they erected additional cairns along the boundary and called for better enforcement of the travel permit system to "put a stop to haphazard use of pastures." Only then could they reestablish the inviolability of the "borderland" (Ma: *jecen obuha ba*, lit. "land that has become a border").[92]

In the end, total exclusion of trespassers was impossible: The border was too long and the guardsmen too few. Difficult terrain exacerbated problems posed by the sheer size of the border and the great distances between *karun*.

Inspection tours, moreover, were expensive. Especially after the crises of the mid-nineteenth century, Qing subjects and officials along the border lacked the capacity, will, and interest to enforce them. The Manchu poem "Songs of Patrolling the Erguna Border" (1851), slyly documents the often blasé attitude of border guards; its lyrics record how guards witnessed a robust trade between Qing subjects and Russians at the border.[93]

We may doubt, then, the purity of the jurisdiction: Though ostensibly a bulwark, the borderland proved porous, and if people were not crossing it, then animals were. Indeed, as hunting pressures on both sides of the border mounted, and ever more hunters worked to get access to the restricted territory, the court found itself in a double bind: As the protector of the borderland, it had to maintain the territory's purity; as a defender of the Uriankhai, it needed to protect the hunt. Both imperial ambitions, ultimately, would inform one another.

THE FUR CRISIS IN URIANKHAI LANDS: AN OVERVIEW

The key institution binding the Uriankhai to their land was the border; the key institution binding the Uriankhai to the hunt was fur tribute. Meeting the obligation was never easy; the Uriankhai had no halcyon days. From the start, in the early summer of 1758 when the Tannu Uriankhai first came under Qing rule, they were in desperate condition. That summer two teams of Qing troops inspected six Tannu Uriankhai *otoġ*, conducted a census, and collect a first payment of tribute. After their inspection, they reported that the Tannu Uriankhai comprised 1,112 households of 5,028 men, women, and children. Of these 1,112 households, 515 were capable of supplying tribute. Of the remaining, 519 were "extremely poor and unable to submit tribute," and seventy-eight were comprised of the elderly and small children. Thus 515 households provided the first Tannu Uriankhai tribute payment: pelts of 155 sables, thirteen lynxes, 346 foxes, thirty-six wolves, nine corsac foxes, two martens, and 2,294 squirrels, as well as a motley assortment of pinions from seven eagles and forty-six hawks, among other valuable knickknacks. The toll tribute took on the community must have been considerable. That same year six Uriankhai noblemen, representing the same six *otoġ*, traveled to the headquarters of the Qing general,

Namjil, and the presiding Mongol, *wang* Cencukjab, to request leniency on further tribute collection; they were experiencing famine, they claimed, and the burden was too extreme.[94] The commanders obliged, and the following year the court forgave all tribute obligations.

After this initial reprieve, however, tribute payments were expected annually. Each year, every Tannu Uriankhai household capable of fulfilling the tribute obligation thus had to submit three "good, naturally colored sables" (Ma: *da bocoi sain seke*). Dyed pelts were not accepted, nor were furs obtained through trade.[95] For every ten sables offered as tribute by the community, the court returned a small bolt of "porous silk" (Ma: *kofon suje*: Ch: *duan*). For every twenty "black squirrels" (Ma: *yacin ulhu*) submitted, the court offered an additional bolt of "fine blue linen" (Ma: *samsu boso*: Ch: *bu*).[96] Although the court technically assessed the Uriankhai by household, no Qing official conducted a census after the inaugural year. Instead, in the blithe language of Qing documents, it expected the Uriankhai to naturally "lead joyful and leisurely lives under Heavenly grace and multiply."[97] Thus, as in other Qing census records, officials simply reported linear population growth over time: on average five new Tannu Uriankhai households, 4.5 new Altai Uriankhai households, and 2.25 new Altan Nuur Uriankhai per year. As the court assessed the Tannu Uriankhai three pelts per household and the Altai and Altan Nuur Uriankhai two per household, the expected number of sable pelts accordingly rose by an average of 28.5 pelts each year: fifteen from the Tannu Uriankhai and 13.5 from the Altai and Altan Nuur Uriankhai combined.

One problem marred the system from the start: Animal populations did not correspond to imperial jurisdictions. For this reason, authorities constantly had to adjust to local ecology. In 1758, when the six Tannu Uriankhai *otoğ* first submitted tribute, the court decided to follow a precedent from a previous power in the region: the Khotogoid Mongols, who had accepted bird pinions and other types of pelts from the Uriankhai, not just for sable. Maintaining a flexible exchange ensured sustainability:

> Having investigated [the matter], when this type of Uriankhai originally could not provide sables as tribute to their noblemen, they gave two foxes, corsac foxes, martens, or wolves as equivalent to one sable. They gave forty squirrels as equivalent to one sable. Hawk pinions were equal to one sable each, and snow leopards, lynx, horses, and eagle pinions were equivalent to three sables each.[98]

TABLE 4.1.

Exchange rates for Uriankhai tribute.

Animal	Value in sable pelts
Lynx	3
Otter	3
Snow leopard	3
Sable	1
Yellow fox	0.5
Corsac fox	0.5
Wolf	0.5
Marten[1]	0.5
Gray squirrel	0.025

[1] The documents give this animal as *suusar* (Mongolian), *harsa* (Manchu), or *sauxue* (Chinese); following Lessing's translation of the Mongolian, I have translated it as "marten," a genus type, not a specific species. Lessing, *Mongolian-English Dictionary*, 741. For the Manchu Norman gives the more specific "yellow-throated marten." Norman, *A Concise Manchu-English Lexicon*, 125. Vainshtein recorded that the Uriankhai submitted "wolverine" as tribute and does not mention *suusar* at all. Vainshtein, *Nomads of South Siberia*, 236. Further research is necessary on the problem.

If sables were scarce, the Tannu Uriankhai could thus swap them at a fixed exchange rate (see Table 4.1).

Likewise, when in 1759 the leader (Ma: *daruga*) of the Sarkiten Uriankhai submitted a tribute of pelts and pinions, but no sables, he explained:

Since the time of my forefathers until now, [my people] have herded [livestock] in the territory near Lake Khövsgöl and the Arig river. Since in the environs of our territory there is absolutely no sable, in past times we presented tribute in accordance with the various things we captured [while hunting].[99]

A later investigation confirmed the claim: His territory "produced no sable." At first, the Qing considered its options: Either move the Tannu Uriankhai to a land with more sable or accept substitutes according to precedent.[100] They chose the latter. Such flexibility was not universal, however. The Altai and Altan Nuur Uriankhai, most importantly, had lower annual lower quotas of sables—only two per household instead of three—but also had a more limited exchange; because they were in lands thought to be relatively rich with sable, the court allowed the Altai Uriankhai to substitute only fox and the Altan Nuur Uriankhai, until 1842, to substitute only squirrel.

Though a household obligation, securing tribute in practice was the work of a core hunting elite. In winter, these hunters formed parties of between four and ten men, though sometimes they traveled in groups of as many as twenty-five. They included both the best and neediest hunters in the community; the wealthy contributed by providing supplies and pack animals in return for half the total haul in furs. By day, when riding was impossible, they moved on foot, using iron crampons and skis. When their dogs picked up an animal's scent, they tracked it down and shot it. By night, they camped about a fire, drinking salted tea and eating roasted squirrels from the day's catch.[101] All were superior marksmen: The weapons of choice, from probably as early as the seventeenth century, were flintlocks, which they purchased through trade. Many hunters, however, made bullets and gunpowder locally; they cast bullets in special stone molds (called *khep* or *ok khevi*) and made gunpowder by reducing a concoction of saltpeter, charcoal, and sheep's droppings.[102] Other weapons also came into play, depending on the animal being hunted: bows made from fir or larch, crossbows made from larch or willow, and more complex M-shaped compound devices. The use of traps was comparatively rare.[103]

Although hunting required mobility, to protect the inviolability of the borderland, the court allowed it only in designated territories. The court kept especially close watch over Tannu Uriankhai hunters who lived south of the *karun* boundary but who crossed the line each winter to obtain furs from the northern mountains. These southern groups sent a party of twenty-five men north into the borderland each winter. Just south of Lake Khövsgöl, at Hathūlbom *karun* (Mo: Qatġulbom, modern-day Hatgal), border guards registered their names and tallied all horses and muskets.[104] Within the borderland, the hunters had standing orders to "thoroughly wipe away their tracks" and leave no trace behind.[105] After the hunt, they reported back for a roll call. Penalties ensued for anyone caught breaking the law: Those who hunted furs outside the designated zone, for example, were sentenced to forty lashes.

Each step of the process was to follow a predictable rhythm. The Tannu Uriankhai nobility met annually in the fall to determine the responsibility of each household within a given banner. The wealthy were assessed as many as twenty sable pelts per household; poorer households were responsible for as few as ten squirrels each. After the hunting season, once the hunting parties returned, banner authorities collected the total number of required furs, and they submitted the full tally to the military governor's office in Uliasutai. In some years, they brought the furs themselves to the garrison; in other years, the military governor's office sent envoys.[106] Once in Uliasutai, the military governors reported to the emperor and forwarded the furs to Beijing.

As with the pearl and ginseng monopolies, enormous volumes of paperwork attended the full process. The military governor's office, for example, registered the total number of pelts, divided into species, for the Tannu, Altai, and Altan Nuur Uriankhai, then forwarded the furs and a Manchu palace memorial to the court. About a month later, when the pelts arrived in Beijing, the Imperial Household Department recorded all pelts received, this time (usually) in Chinese; unlike the Manchu record, however, the Imperial Household Department did not distinguish among Tannu, Altai, and Altan Nuur submissions, but recorded only the combined total. At the end of the year, the court sold the unused or moth-eaten furs left in the Imperial Household Department's treasury to six salt-monopoly districts— Lianghuai, Changlu, Zhejiang, Suzhou, Jiangning, and Huaiguan—which were required to purchase them at market rates (and sometimes higher). We thus have multiple records on the tribute submitted by the Uriankhai, including those compiled in Uliasutai and those by the Imperial Household Department in Beijing. Both types of records are accessible in China's First Historical Archives, though some are held in the National Palace Museum in Taiwan. Between them, they are remarkably complete: For the 152 years in which the Qing state kept records, only fourteen years are missing (see Appendix).[107] For almost the entire period from 1759 to 1911, then, we have two sets of records on the total submission of sable, squirrel, lynx, otter, and other animals on the Uriankhai exchange.

Although this tribute thus became routine, the court constantly had to intervene to make it so. Manchu palace memorials from Uliasutai, in particular, portray the management of tribute as a constant struggle. In 1800, for example, a Tannu Uriankhai banner protested that they had "insufficient land" to live on, as lily bulbs (Mo: *tömüsü*), fish, and animals had grown too scarce to support their community. Their complaint engendered a quick response: The court granted them new territory within the borderlands by the shores of Lake Khövsgöl. In 1802, just two years later, more complaints about animal scarcity led the court to switch course; this time it did not grant new land but ordered a moratorium on trapping in older hunting grounds, near Darkintu *karun*, in modern day Chandmani-Öndör *sum* (see Map 4.1).[108] Between the new territory and the moratorium, the court

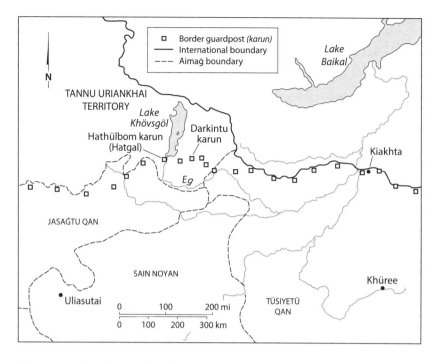

Map 4.1. Lake Khövgsöl and the Tannu Uriankhai border region.

hoped, trappers could continue to secure the annual tribute while animal populations recovered.

Yet complaints of scarcity persisted. In 1805, the Qing court pursued another strategy and fixed a cap on the tribute requirement, abandoning the per capita assessment. For two generations, the court had based the tribute requirement on the number of households capable of submitting it, yet because they had failed to conduct an annual census and expected instead the population to increase linearly over time, the tribute requirement had grown accordingly. By this mechanism alone, between 1774 and 1804, the total tribute demand on the Tannu, Altai, and Altan Nuur Uriankhai had risen by 26 percent, from 3,281 to 4,144 pelts per year. Thus, in 1805, the *amban* conceded that fur tribute could not be assessed like other taxes: Population growth was constant, but "the number of sables and other small animals changed from year to year." As a result, fulfilling the tribute requirement had become "difficult," and the burden had driven the Uriankhai to poverty.[109] After 1805, then, the tribute demand would be fixed at 4,144 pelts per year.[110] The reform represented, in effect, a shift from taxing the productivity of households, which had boundless potential for growth, to taxing the productivity of the land, for which there were ecology limits.

Yet the Uriankhai continued to register complaints. In 1808, just three years after fixing the tribute quota, the court received a report that "now small wild animals have gradually become rare" in the Eg River valley, near Hathūlbom *karun*. From Lake Khövsgöl to Darkintu *karun*, animals were "scarce" (Ma: *seri*). At first, the *ambans*' office requested that the court allow Tannu Uriankhai to hunt farther to the east, near Arhūn Booral *karun*. Doing so, however, might prove "difficult," as Arhūn Booral was much closer to the Russian border than Hathūlbom and border guards already occupied the land.[111] When authorities questioned the guards at Arhūn Booral, they confirmed that the Russian border (Ma: *kili i ba*) was only a half-day's journey on horseback from the *karun*. To protect against strategic risks, then, the court changed tack and decided, after six years of rest, that the Uriankhai again could use the territory around Darkintu to secure tribute.[112] The moratorium of 1802 thus came to an end.

Yet troubles only grew worse, and after a temporary reprieve in the 1810s, conditions deteriorated yet again. In 1822, for example, only eighteen of twenty-five hunters returned to Hathūlbom after the official hunt. When the military governor at Uliasutai ordered an investigation, the leader of the hunting party, Cultumg'umbu, admitted that the seven missing men were hunting in other territories. Although these seven ultimately returned without incident and surrendered their furs, authorities nonetheless ordered each to be whipped forty times and threatened Cultumg'umbu with demotion if trappers left their designated territory again.[113] Meanwhile, Uriankhai hunters kept petitioning for new land and an increase in the size of legal hunting parties that could cross the *karun* line; animals were becoming harder to find, and the customary twenty-five-man parties now seemed "small." By the summer of 1830, the situation remained "extremely worrisome" (Ma: *ele facihiyašara*), and the Tannu Uriankhai based south of the *karun* line requested to expand hunting parties to thirty. The military governor, however, denied them: Because they were still meeting their quota, he found no reason to change the status quo.[114] More reforms did not arrive until 1836, when the court began to suspect corruption in Uliasutai, and it was revealed that some envoys sent to collect tribute had been conducting illegal trade with the Tannu Uriankhai and getting extortionate prices for tea, tobacco, and other gifts. When it was discovered, the emperor ordered the Uriankhai to carry their tribute to Uliasutai themselves.[115]

Problems came to a head that winter, when a dispute erupted between hunters and border guards. Tensions had flared when a Uriankhai snare accidentally killed a border guard's horse, provoking a feud over the restricted territory's boundaries. Where, exactly, could one hunt? Prior to the dispute, there had been a seasonal arrangement: The Uriankhai used the southern slopes of the Khög River valley in summer as pastures and in winter moved south through the passes. There had never been a known problem with the arrangement. As the Mongol *amban* in Khüree, Dorjirabdan, summarized the situation for the emperor: "When we looked into the condition of each side's territory [Ma: *nukte*], the guardsmen's land was limited in size but had ample pastureland for herding livestock, while the Uriankhai's territory was full of forests and steep mountains."

The dispute of 1836, however, finally provoked a high-level response: In the early summer of 1837, the *amban* Dorjirabdan himself personally rode out to the area to assess the situation, take charge, and reestablish a lasting solution. As in the mushroom crisis, such a high-level intervention represented heightened imperial concern, a mounting distrust of local officials, and a perceived need to better clarify boundaries.[116] With the stakes high, Dorjirabdan reassured the emperor that the afflicted territory was of the "utmost importance" and that he would work to "purify the borderland" (Ma: *jecen be bolgo obure*). At the same time, Dorjirabdan also would defend the "livelihood" (Ma: *banjire were*) of the Uriankhai; they were to remain, as always, hunters.

Thus, in the spring of 1837, the *amban* gathered an entourage of secretaries, attendants, and guides and set off on a seven-day journey to Lake Khövsgöl, dispersing gifts of tobacco, tea, and silver along the way.[117] In the end, the Uriankhai's leader, a nobleman named Mandarwa, agreed to allow the customary wintertime boundary to be made permanent, effectively conceding the southern slopes of the valley to the border guards. Dorjirabdan, however, remained confident that this concession was minor and caused "no harm or injury to [the Tannu Uriankhai] way of life." Thus both sides agreed not to cross the new boundary, and the leaders of both communities consecrated the territorial divide with sworn promises in writing to uphold it. Worried that livestock might still cross the line, Dorjirabdan ordered the Uriankhai hunters to stop setting traps in the valley south of the boundary line, creating an enlarged buffer zone between the communities. Once it was agreed, he hired a local lama, named Jamcu, to draw a map of the boundary line, and he ordered that five cairns be erected on the ridgeline to mark the boundary on the ground. Clerks drew up copies of the new agreement, and together with the sworn statements and the map, and the *amban* sent a memorial to Beijing; the court later returned them to the *ambans'* office in Khüree for archiving.[118]

On Jamcu's original color map, a red line cuts across the territory from east to west, marking the borderline between the Uriankhai, to the south, and frontier guards, to the north (see Figure 4.2). Five black triangles—the cairns—dot the line. North of the line sit teepee-shaped markers, which gave the location of the *karun*s, including Hathūlbom *karun* on the shores of Lake Khövsgöl, in the top left. Black dotted lines cut through the landscape and connect the *karun*s; they represented the guardsmen's patrol routes, with one that follows the northern ridgeline and another to its south through the valley of the Kükge River.[119] The boundary, though clear, represented a segregation that was yet to exist; it embodied an imperial aspiration instead.

In many ways, as discussed in Chapter Three, the process of making borders was typical of Qing Mongolia as a whole in this period. Imperial authority was limited on the ground, and people frequently transgressed boundaries. Local-level actors, focused on local-level problems, were generating the demand for new borders, not just the court. The imperial authority was an outsider, and his arrival marked a break in the rhythm of local politics. Ideologically, he was an intermediary, not an advocate: He claimed to respect the identity and integrity of both jurisdictions—even if, in the end, the border guards prevailed. The identity of people, place, and environment was upheld: The Uriankhai had one territory, the guards another.

Indeed, each reform from 1800 to 1837, worked to delimit territories, maintain the idealized identity of the Uriankhai, and restore fur-bearing animals to the land. The laws prohibiting fur dying or fur trade further reveal that it was less important for the court to receive furs from the Uriankhai, per se, than to receive authentic products: furs the Uriankhai had trapped themselves and that came directly from their homelands. Rather than condone a Mongolization of the borderlands, or promote Chinese mercantile activity, the empire aimed to maintain differences: to segregate, define, and allocate. Yet at the center of this process, as in Manchuria and Mongolia, loomed a changing environment. Like pearling and mushroom

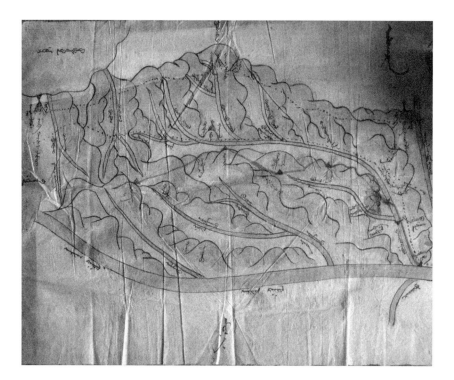

Figure 4.2. Disputed Uriankhai–Borderland boundary line, 1837. The map is oriented with north facing up.

SOURCE: National Central Archives, Ulaanbaatar..

picking, the troubled hunt for fur-bearing animals had moved to the top of the imperial agenda.

DIMENSIONS OF THE FUR CRISIS: A LOOK AT THE NUMBERS

The fact that the fur tribute system endured through the nineteenth century—as if nothing had changed—makes the court's interventions all the more remarkable. If we relied on the Imperial Household Department's records alone, with its faithful record of tribute received, major changes in the Uriankhai tribute system would be invisible, and the Uriankhai might appear unaffected by the passing time. Yet when combined with the Manchu memorials from Uliasutai, the archives paint an altogether different

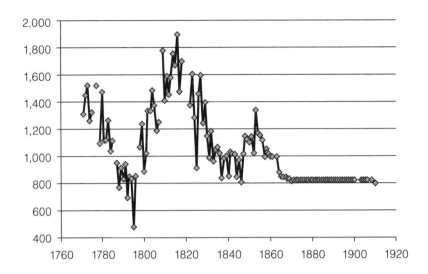

Figure 4.3. Sable tribute—Tannu Uriankhai, 1771–1910.

SOURCE: MWLF and NPM-JJCD. See Appendix.

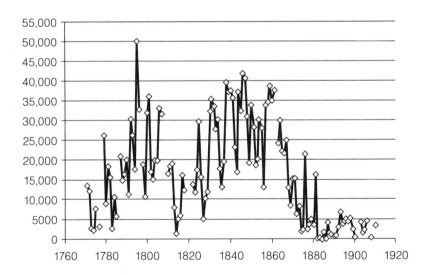

Figure 4.4. Squirrel tribute—Tannu Uriankhai, 1771–1910.

SOURCE: MWLF and NPM-JJCD. See Appendix.

picture. Species by species, it seems, animals were disappearing from the forest: sables first in the 1820s and 1830s, then squirrels in the 1860s, and finally all other valuable fur-bearing animals soon thereafter.

Sable submissions for all three Uriankhai groups combined declined from a high of 3,800 pelts in 1816, to 1,878 pelts in 1831, to a maximum of 1,200 (and often fewer) pelts thereafter. Tannu Uriankhai submissions represented half of the total decline: Their submissions peaked in 1816 at 1,896 pelts but had declined to 992 pelts by 1831 (see Figure 4.3).[120] Complaints about scarcity map onto these periods of declining returns: The period from 1795 to 1805, when reports of scarcity first became frequent, saw sable submissions dip significantly; the same was true during the 1830s, when Dorjirabdan had to intervene at Lake Khövsgöl.

Because of the exchange, the Tannu Uriankhai at least had options: If sables were few, hunters could focus on other types of pelts. In practice, however, tribute tallies suggest that hunters favored the substitution of squirrel pelts above all others, as sable submissions closely correlate with those for squirrel, with a Pearson coefficient of −0.85 between 1800 and 1832 (see Figure 4.4). The preference made sense: Squirrel and sable were the only pelts for which the court offered rewards—a bolt of silk for every ten sable pelts submitted and a bolt of cotton for every twenty squirrels. Hunting sable in return for silk, it seems, was the preferred option: The years when squirrel submissions peaked were the years when complaints about scarcity were most vociferous.

Yet the Uriankhai's options dwindled over time, and particularly from the early 1830s onward. Before 1832, with predictable precision, when sable submissions fell, squirrel submissions rose, and vice versa. After 1832, the correlation between the two becomes weak: sable submissions remained low, but squirrel submissions fluctuated greatly from year to year.[121] The Uriankhai were turning to other animals as tribute instead: fox, lynx, corsac fox, and so on. After the 1860s, as both sable and squirrel dwindled, the Tannu Uriankhai fulfilled their obligation with mostly corsac fox and marten, until the 1880s, when they too disappeared (see Appendix).

The decline of sable in the 1820s and 1830s proved a problem for the Altai and Altan Nuur Uriankhai as well: Altai Uriankhai submissions of sable pelts declined steadily after 1814; Altan Nuur submissions declined all at once in 1830. To make up the difference, both submitted the only options

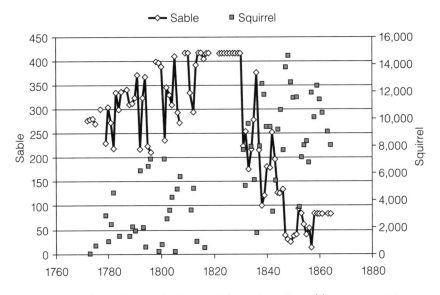

Figure 4.5. Sable and squirrel tribute—Altan Nuur Uriankhai, 1772–1864.
SOURCE: MWLF and NPM-JJCD. See Appendix.

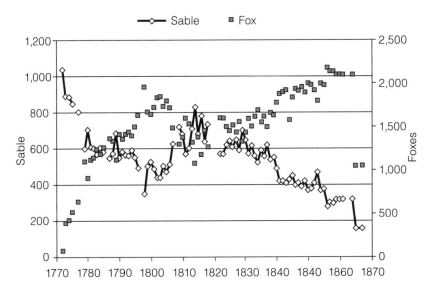

Figure 4.6. Sable and fox tribute—Altai Uriankhai, 1772–1867.
SOURCE: MWLF and NPM-JJCD. See Appendix.

available to them: squirrel for the Altan Nuur Uriankhai, and fox for the Altai Uriankhai (see Figures 4.5 and 4.6). In 1842, to bolster returns, the Qing court allowed the Altan Nuur—whose sable returns had declined by over 90 percent—to substitute snow leopard, otter, lynx, marten, fox, corsac fox, and wolf for sable.[122] Yet, because the Altan Nuur jurisdictions had too few of these animals too, they presented no more than a few dozen of each in the final two decades they submitted tribute.

What was happening? The fewer sable and squirrel pelts the Uriankhai submitted, the fewer rewards they received in return. Perhaps they sold these furs for greater profit on the open market? We know, for example, that the Uriankhai had a history of trading with both Chinese and Russians merchants across the border. They had incentive to do so; the tribute exchange was a bad deal. Based on pawnshop records, the value of a squirrel pelt was as high as 0.08 tael per pelt in the 1840s, while the price of "yellow" Uriankhai sable was as low as 1.00 tael, or twelve times the value of squirrel.[123] Squirrel fur was lowly, but it served as a cheap and passable alternative for consumers, and demand for it was high. On the exchange, however, sable was *forty* times the value of squirrel. Market prices for pelts at Kiakhta—200 miles east of Lake Khövsgöl—show a similar discrepancy. In 1794, one could go to Kiakhta and get more than twice the value of a squirrel pelt on the open market than on the exchange; one likewise received double the value for wolf and corsac fox pelts.[124] Based purely on commercial prices, that is, the Uriankhai lost financially whenever they submitted squirrel pelts as tribute.

The court, conversely, profited from the skewed exchange rates. Each year the Imperial Household Department sold the surplus furs in its treasury, and, by law, commissioners in charge of the empire's six salt-monopoly districts bought it at market rates. In practice, the Imperial Household Department sometimes fixed the rates at a more profitable level, whereby a squirrel pelt was worth about one-fifteenth the value of a sable pelt. Each time the Uriankhai submitted forty squirrel pelts instead of a sable pelt, that is, the Imperial Household Department earned 1.6 taels on the transaction. Thus, as the number of sable submissions declined and squirrel submissions rose, the total value of Uriankhai tribute to the Imperial Household Department doubled from 2,722 taels in 1809 to 5,322 taels in 1847.

The profits help explain some anomalies in the archival record. In 1844, for example, the Imperial Household Department reported receiving the full quota of furs from the Uriankhai: The three groups had sent pelts of 1,503 sables, eight snow leopards, three otters, fifty-nine lynxes, forty-nine martens, 2,255 foxes, 670 steppe foxes, seventy wolves, and 36,360 squirrels. When accounting for exchange values, in short, the Uriankhai had submitted a tribute equivalent in value to 4,144 sable pelts, meeting their quota exactly.[125] That year's memorial from Uliasutai, however, provided a different tally: 1,403 sables, eight snow leopards, three otters, fifty-nine lynxes, forty-nine martens, 1,955 foxes, 670 steppe foxes, seventy wolves, and 46,360 squirrels.[126] Again, when we account for exchange values, the tally adds up to 4,144 sable pelts in value. The numbers do not align: The Imperial Household Department reported receiving 100 more sables, 300 more foxes, and 10,000 fewer squirrels than Uliasutai claimed it sent, even though both reports matched the tribute obligation exactly. The year 1844, moreover, was hardly unique in this regard: Similar discrepancies appear in the years 1800, 1816, 1818, 1823, 1829–1832, 1834, 1837–1844, and 1848.[127] The anomalies are almost always the same: The Imperial Household Department records fewer squirrels and more sables and foxes received than the military governor's office in Uliasutai reports sending. The hidden earnings explain the phenomenon: Squirrel pelts had better value on the open market than sables, so if a corrupt bureaucrat siphoned off squirrel pelts and added extra sables to the treasury, they stood to make hundreds of taels of silver a year. Forensic accounting, in short, suggests that corruption was endemic at the Imperial Household Department. Their records are not to be trusted.[128]

Why, then, were the Uriankhai increasingly choosing to go against their market interest? Even into the late nineteenth century, hunters showed a preference for catching squirrel pelts over other animals, and squirrel pelts even functioned as a local currency among hunters.[129] The most likely explanation, it seems, is ecological: Just as their complaints suggest, animal scarcity was to blame. The synchronicity of scarcity across borders, moreover, suggests local connections to a wider crisis: From the Altais to Khövsgöl to Manchuria and beyond, sables in the wild were in decline in the 1820s and 1830s.

Sables, unlike people, cross boundaries with impunity. They care about their own territories; twentieth-century attempts to protect sables in reserves failed largely because the sables simply left.[130] They reproduce quickly—their population can triple in six years under ideal conditions—

but under hunting pressure they rarely do.[131] Unsurprisingly, then, hunting in one location effected sable populations in another, as hunters across the region were targeting a common pool of animals. If we assume that some trappers and merchants trespassed or traded across imperial boundaries as well, then the assumption becomes stronger: Intensive hunting (or conservation) in one state would have effect in the other. Because hunters in Russia trapped sables for the Kiakhta market, we might even expect the number of sables traded at Kiakhta to correlate with the quantity of sable tribute in Uriankhai lands. If, on the other hand, Russian trappers were not fully engaged with the market—as during the French invasion of 1812—a low (or nonexistent) volume of trade at Kiakhta might belie a growing sable population, and thus we might not expect any correlation between the volumes of tribute and trade.

Indeed, between 1792 and 1830, the scale of the Kiakhta trade and the volume of sable tribute correlate positively, except, notably, in the years surrounding the Napoleonic conflict, when trade declined and tribute reached its peak.[132] It was not by chance that sable submissions declined in Tannu, Altai, and Altan Nuur Uriankhai lands all at once, or that they declined in Manchuria and Sakhalin Island in the same period: The fur crisis transcended the local. Indeed, the integration of the Kiakhta and Canton markets, and the wider synchronicities in the collapse of sea otter populations in North America suggests ways in which sustained demand from China, globalizing markets, and ecological limits had created new and shared dilemmas across the region. Its states all had to respond. Yet the Qing North was not just another American West or Russian Far East, and Khövsgöl was not another California.[133] Rather, it would seem, the coasts of North America were like Khövsgol, the Mongol steppe, or the mussels beds of Manchuria: All, in their own ways, had become ecological peripheries of a Qing-centered world.

CONCLUSION

Today, Lake Khövsgöl is a tourist attraction and a national park. It does not draw crowds like other, more famous sites, but that is the point: Tourists who travel there seek a reprieve from the pace and noise of modern life. Not long before tourists discovered Khövsgöl, imperial explorers did so as well, and in much the same spirit. Douglas Carruthers, in a pioneering British-led expedition in 1910, captured the mood at that time:

> Swampy bottoms, half lake, half forest, looked so mysterious, that if some prehistoric monster had raised its snaky head to have a look at us, it would not have been surprising. We should have felt its presence was all in keeping with its surroundings, and was, in fact, more natural than our own.

There were, of course, people indigenous to this cut-off borderland. But as Carruthers dryly observed of them, "In such a secluded region a peculiar inhabitant can be guessed at."[134] They were the Tannu Uriankhai, and, like their homeland, they seemed from another era. In Carruthers's world, untouched nature and its inhabitants were anomalies; they were atavisms in a world of imperial intrigue, industrial output, and revolutionary growth. To a British adventurer, it was as if the Qing empire had never truly ruled the region, or changed it, at all.

Yet Uriankhai territory was neither isolated nor unaltered. Power, of course, has a way of dilating time: Those perceived to have it see themselves as agents of change; those without can become icons of the unchanged.[135] In the case of Lake Khövsgöl, it was wishful thinking to see it as timeless: The nature of the Uriankhai and their homeland reflected more an imperial artifice than a permanent neglect. If the Uriankhai lived in a world apart, that is, it was because empire helped facilitate the distinction; if their land seemed untouched, it was because guards and bureaucrats helped make it so. The region was not a "wilderness" (Ma: *bigan*) at all; it was, in Manchu terms, a *bolgo jecen*, a "purified borderland." To cross the boundary into Uriankhai land was never to exit time; the boundary itself, like the nature it protected, was an imperial response to a global crisis.

Conclusion

Bannermen razing ginseng fields; mushroom pickers hauled before the Board of Punishments; *amban*s "purifying" the borderland: How do we make sense of these episodes? So much Qing history focuses on the court's efforts to transform the imperial frontiers by making them more productive, more civilized, and more Chinese. Yet none of these events quite fit into that story. What, then, do they tell us, and to what history do they belong?

Manchuria, Mongolia, and the northern borderland all had a special significance to the court; their status was different from other parts of the empire.[1] Although, within each territory, the court governed in diverse ways, aspects of imperial rule converged in the late eighteenth and early nineteenth centuries. In Manchuria, the ideal of the unspoiled Manchu homeland came to overlap with the jurisdictions of the territories' military governors, tying Manchu origins to the Three Eastern Territories. In Mongolia, anxieties about "mixing" provoked new efforts at "purification" and territorial defense. In the borderland, the court remapped the boundaries of the Uriankhai. Imperial representatives established *karun*, compiled registers, dispensed silver, reformed tribute, and empowered territorial authorities to take charge. The empire culled the land of undocumented migrants and punished collaborators.

The territorial project, in all of these ways, involved attempts to remake Qing subjects.[2] The work required more than the removal of pearl thieves, undocumented migrants, and mushroom pickers: It also demanded a changing of hearts. More insidious than "mixing" and migration, it seemed, was the possibility that Mongols and Manchus were losing their ways. To the court, the people of these frontiers were simple; they were hunters, herders, and bannermen, and thus by nature temperate and sincere. To protect their original dispositions, the court condoned only a limited participation in markets; these subjects were supposed to be frugal.[3] Imperial discourse invoked the Spartan spirit of Mongols, Manchus, and "hunters" with words like *innocent* or *pure* (Ma: *gulu*; Mo: *siluǧun*; Ch: *chun*). Those who succumbed to the temptations of the times were fallen; they were "negligent," "blind," or "reckless."

In practice, however, the court's efforts to strengthen territorial rule and reform its subjects were inseparable from an environmental project. To the court, the Uriankhai depended on fur-bearing animals, Manchuria was the land of ginseng and pearls, and Mongols needed mushrooms, marmots, and fish. Yet the nexus between people, place, and product seemed broke: Fur-bearing animals were gone from the taiga, mussels had vanished from riverbeds, and poachers had stripped the steppe of mushrooms, marmots, and fish. Such a transformation was unheard of: There was no precedent for such reckless exploitation. It upended the livelihood of subjects, disrupted the flow of high-value and courtly goods, and violated an imperial "love" of natural things, like mussels.

People, place, and product: The Qing empire reimagined and newly defended the three together amid the great uprooting of the boom years. Ideologically, they proved inseparable; the court defended the difference between pure and corrupted at a territorial and ethnic boundary. It was in its pursuit of "purity," where the native had come to overlap with the alien or altered, that the Qing state produced a type of nature: pristine realms to be unspoiled by the intrusions of time.

Critically, we only see this process unfold with a multilingual and multiarchival approach. Qing elites and the court had strong ideas about what it meant to be a proper Chinese, Manchu, Mongol, or Uriankhai, and they went to great lengths to articulate and maintain the boundaries between them. In court documents especially, the archives tend to reveal where the ideals fell short. The people who emerge from the documents are thus rarely ideal subjects: They are Mongols who sold out for the mushroom trade, Uriankhai who worked the black market, Ula who stole pearls, greedy merchants, debt peddlers, undocumented migrants, farmers of ginseng, poachers, intermarried couples, and vagabonds. It is at the fringes of the Qing world that the distinctions that constituted the empire become clearest.

Along these lines, we can read the specters of planted ginseng, mushroom pickers run amok, and other such impurities as nightmares of a peculiarly *imperial* mind; they recur so frequently in the archives because they set the gears of empire into motion. In Mongolian lands the discourses of ethnic and environmental "purity" were paramount; in the Northeast, invoking the word *purity* was rare. Yet the demands of empire led to convergent institutional and ideological responses in both cases; in both, the court worked to reconstruct the territory as an embodiment of uncorrupted nature.

Perhaps *nature* is not the best word to describe this reconstruction. In English, the word can obscure as much as it reveals: It can mean all that we are, and all that we are not; it can invoke a specifically Christian teleology, a Romantic imagination, or describe the domain of science.[4] Even in the more limited sense of an "unspoiled place," as what William Cronon calls the "wrong" nature, the English *nature* has nuances that Qing constructions certainly lacked; we cannot equate the modern English word, with all its nuances, with any one word from the early Qing. The same holds for *purity*: No one English word captures the nuances of the Manchu *bolgo* or Mongolian *ariġun*.

At the same time, Qing terms were not so exotic. To know whether something, someone, or some place is "natural," we often ask questions about its past: How was it created? Where did it come from? Has someone modified it, or is it free from human alterations? These questions, and what they tell us about the past, deeply informed the court's responses to its environmental crises: Whether in Manchuria, Mongolia, or the borderlands, it seemed the ideal and original order had been altered. Each memorial inscribed this sense of change over time into writing; each raid or reform imbued it with concrete meaning. When we read Qing documents against the grain and seek out documents from alternative archives, it becomes all the clearer that the purity of earlier times was a phantom: Chinese mushroom pickers had been active for generations; fur trapping and ginseng picking extended back centuries; Mongols and Manchus were never so simple; Chinese were never so foreign; the land was never so pristine. Such a reimagining of history, however, should not sound exotic at all: Across Eurasia in this same time period, others were reimagining nature and nation in congruent ways. The Qing state, put simply, was not so unique.[5]

UNSPOILED HOMELANDS BEYOND THE QING

If we step back to consider the Qing invention of nature in a larger, historical context, what do we see? Historians of Europe might find a parallel in the German experience. As the rush for "purity" was underway in the Qing world, Germans, like Mongols, began to insist that production and commerce were severing their connection to the nature of the *Heimat,* or homeland. In response, Romantics reacquainted themselves with the homeland's natural wonders and attempted to recover their lost ways. From the fifteenth century onward, Germans had strived to reconnect to an earlier, more sylvan era.[6] They rediscovered, for example, the *Germania* of Cornelius Tacitus (c. 56–117 CE), which described Romans as luxurious and sensuous and Germans as a more simple kind "without craft or cunning."[7] By the eighteenth century, against the rationalizing tide of the Enlightenment, Johann Gottfried Herder (1744–1803) could look back on Germany's "unspoiled native landscape" for inspiration.[8] A new environmentalism was born: *Heimatschutz,* which gained strength and organizational durability in the late nineteenth century during the second Industrial Revolution. The movement endured into the Nazi era, to an age when national toughness and rustic hardiness again seemed entwined. In Germany, as elsewhere, national and environmental movements went hand in hand.[9] Problems of borders, environmental hazard, moral decline, and political identity were animating the Qing discourse of "purity." They were producing a similar effect among German landscape preservationists; a reimaging of people and place was central to both.[10]

A similar imagined nexus between people and place consumed modern Poles and Lithuanians, who celebrated the forests of Białowieża as the lifeline of the nation. On seeing the forests for the first time in 1820, Julius von Brincken regarded them as "the very picture of ancient Sarmatia: a sylvan arcadia."[11] Amid the November Uprising of 1830–1831, the poet Adam Mickiwevicz likewise celebrated the forests as the vital setting of both his childhood innocence and the nation's primordial past.[12] The early Polish nobility had once dressed in "Sarmatian costume," like nomads, and their early modern successors celebrated them for doing so.[13] (Perhaps we should not be surprised, then, that the Qing emperors saw something of themselves in Poles: An album of tributary nations to the Qing, the *Zhigong tu*, described the Poles [Ma: *bo lo ni ya gurun i niyalama*] as being "like Mongols" and noted their fame for bearbaiting and outfits made from fox and badger furs.[14])

Such efforts to connect to one's natural, national past were hardly unique: Many sensed that something essential was being lost. On the continent, Goethe (1749–1832) saw in the "second creation" of the human world a Faustian deal with the devil; in England, William Wordsworth (1770–1850) brooded that humanity had sold its soul:

> Getting and spending, we lay waste our powers;—
> Little we see in Nature that is ours;
> We have given our hearts away, a sordid boon![15]

Those with power and means reconnected in an old-fashioned way: They hunted and adorned themselves with furs, and like Mongols and Manchus, German, French, Polish, and English elites all used fur to help represent themselves as elite, rustic, martial, and manly. Like emperors, German noblemen consumed imposing quantities of game meat and lavished outsized attention on their *Jagdschlösser*, or hunting lodges. Their hunts were lavish: In 1782, for example, Duke Karl Eugen of Württemberg celebrated the visit of Grand Duke Paul of Russia with a hunting trip that bagged 6,000 deer and 2,500 wild boars. Louis XV once purportedly killed 318 partridges in a mere three hours; Louis XVI killed 8,424 animals in a year.[16] *Vivre en roi, c'est chasser, et chasser régulièrement*: "To live as a king is to hunt, and to hunt regularly."[17] It was true throughout Eurasia: Qing, Mughal, Safavid, and European rulers all agreed.[18]

Early American sensibilities toward the natural environment were no less of the moment: They too were entangled with broader concerns of identity and power. Amid the colonial and industrial transformations of the American landscape, Henry David Thoreau (1817–1862), too, yearned for a purer, simpler, and more virile past: "When I consider that the nobler animals have been exterminated here, —the cougar, panther, lynx, wolverine, wolf, bear, moose, deer, the beaver, the turkey, etc., etc., —I cannot but feel as if I lived in a tamed, and, as it were, emasculated country."[19] Of course, the land was "tamed" before the colonists arrived, as the American wilderness, too, required as much a rewriting of history and political action as it did Qing purity. As Ansel Adams wrote of Yosemite on its founding as a national park: "Unfortunately, in order to keep it pure we have to occupy it."[20] In America, pure and unspoiled nature was elusive without the state.

Unspoiled nature is but an idea and an ambition; no places on Earth are untouched by human agents. We cannot understand even prehistoric landscapes without a human impact, and modern attempts to read humans out of landscapes, without understanding the roles we play in local ecosystems leads to problematic results.[21] As William Cronon argued of modern wilderness: "Far from being the one place on earth that stands apart from humanity, it is quite profoundly a human creation—indeed, the creation of very particular human cultures at very particular moments in human history."[22] Although we may imagine a total distinction between the natural and historical worlds, the two are inseparable.[23] From the American park, to the German forest, to the Soviet reserve, modern nature has survived because, as A. R. Agassiz suggested, states "rigidly preserved" it, whether for participatory politics, primordialism, or technocratic rule.[24] Untouched nature is something created, not destroyed; total wilderness can exist only in a context of total control.

The Qing experience suggests the need to rethink the global history of nature outside of a Eurocentric paradigm. So many attempts to understand "nature" in both China and the West have focused on the term's metaphysical and semantic dimensions, and, on this front, the differences separating Qing and the Western terms are many: When modern translators settled on the Chinese *ziran* and the Mongolian *baigali* to denote "nature," they utterly transformed these words' original meanings.[25] Yet we blind ourselves to parallels between the Qing and wider worlds without better tools for comparison. There were no equivalents for "mile" or "century" in the Qing world either, but people measured distance and time all the same.

Untouched "nature" too serves as a type of standard: We use it to measure and differentiate. In its very juxtaposition with the social and historical, it implies an understanding of origins, creation, permanence, and change; it is neither a domain nor an essence but a relationship to origins; it invokes a type of history. As Carolyn Merchant and William Cronon have argued, *stories* imbue this nature with meaning.[26] In Europe and America, biblical tales and the Edenic myth provided an early touchstone for understanding our natural origins and humanity's "second creation."[27] In the Qing, they did not. Yet, if we insist that the invention of "nature" was peculiar to the modern West, we must also allow that this "nature" belonged to a larger matrix to which Qing "purity," too, had a place. Modern Western debates over "nature," no matter how central they were to the identity of the West, were never entirely unique.[28] We need not understand Mongolia in terms of German or American history, nor argue that the invention of nature must follow a single historical arc. Rather, more modestly, we might begin to see how Germany and America were not so unlike Mongolia, and how they belonged to a common world. Without pigeonholing the Qing, then, we might help provincialize the West.[29]

IMPERIAL LEGACIES

We also may doubt whether modern environmentalism in China and Mongolia is wholly a Western import. For men like H. E. M. James and Douglas Carruthers, who discovered nature in Qing Manchuria and Mongolia in the late nineteenth century, wilderness lacked history; it had survived through time in an original primordial form. Later scholars came to a similar conclusion: The Manchu court preserved these lands from the world beyond, and only with the arrival of homesteaders did history progress. Yet, as this study has emphasized, they were wrong: Qing Manchuria and Mongolia were no less of their time than China proper.

James and others were instead witness to the end of an era. The demographic, political, and economic transformations of the late nineteenth and early twentieth centuries were astounding, and they have captured the imaginations of scholars ever since. The crises of the mid-nineteenth century struck Mongolia and Manchuria particularly hard: When in 1850 troops began to be drafted into the Taiping conflict, participation in the Cicigar *culgan* dropped in half. In 1858 and 1860, with the signing of the Treaties of Aigun and Beijing during the Second Opium War, the Qing court ceded all territory north of the Amur and east of the Ussuri to Russia. In 1881, with the Treaty of St. Petersburg, it granted rights to Russian merchants to live and work in Mongolia. The opening of the treaty ports and the lowering of foreign customs put merchants at new disadvantage to foreign competitors, scrambling commercial networks throughout the North.[30] As the treaty ports grew in stature, so too did their cultural influence; new approaches to nature emerged that represented the power of the sciences.[31] The Qing state struggled to regain control. In 1881, the court signaled a major shift when it legalized ginseng farming to create a new tax revenue in the Northeast.[32] The opening of state-sponsored gold mines in Mongolia and Manchuria in the following decades signaled further change, as the central government entered the business of frontier development. From the 1890s to the 1930s, roughly 25 million people from the Chinese interior immigrated to Manchuria. Commercial and state developers from foreign states built railroads, opened coal mines, industrialized farms, and connected local ecosystems to international wool, lumber, and fertilizer markets. Ginseng pickers became farmers; deer hunters started ranches; sable hunters found new trades.[33]

Yet, despite these myriad changes, the northern reaches of the Qing empire still remain bastions of unspoiled nature in the popular imagination. Associations between national minorities (Ch: *shaoshu minzu*) and unspoiled nature (Ch: *da ziran*) in these regions are boilerplate in the modern People's Republic of China: Buses and clubs play karaoke paeans to Mongolian culture and the steppe; posters depict minorities dancing under pristinely snowcapped mountains; minority-themed restaurants serve wild salmon hotpot; and textbooks describe the Qing emperors as descendants of forest-dwelling tribes. Such stereotypes, of course, are not peculiarly Chinese: They dovetail neatly with the expectations and imagination of foreign tourists who travel to Mongolia and western China.[34] Just as the territorial boundaries of the Qing have gained new meanings in modern times, so too have older divisions between the pure and the corrupted.[35]

Indeed, amid the staggering environmental changes of the post-reform years, many are turning to the "ecological wisdom" of Mongols and other minorities to critique developmentalism.[36] As with Native Americans in the Americas, the invocation of "ecological minorities" in China invokes a specific vision of national heritage. Framing environmental concerns in this way, in fact, carries political weight: China's first environmentalist non-governmental organization (NGO), Friends of Nature, found a place in politics during a campaign to save the Tibetan antelope, or *chiru*—an animal hunted for its underbelly fur to make *shatoosh* scarves. Moved by the *chiru*'s looming extinction, and outraged by reckless overhunting, Liang Congjie, the grandson of the famed revolutionary writer Liang Qichao, helped organize the NGO in 1994; it has worked productively within

China ever since.[37] Environmental protection dovetails with a politics of national renewal.[38]

The national and the natural are everywhere intertwined. In Mongolia, amid a mining boom geared toward the China market, many fear that the most valuable natural resources are being harvested away, and that Mongols themselves are becoming "Chinese": a crude stereotype of a rootless, urban, and emasculated subject.[39] As Franck Billé has argued, many now turn to nature in response: As in the Qing, Mongol identity continues to be rooted in the natural environment and the Mongol countryside (Mo: *hödöö*); it remains the bastion of traditional, rustic, and masculine heritage.[40] Just as striking are efforts to protect this national heritage, in part, by creating nature reserves. Indeed, the expansion of the national parks and reserves in Mongolia and China has almost matched the countries' stunning economic growth over the past two decades: in China alone, the number of these restricted spaces grew from thirty-four in 1978 to over 2,729 by 2014.[41]

Many of these modern parks sit conspicuously on land that the Qing court also attempted to set apart. In China they include Changbaishan National Nature Reserve, which encompasses the mythical homeland of the Manchus, and where the court prohibited any form of hunting, ginseng picking, or pearl collecting. Today, too, government prohibits any form of entry into the reserve except with tickets along designated routes. Likewise, in Mongolia, Gorkhi-Terelj National Park encompasses the old military hunting grounds where no animals could be "spooked," and Bogd Khan Uul, the holy mountain where the *amban*s fought to protect deer and wood from commercial exploitation, is protected as well. Indeed, much of the Left-Wing Front Banner, where Liu Deshan illegally picked mushrooms, today forms Nömrög Strictly Protected Area, a Mongolian natural heritage site. Though grumblings about Chinese poaching continue to be heard in the region, it is difficult for travelers to assess: The Mongolian military maintains a border station nearby, and only licensed biologists may enter the park. The fur-trapping zone of Lake Khövsgöl is protected, too: It sits now within Khövsgöl National Park and houses the Khövsgöl Long-Term Ecological Research Site, one of Mongolia's premier bases for scientific research; tourists generally enter the park via Hatgal, the town built at the *karun* where Uriankhai trappers registered for the annual hunt. In the twenty-first century, visitors can take pictures for cash with a descendant of the Tannu Uriankhai: a reindeer herder who lives in a teepee-shaped tent within the park.[42] In all of these locations, modern "nature" shares a genealogical link to Qing purity.

In all these ways, the Qing empire continues to leave its mark on our modern, globalized world. In *The Unending Frontier*, a pathbreaking work of environmental history, John Richards showed how shared environmental dilemmas transcended national and imperial boundaries in the early modern period, and in a similar vein, scholars such as Kenneth Pomeranz have shown how Qing society inched up to its ecological limits in the early nineteenth century. Across the empire's frontiers—and across what John Richards described as the "unending frontiers" of the early modern world—the production of natural resources boomed, and from Inner to Southeast Asia, and across the Pacific to the Americas, Chinese consumers stood at a pivotal center. A series of commodity rushes enveloped this enormous and diverse region, as consumers gained newfound access to an unprecedented range of goods: sandalwood from Hawaii, bird nests from Borneo, mother-of-pearl from Sulu, copper from Yunnan and Vietnam, nephrite from Xinjiang, jadeite from Burma, sea cucumber from Sulawesi and Fiji, sea otter from California, sable from the Uriankhai, mushrooms from Mongolia, pearls and ginseng from Manchuria. The riches from these trades challenged states to respond. King Kamehameha I in Hawai'i; the Thonburi, Nguyen, and Konbaung kingdoms; the Dutch East India Company; the Russian Empire; and the Qing empire each drew sustenance from, and struggled to claim authority over, the great challenges and opportunities of the age. Each in their own way responded to common dynamics: an expansion of trade; intensified production; new pressures on the land; and, in the most dramatic cases, the extirpation of species.[43]

We cannot understand this history without Qing history and vice versa: Ultimately, frontier history *is* international history, only without the teleology of the nation state and the European states system.[44] Further research on the greater Pacific could offer insights into how to transcend entrenched distinctions between foreign and frontier, north and south, and coast and continent in Chinese history. So many institutions that we associate with border control in the Pacific emerged within Qing territory, only earlier. From California to Australia to Mongolia, nativists even imagined the same Other: the undocumented Chinese migrant.[45]

Much, then, is familiar about the imperial arrangements of the past. Borders and passports, poaching and smuggling, migration and exchange:

We cherish the differences among each other, but what makes us distinct seems perpetually under threat. We are freer to move across boundaries than ever, but the more we move, the more we are monitored and inspected. As some people cross lines, others redouble efforts to build walls. All-under-heaven is united, but uneasily and ambivalently. The environment changes quickly, dramatically, and unnaturally: The problems of empires linger in the modern world.

Appendix

Fur Tribute Submissions, 1771–1910

The First Historical Archives (FHA) in Beijing and the National Palace Museum (NPM) in Taiwan hold tribute records for the Tannu, Altan Nuur, and Altai Uriankhai for the entire period they submitted furs. For the Tannu Uriankhai in particular, Grand Council copies of Manchu palace memorials (Ch: *Junjichu Manwen lufu zouzhe*) are available from 1759 to 1910. The NPM holds copies of these palace memorials for the years 1850 and 1889–1898; the FHA holds the rest.[1] Records from only thirteen years are missing: 1776, 1778, 1786, 1797, 1808, 1819–1821, 1862, 1901–1902, 1907, and 1909.

As discussed in Chapter Four, the military governor's office in Uliasutai compiled tallies for all submitted pelts before their dispatch to Beijing, and the Imperial Household Department compiled a separate tally on their receipt. In Uliasutai, the military governor attached his tally to a Manchu-language palace memorial, and in Beijing, clerks for the Grand Council copied the memorial for their archives. At the time of research these clerical copies are accessible as part of the FHA's *Manwen lufu* collection on microfilm, but today they are available as well through the archive's digital collection. The Imperial Household Department's tallies are in Chinese and accessible through the FHA's *Neiwufu zouxiaodang* collection, available on microfilm. The palace memorials are more detailed than the Imperial Household Department's accounts: They give the quantity and type of pelts submitted by each of the three Uriankhai groups (Tannu, Altan Nuur, and Altai), whereas the Imperial Household Department's records give the aggregate total for all Uriankhai combined (see Chapter Four).

The FHA also holds Manchu-language palace memorials from the military governor of Heilongjiang for the years from 1785 to 1899 on the Cicigar *culgan*. They, too, are accessible on microfilm as part of the *Manwen lufu* collection. The Nationalities Press (*Minzu chubanshe*) published most of these materials in 2001 in the volume *Qingdai Elunchunzu Man-Hanwen dang'an huibian*.[2] The year 1821 was curiously not published but is accessible at the FHA; the years from 1889 to 1894 and 1896 to 1898 have also yet to be published but are available at the National Palace Museum in Taiwan.[3] Taken as a whole, for the period from 1785 to 1899, data for twenty-two years are missing: 1786, 1790, 1799–1813, 1819, 1822, 1857, 1863, and 1876.

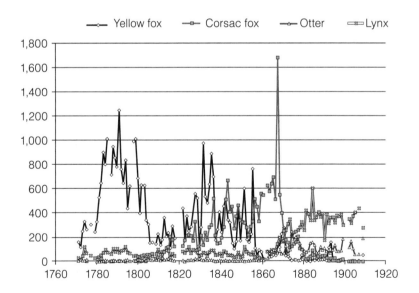

Figure A.1. Tannu Uriankhai submissions of fox, corsac fox, otter, and lynx.

SOURCE: MWLF and NPM-JJCD.

For the Tannu Uriankhai, squirrel pelts served as the primary substitute for sable on the exchange, and fox pelts served as a secondary option. Fox submissions thus followed a similar trajectory as sable: They peaked in 1791 (1,294 pelts) and 1832 (977 pelts), but they dipped dramatically through the 1830s and remained low thereafter, with ten or fewer pelts submitted annually from the 1870s. Corsac fox, marten, and wolf pelts served as the main substitutes for sable, squirrel, and fox beginning in the 1860s. Corsac fox submissions peaked at 1,681 pelts in 1868 but fell dramatically to fewer than 200 annually after 1872; by the 1880s, submissions were no more than 100 pelts per year and usually less than ten per year after 1893. Wolf pelt submissions peaked in 1871; marten submissions peaked in 1864. In the final decades of Qing rule, with all other submissions low, lynx and river otter submissions thus rose dramatically: Otter peaked in 1875 (248 pelts), and lynx peaked in 1885 (604 pelts). Figure A.1 presents the four most important substitutes for sable and squirrel for the Tannu Uriankhai: fox, corsac fox, lynx, and river otter.

Notes

INTRODUCTION

1. James, "A Journey in Manchuria," 539, 542–543.
2. Agassiz, "Our Commercial Relations," 538.
3. "Husos" are a type of sturgeon.
4. Peschurof et al., "Notes on the River Amur," 387.
5. Ravenstein, *The Russians on the Amur*, 96. The quotation comes from a French Catholic missionary, M. de la Brunière, who traveled to the Ussuri region in 1846.
6. Peschurof, 419, 427.
7. Agassiz, 540.
8. Quoted and translated in Elliott, "The Limits of Tartary," 615.
9. Ibid., 616.
10. Chinese history textbooks accordingly begin either with the first human beings or with the advent of agricultural civilization. For Chinese history beginning with human sapiens, see Roberts, *A History of China*, and Bai, *Outline History of China*, 32–34. For recent textbooks that begin with farming, see Huang, *China*, 6, 23, and Ropp, *China in World History*, xiv.
11. For a critical discussion of the region's historical nomenclature, see Elliott, "The Limits of Tartary," 603–646. On the centrality of Manchuria in modern Chinese nationalism, and the resonance of the claim that it is Northeast China, see Mitter, *The Manchurian Myth*.
12. Uyama, "Research Trends," 51. Uyama argues that "the dominant research trend here should be called not only nationalist but also explicitly statist."
13. For works operating in this paradigm, see Lin, *Qingji dongbei yimin shi-bian zhengce zhi yanjiu*; Xu, "Qingmo Heilongjiang yimin yu nongye kaifa"; Yang, *Qingdai dongbeishi*; Zhao, *Jinshi dongsansheng yanjiu lunwenji*; Guan, *Dongbei shaoshu minzu lishi yu wenhua yanjiu*; Wei, *Qingdai jingqi huitun wenti yanjiu*; and Liu, *Qian-Guoerluosi jianshi*. For examples of works operating in the statist paradigm, see Wang, *Dongbei diqu shi shenghuo shi*; Yang, *Mingdai dongbei jiangyu yanjiu*; Isett, *State, Peasant, and Merchant*; Reardon-Anderson, *Reluctant*

Pioneers; Gottschang and Lary, *Swallows and Settlers*; and Lee, *The Manchurian Frontier*. Chinese scholars have more disagreement on the timing of the rise of agriculture in the "Northeast," with many emphasizing that agriculture has existed in the region since prehistory and thus was always Chinese.

14. For the most recent treatment of Manchuria as a frontier that captures this comparative element, see Richards, *The Unending Frontier*. For critical appraisals of the frontier paradigm in the historiography of the American West, see Cronon, *Nature's Metropolis*; Cronon et al., *Under an Open Sky*; Worster, *An Unsettled Country*; White, *"It's Your Misfortune and None of My Own"*; and White, *The Middle Ground*. See also Tsing, "Natural Resources and Capitalist Frontiers," 5101.

15. The field of Chinese environmental history has grown quickly over the past two decades. The most up-to-date critical overviews of the field can be found in Marks, *China*; Wang, *Zhongguo lishishang de huanjing yu shehui*; and Chao, *Shengtai huanjing yu Mingqing shehui jingji*, 1–54. For recent environmental histories of northern frontiers in particular, see Zhao, *Qingdai xibei shengtai bianqian yanjiu*; Zhu, *18-20 shijichu dongbu Neimenggu nongcun luohua yanjiu*; and Han, *Caoyuan yu tianyuan*. For touchstone publications in English, see Elvin and Liu, *Sediments of Time*; Elvin, *The Retreat of the Elephants*; Marks, *Tigers, Rice, Silt, and Silk*; and Perdue, *Exhausting the Earth*.

16. See Burke and Pomeranz, *The Environment and World History*.

17. Ho, *Studies on the Population of China*, 279. Ho Ping-ti estimates that the population of China rose from roughly 150 million in 1700 to 430 million in 1850. For estimated acreage, see Wang, *Land Taxation*, table 1.1, p. 7.

18. The "developmentalist" framework is laid out in Burke and Pomeranz, 3–32, and Pomeranz, "Empire and 'Civilizing' Missions," 34–45.

19. The idea of natural borders was first formalized by Friedrich Ratzel in his influential work, *Politische Geographie* (1897). For contemporaries in agreement, see Brunhes and Vallaux, *La Géographie de l'histoire*, 329–364, and Curzon, *Frontiers*. As August Lösch described the project: "Impressed by the accidental way in which states are created and smashed, we are looking out for a more natural and lasting spatial order of things . . . It is independent economic regions that we here discuss, regions not derived from but equivalent to those political, cultural, geographical units." Lösch, "The Nature of Economic Regions," 107. For a critical survey of the idea of "natural borders," see Fall, "Artificial States," 140–147.

20. See Boldbaatar, *"Mongolchuudyn Baigal,"* 80–98; Gagengaowa and Wuyunbatu, *Menggu minzu de shengtai wenhua*; Ge, *Zhidu shiyuxia de caoyuan shengtai huanjing baohu*; He, *Huanjing yu xiaominzu shengcun*; and Wu and Bao, *Mengguzu shengtai zhihuilun*. For a parallel project on Chinese heritage, see Tucker and Berthrong, *Confucianism and Ecology*. On the German case, see Lekan, *Imagining the Nation in Nature*, and Schama, *Landscape and Memory*.

21. On the southwest, see Giersch, *Asian Borderlands*, and Herman, *Amid the Clouds and Mist*. For Ming antecedents, see Shin, *The Making of the Chinese State*.

22. On the spectrum of state building and identity formation patterns in Qing frontiers, see Crossley et al., *Empire at the Margins*, 1–24.

23. This is not to claim that Chinese and Mongols, for example, did not share a common governing vocabulary. See Atwood, "Worshipping Grace," 86–139.

24. Merchant, "Shades of Darkness," 381. The language of the "vacuum" comes from Fairbank: "In spite of the inevitable overflow of Chinese migrants into the Three Eastern Provinces, Manchuria in effect remained a vacuum down to the late nineteenth century." Fairbank, *Trade and Diplomacy*, 41.

25. Major works on this front include Elliott, *The Manchu Way*; Crossley, *A Translucent Mirror*; Perdue, *China Marches West*; and Rawski, *The Last Emperors*. For a review essay, see Guy, "Who Were the Manchus?" 151–164. For the work that branded this scholarship, see Waley-Cohen, "The New Qing History," 193–206. For recent scholarship from the PRC, see Liu Fengyun, *Qingdai zhengzhi yu guojia renting*.

26. Burbank and Cooper, *Empires in World History*.

27. For a recent examination of Islam and the Qing, see Brophy, "The Junghar Mongol Legacy." On deconstructing the nation in Chinese history, see Duara, *Rescuing History*.

28. Nineteenth-century thinkers held the opposite view: Strength lay in mass militias, so densely populated frontiers were ideal.

29. Farquhar, "The Origins of the Manchus' Mongolian Policy," 198–205; and Di Cosmo and Bao, *Manchu–Mongol Relations*.

30. Elliott, "The Limits of Tartary."

31. For a fascinating new study of Qing environmental history using Manchu-language archives, see Bello, *Across Forest, Steppe, and Mountain*.

32. For recent publications using Manchu sources to write the history of Manchuria, see Tong, *Manyuwen yu Manwen dang'an yanjiu*; Wang, *Yige dengshang longting de minzu*; and Ding et al., *Liaodong yiminzhong de qiren shehui*. For scholars using Mongol and Manchu to study Inner Mongolia, see Liang, *Alashan Menggu yanjiu*; Wurenqiqige, *18–20 shijichu Guihuacheng Tumete caizheng yanjiu*; and Oyunbilig [Wuyunbilige], *Shiqi shiji Menggushi lunkao*.

33. Bartlett, "Books of Revelations," 33; and Crossley and Rawski, "A Profile of the Manchu Language," 63–102.

34. Historians have tackled this issue from multiple perspectives. See Miyazaki, "Shinchō ni okeru kokugo mondai no ichimen," 1–56; Mosca, *From Frontier Policy to Foreign Policy*; and Atwood, "Worshipping Grace," 86–139.

35. Elliott, "Manwen dang'an yu xin Qingshi," 1–18.

36. For a brief overview of the archives and MiDi, see Miyawaki, "Mongoru kokuritsu chūō monjokan shozō no Manjugo, Mongorugo shiryō," 135–141; and Miyawaki, "Report on the Manchu Documents," 6–13.

37. For a critical description of Manchu language archives, see Elliott, "The Manchu-Language Archives," 1–70.

38. I use "eighteenth century" here to refer to China's long eighteenth century, roughly 1681–1840.

39. On the rise of consumer objects as focuses of concern, see Brook, *The Confusions of Pleasure*, and Clunas, *Superfluous Things*. For a fascinating exploration of objects in medical culture into the high Qing, see Bian, *Assembling the Cure*.

40. Relevant, destabilizing works in commodity history are voluminous. For the most recent work in the field, see Beckert, *Empire of Cotton*.

41. Lattimore, *Inner Asian Frontiers*; Khazanov, *Nomads and the Outside World*; Barfield, *The Perilous Frontier*; and Di Cosmo, *Ancient China and Its Enemies*.

42. See Cronon, *Nature's Metropolis*.

43. Ibid., 48–49.

44. On the problematic assumption of the economic view and nomadic dependence, see Di Cosmo, *Ancient China and Its Enemies*.

45. Richards, *The Unending Frontier*.

46. Puett, *The Ambivalence of Creation*. 1–21.

47. For a survey of ideas along these lines, see Ibid.; Cronon, *Changes in the Land*; Guha, *Environmentalism*; Soulé and Lease, *Reinventing Nature?*; Descola, *Beyond Nature and Culture*; and Morton, *Ecology without Nature*.

48. Weller, *Discovering Nature*, 1–18, and Bol and Weller, "From Heaven-and-Earth to Nature," 473–502. Although a constellation of terms circulated in the Qing world that resonated with aspects of the modern idea of "nature"— including "Heaven" (Ch: *tian*; Ma: *abka*; Mo: *tngri*), "landscape" (Ch: *fengshui*), "inborn nature" (Ch: *xing*; Ma: *banin*), "environment" (Mo: *baigali*) and *qi*—as Weller so forcefully argued, it is simply impossible to map the European world of "nature," with all its semantic diversity and implications, neatly onto the Chinese context. For multiple critical looks at the problem of comparison in the history of science and intellectual history, see Vogel et al., *Concepts of Nature*.

49. Merchant, *Reinventing Eden*; and Cronon, "The Trouble with Wilderness," 69–90.

50. The literature on the relationship between identity and origins in the Qing is large. On ethnicity and race, see Crossley, "Manzhou Yuanliu Kao," 761–790; Crossley, *A Translucent Mirror*; and Elliott, *The Manchu Way*. On the interconnections between ethnic, familiar, and corporate associations, see Faure, *Emperor and Ancestor*, and Szonyi, *Practicing Kinship*.

51. Williams, *Keywords*, 169.

52. Cronon, "A Place for Stories," 1347–1376.

53. Latour, *We Have Never Been Modern*, 1–48.

54. Elvin, *The Retreat of the Elephants*; and Burke and Pomeranz, *The Environment and World History*. The important concept of "China-centered" history derives from Cohen, *Discovering History*.

55. For recent work based archival research on Chinese and Manchu documents, see Bello, *Across Forest, Steppe, and Mountain*. For research that captures the diversity of Qing environmental politics, see Perdue, "Nature and Nurture," 245–267.

CHAPTER ONE

1. Pak, *The Jehol Diary*, 189.
2. The queue was a hairstyle marked by a tonsured forehead and braided pigtail.
3. Finnane, "Fashion in Late Imperial China."
4. Difference, at this point, became more genealogical. Crossley, *Orphan Warriors*, 267.
5. Pomeranz, *The Great Divergence*, and Wong, *China Transformed*.
6. For overviews of commercial and social dynamics in the late Ming, see Clunas, *Superfluous Things*, and Brook, *The Confusions of Pleasure*; for the global dimensions of late Ming history, see Brook, *Vermeer's Hat*.
7. Quoted in Finnane, *Changing Clothes in China*, 47.
8. Brook, *Vermeer's Hat*, 70–71.
9. Struve, *Voices from the Ming-Qing Cataclysm*, 51.
10. Clunas, *Superfluous Things*, xv.
11. These issues are studied in depth in Elliott, *The Manchu Way*, and Crossley, *A Translucent Mirror*. On the qualities "plain" (*gulu*) and "pure" (*nomhon*), see Elliott, 284.
12. On the "silver belt" and shared dynamics in the sixteenth and seventeenth centuries, see Kishimoto, "Chinese History and the Concept of 'Early Modernities.'"
13. Kawachi, "Mindai tōhoku Ajia chōhi bōeki," 62–102.
14. Di Cosmo, "The Rise of Manchu Power."
15. Elliott, *The Manchu Way*, 50. Iron smelting began no later than 1599; see Wakeman, *The Great Enterprise*, vol. 1, p. 47. For the argument that fur trade underpinned agriculture, see Kawachi, "Mindai tōhoku Ajia chōhi bōeki," 93–100.
16. For a summary description of these events, see Wakeman, *The Great Enterprise*.
17. The sensibility was not unique to the Qing; it was common throughout Eurasia. Allsen, *The Royal Hunt*. See Conclusion.
18. See Spence, *Emperor of China*, 9.
19. Elliott, *Emperor Qianlong*, 8. All ages in this book are converted from *sui*, which counts the first year of life as year one, the second year as year two, and so on.
20. Spence, *Emperor of China*, 123.
21. Elliott, *The Manchu Way*, 186.
22. Wu, *Qianlong huangdi yushan kaoshu*, 27.
23. Ibid., 28.

24. Spence, *Emperor of China*, 98.
25. On venison trays to members of the Imperial Household Department, see NWFZXD 132.461.76 (JQ18.9.5); on gifts to empresses and concubines, see 132.461.7 (JQ18.9.9). On the prestige surrounding imperial gifts of deer tail, see Bartlett, *Monarchs and Ministers*, 58, 220.
26. NWFZXD 134.471.57 (JQ20.8.23). The Imperial Household Department (Ch: *Neiwufu*; Ma: *Dorgi baita be uheri kadalara yamun*) managed the emperor's personal finances, the imperial family, and members of the inner court, among other activities. See Torbert, *The Ch'ing Imperial Household Department*, and Qi Meiqin, *Qingdai neiwufu*.
27. NWFZXD 132.460.177 (JQ18.7.19), and NWFZXD 134.471.133 (JQ20.7.22).
28. NWFZXD 132.461.79 (JQ18.9.5).
29. NWFZXD 133.462.236 (JQ18.12.15).
30. He ate the salt-fried meat with steppe mushrooms on the afternoon of October 16, 1778 (QL43.8.26).
31. *Jiaqing dongxun jishi*, in *Liaohai congshu*, 1: 2547b.
32. *Yushandan*, passim.
33. Wu, *Qianlong huangdi yushan kaoshu*, 125. Note also Wu, 33.
34. MBRT 1.45.653.
35. Cammann, *China's Dragon Robes*, 21, and Cammann "Origins of the Court," 199–200.
36. Zhao-lian, *Xiaoting zalu*, 1: 392.
37. Tan, *Beiyoulu*, 349.
38. Xu, *Qingbai leichao*, 6126. See the case of the Yongzheng emperor's 108-bead rosary made of eastern pearls, which in 2010 sold for 8.7 million HKD at a Sotheby's auction in Hong Kong. "A Very Important and Magnificent Imperial Pearl Court Necklace."
39. Xu, *Qingbai leichao*, 6129.
40. See, for example, MBRT 3.32.1360–1361.
41. DQHDSL 4: 835a-b.
42. The Manchu word *jušen* is usually translated as "slave," not "Jurchen." "Jurchen" may serve as a better translation in this case. In 1665, the Kangxi emperor presented a sable gown, described as a *jušen seke dokoi unduraku sijigiyan*, to a Mongol nobleman (Ma: *Kalkai dargan cin wang*) on the occasion of a New Year's banquet. The man received a range of other precious gifts, including a dyed sable-fur hat and gold. In this context, it seems unlikely *jušen* meant "slave." See NWFZXD 3.17.233 (KX3.12.27).
43. NWFZXD 3.17.183 (KX3.10.3).
44. MBRT 1.10.160. Cited and translated in Elliott, *The Manchu Way*, 68.
45. NWFZXD 134.467.229 (JQ19.12.8), and 133.463.279 (JQ19.1.2).
46. NWFZXD 133.462.110 (JQ18.12.12). Like precious furs, these woolens were kept in the Fur Treasury. Three types of wool were given: coarse wool, wool sateen, and Tibetan wool.

47. NWFZXD 3.17.233 (KX3.12.27). Another standard gift that came with fur was the *kaiciri*, a toothpick box hung from one's belt.

48. See, for example, the list of items presented in NWFZXD 3.19.71 (KX4.7.3).

49. For extensive lists of tribute items for each individual for each year, see *Daicing gürün ü dotuǧadu yamun* 2: 209, 218, 243, 245, 278, 383, 386, 473, 475, 477–480. In 1680 (KX19), for example, Kharachin, Qonggirad, Khorchin, and Jalaid Mongols all presented birds of prey as tribute.

50. Matsuura, 409. The price of the foxes was 262.1 taels.

51. MWLF 3667.47.171.2651 (JQ9.4.8).

52. Ibid. The document fails to discuss what happened to these tigers in Beijing. Further research will be necessary into the lives of living animals presented as tribute.

53. MWLF 3724.25.176.2118 (JQ12.5.20). Two months later, when the names arrived, the emperor finally bestowed his gifts: Five men received a large roll of silken gauze; nine received small rolls. MWLF 3724.32.176.2160 (JQ12.7).

54. MWLF 3727.28.176.2985 (JQ12.8.17).

55. Elliott, *The Manchu Way*, 284–290.

56. Mitamura, *Shinchō zenshi no kenkyū*, 174–177.

57. Sonoda, *Datta hyōryūki*, 21, 27.

58. MBRT 1.45.653.

59. Ibid., 1.40.592.

60. Ibid., 3.12.1056-1057.

61. Fuge, *Tingyu congtan*, 2: 47. Imperial *efu* also wore a single eastern pearl on their finial. Xu, *Qingbai leichao*, 6132.

62. He, *Shuofang beisheng*, 1.27b.

63. Finnane, *Changing Clothes in China*.

64. MiDi-3833.35 (DG6.9.29).

65. MiDi-3833.33 (DG6.10.1).

66. TGKH 55: 12a.

67. MiDi-3697.34a (JQ25.3.1).

68. James Howard-Johnston argues that, prior to the Abbasid revolution, with its roots in Khorasan, the classical Mediterranean empires associated furs less with legitimate power than with Goths, Huns, Franks, and Vikings. Howard-Johnston, "Trading in Fur," 70–74.

69. Appadurai, "Introduction," 3–63. For a broader critical entry point into material culture studies, see Miller, "Materiality," 1–50.

70. Finnane, "Barbarian and Chinese," 33–43. See page 37 for the quotation.

71. Ibid., 37. Translation by Rorex and Fong, *Eighteen Songs of a Nomad Flute*.

72. Translated in Franke, "Chinese Texts on the Jurchen," 127.

73. Ouyang Xun, *Yiwen leiju*, 67: 1184.

74. Schafer, *The Golden Peaches of Samarkand*, 107. See also Li Qi's "Song below the Border," which commemorated "a thousand horsemen in black sable

furs." Quoted in Ibid., 108. The poem is from the *Quantangshi, han* 2, *ce* 9, 1: 1a. Schafer's use of "Tatar" is more literary than historical; "Tatar frontier" is anachronistic for the Tang period.

75. Finnane, *Changing Clothes in China*, 46; Finnane cites Chen Baoliang, *Mingdai shehui shenghuo shi*, 206–207. I thank Christopher Atwood for the connection between *zhisun* and *jisün*.

76. *Sejong sillok*, 50. In a debate three years earlier, in 1427, on the appropriate role of sable at the Chosŏn court, it was noted that "previous courts valued sable fur most." Ibid., 38. On sumptuary regulations see Kawachi, "Mindai tōhoku Ajia chōhi bōeki," 67.

77. Ch'iu, "Baonuan, huiyao yu quanshi," 555–631. See also Farquhar, "Oirat-Chinese Tribute Relations," 60–68.

78. Kawachi, "Mindai tōhoku Ajia chōhi bōeki," 64–65.

79. Li, *Bencao gangmu*, 51: 2910. Li Shizhen also quotes the Song dynasty scholar Luo Yuan (1136–1184) to characterize sable: "This rodent (Ch: *shu*) likes to eat millet and pine bark. Barbarians [thus] call it the millet rat or pine dog." On categorization and empirical observation in the *Bencao Gangmu*, see Nappi, *The Monkey and the Inkpot*, 12–49.

80. Li, *Bencao gangmu*, 51: 2910.

81. Ibid., 51: 2896.

82. Kawachi, "Mindai tōhoku Ajia chōhi bōeki," 66.

83. See the observations of Zhang Tao in Mitamura, *Shinchō zenshi no kenkyū*, 174–177.

84. *Huang Ming tiaofa shilei zuan*, in Liu and Yang, *Zhongguo zhenxi falü dianji jicheng* 22.16, 4.988. I thank Michael Szonyi for generously providing the reference.

85. On the Mongols as focal points of early modern resistance, see Atwood, "The Mongol Empire."

86. Tan, *Beiyoulu*, 383.

87. D'Orléans, *History of the Two Tartar Conquerors of China*, 24.

88. Rutt, "James Gale's Translation," 102. Kim Ch'angŏp went on the solstitial embassy to Beijing in 1712–1713 and kept a record of the trip in his *Kajae yŏnhaengnok*; his older brother Kim Ch'angjip was the ambassador. See Ledyard, "Hong Tae-yong," 85.

89. Rutt, "James Gale's Translation," 102.

90. Translated in Rutt, "James Gale's Translation," 111–112.

91. Ibid., 143.

92. Finnane, *Changing Clothes in China*, 19–41.

93. Hong, *Tamhŏn yŏngi*, in *Yŏnhaengnok chŏnjip*, 49: 93–95.

94. I have been unable to identify any use of the word prior to the Qing period, though given its Mongolian etymology, *shelisun* may have had earlier precedents in the Yuan or the Ming periods. Cf. the Manchu word *silun*.

95. On Shen Qiliang, see Saarela, "*Shier zitou jizhou*," 10–11.

96. DQQS 3.7a, 3.8a, 3.41a, 3.43a, 4.4a, 4.28b, 5.7b, 5.8a, 5.32b, 6.7a, 6.38a, 6.43b, 11.48a, 11.59b, 13.8a, 13.22a, 13.38b.

97. Tulišen, *Lakcaha jecen de takūraha babe ejehe bithe*, 23. The character used for *lu* is not listed in the *Hanyu dacidian*. It is composed of a fish radical on the left and the character *lu* on the right.

98. Ibid., 52, 54, 61. Chuang Chi-fa notes the discrepancy for *isi* and *shansong*, pointing to *luoye song* (lit. "falling leaf pine") as a more accurate translation of the Manchu. Tulišen, 54n53.

99. Ibid., 52.

100. Ibid., 54.

101. The following discussion is based on the *Han-i araha Manju Monggo gisun-i buleku bithe*, 1: *gurgu i hacin* 2–4. For a description of the text, see Volkova, *Opisanie Man'chzhurskikh khisolografov*, 103. The bilingual edition of 1717 is based on a monolingual 1708 Manchu edition. I thank Baoyintegusi at Inner Mongolia University for the reference.

102. Struve, *Voices from the Ming-Qing Cataclysm*, 1–2.

103. Elliott, *The Manchu Way*, 23.

104. On "Manchu Apartheid," see Wakeman, *The Great Enterprise*, vol. 1, 476.

105. Ibid., 647–650.

106. Struve, *Voices from the Ming–Qing Cataclysm*, 64. Compare with a missionary's claim that the Manchus looked *more* human.

107. Fuge, *Tingyu congtan*, 2: 47. Beyond hats and hairpieces, Manchurian pearls came to figure into a range of jewelry and decorative and ritual items, such as rosaries.

108. QSL SZ, 57: 451.

109. QSL QL, 746: 211b.

110. QSL TZ, 40: 524, 45: 593, 62: 850.

111. QSL SZ, 81: 637.

112. QSL KX, 215: 181; QSL YZ, 76: 1126; QSL GZ, 104: 563.

113. See, for example, QSL YZ, 113: 509, 111: 476, 112: 495–496, 113: 509, 116: 544–545; QSL JQ, 109: 818, 109: 818, 177: 768; QSL DG, 55: 712, 89: 173–174, 132: 19.

114. There were only a few notable cases of Chinese civil officials receiving furs in the seventeenth century. In 1646, in the immediate aftermath of the conquest of Beijing, the court presented eminent Ming scholar-statesmen who had come over to the Qing, such as Hong Chengchou, with 200 sable pelts for his service. QSL SZ, 8: 85.

115. QSL YZ, 17: 284.

116. Ibid., 40: 586. From the entry in the *Veritable Records*, it is unclear whether the *Tongjian gangmu* was in Manchu, Chinese, or both languages. On the Inner Asian history of the text, see Mosca, "The Manchu *Zizhi tongjian gangmu*."

117. QSL GZ, 61: 9.

118. DQHDSL 4: 462b.

119. QSL GZ, 385: 540.

120. These materials have all been published in the series *Gongzhongdang Yongzhengchao zouzhe*. For originals see NPM GZDYZ 402003433 (YZ13.5.28); 402009004 (YZ5.5.12); 402008079 (YZ2.*4.21); 402017576 (YZ7.1.8); 402001497 (YZ5.8.12); 402001498 (YZ7.1.24); 402003919 (YZ13.6.26); 402008503 (YZ5.5.26); 402013700 (YZ4.12.29); 402001067 (YZ13.2.2); 402005221 (YZ7.9.15); 402012234 (YZ7.6.12); 402001060 (YZ11.2.24); 402012139 (YZ1.12.3); 402018465 (YZ2.2.18); 402001746 (YZ7.7.8); 402002398 (YZ11.1.20); 402003678 (YZ2.8.4); 402008792 (YZ7.4.26); 402002055 (YZ13.2.12); 402003512 (YZ13.*4.21); 402014194 (YZ7.12.2); 402005336 (YZ3.8); 402005278 (YZ13.1.4); 402011892 (YZ6.10.27); 402012074-1 (YZ7.11.16); 402015705 (YZ7.1.17); 402009487 (YZ1.6.3); 402011572 (YZ7.3.3); 402008984 (YZ6.1.26); 402014524 (YZ7.11.12); 402014526 (YZ7.12.24); 402014951 (YZ3.2.16); 402004569 (YZ7.4.11); 402004553 (YZ11.3.7); 402009440 (YZ2.5.18); 402009532 (YZ6.12.25); 402009536 (YZ7.7.22); 402009547 (YZ7.11.26); 402021491–402021492 (YZ7.*7.28); 402001427 (YZ9.1.6); 402001718 (YZ3.2.1); 402001738 (YZ13.3.20); 402016168 (YZ12.1.6); 402016177 (YZ12.10.25); 402004206 (YZ7.9.28); 402002419 (YZ7.7.9); 402020722 (YZ2.1.25); 402002442 (YZ7.9.28); 402001740 (YZ12.3.12); 402009269 (YZ5.1.25); 402010327 (YZ4.7.13); 402002135 (YZ7.7.18); 402006208 (YZ4.12.21); 402012575 (YZ2.11.21); and 402012576 (YZ2.12.22).

121. QSL YZ, 71: 1066.

122. QSL GZ, 879: 772, 917: 296, 1100: 734, 1102: 752, and 1119: 944.

123. Ibid., 1130: 112–113, and 1309: 646.

124. Ibid., 383: 39. As with women, most elderly fathers who received sable birthday gifts were the parents of notable officials; cases recorded of commoners receiving gifts were relatively few.

125. Chun, "Sino-Korean Tributary Relations," 90–111.

126. QSL GZ, 201: 582.

127. DQHDSL 6: 866a-b, 897a, 875b, 899b.

128. Crossley, *Orphan Warriors*, 228. See the final words of the book, which references "an inner difference which has no outward sign."

129. Du Halde, *The General History of China*, 120. His masterwork, *The General History of China*, was published first in French in 1735. I have cited the English translation published six years later, in 1741.

130. Ripa, *Memoirs of Father Ripa*, 49.

131. Ibid., 49–50.

132. Leping, *Muwa gisun*, 15b. The text, housed in the Harvard–Yenching Library is undated, though the eighteenth century or the first half of the nineteenth century is a reasonable guess. For a description of the text, see Elliott and Bosson, "Highlights of the Manchu–Mongolian Collection," 85.

133. Xu, *Dumen jilue*, 333.

134. Ibid., 594.

135. Ibid., 613.

136. Ibid., 285–288, 297. Two shops specializing in winter hats were Majuxing, in the Dongxi pailou neighborhood, and Yongzengju, outside Qianmen. Shops named Majuyuan and Dongzhaokui, also located outside Qianmen, specialized in the neck-warmer trade. Note also Leiwanchun tang, in Liulichang, selling deer horn and tiger bone paste.

137. Abe, *Shindaishi no kenkyū*, 371–409. The ubiquity of pawnshops characterized the Qing period, with the number of shops totaling roughly 19,000 in the mid-eighteenth century to 25,000 in the early nineteenth.

138. Translation from Lao She, *Blades of Grass*, 74.

139. Vorha, *Lao She and the Chinese Revolution*, 11. See Muscolino's discussions of financial institutions and the role of credit institutions, including pawnshops, in "overcoming . . . slippage between environmental and business cycles." Muscolino, *Fishing Wars*, 70.

140. NWFZXD 3.17.226 (KX3.12.4).

141. Ibid.

142. Elliott, *The Manchu Way*, 284.

143. QSL YZ, 35: 534a,b.

144. Ibid.

145. Li, *Qiludeng, passim.*

146. Pu, *Xingshi yinyuan chuan*, 1, 12.

147. Ibid., 66.

148. The original author, Cao Xueqin, died around 1763 or 1764 with the manuscript uncompleted. The manuscript was revised and reprinted in 1791.

149. Cao, *Hongloumeng*, 6: 116, 19: 300.

150. Ibid., 63: 988–989. "Yelü" is the family name of the Khitan imperial family in the Liao dynasty.

151. Ibid., 150: 1601.

152. Clunas, *Superfluous Things*, 12.

153. Pu, *Xingshi yinyuan chuan*, 861.

154. *Shuntian fuzhi* (GX12, reprinted GX15), 50 (*shihuozhi er*): 1490.

155. *Lun piyi cuxi maofa*, 129–168.

156. Ibid., 158–161. Curiously, domestic pelts seem to have gone further; a robe required 180 "imported sables," for example, but only 150 of the black domestic variety.

157. He, *Shuofang beisheng, shou* 5.17b

158. *Lun piyi cuxi maofa*, 129–168. The Qing *chuanwo* and *saoshu* do not correspond to any clear, modern categories of animal, and so I have left them in transliteration.

159. Ruan, *Chayu kehua*, in *Biji xiaoshuo daguan*, v. 1.3, p. 9.3-4. On Ruan Kuisheng and his milieu, see Mosca, "Empire and the Circulation of Frontier Intelligence," 178–179.

160. Ruan, *Chayu kehua*, in *Biji xiaoshuo daguan*, v.1.3, p. 9.3–4.

161. On the cartographic project, see Millward, "Coming onto the Map," 61–98.

162. Ke, *Liaojinyuan gongci*, 2: 1.51, 62. Note the protagonist wears an otter-fur coat and sable hat in 2:51.

163. Gu, *Yuanshixuan, chuji*: 54, 66, 97, 109, 364, 405, 879, 904, 925, 974, 1079, 1095, 1195, 1238, 1269, 1326, 1336, 1459, 1489, 1525, 1763, 1891, 1896, 2082, 2190, 2218, 2301; *erchu*: 163, 466, 522, 590, 680, 827, 1363; *sanchu*: 328, 447, 578. For sable coats in a Yuan biography, see Li, *Taiping guangji*, 323: 2562.

164. See Ye, *Qidan guozhi*, 10: 102, 26: 246; *Da Jin guozhi jiaozheng*, 1: 11; Tuo-tuo, *Songshi*, 145: 3407. In the late Ming, the court assumed that the pearls came from saltwater pearl oysters and called them "sea-pearls" (Ch: *haizhu*). *Ming Shenzong shilu*, 519: 9775 and 284: 7223.

165. *Da Jin guozhi jiaozheng, fulu*: 3, 613.

166. Ibid. On gyrfalcons, see Allsen, *The Royal Hunt*, 246.

167. *Qinding Rehe zhi*, 92: 32b. The *Jianping xianzhi* (1931), the gazetteer for a Liaoning county located halfway between Chifeng and Chaoyang in the heart of mushroom-picking country (see Chapter 4), mentioned these three names for the mushroom but added the colloquial "horse dung buds" (Ch: *mafen bao*) as another, elaborating that they were "a type of white autumn mushroom." See *Jianping xianzhi*, 3.9a.

168. *Qinding Rehe zhi*, 92: 32b.

169. *Chengde fuzhi*, 18: 11a,b.

170. Wu, *Youzhengwei zhaiji*, 8: 9a.

171. Bin-liang, *Baochongzhai shiji*, 13: 82a.

172. Ibid.

173. Cui, *Wuwenji*, 3: 15a. The quotation belongs to the historian Cui Shu (1740–1816). Although he wrote that Kalgan's imported steppe mushroom's "name rang out above all," he personally thought the local "chicken leg" mushrooms in Hebei were superior.

174. In Zhili, the gazetteers of Fengrui, Mizhi, Ba, Xushui, Ninghe, Shunyi, Shuntian, Hailong, and Chaoyang counties all compared their local mushrooms to the *koumo*; they were either as good or purportedly better. *Fengrui xianzhi*, 9:45a; *Mizhi xianzhi* 9; *Baxian xinzhi* 4:43; *Ninghe xianzhi* 15:34a; *Shunyi xianzhi* 9:9a; *Shuntian fuzhi* 50:6b; *Hailong xianzhi*, 15:6b; *Chaoyang xianzhi*, 27:5a.

175. Worster, "Transformations."

176. For a recent overview of agricultural expansion and its environmental context, see Marks, *China: Its Environment and History*, 169–222. A touchstone study remains Perdue, *Exhausting the Earth*.

177. Wang, *Land Taxation*, 6–7.

178. For a recent critical survey of the "ecological shadow" of high-Qing consumption, see Marks, *China: Its Environment and History*, 224–227.

179. Korsak, *Istoriko-statisticheskoe obozrienie*, 67, 73, 97, 105.

180. Giersch, *Asian Borderlands*, 107.

181. Ibid., 172–173.

182. On Cochin China, see Li, "The Water Frontier," 3. On Sulu, see Warren, *The Sulu Zone*, 9. On the coastal trade as a whole, see Blussé, "Junks to Java," 211–258.

183. Cranmer-Byng and Wills, "Trade and Diplomacy," 236–237.

184. Millward, *Beyond the Pass*, 185. On jadeite versus nephrite, see Millward, 180. In 1821 the Daoguang emperor canceled the jade tribute on grounds that the treasury already was overstocked.

185. Sun, "From *Baoshi* to *Feicui*," 212–214. The earliest evidence of jade trade with Burma dates to 1719.

186. High and Schlesinger, "Rulers and Rascals," 289–304.

187. Sun, "Ch'ing Government and the Mineral Industries before 1800," 840–842. Qing policies mattered on this front: The Qing government mandated that officials promote the opening of "auxiliary mines" if older ones failed to make quota in 1777, contributing to the growth.

188. Li, "Between Mountains and the Sea," 71–72.

189. Reid, "Chinese Trade and Southeast Asian Economic Expansion," 23–25.

190. Chun, "Sino–Korean Tributary Relations," 108. On tribute, see Rutt 136, 139.

191. HFYD 14: 236; 16: 80, 219, 316; 23: 90, 28: 64, and 29: 156.

192. Sutherland, "A Sino-Indonesian Commodity Chain," 185–188. In the Sulu Sultanate "flotillas of fifty to one hundred" small boats scoured the coast in early summer, with 20,000 men involved in its production. Warren, *The Sulu Zone*, 70.

193. Macknight, *The Voyage to Marege'*, 14, 16, 97.

194. Sutherland, "The Sino–Indonesian Commodity Chain," 177–178, 185. The trade had begun as early as the mid-sixteenth century and survived multiple attempts by the Dutch East India Company, beginning in 1727, to restrict it.

195. Warren, *The Sulu Zone*, 62. Bird's nest trade with Borneo, like other trades, had roots that extended back to at least the early eighteenth century.

196. Gibson, *Otter Skins*, 255.

197. Ibid., 254–257; Warren, *The Sulu Zone*, 72–74, 83; McNeill, "Of Rats and Men," 322; and Matsuda, *Pacific Worlds*, 189.

198. Marks, *China*, 224. On the concept of "shadow ecologies," see Dauvergne, *Shadows in the Forest*.

199. We can integrate, that is, the histories of Southeast Asia's "Chinese Century," the "world that Canton made" in the Pacific, and the histories of Qing frontiers in the post Dzungar period. See Matsuda, *Pacific Worlds*, 176, and Blussé, "Junks to Java," 223.

200. Du Halde, *The General History of China*, 120.

CHAPTER TWO

1. MWLF 4045.37.197.1818 (DG7.3.25).

2. For works operating in this paradigm, see Lin, *Qingji dongbei yimin shibian zhengce zhi yanjiu*; Yang, *Qingdai dongbeishi*; Zhao, *Jinshi dongsansheng yanjiu lunwenji*; Guan, *Dongbei shaoshu minzu lishi yu wenhua yanjiu*; Wei, *Qingdai jingqi huitun wenti yanjiu*; Reardon-Anderson, *Reluctant Pioneers*; Gottschang and Lary, *Swallows and Settlers*; and Lee, *The Manchurian Frontier*.

3. See Timothy Mitchell's analysis of whether mosquitoes can "speak" in Mitchell, *Rule of Experts*, 19–53.

4. Elliott, "The Limits of Tartary," 615–617. For a copy of the text, see Klaproth, *Chrestomathie Mandchou*.

5. Millward, *Beyond the Pass*, 51.

6. On the court's anxieties about assimilation and its significance, see Elliott, *The Manchu Way*, and Crossley, *A Translucent Mirror*.

7. Pomeranz and Topic, *The World That Trade Created*, 41.

8. On the significance of the gradient, see Lattimore, *Nomads and Commissars*, 29. The twenty-inch line is roughly the same gradient that divides the badlands from farmlands in the United States.

9. Today the landscape conforms to both the landscape of the North China plain and the spatial pattern described by G. William Skinner. Skinner, "Marketing and Social Structure," 3–43.

10. Han, *Caoyuan yu tianyuan*.

11. *Qinding Shengjing tongzhi*, juan 33. Cited in Kawakubo, "Shinmatsu ni okeru Kirinshō seihokubu no kaihatsu," 154–166. For an extensive overview of migration and land reclamation through the mid-Qing, see Lin, *Qingji dongbei yimin shibian zhengce zhi yanjiu*, 17–203.

12. Kawakubo, "Shinmatsu ni okeru Kitsurin shō seihokubu no kaihatsu," 149–154. To supply the troops, each garrison also served as an agricultural base, and farmland was opened up around them, using in part slave labor to bolster production.

13. For an overview based in part on Manchu sources, see Wei, *Qingdai jingqi huitun wenti yanjiu*.

14. They also thrived in the smaller Tumen River watershed.

15. Mitamura, *Shinchō zenshi no kenkyū*, 174–177.

16. Jin Xin, "Lun Qingdai qianqi Dawoer, Ewenkezu de shangpin jingji," 129–135; and Kim, "Marginal Constituencies," 141–142.

17. Matsuura, *Shinchō no Amūru seisaku to shōsū minzoku*, 146–187.

18. Matsuura makes this point vividly. On connections to the Korea trade, see Terauchi, "Kyŏngwŏn *kaesi* to Hunchun," 85.

19. Di Cosmo, "The Rise of Manchu Power," 47:30.

20. Mitamura, *Shinchō zenshi no kenkyū*, 156–157, 168–176. To Mitamura, even the story of Nurhaci teaching his subjects how to properly preserve ginseng

is an example of Nurhaci learning how to master markets: His key lesson was how to get the highest price. Mitamura's argument is taken up in Iwai, "Jūroku, jūnana seiki no Chūgoku henkyō shakai," 635–636. More research is needed on Manchuria in earlier eras; the degree to which some of these "early modern" dynamics may have been in play before the Ming remains obscure.

21. The following model of conquest derives from Yanagasiwa, "Shinchō tōchiki no kokuryūkō chiku ni okeru shominzoku no keisei saihen, katei no kenkyū," 7–9.

22. For full accounts of the Eight Banners, see Elliott, *The Manchu Way*, and Ding, *Qingdai baqi zhufang yanjiu.*

23. When a fire struck the Qiqihar "shop street" area in 1741, an estimated 355 housing units (Ch: *jian*) were destroyed, a testimony to the growing size of trade. Jin, "Lun Qingdai qianqi Dawoer, Ewenkezu de shangpin jingji," 129–130.

24. In 1776, the Qianlong emperor reprimanded a memorialist for calling Mukden a "province" (Ch: *sheng*). As he tut-tutted, Mukden was "incomparable with a province" (Ch: *fei gesheng kebi*), and it was a mistake to call the Three Eastern Territories the "Three Eastern Provinces." QSL QL, 1007 (QL41.4). The three territories of Mukden, Ningguta, and Sahaliyan Ula only later became the three provinces of Liaoning, Jilin, and Heilongjiang we know today. Qing territories and today's provinces, however, are not the same; the territories were governed in the Manchu language, and their borders did not overlap with today's provincial borders. At the risk of introducing unnecessary confusion for the reader, I have followed the documents, resisted a final act of translation, and used the Manchu names for the territories in this book.

25. Elliott, "The Limits of Tartary," 603–617. As Elliott shows, Mukden found its way onto Jesuit and Japanese maps almost immediately as "Chinese Tartary" or "Manchuria." Ibid., 619-632.

26. He, *Shuofang beicheng, shou* 6.17a, 8.7b. Kangxi identified the "Sahaliyan-Sunggari corridor" and lands contested by the Russians by the Amur as "extremely close to our dynastic homeland [Ch: *faxiang zhi di*]."

27. Elliot, "The Limits of Tartary," 618–619.

28. Lee, *The Manchurian Frontier*, 32, 50, 56.

29. Ibid., 50. Six publications endorsed by the court between the years 1727 and 1821 estimated the number of men from the regular Eight Banners in Sahaliyan Ula (as opposed to the Butha Eight Banners) at between six and seven thousand men. See Sutō, "Shinchō ni okeru Manshū chūbō no tokushūsei ni kansuru ichi kōsatsu," 185–194.

30. It is impossible to generalize about the myriad practices described by the word. Depending on the context, tribute could involve foreigners choosing to participate or Qing subjects forced to by law; it could be a form of exploitation or largesse; it could involve irregular trips to Beijing or regular visits to your home community. For the most recent overviews, see He Xinhua, *Zuihou de tianchao*, and Kim, "Tribute Data Curation." For discussions of tribute in Qing Inner

Asia in particular, see Di Cosmo, "Nomads on the Qing Frontier," 351–372, and Onuma, "Political Relations," 86–125.

31. Matsuura, *Shinchō no Amūru seisaku to shōsū minzoku*, 227. Korean texts called the "Hūrha" the "Orangkae" (pronounced "Wu-rang-hai" in Mandarin); they are etymological cousins of the Uriankhai discussed in Chapter Four. On the Uriankhai, see Crossley, "An Introduction," 3–24. On the Hūrha, see Terauchi, "Kyŏngwŏn *kaesi* to Hunchun," 76–77.

32. Matsuura, *Shinchō no Amūru seisaku to shōsū minzoku*, 224.

33. Based on a survey of sacked Warka villages in the *Manwen laodang*. MBRT 2.60.278 (TZ6.12.12), 3.5.955 (TZ10.3); 3.7.990 (TZ10.4.10); 3.8.995 (CD1.4); 3.8.995 (CD1.4.15); 3.9.1023 (CD1.5.27); and 3.10.1036 (CD1.5.5).

34. Terauchi, "Kyŏngwŏn *kaesi* to Hunchun," 76–90. Hunchun had been devastated in 1607 during the conflict among Nurhaci, Ula, and Chosŏn Korea.

35. Diao Shuren gives the animals as *haita* and *haidiao*. Diao, "Qingdai Yan-Hun diqu zhufang baqi luelun," 55.

36. Matsuura, *Shinchō no Amūru seisaku to shōsū minzoku*, 285–300.

37. Jin Xin, "Qingdai Dawoer, Ewenke liangzu suo shiyong de falü," 121–128. The *butha* banners coalesced around refugees from the Upper Amur region that fled south to the Nen River Valley during the 1640s, during Hong Taiji's first raids on the Amur, and again during the Russo–Qing conflict of the 1670s and 1680s. Between 1684 and 1691, these transplants, which included remnants of the "Solon" confederation and its mostly Ewenki and Daur communities and the confederation's subject Barga Mongols, were either incorporated into Eight Banner garrisons or placed into "hunter" units. Although at first the Qing court governed them like Mongols and tried their legal cases through the Lifanyuan, through 1695 they were moved gradually to the jurisdiction of the Sahaliyan Ula military governor and tried according to the Qing Code as people of "the interior" (Ma: *dorgi harangga ba*). In 1732, amid the Yongzheng-era intensification of the Dzungar wars, the Qing court endorsed a plan to create the new "Butha Eight Banners." Jin, "Qingdai buteha baqi jianli shijian ji niulu shue xinkao," 83, 85.

38. Jin, "Qingdai buteha baqi jianli shijian ji niulu shue xinkao," 77.

39. The Butha Eight Banners were administered through an *uheri da* (Ch: *zongguan*), a position comparable to Mongol *jasag*s; they were at first an inherited position from Chongde-era collaborators with the Hong Taiji court but gradually bureaucratized from the 1660s to 1732. Jin, "Qingdai qianqi buteha zongguan yange tanxi," 82–95.

40. For a synopsis of these groups and their histories through the mid-eighteenth century, see Ochirin Oyunjargal, *Manzh-Chin ulsaas Mongolchuudig zakhirsan bodlogo*; Yanagasiwa, "Shinchō tōchiki no kokuryūkō chiku ni okeru shominzoku no keisei saihen, katei no kenkyū"; and Kim, "Marginal Constituencies." The Daur appear to be the descendants of the Khitans who assimilated with Mongols after collapse of the Liao dynasty; the name of the Khitan state, in Khitan, was "Daur Gurun"—the Daur Empire. Atwood, *Encyclopedia*, 135–137.

41. Yanagasiwa, "Shinchō tōchiki no kokuryūkō chiku ni okeru shominzoku no keisei saihen katei no kenkyū," 8–9. Also included among the *butha* banners were the Birar, a subdivision of the Oroncon.

42. The following section is based largely on Matsuura, *Shinchō no Amūru seisaku to shōsū minzoku*.

43. Ibid., 297–299, 311–318. We perhaps can imagine, along these lines, a Northeast Asian "Zomia," centered in the Lower Amur region. See Scott, *The Art of Not Being Governed*.

44. Matsuura, *Shinchō no Amūru seisaku to shōsū minzoku*, 227–232, 265– 266. Although the position of *halai da* was supposed to be inherited, in practice the Qing court had little authority to dictate the terms of inheritance, and clans decided inheritors for themselves.

45. Matsuura, *Shinchō no Amūru seisaku to shōsū minzoku*, 146–187.

46. Ibid., 175, 179, 213.

47. Such an arrangement was not atypical: The court laid special claim on other commodities in the Northeast as well, including sturgeon, much as it did so with an array of valuable products throughout the empire, such as jade in Xinjiang, timber in Jiangxi, and furs throughout the north. For jade, see Millward, *Beyond the Pass*, 18. On timber, see Chang, "The Economic Role of the Imperial Household," 255. For sturgeon, see MWLF 3555.18.163.620 (JQ1.11.8); 3555.31.163.685 (JQ1.11.12); 3574.31.164.144 (JQ2.10.26); 3574.48.164.1541 (JQ2.11.4); 3587.34.165.2156 (JQ3.11.2); and 3589.47.165.2199 (JQ3.11.10).

48. Mitamura, 174–175. Mitamura quotes Zhang Tao (fl. 1560–1621): "Eastern pearls and sable bring world-class profits [*tianxia zhi houli*]. Those that come from the River Savages belong to Bujantai's tribe." On Zhang Tao, see Brook, *The Confusions of Pleasure*, 1–13.

49. Hummel, *Eminent Chinese of the Ch'ing Period*, 17.

50. Mitamura, 174, 176. The *Old Manchu Chronicles*, the only surviving Manchu source from this era, describes the conflict with Bujantai in personal and moral terms; Zhang Tao understood it in terms of conflicting interests and control over trade at Kaiyuan and Liaoyang. See MBRT, Taizu fascicles 1–2, passim.

51. Ula bannermen thereafter fell into two categories: those of the upper three banners, who were bondservants of the Imperial Household Department; and those of the lower five banners, who served under Manchu nobility. Unlike Solon and Daur banners, which were ethnically defined, the Ula garrisons were heterogeneous. The court reinforced the Ula garrisons with Solon and Daur troops in 1742 and still others in 1792, while it dispatched Ula bannermen to Ilan Hala, Alcuka, and Ningguta. The Ula dockyards, which were organized through a county system after 1726, were separate. DQHDSL 7: 38a, 12: 120a-b, 12: 211a, 12: 1110b.

52. On the institutional history of the Ula banners, see Jin, "Qingdai de da-sheng wula zongguan yamen," 56–61; Jin, "Guanyu 'dasheng wula zhidian quanshu' xiaoshi, chuban yiji wula shiliao wenku de jianyi," 59–62; Zhao,

"Guanyu Qingdai dasheng wula dongzhu caibuye de jige wenti," 79–85; Wang and Zhai, "Qingdai dasheng wula de dongzhu caibu," 76–80; and Kawakubo, "Shin shiryō 'dasheng wula zhidian quanshu' no hakken ni yosete," 148–151.

53. In 1729, under Yongzheng, the court specified that the supervising commandant be selected from among officials in the capital, but clerks be drawn from the local population. DQHDSL 12: 1080b–1081a.

54. See, for example, MWLF 3541.36.162.872 (JQ1.4.9), and 3549.30.162.2717 (JQ1.9.13).

55. MWLF 3667.47.171.2659 (JQ9.4.30).

56. Graf, "Palearctic freshwater mussel," 71–72. Other species include *Lanceolaria acrorrhyncha, Lanceolaria cylindrical, Nodularia douglasiae, Anondonta beringiana, Anemina arcaeformis, Anemina uscaphys, Inversidens pantoensis, Lamprotula coreana,* and *Lamprotula gottschei.*

57. Ibid., 71–88. Macology has yet to systematically categorize freshwater mussels and remains a divided field. There is no agreement on the number of freshwater pearl species in the greater Amur River basin, nor even on the criteria to delineate such species. The "biological species concept" (BSC), favored in Europe and the United States, uses evolutionary patterns and genealogical lineages as the basic organizing method; the "comparatory method" (CM), favored in Russia, uses the frontal contour of the shells as a typological comparison point. Russian macologists distinguish among fifty-six species in the Amur River region, whereas American scientists distinguish fourteen. The MUSSEL Project Database provides a species correspondence across BSC and CM categories at http://mussel-project.uwsp.edu.

58. I have given the customary translations used in bilingual Qing documents. The *Da Qing quanshu* translates *tana* as *dongzhu* or *dazhu, nicuhe* as simply *zhu,* and *tahūra* as *bang* ("mussel, oyster"). DQQS, 8:1a, 3:37b, and 8:2b. The *Qingwen jian* translates *tana* as *dongzhu, nicuhe* as *zhenzhu,* and *tahūra* as *geli* ("clam"). *Yuzhi Manzhu Menggu Hanzi sanhe qieyin Qingwen jian,* 21:60a, 21:60a, and 31:44a.

59. *Qinding Shengjing tongzhi,* 27: 36b. The *Jilin tongzhi* describes them the same, citing the *Shengjing tongzhi* verbatim. *Jilin tongzhi,* 34: 27b. The *Shengjing tongzhi* says little else about the pearls—only that the mussels (Ch: *bangge*) of the Hun and Tong rivers produce them, that they are harvested between the fourth and eighth lunar months, and that they are submitted as tribute in the first month.

60. *Heilongjiang zhigao,* 15: 32a,b.

61. MWLF 3572.24.164.966 (JQ2.9.13), and 3587.32.165.1553 (JQ3.9.27).

62. MWLF 3549.30.162.2717 (JQ1.9.13), and 3667.47.171.2659 (JQ9.4.30). Tallies from Aihūn and Ningguta were compiled and sent separately.

63. In the published Hunchun records, only the tally from 1806 distinguishes between the latter four types of *tana* pearl. See HFYD 25: 64 (JQ11.8.10). Records for "poor quality" *tana* pearls are found under tallies for 1786 and 1790. In 1786, sixty-five poor-quality *tana* were harvested at Burhatu, sixty-three at

Gahari, and seventy-three at Hailan. In 1790, the figures dropped drastically to eleven at Burhatu and ten at Gahari. HFYD, 15: 155 (QL51.8.15) and 18: 311 (QL55.8.10).

64. Before 1701, each team was responsible for twenty.

65. DQHDSL 10: 278a, 282a.

66. Ibid., 10: 278.1–279.2, 283.2. Newly added pearling teams were created from older teams responsible for other tributary items, such as honey.

67. MWLF 3541.36.162.872 (JQ1.4.9) and 3549.30.162.2717 (JQ1.9.13). In 1796, for example, the teams from Lalin and Alcuka departed on May 16 but did not arrive at the pearl beds at on the Elcuke River until August 7. They harvested pearls through September 4, then departed for the return journey home.

68. HFYD 21: 69 (JQ3.7.6).

69. MWLF 3775.28.179.3221 (JQ14.10.13).

70. In the Qianlong period, pearling teams that took the water route to Ningguta used the Hairan and Šansi Rivers (1786); Hairan, Šansi, and Malhūri Rivers (1790); and the Little Hairan and Hūlan Geo off the Hairan's main branch (1795). HFYD 15: 19 (QL51.5.20), 18.311 (QL55.8.10), and 19.375 (QL60.3.14).

71. HFYD 21: 6 (JQ3.5.1), 23: 167 (JQ10.4.5), 25: 64 (JQ11.8.10), 25: 263 (JQ12.5.1), 26: 117 (JQ17.4.1), 27: 468 (JQ19.8.10), 28: 298 (JQ20.4.24), 29: 271 (JQ23.8.25), and 32: 302 (JQ24.8.10).

72. HFYD 15: 155 (QL51.8.15), 16: 226 (QL52.8.21), 18: 311 (QL55.8.10), 25: 64 (JQ11.8.10), 29: 271 (JQ23.8.25), and 15: 19 (QL51.5.20).

73. NWFZXD 131.560.125 (JQ1.10.26), 131.560.125 (JQ1.10.26), 131.455.45 (JQ6.9.28), 132.462.1 (JQ18.11.1), 133.466.93 (JQ19.10.29), and 135.473.142 (JQ20.11.3); and MWLF 3572.24.164.966 (JQ2.9.13), and 3587.32.165.1553 (JQ3.9.27).

74. The following paragraph derives from Bauer, "Reproductive Strategy," 691–704.

75. Their host fish include salmon, trout, and sturgeon, depending on the species. All of these species were prolific in nineteenth-century Manchuria.

76. I thank George R. Trumbull IV for drawing my attention to the possibility. On mussels as indicators of water ecology, see Carrell et al., "Can Mussel Shells Reveal Environmental History?" 2–10.

77. DQHDSL 10: 280a.

78. Because the value of Manchurian pearls depended both on their size and luster, rewards were adjusted accordingly.

79. DQHDSL 10: 280b.

80. Ibid., 10: 279a.

81. QSL QL, 142: 1045.

82. DQHDSL 12:1081a.

83. Ibid. and DQHDSL 10: 105a, 12: 686b.

84. DQHDSL 2: 950b and 12: 210b.

85. HFYD 19.468 (QL60.6.14).

86. Philippe Le Billon defines lootability as "accessibility to insurgents," a function of the inherent extractability of a material resource and distance from the center of power. Collecting ginseng and pearls in Manchuria was easier for poachers than, say, extracting copper from capital-intensive mines in the Chinese interior. Le Billon, *Wars of Plunder*, 5.

87. HFYD 19.468 (QL60.6.14).

88. Ibid.

89. MWLF 3541.24.162.814 (JQ1.4.10).

90. Ibid.; MWLF 3562.5.163.2235 (JQ2.4.9), 3562.10.163.2255 (JQ2.4.9), and 3571.28.164.742 (JQ2.9.6). That year, the pearling teams managed to collect 742 *tana* and regular pearls.

91. QSL JQ, 56: 741, and DQHDSL 12: 1081b.

92. Ibid.

93. HFYD 15: 155 (QL51.8.15), 16: 226 (QL52.8.21), 18: 311 (QL55.8.10), 25: 64 (JQ11.8.10) 29: 271 (JQ23.8.25), and 15: 19 (QL51.5.20).

94. HFYD, 33: 333 (DG2.2.5).

95. DQHDSL 1: 515a.

96. HFYD 37: 50 (DG5.2.22).

97. MWLF 4045.37.197.1818 (DG7.3.25).

98. See HFYD, 38: 68 (DG8.4.21), 39: 8 (DG8.5.1), and 43: 338 (DG.14.10.15) for the Manchu text of the edict. The edict was also recorded in the *Veritable Records*; see QSL DG, 222: 319.

99. HFYD 46: 286 (DG18.11.28). A diminished tribute system continued on, at least nominally, until 1911. In 1846 and 1848 the moratorium was yet again reinstated, with other moratoriums recorded for 1893, 1895, 1899, 1907, 1909, and 1910. HFYD 58: 230 (DG26.11.20), 61: 273 (DG28.4.9); QSL TZh, 1: 84; QSL GX, 331: 252, 379: 958, 452: 966, 580: 679; and QSL XT, 24: 458, 44–798.

100. For a review of some of these accounts, see Mitamura, *Shinchō zenshi no kenkyū*, 172–173.

101. Kawachi, "Mindai tōhoku Ajia chōhi bōeki," 66. In attempt to starve the beast, the Chosŏn court thus condemned Korean women who wore earmuffs adorned with fur.

102. *Dasheng wula zhidian quanshu*, 149.

103. The scholarship on ginseng in the Qing is voluminous. A touchstone study remains Imamura, *Ninjinshi*; for a comprehensive critical survey, see Chiang Chushan, "Qingdai renshen de lishi: yige shangpin de yanjiu." For an English treatment, see Symons, *Ch'ing Ginseng Management*. For studies based on Manchu archives, see Tong, *Manyuwen yu Manwen dang'an yanjiu*, 258–278, and Wang, "Qingdai dongbei caishenye de xingshuai," 189–192.

104. On deforestation, see Elvin, *The Retreat of the Elephants*, 19–85. The old forests of northern China were not dissimilar in makeup from those of the Great Smoky Mountains of North Carolina and Tennessee today, where ginseng also grows. The poet Gary Snyder makes the imaginative comparison in Snyder,

The Practice of the Wild, 138. Indeed, the Smoky Mountains are today witness-
ing ginseng poaching for the China market. See Zucchino, "Smoky Mountains
National Park."

105. Chiang, "Qingdai renshen de lishi," 39–44.

106. Ibid., 45.

107. Ibid., 103–124.

108. Ibid., 117–119.

109. Ibid., 127–130. The Yongzheng court was active throughout the region
in this period; independent censors on fact-checking missions were frequently
deployed, including on one mission to Sakhalin Island to register fur tribute
bearing communities and another to the Ussuri to monitor ginseng operations.

110. Ibid., 131, 137.

111. MWLF 900.1.19.126 (YZ10.1.6). Likewise, in 1738, the lieutenant governor of Mergen memorialized that ten ginseng poachers, led by one Zhang Jihui,
had been caught near Saddle Mountain (Ma: *enggemu alin*). Two taels of ginseng
root and an additional 0.5 tael of ancillary parts were confiscated. Zhang's team
was equipped with six horses, one bow, a quiver of arrows, two cooking pots, and
two tents; the equipment was dispersed to the troops who arrested them. MWLF
905.4.19.1437 (QL3.10.1).

112. On the importance of 1744 as a turning point and a full description of
the 1744 reforms, see Tong, *Manyuwen yu Manwen dang'an yanjiu*, 264–269.

113. MWLF 3546.46.162.2041 (JQ1.7.17).

114. The Board of Revenue issued these permits in Beijing, then shipped
them to Mukden, Jilin, and Ningguta, where local authorities dispersed them;
all unused permits were returned to the Board of Revenue to be destroyed.

115. Tong, *Manyuwen yu Manwen dang'an yanjiu*, 266–267.

116. MWLF 3651.37.170.1514 (JQ7.12.28).

117. Based on a synopsis of MWLF 3541.22.162.802 (JQ1.4.10),
3544.16.162.1465 (JQ1.5.27), 3546.46.162.2041 (JQ1.7.17), 3562.14.163.2270
(JQ2.4.20), 3564.35.163.2794 (JQ2.5.29), 3567.2.163.3194 (JQ2.*6.6),
3575.34.164.1729 (JQ2.12.7), 3580.42.164.3211 (JQ3.4.16), 3583.3.165.230
(JQ3.5.28), 3584.38.165.718 (JQ3.7.15), 3612.22.167.952 (JQ5.6.21),
3627.2.168.1519 (JQ6.6.10), 3651.37.170.1514 (JQ7.12.28), 3669.45.171.3196
(JQ9.6.6), 3675.10.172.1205 (JQ9.10.27), 3683.17.173.214 (JQ10.5.24),
3691.8.173.2768 (JQ10.11.4), 3703.14.174.2967 (JQ11.6.11), 3710.14.175.1710
(JQ11.11.4), 3720.28.176.1232 (JQ12.5.21), 3723.33.176.1852 (JQ12.7.3),
3726.24.176.2667 (JQ12.8.21), 3730.49.177.420 (JQ12.11.25), and
3742.8.177.3022 (JQ13.5.21).

118. Siolin, for example, was censured for failing to send a report on ginseng
conditions, a nod to imperial anxiety about keeping control over officials in Jilin
involved in the ginseng trade. MWLF 3637.37.169.1217 (JQ7.3.23).

119. A document from 1847 (DG27) put the figure at 44,325 *liang*, thus
giving exactly 75 taels of silver for 591 ginseng licenses. Tong, *Manyuwen yu
Manwen dang'an yanjiu*, 273.

120. Wang, "Qingdai dongbei caishenye de xingshuai," 191.

121. Chiang, "Qingdai renshen de lishi," 151–152.

122. MWLF 3627.2.168.1519 (JQ6.6.10), 3669.45.171.3196 (JQ9.6.6), 3541.22.162.802 (JQ1.4.10), 3544.16.162.1465 (JQ1.5.27), 3562.14.163.2270 (JQ2.4.20), 3564.35.163.2794 (JQ2.5.29), 3580.42.164.3211 (JQ3.4.16), 3583.3.165.230 (JQ3.5.28), 3669.45.171.3196 (JQ9.6.6), 3683.17.173.214 (JQ10.5.24), 3703.14.174.2967 (JQ11.6.11), 3720.28.176.1232 (JQ12.5.21), and 3742.8.177.3022 (JQ13.5.21). In the period from 1796 to 1808, the major drops in permitting were in the years 1797 through 1798 in Ningguta and 1798 through 1801 in Jilin district. In the same period, the combined permits for Alcuka, Bedune, and Ilan Hala districts fell from ninety-nine to sixty-seven. The report for 1798 gave a tally of 211 permits for Alcuka, Bedune, and Ilan Hala combined. MWLF 3583.3.165.230 (JQ3.5.28) and 3669.45.171.3196 (JQ9.6.6). The Alcuka tallies include Lalin jurisdiction from 1804.

123. See, for example, the register of poachers in Chiang, "Qingdai renshen de lishi," 132–135, 139. Note also that the seven-clan Heje were found to be illegally sheltering ginseng poachers in the Ussuri River valley in 1746. Matsuura, *Shinchō no Amūru seisaku to shōsū minzoku*, 327.

124. QSL QL, 1045: 988a.

125. Ibid., 1244: 726a.

126. On the corruption case of 1762, see ibid., 789: 694b.

127. Ibid., 1444: 271b–272a.

128. Ibid., 1444: 272a.

129. Ibid., 1192: 938a,b.

130. MWLF 3596.16.166.0150 (JQ4.5.28).

131. Ibid.

132. MWLF 3730.47.177.408 (JQ12.11.25).

133. MWLF 3575.34.164.1725 (JQ2.12.7).

134. See MWLF 3557.7.163.1051 (JQ1.12.18), 3558.17.163.1332 (JQ2.1.21), 3575.34.164.1725 (JQ2.12.7), 3575.34.164.1725 (JQ2.12.7), 3576.47.164.2023 (JQ3.1.19), 3590.13.165.2228 (JQ3.11.26), 3590.29.165.2315 [JQ3.12], and 3621.28.167.3574 (JQ6.1.11).

135. MWLF 900.2.19.127 (YZ10.1.6).

136. Chiang, "Qingdai renshen de lishi," 163.

137. Cong, "Zhongguo zaipei renshen zhi chuxian yu xingqi," 262–269.

138. Chiang, "Qingdai renshen de lishi," 170, and Kuriyama, "The Geography of Ginseng and the Strange Alchemy of Needs."

139. Documents from the case are republished in "Jiaqingchao shenwu dang'an xuanbian" *Lishi dang'an* 3 (2002), 51–72, and *Lishi dang'an* 4 (2002), 22–42, 63.

140. Chiang, "Qingdai renshen de lishi," 179–180.

141. MWLF 3621.28.167.3574 (JQ6.1.11).

142. MWLF 3651.36.170.1503 (JQ7.12.8).

143. Cong Peiyuan, "Zhongguo zaipei renshen zhi chuxian yu xingqi," 268.

144. Quoted in Chiang Chushan, 168–169. For the original edict, see *Jiaqing Daoguang liangchao shangyu dang*, 8: 26 (JQ8.1.24).

145. Quoted in ibid., 183. For original text, see QSL JQ, 226: 39. The edict was issued in 1810 (JQ15.2).

146. Quoted in ibid., 163.

147. It is not even clear that consumers understood "ginseng" to be a singular item. American and Manchurian varieties, like farmed and wild ones, had entirely different markets: As the Boston merchant Sullivan Dorr explained in 1802, Chinese buyers "say that one root of Tartar Ginseng possesses more virtue than a Catty of ours." Moreover, "neither does it lose its value in consequence of the quantities brought from America for they say their own is infinitaly [sic] better." The American naturalist J. C. Reinhardt, traveling aboard the U.S. frigate *Constitution* to China in 1845, similarly was shocked to learn that Chinese found American and Manchurian ginseng to be "altogether distinct." He heard that the natural Manchurian variety grew in a land of tigers, and it had numinous powers—he was even informed it "cannot be seen in the day-time, but at night a flame issues from it." Reinhardt, "Report," 554.

148. Anderson, *Imagined Communities*.

149. The Manchu and Qing homeland did not need to be linked to a territorial unit. Tulišen, for example, in his *Lakcaha jecen de takūraha babe ejehe bithe/ Yiyu lu*, took the "land where the phoenix took flight and the dragon ascended" to be simply the "northeast" (Ma: *dergi amergi ergi*). Tulišen, *Lakcaha jecen de takūraha babe ejehe bithe*, 5. More common was to describe the region as the land "beyond the boundary" (Ma: *jasei tulergi*); rules for trafficking sable, for example, applied to both "beyond the boundary" and the "Mongol steppe" equally. See the memorial dated QL.11.22 in *Gongzhongdang Qianlongchao zouzhe* 75.496–497. I am indebted to Benjamin Levey for the reference.

150. On the Manchu construction of both, see Elliott, "The Limits of Tartary," 603–624.

151. *Yongzheng shangyu neige, juan* 89 (YZ7.12.7).

152. QSL QL, 576: 345.

153. Ibid., 142: 1045.

154. Ibid., 674: 543, 676: 555.

155. *Dasheng wula zhidian quanshu*, 118.

156. See, for example, QSL JQ, 113: 501, 256: 455; and QSL DG, 25: 445, 37: 670, 476: 1001.

157. See *Donghua xulu*, DG14: 8b-9a; *Qingchao xu wenxian tongkao*, 8590a; and *Jilin tongzhi* 3.16a, 20a.

158. *Jilin tongzhi* 2: 17a, citing an 1816 memorial; see also *Jilin tongzhi* 3: 16a.

159. See, for example, *Qingchao xu wenxian tongkao*, 8590a.

160. He Changling, *Qing jingshi wenbian*, 80: 11, and Wei Yuan, *Shengwu ji, juan* 14 *fulu*.

161. Many of these publications were explicitly focused on territorial and diplomatic concerns, including statecraft compendia such as the *Qing jingshi*

wenbian, and the diplomatic travelogues of the late nineteenth century, such as the *Xixun dashiji* and the *Genzi haiwai ji*. The enlarged territorial homeland of the Qing court, in other words, was from the start included in the formation of the new Chinese nation-space.

162. QSL QL, 1035: 868; for a later reference, see QSL JQ, 113: 496.

CHAPTER THREE

1. QSL DG, 161: 488a.

2. *Xuzeng xing'an huilan*, 6: 4192.

3. According to the *Lifanyuan zeli*, "Bannermen and civilians who live within the [Great Wall] boundary may not cross the boundary and plow fields in Mongol lands. Punish those who break the prohibition in accordance with laws for illicitly farming pastureland." In parallel fashion, a similar rule existed for "illicitly inviting Mongols from other banners to cross the border and homestead on state land" (Ma: *siden i ongko ba*; Mo: *alban u belciger ġajar*). GMQJ 34: 8a, 10: 9a–10b; and TGKH 10: 1a,b, 34: 8a, 10: 14a–15a.

4. Beneath the banner were local units called "arrows" (Ma: *niru*; Mo: *sumu*; Ch: *zuoling*). The number of arrows per banner and banners per *aimaġ* were irregular; on average, the Inner Mongol banners contained 23.6 arrows, whereas in Outer Mongolia the banner itself was often the smallest unit of territorial governance, with fifty-five of eighty-six banners lacking arrow subdivisions altogether. Farquhar, "The Ch'ing Administration of Mongolia," 71. For a full treatment of local administration in Mongolia, see Oka, *Shindai Mongoru monki seido no kenkyū*. The topic is indispensible: Further research on environmental history at the most local levels is needed.

5. Sneath, *The Headless State*.

6. Khalkha Mongols claimed descent from Geresenje Jalair Khung-Taiji (d. 1548), the son of Dayan Khan (r. 1480?–1517?). Most Mongols in Mongolia today identify as members of the Khalkha ethnicity (Mo: *yastan*). Atwood, *Encyclopedia of Mongolia*, 299–301.

7. I have translated the Mongol *obuġa* as *cairn* in most locations in the text, despite limits to the translation. The Mongol *obuġa*, unlike the English "cairn," is imbued with spiritual dimensions and cultural importance specific to the Mongol context, a sense that *cairn* fails to capture. See Bawden, "Two Mongol Texts," 23–41.

8. Li, *Waimeng zhengjiao zhidu kao*, 75.

9. Elverskog, *Our Great Qing*, 127–165. A parallel hierarchy existed for Mongols who lived within the jurisdiction of Buddhist monasteries.

10. Li, *Waimeng zhengjiao zhidu kao*, 109–110.

11. Zhang, *Jinshang xingshuai shi*, 43, 46, 73–74. The checkpoints doubled as customs offices.

12. To avoid detection, some on the Russo–Qing border even tried making their footprints look like animal tracks. Personal communication, Sayana Namsaraaeva.

13. MıDı-3840.55a (DG7.9). Pilgrims, like merchant caravans, would have been common sights on the road. See Charleux, *Nomads on Pilgrimage*, and Tuttle, "Tibetan Buddhism," 163–214.

14. See MıDı-3840.32 (DG7.2.7):

15. See, for example, the language in MıDı-3840.18 (XF7.9.20).

16. Sanjdorji, *Manchu Chinese Colonial Rule*, 70–82.

17. Cited in MıDı-3935.15b (DG11.7.28).

18. MıDı-4079.53 (DG17.2.29). The *ambans'* office's seal gave these documents their authority. On imperial seals in Qing Mongolia, see Mostaert, "L''ouverture du sceau,'" 315–337.

19. The length of stay was calibrated to travel times and the estimated time needed for business. A permit for a trip from Hohhot to a Khalkha banner was good for one year. One hundred days was given for the Khuree–Kiakhta round trip. Two hundred days were allotted for Khuree–Uliasutai permits, and one year was usually allotted for trade in certain banners. MıDı-4079.13a (DG17.10.4); MıDı-4079.15a (DG17.12.24); and MıDı-4079.26 (DG17.3.30).

20. MıDı-4319.45a (DG27.12).

21. MıDı-3697.6 (JQ24.12.20).

22. MıDı-4079.53 (DG17.2.29).

23. MıDı-4079.15a (DG17.12.24). The state profited from the arrangement; each year, the government rented out the land allotted to merchants in Kiakhta for 400 silver taels per annum and in Khuree for 300 taels. MıDı-3697.16a (JQ25.10).

24. Zhang, *Jinshang xingshuai shi,* 80, and MıDı-843.1 (DG4.8.9). A register was made of all mixed Chinese-Mongol households comprised of Chinese fathers and Mongol mothers; the Mongol mothers, for their part, all belonged to ecclesiastical estates as members of the Great Šabi. The register took their names, home jurisdiction (county for the Chinese, *otoġ daruġa* for the Mongols), and ages, as well as the names, gender (male, female, and infant), and age of all children and dependents, including adopted children, children-in-law, nieces, and nephews. Their children were registered with Mongol names and subject to their mother's jurisdiction.

25. See, for example, the cases discussed in MıDı-3833.23a (DG6.3.20); MıDı-3833.27a (DG6.4.6); and MıDı-3874.12b (DG8.3.23).

26. MıDı-3874.13a (DG8.11.21).

27. MıDı-3913.9a (DG9.1.20).

28. MıDı-3874.9b (DG8.12.15).

29. MıDı-3913.9a (DG9.1.20).

30. MıDı-3913.9b (DG9.1.29). The last phrase juxtaposes the Manchu words *urse* ("people") and *irgese* ("Chinese").

31. MɪDɪ-3874.9b (DG8.12.15), and MɪDɪ-3913.9a (DG9.1.20).

32. MɪDɪ-4144.3 (DG10.8).

33. The problem of parks and "purity" is discussed at length below.

34. MɪDɪ-4144.2a (DG10.10.7).

35. MɪDɪ-4166.15a (DG21.12.28).

36. Deer horn was not always the uniquely precious commodity it would become; the *Shengjing tongzhi* makes note of the antler as a valuable part of the elk
(Ch: *milu*) but includes it among the full range of other anatomical parts, such as
tail, of seemingly equal importance. *Qinding shengjing tongzhi*, 27: 30a.

37. MɪDɪ-3697.1 (JQ25.5.13).

38. See, for example, MɪDɪ-3697.2 (JQ25.4.28); MɪDɪ-3697.1 (JQ25.5.13);
and MɪDɪ-3935.3 (DG11.12.14). Between May 31, 1820, and June 20, 1820,
alone, the trade supervisor's office registered the sale of thirty-three sets of deer
horns to nine different merchant houses. Their average value was ninety bricks
of tea, though the range in prices varied from eleven to 165 tea bricks per pair.
Eleven years later, in 1831, the price and volume of deer horn had risen consider-
ably, but the number of houses engaged in the trade had whittled down to three:
Linshengyuan, Xinglongyong, and Tianchunyong (known, in Mongol, by the
names Buyandalai, Sanggaidalai, and Bayandorji). In eighty-three days between
May 14 and August 10, a total of fifty-nine pairs of deer horns were sold in
exchange for 6,259 bricks of tea. In 1820 the average rack of deer horn sold for
ninety bricks of tea, but in 1831 a rack sold for 106 bricks (with prices ranging
from twenty to 202 bricks of tea per pair). The rising prices may have been a
result of shrinking supplies, as deer became increasingly scarce. An average day
in 1820 brought in 1.65 antler racks; in 1831 the figure was 0.71 rack per day for
the year, and 0.85 rack per day in the high season. The average per diem haul had
dropped by half.

39. MɪDɪ-4320.54 (DG27.12.20).

40. The *otoġ* was a Mongol unit of governance that predated Qing rule, and it
survived primarily as an administrative unit for herders on Buddhist ecclesiastical estates (Mo: *šabi*). On the institution, see Atwood, *Encyclopedia of Mongolia*,
430–431.

41. MɪDɪ-3822.23 (DG6.4.20).

42. We should be careful not to read the growth of commercial licensing in
Outer Mongolia as a form of "developmentalism." Deer horn is instructive in this
regard, as the deer-horn rush led to similar licensing schemes in Xinjiang and the
Northeast, but for entirely different reasons. In the Northeast, the court endorsed
a plan in 1831 by the acting military governor of Mukden, Fugiyūn (1749–1834),
to license the deer-horn trade, pitched as a way to help cultivate the Manchu Way
by affording bannermen the opportunity to capitalize on their hunting skills.
Licensing the trade in Xinjiang's Ili valley had an altogether different function.
There, the military governor, Teišunboo, proposed licensing in 1833, reasoning
that with proper enforcement and taxing mechanisms, local Mongols would
benefit, and the state could generate funds for public irrigation. In Mongolia, the

court aimed to stem poaching in restricted grounds; in Manchuria, the hope was to support impoverished bannermen; in Xinjiang, it was to drum up tax revenue. QSL DG, 202: 1171a,b, 249: 761a,b.

43. The region was known as Ulaġanqada in Mongolian and Ulan Hada in Manchu.

44. Northern Zhili was growing exponentially fast when Liu Deshan arrived; the reported population of Chengde prefecture, doubled from roughly 500,000 to a million between 1776 and 1820 alone. Li, *Fighting Famine*, 80. On unattached, migrant men in general as villains of the Qing world, see Kuhn, *Soulstealers*; and Sommer, *Sex, Law, and Society*.

45. M1D1-3913.5a (DG9.11.15) and M1D1-3913.10 (DG10.4.16). This was not the first corruption case involving blank, *yamen*-sealed paper. Just four years prior, in 1825, twenty fake documents with official letterhead had been illegally issued, with twelve put to use, leading to another corruption scandal in Chaoyang county. See M1D1-3913.10 (DG10.4.16).

46. *Chaoyang xianzhi*, 27: 5a.

47. A recent survey listed 217 species of mushroom in Mongolia, of which only twenty-six could be found on the steppe. Gombobaatar et al, *Convention on Biological Diversity*, 26–27.

48. Ibid., 26. In 2013, the Mongolian government added *Tricholoma mongolicum* to a red list and took steps to protect it in protected zones. Poaching remains a significant problem, however, as demand in China remains high; on the open market, Mongolian steppe mushrooms sell for as much as $70 a kilogram. See PIRE Mongolia Blog, "The Bounty of the Steppe," July 25, 2011.

49. Some modern Chinese guidebooks even claim they fight cancer. Tanesaka et al., "Mongoru sōgenni jiseisuru *tricholoma mongolicum* Imai," 33, and Mao, *Zhongguo daxing zhenjun*, 69.

50. In his notice to the field, Imai described its distinctive anatomy in detail but provided little on its ecology or taste, offering only that "the fungus grows on grassy ground in fields from late June to September, and most abundantly early in August and early in September . . . taste and odour [are] mild and agreeable." Imai, "On an Edible Mongolian Fungus 'Pai-mo-ku,'" 280–282.

51. Reading et al., "The Commercial Harvest," 59.

52. Tourism languishes in the region today in large part because of the mosquitoes. Personal communication, Christopher Atwood. According to one report, the viciousness and omnipresence of the bloodsucking insects in the region is "almost legendary." Kaczensky, "First Assessment," 11.

53. Kaczensky, "First Assessment," 9.

54. M1D1-3874.25

55. M1D1-3742.2–5 [undated]. The most popular sites were the Delger River (fourteen camps, 146 men), Qadantai (eight camps, sixty-seven men), the source of the Buyan River (six camps, fifty-six men), Pimbal (five camps, thirty-six men), Mekegertü (four camps, twenty-five men), Qailongtai (three camps, twenty-five men), Aru Balgal (three camps, twenty-four men), and Bacingtu

(three camps, twenty-four men). The names of the most popular mushroom-picking locations suggests the centrality of river systems in the zone between steppe and forest, with a range of names that include words like "river" (Mo: *gool*), "headwater" (*gool un ekh*), or "spring" (*bulag*). For a map of these locations, see Haltod, *Mongolische Ortsnamen*, 2: 80.

56. The following discussion is based on M1D1-3874.1–7 [undated].

57. M1D1-3874.2.

58. Because the confession was in Manchu, we lack the characters for these shops. Deyu and Xitai were located in *šeobei hutong*, which I have been unable to locate precisely, but were "outside *šubei* gate," that is, outside Chongwenmen, on the southwest side of the Beijing city wall.

59. *Shuntian fuzhi* 50.6b.

60. Wu, *Manzu shisu yu Qinggong yushan*, 102.

61. Ibid.

62. Yuan, *Suiyuan shidan*, 3: 30.

63. For banner salaries and their complexities, see Elliott, *The Manchu Way*, 192; for average, see Pomeranz, *The Great Divergence*, 100–102.

64. Consumer prices over time for mushrooms do not exist in any complete form. In the Republican period, local gazetteers show *koumo* to have been the most valuable type of mushroom, taxed at three times the rate of wood ear (Ch: *mu'er*) and twice the rate of elm oyster; by weight, it was one-and-half times the tax value of sea cucumbers—a rare delicacy. See *Nongan xianzhi*, 6.8b, and *Binxian xianzhi*, 150. A gazetteer published for Xiuyan county (Liaoning) reported that the price of *koumo* in 1927 was higher than any other comparable product; the price per catty of *mu'er* was 0.008 yuan per catty and sea cucumber was 0.05 yuan per catty, but *koumo* was a stunning eighteen yuan per catty, over 2,000 times the price. *Xiuyan xianzhi*, 3.20b.

65. Customs rates provide only a faint indication of market value, as they were infrequently adjusted. In the years 1669 (KX8) and 1780 (QL45), the mushrooms were taxed at a rate of 0.402 silver tael per 100 catties, or approximately 0.66 tael per kilo. A new sable-fur or a leopard-skin coat (Ch: *ao*) was taxed at the same rate, and a catty of sea cucumber was taxed at half the rate. In 1902, the customs rate was recorded at 0.9 tael per 100 catties (about 1.5 taels per kilo)—still double the sea cucumber rate but 100 times lower than the rate for low-grade wild ginseng. See *Chongwenmen shangshui yamen xianxing shuize*, v. 6.1, 6.2 and 7.

66. M1D1-2875.2 (QL27.6.4).

67. For this reason, David Sneath described Mongolia as a "headless state" where the Mongol aristocracy ruled. Sneath, *The Headless State*.

68. Dasigeleng (Ch: Da-shi-ge-lei-ke), *jasaġ* of the Left-Wing Front Banner of Secen Qan *aimaġ*, was a fourth generation descendant of Cebden, the man who first held the title. Bao and Qichaoketu, *Menggu huibu wanggong biaozhuan*, 165, and Jin et al., *Qingdai Menggu zhi*, 101.

69. Quoted in M1D1-3744.7a (DG2.10).

70. M1D1-3744.7a (DG2.10), and M1D1-3913.20 (DG9.1.19).

71. M1D1-3744.8a (DG2.6.27).

72. Sonomdarjya (Ch: Suo-nuo-mu-da-er-jia, Suo-nuo-mu-da-er-ji-ya), *jasaġ* of the Left-Wing Front Banner of Secen Qan *aimaġ*, was the sixth-generation descendant of Cebden. Another man, Dorjibolam, held the post briefly between 1820 and 1822. Bao and Qichaoketu, *Menggu huibu wanggong biaozhuan*, 303, and Jin et al., *Qingdai Menggu zhi*, 101.

73. M1D1-3744.7a (DG2.10).

74. Ibid.

75. M1D1-3811.5a (DG5.8.20).

76. M1D1-3811.4a (DG5.4). Such an arrangement may have existed informally in earlier years. See below.

77. M1D1-3811.5a (DG5.8.20), and M1D1-3811.4a (DG5.4).

78. M1D1-3811.5a (DG5.8.20), and M1D1-3833.15 (n/a).

79. M1D1-3811.5a (DG5.8.20).

80. Ibid. and M1D1-3833.25a (DG6.1.21). The names of the locations were given in Manchu as *šereneke kūwangbaci i hotduk* and *salkitu*.

81. M1D1-3833.58a (DG6.6.9).

82. M1D1-3913.14b (DG9.1?).

83. Ibid., and M1D1-3913.17a (DG8.11.1).

84. M1D1-3913.14b (DG9.1?).

85. M1D1-3913.17a (DG8.11.1). The trade supervisor's office found Hui Wanzong's name and home jurisdiction in an earlier register. He was from Chang'ai county, Shandong (Laizhou prefecture). Like Liu Deshan, he was a migrant from Shandong to Chifeng.

86. M1D1-3913.18a (DG9.5.2). Two foremen working beneath him, Jiao Shi and Kui Qiufan, wore the cangue for two months.

87. M1D1-3913.10 (DG10.4.16).

88. M1D1-3913.18a (DG9.5.2).

89. M1D1-3913.10 (DG10.4.16).

90. M1D1-3913.5a (DG9.11.15).

91. Hui Wanzong originally was ordered to receive a stiffer corporal punishment without the exile sentence, but because he resisted arrest, the punishment was made more severe. M1D1-3913.10 (DG10.4.16).

92. Ibid.

93. As written in the *Qing Code*: "When, because there is no precisely applicable statute or substatute, a statute or substatute which is most closely applicable is cited, the Board of Punishments will then assemble the Three High Courts . . . to deliberate and determine sentence. This sentence will then be submitted to the throne with detailed explanation that inasmuch as the Code lacks a precisely applicable article, the present judgment is being pronounced 'by analogy to' [*bizhao*] a certain statute or substatute or that, in the same manner, a one-degree increase or reduction of the statutory penalty is being pronounced. The imperial

rescript will then be awaited and action taken accordingly." Morris and Bodde, *Law in Imperial China*, 176.

94. Ibid.

95. M1D1-3697.29 (JQ25.2.7), M1D1-3697.26 (JQ25.9.13), and M1D1-3913.10 (DG10.4.16). The punishments were comparable to similar serious crimes. If a Chinese man swore at the *amban* he was sentenced to wear the cangue a month, received 100 strokes with the heavy staff, and was banished back to the Chinese interior. Likewise, if a Chinese man was expelled from Mongolia but later returned, he was sentenced to wear the cangue in the marketplace for two months, after which he was whipped 100 times and expelled again.

96. M1D1-3744.7a (DG2.10).

97. M1D1-3822.58a (DG6.6.9).

98. M1D1-3855.7a (DG7.6.4), and M1D1-2874.14 (DG8.12.6).

99. See, for example, M1D1-3744.8a (DG2.6.27), M1D1-3744.7a (DG2.10), and M1D1-3855.11a (DG7.10).

100. M1D1-3913.20 (DG9.1.19).

101. M1D1-3874.25 (DG8.1.22), and M1D1-3913.22 (DG10.8.5).

102. M1D1-4031.2 (DG11.9.16), and M1D1-3874.25.

103. M1D1-3833.13 (DG6.9.28).

104. See M1D1-3833.11 (DG6.11.30), M1D1-3855.9a (DG7.7.30), M1D1-3874.1 (DG8.11.21), M1D1-3913.24 (DG10.*4.10), and M1D1-4031.5 (DG15.6.14).

105. M1D1-3833.11 (DG6.11.30).

106. The language is ubiquitous in all documents on mushroom picking throughout the decade of the mushroom-picking crisis.

107. M1D1-3874.50 (DG8.8.13).

108. Ibid.

109. Ibid., and M1D1-3913.14b (DG9.1?).

110. See, for example, M1D1-3874.14 (DG8.12.6) and M1D1-3874.14 (DG8.12.6).

111. M1D1-3874.25 and M1D1-3913.22 (DG10.8.5).

112. Cited and translated in Elliott, *The Manchu Way*, 287. For the original Manchu, see *Shangyu baqi/Dergi hese jakūn gūsade wasimbuhangge*, 5:36b.

113. *Wuliyasutai zhilue*, 65. The writer of the *Wuliyasutai zhilue* was not convinced, however, that Mongol ways were entirely righth-eaded. He recorded that Mongol medicine practiced by lamas left something to be desired; likewise, for his Chinese-reading audience, he noted left the curiosity that Mongols did not clothe the dead but left them in the wilderness to be devoured by wild animals.

114. Chuang, *Qingdai zhungaer shiliao*, 148-149.

115. See M1D1-3744.7a (DG2.10).

116. M1D1-4031.1 (DG11.2.11), and M1D1-4031.3 (DG13.2.11).

117. M1D1-3833.25a (DG6.1.21).

118. M1D1-3855.7a (DG7.6.4), and M1D1-3855.9a (DG7.7.30).

119. Crossley, "Making Mongols," 58–82.

120. M1D1-3833.18a (DG6.4.15), M1D1-3833.20 (DG6.7.19), M1D1-3833.24 (DG6.8.2), M1D1-3833.25a (DG6.1.21), M1D1-3822.58a (DG6.6.9), M1D1-3855.3a (DG7.1), M1D1-3855.9a (DG7.7.30), M1D1-3855.3a (DG7.1), M1D1-3855.7a (DG7.6.4), M1D1-3855.3a (DG7.1), M1D1-3855.12a (DG7.10), M1D1-3855.6a (DG7.1.11), M1D1-3845.15a (DG7.3), M1D1-3855.11a (DG7.10), and M1D1-3855.7a (DG7.6.4).

121. M1D1-3822.58a (DG6.6.9).

122. M1D1-3833.20 (DG6.7.19).

123. Ibid.

124. Ibid. On the authorities that confronted them, see M1D1-3855.9a (DG7.7.30).

125. M1D1-3855.7a (DG7.6.4), and M1D1-3855.9a (DG7.7.30). The original draft of this document left out "cutting down trees" (Ma: *moo sacime*); the phrase was inserted in a later draft.

126. M1D1-3833.13 (DG6.9.28), and M1D1-4031.2 (DG11.9.16).

127. M1D1-3742.3.

128. He led a camp of eight men in 1827, using supplies of grain provided by a man in Kiskiktu named Ding Si.

129. Compare with Lattimore, *Inner Asian Frontiers of China*, 481. For Lattimore, Chinese acculturation to Mongol ways was a necessary outcome of life and work on the steppe: "The steppe was not suitable for occupation by unmodified Chinese communities" (473).

130. See the case of two wood sellers from Chifeng in Sonomdaryja's banner in M1D1-3822.58a (DG6.6.9).

131. M1D1-3855.8 (DG7.*5.18).

132. M1D1-3833.13 (DG6.9.28), and M1D13874.28 (DG8.F3.24).

133. M1D1-3811.5a (DG5.8.20), and M1D1-3833.15 (n/a).

134. *Han-i araha Manju Monggo gisuni buleku bithe*, 6: 65a (*tondo bolgo i hacin*).

135. DQQS 6: 8b. The first definition, *qing*, is the same character as the name of the dynasty, the Qing. Manchu and Mongol documents, however, never translated "Qing" but transliterated the state's name from *Da Qing* to *Daicing*. In contrast, the state name "Jin," used by the Jurchen courts of the medieval (1115–1234) and pre-Qing (1616–1636) periods was always rendered as "gold" (Ma: *aisin*; Mo: *altan*) in Qing documents. See High and Schlesinger, "Rulers and Rascals," 301n27. For a contemporary translation of "Qing" as meaning *arigun*, see Enhbayaryn Jigmeddorj, *Khalkh-Manjiin uls töriin khariltsaa*, 27.

136. *Yuzhi Manzhu Menggu Hanzi sanhe qieyin Qingwen jian*, 6: 40a; and Tamamura et al., *Gotai shin bunkan yakukai*, no. 2593, 3573, and 5476. A fourth definition of *bolgo*, listed under "Humans—sounds," is given as "tonal harmony" (Ch: *shengqing*; Mo: *iraġu*). See *Yuzhi Manzhu Menggu Hanzi sanhe qieyin Qingwen jian*, 14: 23b. The verbal relatives of *bolgo* show an even broader semantic range, including Buddhist dimensions; the verb "to abstain or fast" (Ma:

bolgomimbi), for example, found under "Monks and Priests—Buddha-related" (Ch: *sengdaobu folei*), denoted "purification" through self-denial (Ch: *zhai*; Mo: *arǧiulamui*). *Yuzhi Manzhu Menggu Hanzi sanhe qieyin Qingwen jian*, 19: 3b.

137. In Southeast Asia during WWII, a *suqing* policy—known today as *Sook Ching*—was a form of ethnic "purging" or "cleansing" by the Japanese army directed at overseas Chinese. See Blackburn, "The Collective Memory," 73. In contexts in which the aesthetic meaning is primary, as when Tulišen described a mountain as "pure and beautiful" (Ma: *bolgo saikan*), he rendered the Chinese as "contending for beauty" (Ch: *jingxiu*). See Tulišen, *Lakcaha jecen de takūraha babe ejehe bithe*, 96.

138. See the use of *qingjing shengdi* in the Chinese translation of Umuna's account to Kangxi of his trip up Changbaishan. Yang, "Liubian jilue," in Zhou, *Longjiang sanji*, 30.

139. The phrase appears in Mongol language laws but not in their Manchu language translation. Compare GMQJ 5a–b and TGKH 53.5a–6a. On gold mines in particular, see High and Schlesinger, "Rulers and Rascals," 293–295.

140. M1D1-3840.27 (DG7).

141. Ibid., M1D1-3675.2 (JQ24.4.4), and M1D1-3833.39 (DG6.7.18).

142. The mountain is today protected as a national park. The president's mansion lies at its northern foot, and, after the disorder following the 2009 elections, riot police trained there. Brian Baumann, personal communication.

143. M1D1-3840.27 (DG7), and M1D1-3675.30 (JQ24).

144. M1D1-3675.2 (JQ24.4.4), and M1D1-3840.27 (DG7).

145. The literature on imperial hunting grounds in the Qing is large, though most focuses exclusively only on the emperor's personal hunting grounds at Mulan. Works include Luo Yunzhi, *Qingdai Mulan weichang de tantao*; Menzies, *Forest and Land*, 55–64; and Elliott and Ning Chia, "The Qing Hunt at Mulan," 66–83. For a detailed study of imperial hunting across Eurasia, including conservation practices, see Allsen, *The Royal Hunt*.

146. There were several such sites used as game parks for military training. One was northeast of Khüree, in land under the formal jurisdiction of the Jibzundamba Khutugtu. There were other hunting grounds in the far east of Secen Qan *aimaǧ*, on the border with Hulun Buir, near the mushroom fields. For descriptions and geography, see M1D1-3416.19 (JQ10.8), and M1D1-3416.5 (JQ10.4).

147. M1D1-3416.7a (JQ10.8).

148. M1D1-3834.8 (DG6.6.18).

149. M1D1-4166.9a (DG21.1.19).

150. M1D1-2875.2 (QL27.6.4).

151. See, for example, ibid.

152. M1D1-3750.1 (DG3.6.9).

153. M1D1-3416.11 (JQ10.6).

154. M1D1-3416.1a (JQ10.8).

155. M1D1-4079.57 (DG17?).

156. MiD1-3840.6 (DG7.8.18).

157. MiD1-4079.57 (DG17?).

158. Ibid.

159. Humphrey, "Chiefly and Shamanist Landscapes," 142–149. Humphrey contrasts "chiefly landscapes," such as mountains associated with the Mongol khans, with to "shamanist landscapes," which were generally associated with the earth (for example, caves), females, and peripheral lands outside state control. On gender, power, and religious landscapes more broadly in the Mongol context, see Humphrey, *Shamans and Elders.*

160. In this sense, Qing "purity" was similar in spirit to how Mary Douglas conceived it, as a process of making borders and clarifying social roles. In Douglas's words: "Ideas about separating, purifying, demarcating and punishing transgressions have as their main function to impose system on an inherently untidy experience." Douglas, *Purity and Danger,* 4.

161. See MiD1-3675.1a (JQ24.5.14) for the language; a replica of this document can be found in MiD1-3675.46. *Karun* staffed by six guards stretched every thirty to forty *li* on the boundary of the imperial game park at Soyolji, on the eastern rim of Secen Qan *aimaġ.* MiD1-2875.3 (QL27.7.17).

162. MiD1-4166.14a (DG21.9.10), and MiD1-3750.3 (DG3.5.17).

163. MiD1-3750.8b (DG3.6.12).

164. See, for example, MiD1-4319.46 (DG27.6). Incidents of badger hunters starting fires were not uncommon. In 1762, for example, a guardsman named Batu at the imperial game park at Soyolj, in Secen Qan *aimaġ,* sparked a costly fire that swept through the region; he was later found to have been smoking out badgers (Ma: *manggisu*) on the sandy banks of the Nömrög River, just to the north of the park. He and other guards scrambled to stamp it out but failed. When the wind picked up, it quickly carried the fire to the southeast, and by evening almost sixty *li* of land had burned. Batu originally claimed he had been smoking tobacco and that a smoldering pipe ember had ignited the prairie, but authorities later discovered he was badger hunting. MiD1-2875.3 (QL27.7.17), and MiD1-2875.1 (QL27.9.16).

165. MiD1-3675.67 (JQ24.3.13).

166. The documents give the Manchu word; the Chinese law calls for the Chinese. I have not discovered in what language these criminals were tattooed.

167. MiD1-3416.5 (JQ10.4).

168. MiD1-2875.3 (QL27.7.17) and MiD1-2875.1 (QL27.9.16).

169. QSL QL, 947: 838.

170. MiD1-3416.19 (JQ10.8).

171. Ibid. Among the memorials housed in the Mongolian Central Archives, this *nikasa* was the lone case after the Qianlong period in which "*nikan*" or "*nikasa*" appeared in one of these documents. Instead, the common term for Chinese was "*irgen*" or "*irgese*"—literally a civilian subject whose jurisdiction was outside the banners (Ch: *min*), but specifically in this context a Chinese person whose home jurisdiction remained in the *junxian* system. *Irgen* had the flexibility

to apply, for example, to Chinese Muslims, whereas *nikasa*, from what I have seen, may not have carried the same openness. Further research is needed into the use of *nikan*. At least in the case of trade licenses at Kiakhta, early Qianlong period documents use the term, whereas later ones do not. See MıDı-128.1 (QL22), MıDı-128.2 (QL22), and MıDı-128.3 (QL22). See also MıDı-2875.2 (QL27.6.4), discussed earlier, for a typical Qianlong-period usage: the *nikasa* picking mushrooms and starting a prairie fire.

172. On legibility, see Scott, *Seeing Like a State*.

173. Timkovskii, *Travels of the Russian Mission*, 426.

174. Ibid., 427.

CHAPTER FOUR

1. For an attempt in this direction, see Richards, *The Unending Frontier*, 463–546.

2. A major exception to this rule has been the work of Lai Hui-min. See Lai, "Qianlongchao Neifuyuan pihuo maimai yu jingcheng shishang," 101–134. On the Tannu Uriankhai as part of Chinese history, see Fan, *Tangnu Wulianghai lishi yanshi*.

3. See, for example, He, *Shuofang beisheng*, 3: 21a, 5: 1a–8b; and Qi Yunshi, *Huangchao fanbu yaolue*, 5: 2b.

4. On the fur trade in late antiquity, see Howard-Johnston, "Trading in Fur," 66–68, and Liu, *Ancient India and Ancient China*, 9, 19.

5. On the Song in particular, see Zeng, "Songdai maopi maoyi." For an entry point into fur trade under the Mongols, see Martin, "The Land of Darkness," 401–422.

6. On the Western circuit, see Martin, *Treasure in the Land of Darkness*; Veale, *The English Fur Trade*; and Bennigsen and Lemerchier-Quelquejay, "Les marchands de la cour ottomane," 363–390. On the legacy of Mongol institutions in the formation of these early modern networks, see Atwood, "The Mongol Empire," 27.

7. The literature on the modern fur trade is vast. For introductions to the Russian and North American trades, see Fisher, *The Russian Fur Trade*; Gibson, *Russian Fur Trade*; Bockstoce, *Furs and Frontiers*; White, *The Middle Ground*; and Richards, *The Unending Frontier*, 463–546.

8. Veale, *The English Fur Trade*, 57–60, 171–175.

9. On the early growth of the Northeast Asian fur trade, see Kawachi, "Mindai tōhoku Ajia chōhi bōeki," 62–120. On the "northern silk road," see Yang, *Ming-Qing dongbeiya shuilu sichou zhi lu*.

10. Based on comparison of the statistics presented in Poland, *Fur-Bearing Animals*, xxi–xxxiii, and Gibson, *Otter Skins*, 315.

11. Reidman and Estes, *The Sea Otter*, 31–59, 73.

12. Yazan, "Relations between the Marten," 36–45, and Tarasov, "Intraspecific Relations," 46.

13. Monakhov, "*Martes zibellina*," 81.

14. Gibson, *Otter Skins*, 22–23. On the role of the Ostrovnoe Fair in opening the Arctic fur trade, see Bockstoce, *Furs and Frontiers*, 92–102.

15. For an overview, see Gibson, *Otter Skins*, passim; on the environmental interconnections across the North Pacific rim, see Jones, "Running into Whales," 349–377.

16. For an overview of the Kiakhta trade, see Lai Hui-min, "Shijiu shiji Qiaketu maoyi de Eluosi fangzhipin," 1–46, and Mi Zhenbo, *Qingdai Zhong-E Qiaketu bianjing maoyi*.

17. Gibson, *Otter Skins*, 28; Ogden, "Russian Sea-Otter and Seal Hunting," 235; and Bockstoce, *Furs and Frontiers*, 5.

18. Richards, *The Unending Frontier*, 463–516, and Gibson, *Otter Skins*, 82, 101, 179. On the Spanish fur trade in particular, see Ogden, "The Californias," 444–469.

19. Richards, *The Unending Frontier*, 517–546, and Fisher, *The Russian Fur Trade*.

20. Ibid., 315, 317. Taken together, price and supply shared a Pearson coefficient of between −0.77 and −0.80, depending, respectively, on the low and high prices recorded.

21. Ibid., 178–179, 204–211, 315, and Ogden, "Russian Sea-Otter and Seal Hunting," 235.

22. Tegoborski, *Commentaries*, v. 2, 470–472.

23. On Russian–American partnerships, see Ogden, "Russian Sea-Otter."

24. For detailed analysis, see Gibson, *Otter Skins*, 201–202; Zhou, "Yiwu yu shangwu—yi Guangzhou kouan maopi jinyun shijian wei li," 85–91; and Zhou "Qingdai maopi maoyizhong de Guangzhou yu Qiaketu," 85–94.

25. The following discussion is based on statistics culled from Nagazumi, *Tōsen yushutsunyūhin sūryō ichiran*, 254–328. On the Hokkaido trade and its significance, see Walker, *The Conquest of Ainu Lands*, 94–97.

26. Between 1785 and 1810, there is a weak correlation between sea otter pelt prices in Canton and the supply of Japanese exports, which represented no more than one percent of the total supply of sea otter pelts on the southern coast; the Pearson coefficients for the period between 1785 and 1810 are −0.30 (low price) and −0.34 (high price). Between 1810 and 1821, when Japanese exports rose to as much as fifteen percent of total supply, the year-to-year supply of pelts began to more strongly correlate with price fluctuations in Canton, with Pearson coefficients of −0.69 (low price) and −0.70 (high price). Of course, given the limited number of years in play, we can only draw so many conclusions from the evidence. More research is needed on the problem.

27. Matsuura, *Shinchō no Amūru seisaku to shōsū minzoku*. Other focused surveys include Cong, *Dongbei sanbao jingji jianshi*, and Huen Fook-fai, "The Manchurian Fur Trade," 41–73.

28. Matsuura, *Shinchō no Amūru seisaku to shōsū minzoku*, 353–354.

29. For a detailed look at the number of households and pelts submitted through Ningguta, as well as the mechanics of the system, see ibid., 203, 240, 248–263, 326, 384–390, 421.

30. Ibid., 408–416. Many of the documents with tribute submission data are published in Chinese translation in *Sanxing fudutong yamen Manwen dang'an yibian* and *Qingdai Sanxing fudutong yamen Man-Hanwen dang'an xuanbian*.

31. Ibid., 394–396, 405–406, 411.

32. Ibid., 196–204, 349–354, 362, 392, 446. On the enduring importance of smallpox in Mongolian and Manchurian history in the late imperial period, see Serruys, "Smallpox."

33. Ibid., 188–220, 356–360, 370–371, 398, 441–454. On dwindling stocks of fur in Sakhalin, see in particular 210, 211.

34. The Imperial Household Department accepted no pelts graded below third class.

35. Cong, *Dongbei sanbao jingji jianshi*, 207–209.

36. TGKH 53: 5a–8a; GMQJ 53: 5a–8b. The court specifically prohibited Mongols from buying sable in "Solon" lands. The punishments for allowing illegal sable and ginseng trade in a Mongol banner were comparable to those for sheltering illegal migrants: A Mongol commoner who bought sable pelts on the black market received 150 lashes; a nobleman received a year of suspended stipends and a penalty of two "nines" of livestock; a Mongol who had acted as middleman to buy on behalf of another was whipped eighty times. Officials who failed to properly investigate a case of smuggling or poaching were punished, too: Mongol noblemen received a fine valued at a year's worth of stipends, and banner authorities had to pay three "nines" of livestock.

37. On the 1795 reforms, see Cong, *Dongbei sanbao jingji jianshi*, 208.

38. The following analysis of tributary records is based on *Manwen lufu* held in the First Historical Archives in Beijing, Manchu palace memorials held in the National Palace Museum in Taipei, and published archives from Harbin and Beijing in *Qingdai Elunchunzu Man-Hanwen dang'an huibian*. See Appendix.

39. The Pearson coefficient is 0.32 between 1814 and 1830. For 1831 to 1850 it is 0.51; for 1851 to 1870 it is 0.93.

40. Atwood, *Encyclopedia*, 9.

41. Vainshtein, *Nomads of South Siberia*, 47–48, 188–189. The elevation at which these ecosystem shifts occurred varied. In the Sayan mountains, for example, the steppe grasses pushed no higher than 1,000 meters, but they reached as high as 2,000 meters on the southern slopes of the Tannu-Ola. Ibid., 47.

42. Ibid., 49, 121, 145–165.

43. For background on the Chinggünjab rebellion, see Bawden, "Some Documents," 1–23.

44. MWLF 1663.29.46.3298 (QL22.12.5).

45. One document states that the Dzungars had lowered the expected quota to four pelts from a previous high of six. MWLF 1663.29.46.3298 (QL22.12.5).

46. Ibid.

47. On the meaning of *ejen* in Qing relations, see Onuma, "Political Relations" 86–125. On grace, see Atwood, "Worshipping Grace."

48. Similar stock phrases in the documents include "become the subject/tributary of the great lord" (Ma: *amba ejen i albatu obumbi*), MWLF 1748.35.52.799 (QL24.3.7), and "entering into service" (Ma: *alban de dosimbuha*), MWLF 1786.20.54.2057 (QL24.9.29).

49. MWLF 1663.29.46.3298 (QL22.12.5). The noble leader of the Altan Nuur Uriankhai at the time of their creation was Cadak.

50. Notably, the Uriankhai remain in an ambiguous position vis-à-vis the Mongols today, maintaining a distinct identity as an "ethnic group" (Mo: *yastan*) but not fully recognized "nationality" (Mo: *ündesten*), like the Kazaks. Billé, *Sinophobia*, 81.

51. MWLF 3601.28.166.1520 (JQ4.9.21).

52. MWLF 1786.20.54.2057 (QL24.9.29).

53. Vainshtein, *Nomads of South Siberia*, 166–167.

54. MWLF 1734.7.51.1373 (QL23.12.13).

55. MWLF 1786.20.54.2057 (QL24.9.29). Others, too, like a group of over twenty Tes Uriankhai, under the *jaisang* Onom, were described as having "gone in search of game and fish," and were so impoverished that the Qing court stripped Onom of his rank, and combined his households with thirty Kirgis households to create a new *otoġ*.

56. On the text, which is undated but can reasonably be traced to the first half of the nineteenth century, see David Farquhar, "The Ch'ing Administration of Mongolia up to the Nineteenth Century," 311–312n92.

57. Their homeland was also an "extreme frontier" (Ch: *dichu jibian*); as the *Wuliyasutai zhilue* recorded, "The warmth comes late, and the cold comes early. The summers are not hot, and the winters are severe, so much so that simply moving about causes one to wheeze (Ch: *xingdong zuochuan*)." *Wuliyasutai zhilue*, 66.

58. MWLF 3601.28.166.1520 (JQ4.9.21).

59. Ibid.

60. *Wuliyasutai zhilue*, 67.

61. Vainshtein, *Nomads of South Siberia*, 224.

62. MWLF 3667.14.171.2447 (JQ9.4.3)

63. MWLF 3695.35.174.637 (JQ11.26).

64. The author adds a caveat, however: "The land is vast with endless mountains and rivers, and each locality has its own products. If I thus recorded in detail all the regular grasses, trees, wild birds, wild animals, and unusual objects, there would be a great number of types. I fear there would be errors and mistakes . . ." *Wuliyasutai zhilue*, 70.

65. Ibid., 70–72.

66. Perdue, *China Marches West*, 161–173, 409–461.

67. Significantly, the treaty also maintained special provisions on fur trappers. The Treaty of Bura and the Treaty of Kiakhta adopted the same language:

"The Uriankhy, to whichever side they pay five sables of *yasak*, on that side they shall remain and continue to pay [the *yasak*]. Those Uriankhy, however, who paid one sable to each side, from the day the frontier is established, will never again be required [to pay it]." Translated in Mancall, *Russia and China*, 285.

68. These principles became domestic law, with the same language used in the Treaty of Kiakhta inscribed into the *Laws and Precedents for the Board Governing Outer Dependencies* (Ch: *Lifanyuan zeli*), the compendium of laws governing Outer Mongolia. The text was published on six different occasions: 1789 (juan 12, as the Menggu lüli), 1817 (juan 63), 1826 (juan 63), 1841 (juan 63), 1891 (juan 64), and 1908 (juan 64). See Farquhar, "The Ch'ing Administration," 206–207n176, and Legrand, *L'Administration*.

69. *Da Qing huidian* 66: 2a. Cited in Li, *Waimeng zhengjiao zhidu kao*, 55. The phrase was boilerplate Qing administrative language for Outer Mongolia from at least the mid-eighteenth century.

70. M1D1-3834.7a (DG6.1.12), for example, explicitly contrasts "borderland" (Ma: *jecen i ba*) with "Mongol land" (Ma: *monggo i ba*).

71. Russian diplomats later pointed to this peculiarity of the Qing borderlands to justify imperial expansion, including into Tannu Uriankhai lands, in the late nineteenth and early twentieth centuries. Ewing, "The Forgotten Frontier," 189.

72. TGKH 63: 4b–5a.

73. Ibid.; GMQJ 63: 5a.

74. On the border guards, see Jigmeddorji, *Manzhiĭn üeiĭn ar mongol dakh' khiliĭn kharuul.*

75. *Wuliyasutai zhilue*, 45. Additional assistant officers staffed some of the *karun* as well.

76. Ibid.

77. M1D1-3750.11 (DG3.10).

78. M2D1-176.78a-b (DG15.*6), M2D1-177.12a (XF1.6), and M2D1-177.35b (XF2.6). The language in the three documents is identical. The emperor responded "acknowledged" (Ma: *saha*) in each case.

79. M1D1-3834.1a (DG6.7).

80. Ibid.

81. A similar border was maintained between Manchuria and Korea, and it was not unusual for Korean travelers passing through on their way to Manchuria to write as if they were isolated on an ancient and broken steppe: "Going to bed I think of home. It is truly silent [at the water's edge]. There is no one to be seen, only dense grass and mature forest. I suddenly recall Du Fu's poem, 'I travel amongst northern barbarians [Ch: *hu*], as if in an empty valley.'" Zhang, *Hanguo shiliao sanzhong*, 185.

82. For a discussion of the scale and logistics of the effort, see Perdue, "Military Mobilization," 757–793.

83. Chuang, *Qingdai zhungaer shiliao*, 46.

84. Tulišen, *Lakcaha jecen de takūraha babe ejehe bithei*, 14.

85. *Taiga* is the word used in all texts. The English word *taiga* derives ultimately from the Mongol.

86. TGKH 63: 3a,b; and GMQJ 63:3a,b.

87. The *Manwen laodang* characteristically celebrates Nurhaci and Hong Taiji for their superior ability to use terrain to their advantage, for example, by manipulating ill-fated Ming armies into quagmires and marshes then ambushing them. Qing generals were to avoid such quagmires at all costs. Cf. MBRT 1.8.126.13, 3.38.1484.6, 3.4.940.15, and 3.8.1007.6c.

88. *Han-i araha Manju Monggo gisun-i bileku bithe, Na-i hacin* 2.

89. In the summer of 1815 alone, for example, three separate incidents triggered bursts of diplomatic correspondences and paperwork. The first involved five horses crossing into Qing territory; the second, Russian children who chased a loose bellwether into it; then another case of escaped horses. The displaced animals and children were all returned according to proper procedure. M1D1-407.14a (QL51), M1D2-307.7 (JQ20.5.14), M1D2-307.9 (JQ20.7.18), and M1D2-307.10. This final document is a bilingual Russian–Mongol diplomatic correspondence dispatched to the captain Teksurun at Boora *karun*. The document follows the general form of Qing documents, but it dates the letter June 8, 1815, using the Julian calendar (June 20, 1815, Gregorian), not with the Qing calendar as JQ20.5.14.

90. M1D1-3834.1a (DG6.7).

91. The Mongols were locals from Mingjurdorji's banner. M1D1-3822.1a (DG6.9.1). The winter of 1825–1826 was a disaster throughout Mongolia. Border guards around Hathūlbom *karun* perhaps suffered the worst, when flooding, followed by a blizzard, washed away the Eg River at its source at the southern tip of Lake Khövsgöl. When the snow melted the following spring, a wall of mud and rocks remained, leaving the Eg dammed at its source. Downstream communities that depended on the water for its pastures—including the guardsmen at Hathūlbom—were in desperate straits; their only short-term solution was to remove to different pastures. But when they issued a panicked plea to the *amban*'s office, the response returned was ice cold: Leaving the *karun* was out of the question. Instead, they were upbraided for bringing misfortune on themselves by failing to pay proper respects to mountain and river sprits. The *amban* ordered that all the soldiers and lamas in the community gather together to read sutras, pray for good fortune, and pay more earnest respect to Lake Khövsgöl, local mountains, and the Eg river. Then, with Heaven's help, water would come forth on its accord. M1D1-3834.2a (DG6.3.21).

92. M1D1-3834.7a (DG6.1.12).

93. Kim, "Marginal Constituencies," 141–142.

94. MWLF 1734.7.51.1373 (QL23.12.13).

95. Ibid.

96. QSL QL, 552: 1061b.

97. M1D1-3909.2 [JQ10].

98. MWLF 1748.35.52.799 (QL24.3.7).

99. Ibid.

100. Ibid.

101. Vainshtein, *Nomads of South Siberia*, 173–176, 187. Squirrels were the easiest prey to catch. Over time, sables became perhaps the hardest: By the late eighteenth and early nineteenth centuries, it often took over two weeks of stalking to catch one.

102. Ibid., 168–169. A hunter's "quivers" (*saadak*) were thus his powder flask, powder measure, and bullet pouch draped about his belt. In the early twentieth century, a rifle sold for roughly 200 to 250 squirrel pelts.

103. Ibid., 169–172, 175. For those without flintlocks, the preferred weapons for hunting squirrels were simple bows or compound devices. When their dogs caught a scent of a squirrel, they dismounted and shot a "whistling" arrow to startle the squirrel into the open, then used a regular arrow for the kill shot. Crossbows were popular for catching squirrels and larger animals, including foxes, wolves, sables, and squirrels.

104. Until 1802 they also passed through Darkhintu *karun*.

105. M1D1-3976.7b (DG13.12.10).

106. Vainshtein, *Nomads of South Siberia*, 167, 236. In the late nineteenth and early twentieth centuries, households could legally submit cattle in place of furs to fulfill their *alban* obligation.

107. For a complete listing and discussion of the sources, see Appendix. I am profoundly grateful to Lai Hui-min for guiding me to the *Neiwufu zouxiaodang* (NWFZXD), held today at the First Historical Archives in Beijing.

108. M1D1-3427.18a (JQ13.11.3), and M1D2-223.2b (JQ13.*5.24). Darkintu is spelled *Darkintū* in Manchu documents; in modern Mongolian it is *Darhintu qaruul*.

109. M1D1-3909.2 [JQ10].

110. M2D1-176.88b (DG15.8).

111. Further complicating the matter was the fact that Arhūn Booral *karun* lay under the jurisdiction of the *ambans'* office in Ikh Khüree, whereas Hathūlbom belonged to the military governor's office in Uliasutai.

112. M1D1-3427.18a (JQ13.11.3).

113. M1D1-3976.5a (DG13.5.24).

114. M1D1-3909.1 (DG10.7.6). That spring, officials confirmed that a hunting party of twenty-five left from Hathūlbom. See M1D1-3909.3 (DG10.8.19).

115. In time, this policy proved just as ruinous, as "multiple times" the Uriankhai became the targets of banditry, and trappers took on debts just to cover the journey's expenses. In 1851, the court restored the envoy system, blaming the reformed delivery system for "deficits" in fur tribute. See M2D1-177.1a (XF1.2.15). Tribute continued to be delivered to Beijing in this way until 1911. Humphrey, "Introduction," 24. See M2D1-177.1a (XF1.2.15).

116. We can thus update Thomas Ewing's claim, made without the benefit of access to archival records, that "there is no evidence that Tannu-Urjankhai was

ever visited by a senior Ch'ing official (except perhaps in 1726)." Ewing, "The Forgotten Frontier," 189.

117. The following account is taken from M1D1-4092.1 (DG17.4.20).

118. Ibid., M1D1-4092.5 [undated], and M1D1-4092.7 (DG17.3).

119. On the top right corner is written the Manchu word "*asara*"—"store away [for the files]."

120. 1853 was an exceptional and outstanding year in this regard, with a 1,348 sable pelts submitted.

121. The Pearson coefficient is −0.21 from 1833 to 1867.

122. MWLF 4238.27.211.1940 (DG22.8.29).

123. *Zhongguo gudai dangpu jianding miji*, 447.

124. Calculating the value of tribute exchanges to the Uriankhai is complicated by what they received in return: silk for sable and cotton for squirrel. Within China proper, where price histories are easier to reconstruct, silk was worth no more than seven times the value of fine cotton by weight: In the mid-eighteenth-century, the price of cotton was roughly 0.3 to 0.8 tael of silver per *jin* (at about 1.33 taels per bolt), and 2.08 taels per *jin* of silk in the same period; the prices of both commodities rose at roughly the same rates, roughly doubling between the 1730s and the 1790s. If the seven-to-one exchange rate for cotton and silk held in Uriankhai lands, then squirrel was more valuable as tribute than the official tribute exchange suggested: Fourteen squirrel pelts should have equaled one sable, not forty. More research on prices in Uriankhai in this period is needed, though, to fully understand the market, fur and textile prices, and by extension the degree to which tribute exchanges were exploitative. On silk and cotton prices, see Kishimoto, *Shindai Chugoku no bukka to keizai*, 143–153, and Pomeranz, *The Great Divergence*, 317–319.

125. NWFZXD 155.624.199 (DG24.10.14).

126. MWLF 4264.2.213.931 (DG24.8.13).

127. The reverse, though, happened in 1814: The number of squirrels reported as received was higher than those recorded as sent, and the number of sables was higher. In other years, the math simply did not add up at all in the Imperial Household Accounts; no one, it seems, was checking the math.

128. I owe a debt of gratitude to Beatrice Bartlett for first alerting me to this possibility.

129. Vainshtein, *Nomads of South Siberia*, 167–168. Vainshtein notes that squirrel pelts functioned as money for the Tannu Uriankhai in the late nineteenth and early twentieth centuries; they estimated prices in terms of units of ten squirrel pelts.

130. Tarasov, "Intraspecific Relations," 2.47.

131. Sables have a two-year reproductive cycle, with an average litter size of three. In one study, 23.4 percent of females were pregnant after two years in the Sayan mountains. By this math, in ideal conditions, a population of 100 would grow to 289 members after six years. On reproduction and ecology, see Monakhov, "*Martes zibellina*," 80–81.

132. Based on a comparison of Tannu Uriankhai sable submissions recorded in MWLF (see Appendix) and the statistics on the total value of the Kiakhta trade supplied in Korsak, *Istoriko-statisticheskoe obozrienie*, 67, 73, 97, 105. Between 1792 and 1830 the Pearson coefficient is 0.62; between 1792 and 1810, the Pearson coefficient is 0.80. Given the limited data, however, more research is needed into the problem. Note that Japanese junk boat trade in sea otters peaked in this period as well. Nagazumi, *Tōsen yushutsunyūhin sūryō ichiran*, 254–328.

133. The comparison is not extreme; people saw Manchuria in exactly such terms in the late nineteenth century. See Gamsa, "California on the Amur," 236–266.

134. Carruthers, "Exploration in North-West Mongolia and Dzungaria," 524, 526.

135. On such "tropes of anachronism" in the Qing, see Teng, *Taiwan's Imagined Geography*, 60–80. For the broader historiographical dimensions, see Goody, *The Theft of History*.

CONCLUSION

1. On the importance of differing perceptions of cultural distinctions in the perception of nature in Qing frontiers, see Perdue, "Nature and Nurture," 245–267.

2. On the connected processes of making bordered space, consolidating sovereignty, and streamlining government hierarchies, see Thongchai, *Siam Mapped*, 100–107.

3. On frugality and the Manchus in particular, see Elliott, *The Manchu Way*, 276, 347.

4. The range of critical perspectives on the significance of the term is accordingly complex and varied. For touchstone theoretical interventions, see Latour, *We Have Never Been Modern*, 1–48; Soulé and Lease, *Reinventing Nature*; and Descola, *Beyond Nature and Culture*.

5. We should not expect it to have been unique, either. On the integrative and comparative dimensions of the history of the Qing empire, see Perdue, *China Marches West*; Crossley, *A Translucent Mirror*; and Di Cosmo, "Qing Colonial Administration."

6. Schama, *Landscape and Memory*, 75–134.

7. Ibid., 77.

8. Ibid., 103; and Lekan, *Imagining the Nation in Nature*, 26–28.

9. Uekoetter, *The Green and the Brown*.

10. On German landscape preservation, see Lekan, *Imagining the Nation in Nature*, 4.

11. Schama, *Landscape and Memory*, 48.

12. Ibid., 57.

13. Schama, *Landscape and Memory*, 38.

14. Chuang, *Xie Sui 'Zhigongtu' Manwen tushuo xiaozhu*, 73.

15. In Hayden, *William Wordsworth*, 166.

16. Blanning, *The Pursuit of Glory*, 394–395, 405. The year was 1775.

17. Salvadori, *La Chasse sous l'ancien régime*, 203, cited in Blanning, *The Pursuit of Glory*, 393.

18. Allsen, *The Royal Hunt*. Just as Qing subjects knew the number of tigers and deer the Kangxi shot, so too did Mughal and Safavid subjects circulate stories about their own rulers: Thus we know that the Mughal emperor Jahāngīr (r. 1605–1627), for example, shot 17,167 animals in his lifetime.

19. Cited in Cronon, *Changes in the Land*, 4.

20. Quoted in Schama, *Landscape and Memory*, 9.

21. Martin and Wright, *Pleistocene Extinctions*; Scott, *Seeing Like a State*; and Fairhead and Leach, *Misreading the African Landscape*.

22. Cronon, "The Trouble with Wilderness," 69.

23. Latour, *We Have Never Been Modern*, 1–48.

24. For American wilderness as a European preserve, see Richards, *The Unending Frontier*, 516. On Russian preserves, see Weiner, *Models of Nature*.

25. Both *ziran* and *baiğali* remain nuanced terms. On *ziran*, see Weller, 20–21. On *baiğali*, see Humphrey and Sneath, *The End of Nomadism?* 2–3.

26. Merchant, *Reinventing Eden*, and Cronon, "A Place for Stories," 1347–1376.

27. For an overview, see Merchant, *Reinventing Eden*; see also Hughes, *Human-Built World*, 17–43, and Nye, *America as Second Creation*.

28. Puett, *The Ambivalence of Creation*.

29. The touchstone theoretical analysis of such a project remains Chakrabarty, *Provincializing Europe*. European exceptionalism remains dominant in theoretical scholarship; Descola, for example, not only argues that nature was wholly a product of the modern West, but claims has been the "idea of nature is unknown" in China and Japan. Descola, *The Ecology of Others*, 82. For counter-perspectives from Tokugawa Japan, see Thomas, *Reconfiguring Modernity*, and Marcon, *The Knowledge of Nature*.

30. Zhang, *Mingqing jinshang ji minfeng*, 60–63.

31. The literature on this topic is large. For critical entry points, see Rogaski, *Hygienic Modernity*, and Fan, *British Naturalists*.

32. Cong, "Zhongguo zaipei renshen zhi chuxian yu xingqi," 268.

33. For a synopsis of these events, see Lee, *The Manchurian Frontier*. On domesticated deer and deer-horn production in the Altai region among descendants of the Altan Nuur Uriankhai, see "National Treasures."

34. For a critical overview of such representations, see Gladney, *Dislocating China*.

35. Much work exists on the legacies of the Qing. On the enduring importance of the empire's territorial boundaries, classification schemes for people, and legal system, see Ho, "The Significance of the Ch'ing Period," 189–195;

Crossley, *A Translucent Mirror*, 337–361; and Cassel, "Excavating Extraterritoriality," 156–182.

36. On ecological wisdom, see Gagengaowa and Wuyunbatu, *Menggu minzu de shengtai wenhua*; Ge, *Zhidu shiyuxia de caoyuan shengtai huanjing baohu*; He, *Huanjing yu xiaominzu shengcun*; and Wu and Bao, *Mengguzu shengtai zhihuilun*.

37. Shapiro, *China's Environmental Challenges*, 113.

38. As the film director Su Xiaokang recently argued, preserved landscapes have a power to connect people to their past. Su and Link, "A Collapsing," 215.

39. Billé, *Sinophobia*.

40. Ibid., 22, 102, 117.

41. Harris, *Wildlife Conservation*, 111.

42. Personal encounter by the author in 2004. One tourist guidebook expressed doubts about the authenticity of traditional reindeer herders crassly playing to the market. Kohn, *Lonely Planet*, 155.

43. This argument derives from Richards, *The Unending Frontier*.

44. Walker, "Foreign Affairs and Frontiers in Early Modern Japan," 44–62.

45. Although research on these points remains to be done, scholarship already points in this direction. For a recent history that integrates Qing history into the dynamics of Chinese emigration, see Kuhn, *Chinese Among Others*. For a wider view on gold rush politics in the boom years in particular, see Ngai, "Chinese Gold Miners," 1082–1105; High and Schlesinger, "Rulers and Rascals," 289–304; and Chew, *Chinese Pioneers*. On fears of Chinese immigration in this period and modern border regimes, see McKeown, *Melancholy Order*.

APPENDIX

1. For the records in Taiwan, see NPM-JJCD 174661 (DG30.8.21), 170779 (GX15.11.1), 171123 (GX16.10.20), 171477 (GX17.10.24), 171885 (GX18.10.28), 172227 (GX19.10.29), 172806 (GX20.11.6), 173223 (GX22.11.13), 173605 (GX23.11.11), and 173869 (GX24.10.12). For records in Beijing, see MWLF 2441.14.94.209 (QL36.5.29), 2456.24.95.488 (QL37.5.17), 2521.24.99.468 (QL38.4.20), 2854.26.103.11 (QL39.5.19), 2635.14.106.769 (QL40.5.24), 2717.7.111.2133 (QL42.5.22), 2795.10.116.2662 (QL44.5.19), 2830.31.118.2902 (QL45.5.17), 2881.25.121.2676 (QL46.5.24), 2932.36.124.3606 (QL47.5.28), 2967.2.127.1255 (QL48.6.2), 3025.39.131.1532 (QL49.6.4), 3073.10.134.1629 (QL50.5.25), 3169.18.140.715 (QL52.6.19), 3197.5.142.678 (QL53.6.24), 3248.41.14.2616 (QL54.7.26), 3300.22.148.3323 (QL55.6.7), 3346.20.151.1728 (QL56.5.28), 3391.33.153.3169 (QL57.6.2), 3434.26.156.1537 (QL58.6.13), 3473.3.158.2326 (QL59.6.24), 3504.36.160.1392 (QL60.6.6), 3544.28.162.1510 (JQ1.6.4), 3582.49.165.202 (JQ3.6.19), 3599.33.166.1018 (JQ4.7.3), 3613.31.167.1223 & 3613.29.167.1206 (JQ5.7.10), 3628.29.168.1988 (JQ6.7.5), 3642.34.169.2452 (JQ7.6.25), 3659.36.171.225 (JQ8.7.2), 3671.41.172.161 (JQ9.7.13), 3686.9.173.1160 (JQ10.7.1), 3705.25.175.83 (JQ11.7.12), 3427.32.176.2180 (JQ12.7.20), 3770.20.179.2259 (JQ14.8.11), 3788.25.180.2858

(JQ15.6.20), 3802.20.181.2772 (JQ16.6.6), 3819.19.182.3116 (JQ17.6.26), 3833.15.183.2840 (JQ18.7.11), 3849.20.184.3328 (JQ19.7.12), 3863.27.185.3290 (JQ20.6.15), 3878.52.187.373 (JQ21.*6.13), 3909.10.189.947 (JQ23.7.7), 3925.41.190.1057 (JQ24.6.20), 3975.15.193.600 (DG2.7.20), 3990.43.194.459 (DG3.8.11), 4006.1.195.152 (DG4.*7.8), 4021.46.195.3507 (DG5.7.7), 4037.20.196.3360 (DG6.7.20), 4049.12.197.2763 (DG7.8.10), 4062.21.198.2806 (DG8.8.8), 4078.27.199.3044 (DG9.8.13), 4092.53.200.2959 (DG10.8.7), 4105.52.201.2413 (DG11.8.26), 4118.42.202.2038 (DG12.9.14), 4139.41.203.1625 & 4130.27.203.1557 (DG13.8.13), 4142.49.204.1142 (DG14.8.9), 4157.3.205.115 (DG15.8.6), 4169.29.206.824 (DG16.8.18), 4179.33.207.399 (DG17.8.20), 4190.36.208.87 (DG18.8.29), 4201.41.208.3288 (DG19.8.22), 4211.26.209.2501 (DG20.8.12), 4225.6.210.2462 (DG21.8.25), 4238.27.211.1940 (DG22.8.29), 4251.43.212.530 (DG23.8.20), 4264.2.213.931 (DG24.8.13), 4274.38.214.32 (DG25.8.16), 4286.32.214.3004 (DG26.8.17), 4296.62.215.2360 (DG27.8.16), 4309.13.216.2107 (DG28.9.13), 4321.4.217.1624 (DG29.8.24), 4343.10.219.337 (XF1.9.11), 4355.50.220.113 (XF2.8.17), 4369.45.221.735 (XF3.9.18), 4385.28.222.1304 (XF4.9.25), 4399.15.223.1417 (XF5.9.16), 4410.29.224.1372 (XF6.9.16), 4422.19.225.1463 (XF7.9.26), 4431.45.226.1217 (XF8.10.7), 4441.46.227.1353 (XF9.9.23), 4451.26.228.1641 (XF10.9.26), 4459.17.229.1453 (XF11.9.26), 4471.43.231.14 (TZ2.10.6), 4477.52.231.3014 (TZ3.10.3), 4483.70.232.2366 (TZ4.10.22), 4489.22.235.1324 (TZ5.11.9), 4494.7.234.14 (TZ6.10.9), 4500.5.234.2718 (TZ7.11.28), 4504.14.235.1015 (TZ8.11.13), 4508.16.235.2782 (TZ9.10.5), 4514.61.236.2222 (TZ10.12.6), 4518.21.237.629 (TZ11.10.25), 4520.33.237.1649 (TZ12.10.25), 4523.2.237.2937 (TZ13.9.9), 4526.3.238.1861 (GX1.10.3), 4528.1.238.2085 (GX2.11.3), 4530.54.238.3305 (GX3.9.26), 4533.57.239.1300 (GX4.9.24), 4536.42.239.2672 (GX5.9.12), 4539.28.240.326 (GX6.9.28), 4542.62.240.1892 (GX7.9.20), 4545.31.240.3188 (GX8.9.20), 4549.8.241.1566 (GX9.9.24), 4853.1.241.3489 (GX10.9.10), 4556.62.242.1744 (GX11.9.28), 4589.68.242.3457 (GX12.10.4), 4564.20.243.2100 (GX13.10.7), 4567.69.244.244 (GX14.10.12), 4571.7.244.1482 (GX21.10.9), 4574.88.244.2965 (GX25.10.21), 4576.77.245.388 (GX26.9.21), 4579.47.245.1772 (GX29.9.6), 4881.6.245.2802 (GX30.9.19), 4582.95.246.404 (GX31.9.24), 4583.111.246.1061 (GX32.9.12), 4587.42.246.3074 (GX34.9.26), and 4589.89.247.965 (XT2.9.18).

2. *Qingdai Elunchuzu Man-Hanwen dang'an huibian*, no. 199 (QL50.6.6), 200 (QL52.6.6), 201 (QL53.6.6), 202 (QL54.*5.26), 203 (QL56.6.8), 204 (QL57.6.28), 205 (QL58.6.10), 206 (QL59.6.16), 207 (QL60.6.12), 209 (JQ1.6.16), 210 (JQ2.*6.6), 211 (JQ3.6.7), 213 (JQ19.6.12), 214 (JQ20.6.13), 215 (JQ21.*6.1), 216 (JQ22.6.7), 217 (JQ23.6.18), 218 (JQ25.6.7), 219 (DG3.6.12), 220 (DG4.6.28), 221 (DG5.6.8), 222 (DG6.6.14), 223 (DG7.*5.27), 224 (DG8.6.10), 225 (DG9.6.22), 226 (DG10.6.22), 227 (DG11.6.19), 228 (DG12.6.24), 229 (DG13.6.25), 230 (DG14.6.20), 231 (DG15.6.11), 232 (DG16.6.15), 233 (DG17.6.26), 234 (DG18.6.15), 235 (DG19.6.20), 236 (DG20.6.26), 237 (DG21.6.17), 238 (DG22.6.26), 239 (DG23.7.8), 240 (DG24.6.26), 241

(DG25.6.27), 242 (DG26.6.20), 243 (DG27.6.20), 244 (DG28.7.1), 245 (DG29.6.25), 246 (DG30.7.4), 247 (XF1.6.28), 248 (XF2.6.25), 249 (XF3.7.1), 250 (XF4.7.15), 251 (XF5.7.3), 252 (XF6.7.12), 254 (XF8.7.3), 255 (XF9.7.20), 258 (XF10.6.26), 259 (XF11.7.11), 260 (TZ1.7.27), 261 (TZ3.7.1), 262 (TZ4.6.20), 263 (TZ5.7.8), 264 (TZ6.6.25), 265 (TZ7.7.13), 266 (TZ8.6.24), 267 (TZ9.7.28), 268 (YZ10.7.18), 269 (TZ11.7.18), 271 (TZ12.6.28), 272 (TZ13.8.2), 275 (GX1.8.9), 279 (GX3.7.21), 282 (GX4.7.10), 283 (GX5.7.1), 284 (GX6.7.25), 286 (GX7.7.2), 288 (GX8.7.26), 290 (GX9.8.12), 291 (GX10.7.27), 293 (GX11.8.3), 295 (GX12.7.26), 296 (GX13.7.28), 298 (GX14.7.19), 304 (GX21.8.10), and 307 (GX25.9.4).

   3. MWLF 3960.19.192.877 (DG1.7.10); and NPM-JJCD 170731 (GX15.8.13), 171049, 171050 (GX16.8.1), 171397 (GX17.7.20), 171770 (GX18.7.11), 172155 (GX19.8.10), 172728 (GX20.8.10), 173163 (GX22.8.10), 173508 (GX23.8.29), and 173790 (GX24.8.23).

List of Chinese Terms

aiye diao 艾葉貂
ao 襖
bai mogu 白蘑菇
bang 蚌
bang'e 蚌蛤
Beiyou lu 北遊錄
beizhu 北珠
Bencao gangmu 本草綱目
biji 筆記
bijia 比甲
bizhao 比照
bu 布
Buteha wula 布特哈烏拉
cheng'an 成案
Chengde fuzhi 承德府志
chi 尺
chuanwo 穿窩
chun 淳 or 純
chunfeng 淳風
cun 寸
Da Qing 大清
Da Qing quanshu 大清全書
Da Xing'an ling 大興安嶺
da ziran 大自然
dahu 褡護
dangshen 黨蔘
dao tianye gumai 盜田野穀麥
dazhu 大珠
diaochan 貂蟬
diaopi 貂皮

diaoqiu 貂裘
diaoshu 貂鼠
dichu jibian 地處極邊
diling zhongchan 地靈鍾產
Dongsansheng 東三省
dongzhu 東珠
doushu 豆鼠
duan 緞
Dumen jilue 都門紀略
Duyusi 都虞司
erdiao 珥貂
fanli 藩籬
faxiang zhi di 發祥之地
fei gesheng kebi 非各省可比
fen 分
fengjin zhengce 封禁政策
fengshui 風水
fengsu chunpu 風俗純樸
Fengtian 奉天
fu huaxia zhi chunfeng 復華夏之
　淳風
fudutong 副都統
fuduyushi 副都御史
ganjing 乾淨
ge 蛤
geli 蛤蜊
genben 根本
genben zhi di 根本之地
genben zhongdi 根本重地
gong 貢 (tribute)

gong 公 (duke)
Guangzhi 廣志
Guanshenju 管參局
haita 海獺
haidongqing 海東青
haidiao 海貂
haizhu 海珠
Heilongjiang 黑龍江
Heilongjiang zhigao 黑龍江志稿
Hongloumeng 紅樓夢
hongpiao 紅票
Houluanshui qiufeng shi 後灤水
　秋風詩
houtou 猴頭
hu 胡
Hubu 戶部
Hujia shiba pai 胡笳十八拍
huli 狐狸
humao 胡帽
jian 間
jiangjun 將軍
jiangyi 江夷
jie 潔
jie xi manzhou 皆係滿洲
jiejing 潔淨
Jin 金 (dynastic name)
jin 斤 (unit of measurement)
jindi 禁地
jing 淨
jingxiu 競秀
jinshan zhaopiao 進山照票
jinshi 進士
jun 菌
jun chu shazhong mei 菌出沙中美
Junjichu manwen lufu zouzhe
　軍機處滿文錄副奏摺
junxian 郡縣
kalun 卡倫
ke 克
koumo 口蘑
koumo feilong tang 口蘑飛龍湯

koumo huijiding 口蘑燴雞丁
koumo shaorou kui 口蘑燒肉塊
koumo yanjianrou 口蘑鹽煎肉
kulun banshi dachen 庫倫辦事大
　臣
li 里
liang 兩
lingcui 領催
liumin 流民
lu 魯
Luanjing zayong 灤京雜詠
lujin shaokoumo 鹿筋燒口蘑
Lun piyi cuxi maofa 論皮衣粗細
　毛法
luoye song 落葉松
mafen bao 馬糞苞
magua 馬褂
Manzhou genben zhongdi 滿洲根
　本重地
maye 麻葉
meilu 梅鹿
mengchang 盟長
Menggu fuxing chunpu 蒙古賦性
　淳樸
milu 麋鹿
min 民
min yi renshen wei difang hai 民以
　人參為地方害
mogu 蘑菇
mu 畝
mu'er 木耳
Neiwufu 內務府
Neiwufu zouxiaodang 內務府奏
　銷檔
pao 袍
paozi 袍子
pu 樸
qi 氣 (*qi*)
qi 旗 (banner)
qili zihou 其力自厚
Qiludeng 崎路燈

Qinding Rehe zhi 欽定熱河志
qing 清
qingjing 清淨
qingjing shengdi 清淨聖地
qingshu kewu 情殊可惡
qingtu 清土
Sanxing 三姓
saoshu 騷鼠
saoxue 掃雪
sengdaobu folei 僧道部佛類
shajun 沙菌
Shangdu 上都
Shangjing 上京
Shangjing shiyong 上京十詠
Shangjing zashi 上京雜詩
shaojiu 燒酒
shaoshu minzu 少數民族
shelisun 猞狸猻
sheng 省
Shengjing 盛京
Shengjing tongzhi 盛京通志
shengqing 聲清
Shengwu ji 聖武記
shenpiao 參票
shu 鼠
si 私
Songhua 松花
sui 歲
Suiyuan shidan 隨園食單
suqing 肅清
suqing bianjie 肅清邊界
ta 獺
tao 套
tian 天
tianxia zhi houli 天下之厚利
Tongjian gangmu 通鑑綱目
tusi 土司
waitao 外套
wang 王
weichang 圍場

weijing 味精
wodao 猧刀
xianpiao 限票
xiaoqixiao 驍騎校
xiashan zhaopiao 下山照票
xieling 協領
xing 性
xingdong zuochuan 行動作喘
Xingshi yinyuan zhuan 醒世姻緣
傳
xisu chunzheng 習俗淳正
xiu 秀
Xuzeng xing'an huilan 續增刑案
匯覽
yamen 衙門
yao 要
yaopai 腰牌
yapiao 押票
yingpan mogu 營盤蘑菇
Yiyulu 異域錄
youmu 遊牧
*Yuzhi Manzhu Menggu Hanzi sanhe
qieyin Qingwenjian* 御製滿珠
蒙古漢字三和切音清文鑒
Yuzhi wuti Qingwen 御製五題清
文鑒
zhai 齋
Zhangwu zhi 長物志
zhengzhu 正珠
zhenzhu 真珠 (true pearl)
zhenzhu 珍珠 (translation for
nicuhe)
zhisun 隻孫
zhongtu 中土
zhu 珠
zhuxuan 珠軒
ziran 自然
zongguan 總管
zongguan yichang 總管翼長
zuoling 佐領

Works Cited

ABBREVIATIONS

DFZ: *Airusheng difangzhi shuju ku*
DQHDSL: *Da Qing huidian shili*
DQQS: *Daicing gurun-i yooni bithe/Da Qing quanshu*
GMQJ: *Jarliġ-iyar toġtoġaġsan ġadaġadu monġġol-un törö-yi jasaqu yabudal-un yamun-u qauli juil-un bicig*
HFYD: *Hunchun fudutong yamen dang'an*
M1D1: Archive for the *amban*'s office in Khüree, fond M-1, *devter* 1 (National Central Archives, Ulaanbaatar)
M1D2: Archive for the *amban*'s office in Khüree, fond M-1, *devter* 2 (National Central Archives, Ulaanbaatar)
M2D1: Archive for the military governor of Uliasutai, fond M-2, *devter* 1 (National Central Archives, Ulaanbaatar)
MBRT: *Manbun rōtō*
MWLF: *Junjichu Manwen lufu zouzhe* (First Historical Archives)
NPM-GZDYZ: *Gongzhongdang Yongzhongchao zouzhe* (National Palace Museum)
NPM-JJCD: *Junjichu dang zhejian* (National Palace Museum)
NWFZXD: *Neiwufu zouxiaodang* (First Historical Archives)
QSL: *Da Qing lichao shilu.* Compiled by reign. (TZ: *Taizong shilu*; SZ: *Shizu shilu*; KX: *Shengzu shilu*; YZ: *Shizong shilu*; QL: *Gaozong shilu*; JQ: *Renzong shilu*; DG: *Xuanzong shilu*; XF: *Wenzong shilu*; TZh: *Muzong shilu*; GX: *Dezong shilu*; XT: *Sundi shilu*)
TGKH: *Hese-i toktobuha tulergi golo be dasara jurgan-i kooli hacin i bithe*
ZJGK: *Zhongguo jiben guji ku*

ARCHIVAL SOURCES

Archive for the *ambans*' office in Khüree). Fond M-1, *devter* 1. National Central Archives, Ulaanbaatar.
Archive for the *ambans*' office in Khüree. Fond M-1, *devter* 2. National Central Archives, Ulaanbaatar.

Archive for the military governor of Uliasutai. Fond M-2, *devter* 1. National Central Archives, Ulaanbaatar.

Gongzhongdang Yongzhengchao zouzhe [Secret palace memorials of the Yongzheng reign]. National Palace Museum, Taipei.

Han-i araha Manju Monggo gisun-i buleku bithe / Qaġan-u bicigsen Manju Mongġol ügen-ü toil bicig [The Khan's Manchu-Mongol Dictionary], 1717. Institute of Eastern Manuscripts, Russian Academy of Science, St. Petersburg.

Hese-i toktobuha tulergi golo be dasara jurgan-i kooli hacin i bithe [Imperially Commissioned Statutes of the Board of Outer Dependencies] 1841. Chinese Collection, British Library. London.

Jarliġ-iyar toġtoġaġsan ġadaġadu mongġol-un törö-yi jasaqu yabudal-un yamun-u qauli juil-un bicig [Imperially Commissioned Statutes of the Board of Outer Dependecies] 1826. East Asia Collection, Staatsbibliothek. Berlin.

Junjichu Manwen lufu zouzhe [Manchu Palace Memorial Record Books of the Grand Council]. First Historical Archives, Beijing.

Leping. "Muwa Gisun" [Plain talking]. MS no. TMA 5806.09/0622. Rare Book Collection, Harvard-Yenching Library, Harvard University. Cambridge, MA.

Neiwufu zouxiaodang [Accounts of the Imperial Household Department]. First Historical Archives, Beijing.

PUBLISHED SOURCES

Abe Takeo, *Shindaishi no kenkyū* [Research on Qing history]. Tokyo: Sōbunsha, 1972.

Agassiz, A. R. "Our Commercial Relations with Chinese Manchuria." *The Geographical Journal* 4.6 (1894): 534–556.

Airusheng difangzhi shuju ku [Erudition Chinese Local Gazetteers Database]. Beijing: Beijing Airusheng shuzihua jishu yanjiu zhongxin, 2009. http://server.wenzibase.com/dblist.jsp.

Allsen, Thomas. *The Royal Hunt in Eurasian History*. Philadelphia: University of Pennsylvania Press, 2006.

Anderson, Benedict. *Imagined Communities*. London: Verso, 1983.

Appadurai, Arjun. "Introduction: Commodities and the Politics of Value." In *The Social Life of Things: Commodities in Cultural Perspective*, eds. Arjun Appadurai et al. London: Cambridge University Press, 1986.

Atwood, Christopher. "'Worshipping Grace': The Language of Loyalty in Qing Mongolia." *Late Imperial China* 21.2 (2000): 86–139.

———. *Encyclopedia of Mongolia and the Mongol Empire*. New York: Facts on File, 2004.

———. "The Mongol Empire and Early Modernity." Paper presented at "Asian Early Modernities: Empires, Bureaucrats, Confessions, Borders, Merchants." Istanbul, 2013.

Bai Shouyi. *Outline History of China*. Beijing: Foreign Language Press, 1982.

Bao Wenhan and Qichaoketu. *Menggu huibu wanggong biaozhuan* [Bibliographic charts of Mongol and Muslim nobility]. Hohhot: Neimenggu daxue chuban-she, 1998.

Barfield, Thomas J. *The Perilous Frontier: Nomadic Empires and China, 221 BC to AD 1757.* Cambridge, MA: Blackwell Publishers, 1989.

Bartlett, Beatrice S. "Books of Revelations: The Importance of the Manchu Language Archival Record Books for Research on Ch'ing History." *Late Imperial China* 6.2 (1985), 25–36.

———. *Monarchs and Ministers: The Grand Council in Mid-Ch'ing China, 1723–1820.* Berkeley: University of California Press, 1991.

Bauer, G. "Reproductive Strategy of the Freshwater Pearl Mussel *Margaritifera margaritifera.*" *Journal of Animal Ecology* 56 (1987): 691–704.

Bawden, Charles. "Two Mongol Texts Concerning Obo-Worship." *Oriens Extremus* 5 (1958): 23–41.

———. "Some Documents Concerning the Rebellion of 1756 in Outer Mongolia." *Bianzheng yanjiusuo nianbao* (1970): 1–23.

Baxian xinzhi [New gazetteer for Ba County], ed. Liu Chongben. 1934. Digital reprint, DFZ.

Beckert, Sven. *Empire of Cotton: A Global History.* New York: Alfred A. Knopf, 2014.

Bello, David. "The Cultured Nature of Imperial Foraging in Manchuria." *Late Imperial China* 31.2 (2010): 1–33.

———. "Relieving Mongols of their Pastoral Identity: Disaster Management on the Eighteenth-Century Qing China Steppe." *Environmental History* 19.3 (2014): 480–504.

———. *Across Forest, Steppe, and Mountain: Environment, Identity, and Empire in Qing China's Borderlands.* New York: Cambridge University Press, 2016.

Bennigsen, Alexandre, and Chantal Lemerchier-Quelquejay. "Les marchands de la cour Ottoman et le commerce des fourrures moscovites dans la seconde moitié du XVIe siècle." *Cahiers du monde russe et soviétique* 11.3 (1970): 363–390.

Bian He. "Assembling the Cure: *Materia Medica* and the Culture of Healing in Late Imperial China." PhD dissertation, Harvard University. 2014.

Billé, Franck. *Sinophobia: Anxiety, Violence, and the Making of Mongolian Identity.* Honolulu: University of Hawaii Press, 2015.

Bin-liang, *Baochongzhai shiji* [Collected poems from Baochong studio]. Chongfu Hunan edition, 1879. Digital reprint, ZJGK.

Binxian xianzhi [Gazetteer for Bin County], ed. Zhu Yidian. Minguo. Digital reprint, DFZ.

Blackburn, David. "The Collective Memory of the Sook Ching Massacre and the Creation of the Civilian War Memorial in Singapore." *Journal of the Malaysian Branch of the Royal Asiatic Society*, 73.2 (2000): 71–90.

Blanning, Tim. *The Pursuit of Glory: Europe, 1648–1815.* New York: Viking, 2007.

Blussé, Leonard. "Junks to Java: Chinese Shipping to the Nanyang in the Second Half of the Eighteenth Century." In *Chinese Circulations: Capital, Commodities, and Networks in Southeast Asia*, eds. Eric Tagliacozzo and Wen-Chin Chang. Durham, NC: Duke University Press, 2011.

Bockstoce, John R. *Furs and Frontiers in the Far North*. New Haven, CT: Yale University Press, 2009.

Bol, Peter K., and Robert P. Weller. "From Heaven-and-Earth to Nature: Chinese Concepts of the Environment and Their Influence on Policy Implementation." In *Confucianism and Ecology: The Interrelation of Heaven, Earth, and Humans*, eds. Mary Evelyn Tucker, John Berthrong, et al. Cambridge, MA: Harvard University Press, 1998.

Boldbaatar, Zh. "Mongolchuudyn Baigal' Orchnoo Hamgaalah Zan Zanshil, Huul' Togtoomjiin Högzhliin Tüühen Toim" [Outline history of the Mongols' development of customs and laws of environmental protection]." *Tüüh: Erdem Shinzhilgeenii Bichig* 188.14 (2002): 80–98.

Brook, Timothy. *The Confusions of Pleasure: Commerce and Culture in Ming China*. Berkeley: University of California Press, 1999.

———. *Vermeer's Hat: The Seventeenth Century and the Dawn of the Global World*. New York: Bloomsbury Press, 2008.

Brophy, David. "The Junghar Mongol Legacy and the Language of Loyalty in Qing Xinjiang." *Harvard Journal of Asiatic Studies* 73.2 (2013): 231–258.

Brunhes, Jean, and Camille Vallaux. *La Géographie de l'histoire: géographie de la paix et de la guerre sur terre et sur mer*. Paris: F. Alcan, 1921.

Burbank, Jane, and Frederick Cooper. *Empires in World History: Power and the Politics of Difference*. Princeton, NJ: Princeton University Press, 2010.

Burke, Edmund III, and Kenneth Pomeranz. *The Environment and World History*. Berkeley: University of California Press, 2009.

Cammann, Schuyler. "Origins of the Court and Official Robes of the Ch'ing Dynasty." *Artibus Asiae* 12.3 (1949): 189–201.

———. *China's Dragon Robes*. New York: The Ronald Press Company, 1952.

Cao Xueqin. *Hongloumeng jiaozhu* [Annotated Dream of the Red Chamber]. Taipei: Liren shuju, 1984.

Carrell, Birgitta, et al. "Can Mussel Shells Reveal Environmental History?" *Ambio* 16.1 (1987): 2–10.

Carruthers, Douglas. "Exploration in North-West Mongolia and Dzungaria." *The Geographical Journal* 39.6 (1912): 521–551.

Cassel, Pär. "Excavating Extraterritoriality: The 'Judicial Sub-Prefect' as a Prototype for the Mixed Court in Shanghai." *Late Imperial China* 24.2 (2003): 156–182.

Chakrabarty, Dipesh. *Provincializing Europe: Postcolonial Thought and Historical Difference*. Princeton, NJ: Princeton University Press, 2008.

Chang Te-Ch'ang. "The Economic Role of the Imperial Household in the Ch'ing Dynasty." *The Journal of Asian Studies* 31.2 (1972): 243–273.

Chao Xiaohong. *Shengtai huanjing yu Mingqing shehui jingji* [Ecology and environment in Ming-Qing society and economy]. Hefei shi: Huangshan shushe, 2004.

Chaoyang xianzhi [Gazetteer for Chaoyang County], ed. Shen Mingshi. 1930. Digital reprint, DFZ.

Charleux, Isabelle. *Nomads on Pilgrimage: Mongols on Wutaishan (China), 1800–1940*. Boston: Brill, 2015.

Chen Baoliang. *Mingdai shehui shenghuo shi* [History of social life in the Ming period]. Beijing: Zhongguo shehui kexue chubanshe, 2004.

Chengde fuzhi [Gazetteer for Chengde Prefecture], eds. Hai Zhong and Lin Congshang. 1831. Digital reprint, DFZ.

Chew, Daniel. *Chinese Pioneers on the Sarawak Frontier, 1841–1941*. New York: Oxford University Press, 1990.

Chiang Chushan. "Qingdai renshen de lishi: yige shangpin de yanjiu" [The history of ginseng in the Qing period: research on a commodity]. PhD thesis, National Tsing Hua University, 2006.

Ch'iu Chung-lin. "Baonuan, huiyao yu quanshi: mingdai zhengui maopi de wenhuashi [Warmth, ostentatiousness, and power: A cultural history of precious furs in the Ming dynasty]. *Zhongyang yanjiuyan lishi yuyan yanjiusuo jikan* 80.4 (2009): 555–631.

Chongwenmen shangshui yamen xianxing shuize [Active customs regulations of the Chongwenmen customs office]. Beijing: Quanguo tushuguan wenxian suowei fuzhi zhongxin, 2008.

Chosŏn wangjo sillok [Veritable records of the Chosŏn dynasty]. 48 vols. Seoul: Kuksa p'yŏnch'an wiwŏnhoe, 1955–1958.

Chuang Chi-fa. *Qingdai zhungaer shiliao chubian* [Historical materials from the Qing period on the Dzungars, collection one]. Taipei: Wenshizhe chubanshe, 1977.

———. *Xie Sui 'Zhigongtu' Manwen tushuo xiaozhu* [Annotated and Illustrated Manchu edition of the Xie Sui *Zhigongtu*]. Taipei: *Guoli gugong bowuyuan yinhang*, 1989.

Chun Hae-jong. "Sino–Korean Tributary Relations in the Ch'ing Period." In *The Chinese World Order*, ed. John K. Fairbank. Cambridge, MA: Harvard University Press, 1968.

Clunas, Craig. *Superfluous Things: Material Culture and Social Status in Early Modern China*. Cambridge, UK: Polity Press, 1991.

Cohen, Paul A. *Discovering History in China: American Historical Writing on the Recent Chinese Past*. New York: Columbia University Press, 1984.

Cong Peiyuan. "Zhongguo zaipei renshen zhi chuxian yu xingqi" [The appearance and rise of ginseng cultivation in China]. *Nongye kaogu* 1 (1985): 262–269, 291.

———. *Dongbei sanbao jingji jianshi* [Simple economic history of the "three treasures" of Manchuria]. Beijing: Zhongguo huanjing kexue chubanshe, 1990.

Corning, Howard. "Letters of Sullivan Dorr." *Proceedings of the Massachusetts Historical Society* 67 (1941–1944): 178–364.

Cranmer-Byng, John L. and John E. Wills. "Trade and Diplomacy under the Qing." In *China and Maritime Europe, 1500–1800*, ed. John E. Wills. New York: Cambridge University Press, 2011.

Cronon, William. *Changes in the Land: Indians, Colonists, and the Ecology of New England*. New York: Hill and Wang, 1983.

———. *Nature's Metropolis: Chicago and the Great West*. New York: W. W. Norton, 1992.

———. "A Place for Stories: Nature, History, and Narrative." *Journal of American History* 78.4 (1992), 1347–1376.

———. "The Trouble with Wilderness; or, Getting Back to the Wrong Nature." In *Uncommon Ground: Rethinking the Human Place in Nature*, ed. William Cronon. New York: W. W. Norton, 1996.

Cronon, William, George Miles, and Jay Gitlin. *Under an Open Sky: Rethinking America's Western Past*. New York: W. W. Norton, 1992.

Crossley, Pamela Kyle. "An Introduction to the Qing Foundation Myth," *Late Imperial China*, 6.1 (1985), 3–24.

———. "Manzhou Yuanliu Kao and the Formalization of the Manchu Heritage." *The Journal of Asian Studies* 46.4 (1987): 761–790.

———. *Orphan Warriors: Three Manchu Generations and the End of the Qing World*. Princeton, NJ: Princeton University Press, 1990.

———. *A Translucent Mirror: History and Identity in Qing Imperial Ideology*. Berkeley: University of California Press, 1999.

———. "Making Mongols." In *Empire at the Margins: Culture, Ethnicity, and Frontier in Early Modern China*, eds. Pamela Kyle Crossley, Helen Siu, and Donald Sutton. Berkeley: University of California Press, 2006.

Crossley, Pamela Kyle, and Evelyn S. Rawski, "A Profile of the Manchu Language in Ch'ing History," *Harvard Journal of Asiatic Studies* 53.1 (1993): 63–102.

Crossley, Pamela Kyle, Helen Siu, and Donald Sutton. *Empire at the Margins: Culture, Ethnicity, and Frontier in Early Modern China*. Berkeley: University of California Press, 2006.

Cui Shu, *Wuwenji* [A collection of the unheralded]. In *Cui Dongbi yishu*. Digital reprint, ZJGK.

Curzon, George Nathaniel. *Frontiers: Delivered in the Sheldonian Theatre, Oxford, November 2, 1907*. Westport, CT: Greenwood Press, 1976.

Da Jin guozhi jiaozheng [Annotated gazetteer of the great Jin state]. Beijing: Zhonghua shuju, 1986.

Da Qing huidian [Collected statutes of the Qing], comp. Sun Jiading, 1899.

Da Qing huidian shili [Collected statutes and precedents of the Qing dynasty], eds. Kun'gang et al. 1899. Reprint, Beijing: Zhonghua shuju, 1991.

Da Qing lichao shilu [The veritable records of the Qing dynasty]. Beijing: Zhonghua shuju, 1986.

Daicing gürün ü dotuġadu yamun u mongol bicig un ger ün dangsa [Mongol language archives of the Qing Grand Secretariat]. Hohhot: Neimenggu renmin chubanshe, 2005.

Daicing gurun-i yooni bithe/Da Qing quanshu [Complete book of the Great Qing], comp. Shen Qiliang. 1683. Reprinted, 1713.

Dasheng wula zhidian quanshu, dasheng wula difang xiangtu zhi [The complete gazetteer and statutes of the Hunter Ula and the native place gazetteer of the Hunter Ula], ed. Jin Enhui et al. Changchun: Jilin wenshi chubanshe: 1988.

Dauvergne, Peter. *Shadows in the Forest: Japan and the Politics of Timber in Southeast Asia.* Cambridge, MA: MIT Press, 1997.

Daws, Gavan. *Shoal of Time: A History of the Hawaiian Islands.* Honolulu: University of Hawaii Press, 1968.

Descola, Philippe. *Beyond Nature and Culture.* Chicago: University of Chicago Press, 2013.

———. *The Ecology of Others.* Chicago: Prickly Paradigm Press, 2013.

Di Cosmo, Nicola. "Qing Colonial Administration in Inner Asia." *The International History Review,* 20.2 (1998): 253–304.

———. *Ancient China and Its Enemies: the Rise of Nomadic Power in East Asian History.* New York: Cambridge University Press, 2002.

———. "Nomads on the Qing Frontier: Tribute, Trade or Gift-Exchange?" In *Political Frontiers, Ethnic Boundaries, and Human Geographies in Chinese History.* eds. Nicola di Cosmo and Don J. Wyatt, 351–372. New York: Routledge Curzon, 2003.

———. "The Rise of Manchu Power in Northeast Asia (c. 1600–1636)." October 12, 2007. Video Clip. Retrieved on March 12, 2012, from YouTube at www.youtube.com, http://www.youtube.com/watch?v=Gl1-vop7ipY).

Di Cosmo, Nicola, and Dalizhabu Bao, *Manchu–Mongol Relations on the Eve of the Qing Conquest: A Documentary History.* Brill: Boston, 2003.

Diao Shuren. "Qingdai Yan-Hun diqu zhufang baqi luelun" [General description of Eight Banner garrisons in the Yanji-Hunchun region during the Qing period]. *Dongjiang xuekan—zhexue shehui kexue ban* 4 (1992): 55–61.

Ding Yizhuang. *Qingdai baqi zhufang yanjiu* [Research on banner garrisons in the Qing]. Shenyang: Liaoning minzu chubanshe, 2002.

Ding Yizhuang, Guo Songyi, Kang Wenlin [Cameron Campbell], and Li Zhongqing [James Lee]. *Liaodong yiminzhong de qiren shehui* [Banner society and migrants in Liaodong]. Shanghai: Shanghai shehui kexueyuan chubanshe, 2004.

Donghua xulu (Jiaqing chao) [Continuation of the Records from within the Eastern Gate—the Jiaqing reign], ed. Wang Xianqian. Changsha Wangshi edition, 1884. Digital reprint, ZJGK.

D'Orléans, Pierre Joseph. *History of the Two Tartar Conquerors of China, Including the Two Journeys into Tartary of Father Ferdinand Verbiest, in the Suite of the Emperor Kang-Hi.* New York: Burt Franklin, 1964.

Douglas, Mary. *Purity and Danger; An Analysis of Concepts of Pollution and Taboo*. London: Routledge & K. Paul, 1966.

Du Halde, Jean-Baptiste. *The General History of China*. London: J. Watts, 1741.

Duara, Prasenjit. *Rescuing History from the Nation: Questioning Narratives of Modern China*. Chicago: University of Chicago Press, 1995.

Elliott, Mark C. "The Limits of Tartary: Manchuria in Imperial and National Geographies." *The Journal of Asian Studies* 59.3 (2000): 603–646.

———. "The Manchu-Language Archives of the Qing Dynasty and the Origins of the Palace Memorial System." *Late Imperial China* 22.1 (2001): 1–70.

———. *The Manchu Way: The Eight Banners and Ethnic Identity in Late Imperial China*. Stanford, CA: Stanford University Press, 2001.

———. "Manwen dang'an yu xin Qingshi." *National Palace Museum Quarterly* 24.2 (2006): 1–18.

———. *Emperor Qianlong: Son of Heaven, Man of the World*. New York: Longman, 2009.

Elliott, Mark C., and James Bosson. "Highlights of the Manchu-Mongolian Collection." In *Treasures of the Yencheng*, ed. Patrick Hanan. Cambridge, MA: Harvard–Yenching Library, Harvard University, 2003.

Elliot, Mark C. and Ning Chia. "The Qing Hunt at Mulan." In *New Qing Imperial History: The Making of Inner Asian Empire at Qing Chengde*, eds. James A. Millward, Ruth W. Dunnell, Mark C. Elliott, and Philippe Forêt. New York: RoutledgeCurzon, 2004.

Elverskog, Johan. *Our Great Qing: The Mongols, Buddhism and the State in Late Imperial China*. Honolulu: University of Hawaii Press, 2006.

Elvin, Mark. *The Retreat of the Elephants*. New Haven, CT: Yale University Press, 2004.

Elvin, Mark, and Liu Ts'ui-jung, eds. *Sediments of Time: Environment and Society in Chinese History*. New York: Cambridge University Press, 1998.

Enhbayaryn Jigmeddorj. *Khalkh-Manzhiĭn uls töriĭn khariltsaa* [Khalkha-Manchu political relations]. Ulaanbaatar: Mongol uls shinzhlekh khaany akademi tüükhin khüreelen, 2008.

Ewing, Thomas E. "The Forgotten Frontier: South Siberia (Tuva) in Chinese and Russian History, 1600–1920." *Central Asiatic Journal* 25.3–4 (1981): 174–212.

Fairbank, John King. *Trade and Diplomacy on the China Coast: The Opening of the Treaty Ports, 1842–1854*. Cambridge, MA: Harvard University Press, 1964.

Fairhead, James, and Melissa Leach. *Misreading the African Landscape: Society and Ecology in a Forest-Savanna Mosaic*. New York: Cambridge University Press, 1996.

Fall, Juliet J. "Artificial States? On the Enduring Geographical Myth of Natural Borders." *Political Geography* 29 (2010): 140–147.

Fan Fa-ti. *British Naturalists in Qing China: Science, Empire, and Cultural Encounter*. Cambridge, MA: Harvard University Press, 2004.

Fan Mingfan, *Tangnu Wulianghai lishi yanshi* [Research on the history of the Tannu Uriankhai]. Beijing: Zhongguo shehui kexue chubanshe, 2007.

Farquhar, David Millar. "Oirat-Chinese Tribute Relations, 1408–1446." In *Studia Altaica: Festschrift für Nikolaus Poppe zum 60 Geburtstag am 8 August 1957*. Wiesbaden: O. Harrassowitz, 1957.

———. "The Ch'ing Administration of Mongolia Up to the Nineteenth Century." PhD dissertation, Harvard University, 1960.

———. "The Origins of the Manchus' Mongolian Policy." In *The Chinese World Order*. ed. John K. Fairbank. Cambridge, MA: Harvard University Press, 1968.

Faure, David. *Emperor and Ancestor: State and Lineage in South China*. Stanford, CA: Stanford University Press, 2007.

Feng Ming-chu. *Qianlong huangdi de wenhua daye* [Emperor Ch'ien-lung's Grand Cultural Enterprise]. Taipei: Guoli gugong bowuyuan, 2002.

Fengrui xianzhi [Gazetteer for Fengrui County], ed. Hao Zenghu. 1891. Digital reprint, DFZ.

Finnane, Antonia. *Changing Clothes in China: Fashion, History, Nation*. New York: Columbia University Press, 2008.

———. "Barbarian and Chinese: Dress as Difference in Chinese Art." *Humanities Australia* 1 (2010): 33–43.

———. "Fashion in Late Imperial China." In *The Fashion History Reader: Global Perspectives*, eds. Giorgio Riello and Peter McNeill. New York: Routledge, 2010.

Fisher, Raymond H. *The Russian Fur Trade, 1550–1700*. Berkeley: University of California Press, 1943.

Franke, Herbert. "Chinese Texts on the Jurchen: A Translation of the Jurchen Monograph in the San-ch'ao pei-meng hui-pien." *Zentralasiatische Studien* 9 (1975): 119–186.

Fuge, *Tingyu congtan* [Discussions at Tingyu]. Beijing: Zhonghua shuju, 1984.

Gagengaowa and Wuyunbatu. *Menggu minzu de shengtai wenhua* [The ecological culture of the Mongol nationality]. Hohhot: Neimenggu jiaoyu chubanshe, 2003.

Gamsa, Mark. "California on the Amur, or the 'Zheltuga Republic' in Manchuria (1883–86)." *The Slavonic and East European Review* 81.2 (2003): 236–266.

Ge Zhiyi. *Zhidu shiyuxia de caoyuan shengtai huanjing baohu* [Systematic analysis on protecting the ecology and environment of the steppe]. Shenyang: Liaoning minzu chubanshe, 2008.

Gibson, James R. *Otter Skins, Boston Ships, and China Goods: The Maritime Fur Trade of the Northwest Coast, 1785–1841*. Seattle: University of Washington Press, 1992.

Giersch, Charles Patterson. *Asian Borderlands: The Transformation of Qing China's Yunnan Frontier*. Cambridge, MA: Harvard University Press, 2006.

Gladney, Dru. *Dislocating China: Reflections on Muslims, Minorities, and Other Subaltern Subjects*. Chicago: University of Chicago Press, 2004.

Gombobaatar, S., et al. *Convention on Biological Diversity: The 5th National Report of Mongolia*. Ulaanbaatar: Ministry of Environment and Green Development, 2014. Retrieved from www.cbd.int.

Gongzhongdang Qianlongchao zouzhe [Palace memorials of the Qianlong reign from the palace archives]. Taipei: Guoli gugong bowuyuan, 1982–1989.

Goody, Jack. *The Theft of History*. New York: Cambridge University Press, 2006.

Gottschang, Thomas R., and Diana Lary. *Swallows and Settlers: The Great Migration from North China to Manchuria*. Ann Arbor: Center for Chinese Studies, University of Michigan, 2000.

Graf, Daniel L. "Palearctic Freshwater Mussel (*Mollusca: Vivalvia: Unionoida*) diversity and the Comparatory Method as a Species Concept." *Proceedings of the Academy of Natural Sciences of Philadelphia* 156 (2007): 71–88.

Gu Sili. *Yuanshixuan* [Selection of Yuan poetry]. Beijing: Zhonghua shuju, 1987.

Guan Jie. *Dongbei shaoshu minzu lishi yu wenhua yanjiu* [Research on the history and cultures of the ethnic minorities of the Northeast]. Shenyang: Liaoning minzu chubanshe, 2007.

Guha, Ramachandra. *Environmentalism: A Global History*. New York: Longman, 2000.

Guy, R. Kent. "Who Were the Manchus? A Review Essay." *The Journal of Asian Studies* 61.1 (2002): 151–164.

Hailong xianzhi [Gazetteer for Hailong County], ed. Wang Chunpeng. 1937. Digital reprint, DFZ.

Haltod, Magadbürin. *Mongolische Ortsnamen*. Wiesbaden: F. Steiner, 1966.

Han Maoli. *Caoyuan yu tianyuan: Liao-Jin shiqi xiliaohe liuyu nongmuye yu huanjing* [Grassland and rurality: The recurrence of agriculture and livestock-raising and its environment in the area of the Liao river during the Liao and Jin dynasties]. Beijing: SDX Joint Publishing Company, 2006.

Harris, Richard B. *Wildlife Conservation in China: Preserving the Habitat of China's Wild West*. Armonk, NY: M. E. Sharpe, 2008.

Hayden, John O., ed. *William Wordsworth: Selected Poems*. New York: Penguin Books, 1994.

He Changling, comp. *Qing jingshi wenbian* [Qing documents on statecraft]. Sibulou edition, 1887. Digital reprint, ZJGK.

He Qiutao. *Shuofang beisheng* [Defense of the north]. 1881. Reprint, Shanghai: Shanghai guji chubanshe, 2002.

He Qun. *Huanjing yu xiaominzu shengcun: Elunchun wenhua de bianqian* [Environment for the survival of an ethnic minority: Oronqen people in China]. Beijing: Shehui kexue wenxian chubanshe, 2006.

He Xinhua. *Zuihou de tianchao: Qingdai chaogong zhidu yanjiu* [The last celestial empire: A study of the tributary system in the Qing dynasty]. Beijing: Renmin chubanshe, 2012.

Heilongjiang zhigao [Draft gazetteer of Heilongjiang], comp. Zhang Boying et al. 62 *juan*, appendix, 4 *juan*. Taipei: Wenhai chubanshe, 1965.

Herman, John E. *Amid the Clouds and Mist: China's Colonization of Guizhou, 1200–1700.* Cambridge, MA: Harvard University Asia Center, 2007.

High, Mette, and Jonathan Schlesinger. "Rulers and Rascals: The Politics of Gold in Mongolian Qing History." *Central Asian Survey* 29.3 (2010): 289–304.

Ho Ping-ti, *Studies on the Population of China, 1368–1953.* Cambridge, MA: Harvard University Press, 1959.

———. "The Significance of the Ch'ing Period in Chinese History." *Journal of Asian Studies* 26.2 (1967): 189–195.

Hong Tae-yong, *Tamhŏn yŏngi* [Notes from my journey to Beijing]. In *Yŏnhaengnok chŏnjip* [Complete collection of the Records of Trips to Beijing], ed. Im Ki-jung. Seoul: Tongguk taehakkyo ch'ulp'anbu, 2001.

Howard-Johnston, James. "Trading in Fur, from Classical Antiquity to the Early Middle Ages." In *Leather and Fur: Aspects of Early Medieval Trade and Technology*, eds. Esther Cameron et al. London: Archetype Publications Ltd., 1998.

Huang Ming tiaofa shilei zuan. [Legal matters of the August Ming by category]. In *Zhongguo zhenxi falü dianji jicheng.* Eds. Liu Hainian and Yang Yifan. Beijing: Kexue chubanshe, 1994.

Huang, Ray. *China: A Macro-History.* Armonk, NY: M. E. Sharpe, 1997.

Huen, Fook-fai. "The Manchurian Fur Trade in the Early Ch'ing." *Papers on China,* 24 (1971): 41–73.

Hughes, Thomas P. *Human-Built World: How to Think about Technology and Culture.* Chicago: The University of Chicago Press, 2004.

Hummel, Arthur W. *Eminent Chinese of the Ch'ing Period (1644–1912).* Washington: United States Government Printing Office, 1943–1944.

Humphrey, Caroline. "Introduction." In *Nomads of South Siberia*, ed. Caroline Humphrey. New York: Cambridge University Press, 1980.

———. "Chiefly and Shamanist Landscapes in Mongolia." In *The Anthropology of Landscape: Perspectives on Place and Space*, ed. Eric Hirsch et al. New York: Oxford University Press, 1995.

Humphrey, Caroline, and Urgunge Onon. *Shamans and Elders: Experience, Knowledge, and Power among the Daur Mongols.* Oxford, UK: Clarendon Press, 1996.

Humphrey, Caroline, and David Sneath. *The End of Nomadism? Society, State, and the Environment in Inner Asia.* Durham, NC: Duke University Press, 1999.

Hunchun fudutong yamen dang [Records of the office of the lieutenant governor of Hunchun]. Guilin: Guangxi shifan daxue chubanshe, 2007.

Imai Sanshi. "On an Edible Mongolian Fungus 'Pai-mo-ku.'" *Proceedings of the Imperial Academy of Japan* 13 (1937): 280–282.

Imamura Tomo. *Ninjinshi* [Ginseng history]. Tokyo: Chōsen Sōtokufu Senbai-kyoku, 1934–1940.

Isett, Christopher M. *State, Peasant, and Merchant in Qing Manchuria, 1644–1862.* Stanford, CA: Stanford University Press, 2006.

Iwai Shigeki. "Jūroku, jūnana seiki no Chūgoku henkyō shakai" [Frontier society in sixteenth- and seventeenth-century China]. In *Minmatsu Shinsho no shakai to bunka*, ed. Ono Kazuko. Kyoto: Kyōtō Daigaku Jinbun Kagaku Kenkyūjo, 1996.

James, H. E. M. "A Journey in Manchuria." *Proceedings of the Royal Geographical Society and Monthly Record of Geography* 9.9 (1887): 531–567.

Jianping xianzhi [Gazetteer for Jianping County], ed. Yao Wenyan. 1931. Digital reprint, DFZ.

Jiaqing Daoguang liangchao shangyu dang [Record of imperial edicts from the Jiaqing and Daoguang courts]. Guilin: Guangxi shifan daxue chubanshe, 2000.

Jiaqing dongxun jishi [Record of the Jiaqing eastern tour]. In *Liaohai congshu* [Collected writings on the distant seas]. Ed. Jin Yufu. Taipei: Yiwen yinshu guan: 1971.

"Jiaqingchao shenwu dang'an xuanbian (shang)" [Archival selections on ginseng management in the Jiaqing reign period, part 1]. *Lishi dang'an* 3 (2002): 51–72.

"Jiaqingchao shenwu dang'an xuanbian (xia)" [Archival selections on ginseng management in the Jiaqing reign period, part 2]. *Lishi dang'an* 4 (2002): 22–42, 63.

Jigmeddorji. *Manzhiin üeiin ar mongol dakh' khiliin kharuul* [The border guards of the Qing dynasty in Outer Mongolia]. Ulaanbaatar: Instituti Historiae Scientiarum Mongoli, 2006.

Jilin tongzhi [Comprehensive gazetteer of Jilin], ed. Li Guilin. 1891. Digital reprint, ZJGK.

Jin Enhui. "Qingdai de dasheng wula zongguan yamen" [The office of the supervising commandant of the Hunter Ula in the Qing period]. *Dongbei shida xuebao* 3 (1980): 56–61.

———. "Guanyu 'dasheng wula zhidian quanshu' xiaoshi, chuban yiji wula shiliao wenku de jianyi" [On the annotation and publication of the *Dasheng wula quanshu*, with suggestions]. *Shentu tongxun* 3 (2008): 59–62.

Jin Hai et al. *Qingdai Menggu zhi* [Gazetteer of Qing Mongolia]. Hohhot: Neimenggu renmin chubanshe, 2009.

Jin Xin. "Lun Qingdai qianqi Dawoer, Ewenkezu de shangpin jingji" [Research on development of Daur and Ewenki's commodity economy in the early period of Qing dynasty]. *Manyu yanjiu* 54 (2012): 127–141.

———. "Qingdai buteha baqi jianli shijian ji niulu shue xinkao" [A new study on the establishing time of the butha eight banner and the number of its niru in the Qing dynasty]. *Minzu yanjiu* 6 (2012): 75–85.

———. "Qingdai Dawoer, Ewenke liangzu suo shiyong de falü" [Study on the national laws Ewenki and Daur followed in the Qing dynasty]. *Manyu yanjiu* 57.2 (2013): 121–128.

———. "Qingdai qianqi buteha zongguan yange tanxi" [A new exploration on the evolutionary course of Butha Zong Guan in the early Qing dynasty]. *Minzu yanjiu* 4 (2013): 82–95.

Jones, Ryan Tucker. "Running into Whales: The History of the North Pacific from below the Waves." *American Historical Review* 118.2 (2013), 349–377.

———. *Empires of Extinction: Russians & the North Pacific's Strange Beasts of the Sea, 1741–1867*. New York: Oxford University Press, 2014.

Kaczensky, Petra. "First Assessment of Nomrog and Dornod Mongol Strictly Protected Areas in the Eastern Steppe of Mongolia for the Re-introduction of Przewalski's Horses." *International Takhi Group*. 2005. Retrieved from www.takhi.org/media/forschung/2005FirstassessmentofNomrogand DornodMongolStrictlyProtectedAreasintheEesternSteppeofMongoliaforthere- introductionofPrzewalskishorses.PetraKaczensky.pdf.

Kawachi Yoshihiro. "*Mindai tōhoku Ajia chōhi bōeki*" [Sable trade in Northeast Asia in the Ming Period]. *Tōyoshi Kenkyū* 30.1 (1971): 62–120.

Kawakubo Teirō. "Shinmatsu ni okeru Kirinshō seihokubu no kaihatsu" [The opening of northwestern Jilin in the late Qing]. *Rekishigaku kenkyū* 5.2 (1935): 147–184.

———. "Shin shiryō 'dasheng wula zhidian quanshu' no hakken ni yosete" [The discovery of new historical material: The *dasheng wula zhidian quanshu*]. *Tōhōgaku* 66 (1983): 148–151.

Ke Jiusi. *Liaojinyuan gongci* [Palace poems from the Liao, Jin, and Yuan dynas- ties]. Beijing: Beijing guji chubanshe, 1988.

Khazanov, Anatoly. *Nomads and the Outside World*. Madison: University of Wisconsin Press, 1994.

Kim, Loretta. "Marginal Constituencies: Qing Borderland Policies and Vernacu- lar Histories of Five Tribes on the Sino-Russian Frontier." PhD dissertation, Harvard University, 2009.

———. "Tribute Data Curation." *History in Data*. September, 2014. http:// digital.lib.hkbu.edu.hk/history/tribute.php

Kishimoto Mio. *Shindai Chugoku no bukka to keizai* [Economic and price changes in Qing China]. Tokyo: Kenbun Shuppan, 1997.

———. "Chinese History and the Concept of 'Early Modernities,'" paper presented at "An International Conference on the Early Modern World," Uni- versity of Chicago, June 3, 2005. Retrieved on February 22, 2015, from http:// earlymodernworld.uchicago.edu/kishimoto.pdf.

Klaproth, Julius. *Chrestomathie Mandchou ou Recueil de Textes Mandchou*. Paris: Imprimerie Royale, 1828.

Kohn, Michael. *Lonely Planet: Mongolia*. London: Lonely Planet, 2008.

Korsak, Aleksandr. *Istoriko-statisticheskoe obozrienie torgovykh snoshenii Rossii s Ki- taem* [A historical and statistical review of trade relations between Russia and China]. Kazan: Izd. Knigoprodavtsa Ivan Dubrovina, 1856.

Kuhn, Philip. *Soulstealers: The Chinese Sorcery Scare of 1768*. Cambridge, MA: Harvard University Press, 1990.

———. *Chinese Among Others: Emigration in Modern Times.* New York: Rowman & Littlefield, 2008.

Kuriyama Shigehisa. "The Geography of Ginseng and the Strange Alchemy of Need." Talk presented at the Reischauer Institute Japan Forum, January 27, 2012.

Lai Hui-min. "Qianlongchao Neifuyuan pihuo maimai yu jingcheng shishang" [Fur trade by the Imperial Household Department and fashion in Beijing during the reign of Emperor Qianlong]. *Zhongyang yanjiuyuan jindaishi yanjiusuo jikan* 21.1 (2003): 101–134.

———. "Shijiu shiji Qiaketu maoyi de Eluosi fangzhipin" [Russian textiles in the nineteenth-century Kiakhta trade]. *Zhongyang yanjiuyuan jindaishi yanjiusuo jikan* 79 (2013), 1–46.

Lao She, *Blades of Grass: The Stories of Laoshe.* William A. Lyell and Sarah Weiming Chen, trans. Honolulu: University of Hawai'i Press, 1999.

Latour, Bruno. *We Have Never Been Modern.* Cambridge, MA: Harvard University Press, 1993.

Lattimore, Owen. *Inner Asian Frontiers of China.* New York: American Geographical Society, 1940.

———. *Nomads and Commissars: Mongolia Revisited.* New York: Oxford University Press, 1962.

Le Billon, Philippe. *Wars of Plunder: Conflicts, Profits, and the Politics of Resources.* London: Hurst and Company, 2012.

Ledyard, Gari. "Hong Tae-yong and His Peking Memoir." *Korean Studies* 6 (1982): 63–103.

Lee, Robert H. G. *The Manchurian Frontier in Ch'ing History.* Cambridge, MA: Harvard University Press, 1970.

Legrand, Jacques. *L'administration dans la domination Sino-Mandchou en Mongolie Qalq-a: version mongole du Lifan Yuan Zeli.* Paris: Collège de France, Institut des Hautes Études Chinoises, 1976.

Lekan, Thomas. *Imagining the Nation in Nature: Landscape Preservation and German Identity, 1885–1945.* Cambridge, MA: Harvard University Press, 2004.

Lessing, Ferdinand D. *Mongolian-English Dictionary.* Berkeley: University of California Press, 1960.

Li Fang. *Taiping guangji* [Extensive records of the Taiping era]. Beijing: Zhonghua shuju, 1961.

Li Huazi. *Qingchao yu Chaoxian guanxi shi yanjiu* [Research on the history of Qing-Chosŏn relations]. Yanji: Yanbian daxue chubanshe, 2006.

Li, Lillian M. *Fighting Famine in North China: State, Market, and Environmental Decline, 1690s–1990s.* Stanford, CA: Stanford University Press, 2007.

Li Lüyuan. *Qiludeng* [Lantern at the road fork]. Taipei: Xinwenfeng chuban gongsi, 1979.

Li Shizhen. *Bencao gangmu* [Compendium of materia medica]. Beijing: Renmin wesheng chubanshe, 1975.

Li Tana. "The Water Frontier: An Introduction." In *Water Frontier: Commerce and the Chinese in the Lower Mekong Region, 1750–1880*, eds. Nola Cooke and Li Tana. Lanham, MD: Rowman and Littlefield Publishers, 2004.

———. "Between Mountains and the Sea: Trades in Early Nineteenth-Century Northern Vietnam." *Journal of Vietnamese Studies* 7.2 (2012): 67–86.

Li Yushu. *Waimeng zhengjiao zhidu kao* [Study of the government and religious systems of Outer Mongolia]. Taipei: Zhongyang yanjiuyuan jindaishi yanjiu suo, 1962.

Liang Lixia. *Alashan Menggu yanjiu* [Research on the Alashan Mongols]. Beijing: Minzu Chubanshe, 2005.

Lin Shixuan. *Qingji dongbei yimin shibian zhengce zhi yanjiu* [Research on the Qing policy for defending the frontier with migrants]. Taipei: Guoli zhenzhi daxue lishi xuexi, 2001.

Liu Fengyun. *Qingdai zhengzhi yu guojia renting* [Politics and national identity in the Qing dynasty]. Beijing: Shehui kexue wenxian chubanshe, 2012.

Liu Jiaxu. *Qian Guoerluosi jianshi* [Basic history of the Front Gorlos]. Shenyang: Liaoning minzu chubanshe, 2005.

Liu Xinru. *Ancient India and Ancient China: Trade and Religious Exchanges, AD 1–600*. New York: Oxford University Press, 1994.

Lösch, August. "The Nature of Economic Regions." In *Regional Development and Planning: A Reader*, ed. John Friedmann. Cambridge, MA: M.I.T. Press, 1964.

Lun piyi cuxi maofa [Rules for Fine Furs]. Reprint, *Zhongguo gudai dangpu jianding miji* [Compilation of ancient Chinese pawnshop appraisals]. Beijing: Quanguo tushuguan wenxian suowei fuzhi zhongxin, 2001.

Luo Yunzhi. *Qingdai Mulan weichang de tantao* [Investigation into the Mulan hunting grounds in the Qing]. Taipei: Wenshizhe chubanshe, 1989.

Macknight, Charles Campbell. *The Voyage to Marege': Macassan Trepangers in Northern Australia*. Carlton, Australia: Melbourne University Press, 1976.

Manbun rōtō [Old Manchu Records], ed. Kanda Nobuo et al. Tokyo: Tōyō Bunko, 1955–1963.

Mancall, Mark. *Russia and China; Their Diplomatic Relations to 1728*. Cambridge, MA: Harvard University Press, 1971.

Mao Xiaolan. *Zhongguo daxing zhenjun* [The macrofungi of China]. Zhengzhou: Henan kexue jishu chubanshe, 2000.

Marcon, Federico. *The Knowledge of Nature and the Nature of Knowledge in Early Modern Japan*. Chicago: The University of Chicago Press, 2015.

Marks, Robert. *Tigers, Rice, Silk, and Silt: Environment and Economy in Late Imperial South China*. New York: Cambridge University Press, 1997.

———. *China: Its Environment and History*. New York: Rowman and Littlefield Publishers, 2012.

Martin, Janet. "The Land of Darkness and the Golden Horde: The Fur Trade under the Mongols, XIII–XIVth Centuries." *Cahiers du Monde russe et soviétique* 19.4 (1978): 401–421.

———. *Treasure in the Land of Darkness: The Fur Trade and Its Significance for Medieval Russia.* New York: Cambridge University Press, 1986.

Martin, P. S., and H. E. Wright. *Pleistocene Extinctions: The Search for a Cause.* New Haven, CT: Yale University Press, 1967.

Matsuda, Matt K. *Pacific Worlds: A History of Seas, Peoples, and Cultures.* New York: Cambridge University Press, 2012.

Matsuura Shigeru. *Shinchō no Amūru seisaku to shōsū minzoku* [Ethnic minorities and policies of the Qing Amur]. Kyoto: Kyōto Daigaku Gakujutsu Shuppankai, 2006.

McKeown, Adam. *Melancholy Order: Asian Migration and the Globalization of Borders.* New York: Columbia University Press, 2008.

McNeill, J. R. "Of Rats and Men: A Synoptic History of the Island Pacific." *Journal of World History* 5.2 (1994): 299–349.

Menzies, Nicholas. *Forest and Land Management in Imperial China.* New York: St. Martin's Press, 1994.

Merchant, Carolyn. *Reinventing Eden: The Fate of Nature in Western Culture.* New York: Routledge, 2003.

———. "Shades of Darkness: Race and Environmental History." *Environmental History* 8.3 (2003): 380–394.

Mi Zhenbo. *Qingdai Zhong-E Qiaketu bianjing maoyi* [Qing Kiakhta trade of the Sino-Russian border]. Tianjin: Nankai daxue chubanshe, 2003.

Miller, Daniel. "Materiality: An Introduction." In *Materiality*, ed. Daniel Miller. Durham, NC: Duke University Press, 2005.

Millward, James. *Beyond the Pass: Economy, Ethnicity, and Empire in Qing Central Asia, 1795–1864.* Stanford, CA: Stanford University Press, 1998.

———. "'Coming onto the Map': 'Western Regions' Geography and Cartographic Nomenclature in the Making of Chinese Empire in Xinjiang." *Late Imperial China* 20.2 (1999): 61–98.

Ming shenzong shilu. See *Ming shilu.*

Ming shilu [Veritable records of the Ming dynasty]. Taipei: Zhongyang yanjiuyuan lishi yuyan yanjiusuo, 1966. [Wanli reign = *Shengzong shilu*]

Mitamura Taisuke, *Shinchō zenshi no kenkyū.* Kyoto: Tōyōshi kenkyūkai, 1965.

Mitchell, Timothy. *Rule of Experts: Egypt, Techno-Politics, Modernity.* Berkeley: University of California Press, 2002.

Mitter, Rana. *The Manchurian Myth: Nationalism, Resistance and Collaboration in Modern China.* Berkeley: University of California Press, 2000.

Miyawaki Junko. "Report on the Manchu Documents Stored at the Mongolian National Central Archives of History." *Saksaha* 4 (1999): 6–13.

———. "Mongoru kokuritsu chūō monjokan shozō no Manjugo, Mongorugo shiryō—toku ni Ifu-furē-Manju daijin no yakusho (Korin ichiji daijin gamon) bunsho ni tsuite" [On the Mongolian National Central Archive's Manchu and

Mongol language historical materials, especially documents from the Khüree ambans' yamen]. *Shi shiryō habu: chiiki bunka kenkyū* 2 (2009), 135–141.

Miyazaki Ichisada. "Shinchō ni okeru kokugo mondai no ichimen" [A look at the question of national language during the Qing]. *Tōhōshi ronsō* 1 (1947): 1–56.

Mizhi xianzhi [Gazetteer for Mizhi County], ed. Gao Zhaoxu. Guangxu reign period. Digital reprint, DFZ.

Monakhov, Vladimir G. "*Martes zibellina* (Carinvora: Mustelidae)." *Mammalian Species* 43 (1): 75-86.

Morris, Clarence, and Derk Bodde. *Law in Imperial China*. Cambridge, MA: Harvard University Press, 1967.

Morton, Timothy. *Ecology without Nature: Rethinking Environmental Aesthetics*. Cambridge, MA: Harvard University Press, 2007.

Mosca, Matthew W. "Empire and the Circulation of Frontier Intelligence: Qing Conceptions of the Ottomans." *Harvard Journal of Asiatic Studies* 70.1 (2010): 147–207.

———. *From Frontier Policy to Foreign Policy*. Stanford, CA: Stanford University Press, 2013.

———. "The Manchu *Zizhi tongjian gangmu* and the Eurasian Transmission of Confucian Historiography." Paper at the Annual Conference of the Association for Asian Studies. Philadelphia, March 29, 2014.

Mostaert, Antoine. "L' 'ouverture du sceau' et les addresses chez les Ordos." *Monumenta Serica* 1 (1935–36): 315–337.

Muscolino, Micah S. *Fishing Wars and Environmental Change in Late Imperial and Modern China*. Cambridge, MA: Harvard University Asia Center, 2009.

Nagazumi Yōko. *Tōsen yushutsunyūhin sūryō ichiran, 1637–1833-nen* [A quantitative look at Chinese maritime imports and exports, 1637–1833]. Tokyo: Sōbunsha, 1987.

Nappi, Carla. *The Monkey and the Inkpot*. Cambridge, MA: Harvard University Press, 2010.

"National Treasures." In *Russia: A Journey with Jonathan Dimbleby*. DVD. Directed by David Wallace. BBC: 2008.

Ngai, Mae M. "Chinese Gold Miners and the 'Chinese Question' in Nineteenth-Century California and Victoria." *Journal of American History* 101.4 (2015): 1082–1105.

Ninghe xianzhi [Gazetteer for Ninghe County], ed. Tan Songling. 1880. Digital reprint, DFZ.

Nongan xianzhi [Gazetteer for Nongan County], ed. Zhu Yidian. 1927. Digital reprint, DFZ.

Norman, Jerry. *A Concise Manchu-English Lexicon*. Seattle: University of Washington Press, 1978.

Nye, David E. *America as Second Creation: Technology and Narratives of New Beginnings*. Cambridge, MA: The MIT Press, 2003.

Ochirin Oyunjargal. *Manzh-Chin ulsaas Mongolchuudig zakhirsan bodlogo: Oiraduudin zhisheen deer* [The Manchu-Qing policy of managing Mongols: The case of the Oirats]. Ulaanbaatar: Arvin Sudar, 2009.

Ogden, Adele. "The Californias in Spain's Pacific Otter Trade, 1775–1795." *Pacific Historical Review* 1.4 (1932): 444–469.

———. "Russian Sea-Otter and Seal Hunting on the California Coast, 1803–1841." *California Historical Society Quarterly* 12.3 (1933): 217–239.

Oka Hiroki. *Shindai Mongoru monki seido no kenkyū* [Research on the league-and-banner system of Qing Mongolia]. Tokyo: Tōhō Shoten, 2007.

Onuma Takahiro. "Political Relations between the Qing Dynasty and Kazakh Nomads in the Mid-18th Century: Promotion of the '*ejen-albatu* Relationship' in Central Asia." In *A Collection of Documents from the Kazakh Sultans to the Qing Dynasty*, ed. Noda Jin and Onuma Takahiro. Tokyo: The University of Tokyo, 2010.

Ouyang Xun. *Yiwen leiju* [Collection of literature arranged by categories]. Shanghai: Shanghai guji chubanshe, 1999.

Oyunbilig [Wuyunbilige]. *Shiqi shiji Menggushi lunkao* [Essays on seventeenth-century Mongol history]. Hohhot: Neimenggu renmin chubanshe, 2009.

Pak Chi-wŏn. *The Jehol Diary*. Folkestone, UK: Global Oriental, 2010.

Pederson, Neil, et al. "Hydrometeorological Reconstructions for Northeastern Mongolia Derived from Tree Rings: 1651–1995." *Journal of Climate* 14 (2000): 872–881.

Perdue, Peter C. *Exhausting the Earth: State and Peasant in Hunan, 1500–1850*. Cambridge, MA: Harvard University Press, 1987.

———. "Military Mobilization in Seventeenth and Eighteenth-Century China, Russia, and Mongolia." *Modern Asian Studies* 30.4 (1996): 757–793.

———. *China Marches West: The Qing Conquest of Central Eurasia*. Cambridge, MA: The Belknap Press of Harvard University Press, 2005.

———. "Nature and Nurture on Imperial China's Frontiers." *Modern Asian Studies* 43.1 (2009): 245–267.

Peschurof, M. M. et al. "Notes on the River Amur and the Adjacent Districts." *Journal of the Royal Geographical Society of London* 28 (1858): 376–446.

PIRE Mongolia Blog. "The Bounty of the Steppe." *Wordpress*. July 25, 2011. Retrieved on August 20, 2015, from https://piremongolia.wordpress.com.

Poland, Henry. *Fur-Bearing Animals in Nature and in Commerce*. London: Gurney & Jackson, 1892.

Pomeranz, Kenneth. *The Great Divergence: China, Europe, and the Making of the Modern World Economy*. Princeton, NJ: Princeton University Press, 2000.

———. "Empire and 'Civilizing' Missions, Past and Present." *Daedalus* 134.2 (2005): 34–45.

Pomeranz, Kenneth, and Steven Topic. *The World That Trade Created: Society, Culture, and the World Economy, 1400 to the Present*. Armonk, NY: M. E. Sharpe, 2006.

Pu Songling. *Xingshi yinyuan chuan* [A romance to awaken the world]. Taipei: Lianjing, 1986.

Puett, Michael. *The Ambivalence of Creation: Debates Concerning Innovation and Artifice in Early China*. Stanford, CA: Stanford University Press, 2001.

Qi Meiqin. *Qingdai neiwufu* [The Qing Imperial Household Department]. Shenyang: Liaoning minzu chubanshe, 2008.

Qi Yunshi. *Huangchao fanbu yaolue* [Outline of the tribes of our august dynasty]. In *Xuxiu siku quanshu*, vol. 740. Shanghai: Shanghai guji chubanshe, 2002.

Qingchao xu wenxian tongkao [Continuation of the *Wenxian tongkao* encyclopedia for the period 1786–1911], ed. Liu Jinzao. Jingshitong edition, 1921. Digital reprint, ZJGK.

Qingdai Elunchunzu Man-Hanwen dang'an huibian [Collection of Manchu- and Chinese-language archives of the Oroncon nationality in the Qing period]. Beijing: Minzu chubanshe, 2001.

Qingdai Sanxing fudutong yamen Man-Hanwen dang'an xuanbian [Selected Manchu- and Chinese-language Qing period archives of the office of the lieutenant governor of Sanxing]. Shenyang: Liaoning guji chubanshe, 1995.

Qinding Rehe zhi [Imperially ordained gazetteer for Rehe], ed. Heshen. 1781. Digital reprint, DFZ.

Qinding shengjing tongzhi [Imperially ordained comprehensive gazetteer for Mukden], comp. Wei Shu. 1736. Reprint, Taipei: Wenhai chubanshe, 1965.

Ratzel, Friedrich. *Politische Geographie*. Munich: R. Oldenbourg, 1897.

Ravenstein, Ernst Georg. *The Russians on the Amur: Its Discovery, Conquest, and Colonization, with a Description of the Country, Its Inhabitants, Productions, and Commercial Capabilities; and Personal Accounts of Russian Travellers*. London: Trübner and Co., 1861.

Rawski, Evelyn. *The Last Emperors: A Social History of Qing Imperial Institutions*. Berkeley: University of California Press, 1998.

Reading, Richard, et al. "The Commercial Harvest of Wildlife in Dornod Aimag, Mongolia." *Journal of Wildlife Management* 62.1 (1998): 59–71.

Reardon-Anderson, James. *Reluctant Pioneers: China's Expansion Northward, 1644–1937*. Stanford, CA: Stanford University Press, 2005.

Reid, Anthony. "Chinese Trade and Southeast Asian Economic Expansion in the Later Eighteenth and Early Nineteenth Centuries: An Overview." In *Water Frontier: Commerce and the Chinese in the Lower Mekong Region, 1750–1880*, eds. Nola Cooke and Li Tana. Lanham, MD: Rowman and Littlefield Publishers, 2004.

Reidman, Marianne L. and James A. Estes. "The Sea Otter (*Enhydra lutris*): Behavior, Ecology, and Natural History." *Biological Report* 90.14: 1990.

Reinhardt, J.C. "Report of J.C. Reinhardt, Naturalist." *Proceedings of the National Institution for the Promotion of Science* 4 (1846): 533–567.

Richards, John F. *The Unending Frontier*. Berkeley: University of California Press, 2006.

Ripa, Matteo. *Memoirs of Father Ripa, during Thirteen Years' Residence at the Court of Peking in the Service of the Emperor of China; with an Account of the Foundation of the College for the Education of Young Chinese at Naples.* London: J. Murray, 1855.

Roberts, J. A. G. *A History of China.* New York: Palgrave Macmillan, 2011.

Rogaski, Ruth. *Hygienic Modernity: Meanings of Health and Disease in Treaty-Port China.* Berkeley: University of California Press, 2004.

Ropp, Paul. *China in World History.* New York: Oxford University Press, 2010.

Rorex, Robert A., and Wen Fong. *Eighteen Songs of a Nomad Flute: The Story of Lady Wen-chi.* New York: Metropolitan Museum of Art, 1974.

Ruan Kuisheng. *Chayu kehua* [Talks with guests over tea]. 12 *juan.* Taipei: Xinyu, 1973.

Rutt, Richard. "James Gale's Translation of the Yonhaeng-nok, an Account of the Korean Embassy to Peking, 1712–1713." *Transactions of the Royal Asiatic Society, Korea Branch* 49 (1974): 55–144.

Saarela, Mårten Söderblom. "*Shier zitou jizhou* (Collected notes on the twelve heads): A Recently Discovered Work by Shen Qiliang." *Saksaha* 12 (2014): 9–31.

Salvadori, Philippe. *La Chasse sous l'ancien régime.* Paris: Fayard, 1996.

Sanjdorji, M. *Manchu Chinese Colonial Rule in Northern Mongolia.* New York: St. Martin's Press, 1980.

Sanxing fudutong yamen Manwen dang'an yibian [Translated selections from the Manchu archives of the office of the lieutenant governor of Sanxing]. Shenyang: Liaoshen shushe, 1984.

Schafer, Edward H. *The Golden Peaches of Samarkand: A Study in T'ang Exotics.* Berkeley: University of California Press, 1963.

Schama, Simon. *Landscape and Memory.* New York: Alfred A. Knopf, 1995.

Scott, James C. *Seeing Like a State: How Certain Schemes to Improve the Human Condition Have Failed.* New Haven, CT: Yale University Press, 1998.

———. *The Art of Not Being Governed: An Anarchist History of Upland Southeast Asia.* New Haven, CT: Yale University Press, 2009.

Sejong sillok. See *Chosŏn wangjo sillok.*

Serruys, Henry. "Smallpox in Mongolia during the Ming and Ch'ing Dynasties." *Zentralasiatische Studien des Seminars für Sprach- und Kulturwissenschaft Zentralasiens der Universitet Bonn* 14 (1980): 41–63.

Shangyu baqi/Dergi hese jakūn gūsade wasimbuhangge [Edicts to the Eight Banners]. 10 *ce.*

Shapiro, Judith. *China's Environmental Challenges.* Malden, MA: Polity Press, 2012.

Shin, Leo Kwok-yueh. *The Making of the Chinese State: Ethnicity and Expansion on the Ming Borderlands.* New York: Cambridge University Press, 2006.

Shuntian fuzhi [Gazetteer for Shuntian Prefecture], ed. Zhang Zhidong. 1889. Digital reprint, DFZ.

Shunyi xianzhi [Gazetteer for Shunyi County], ed. Yang Dexin. 1933. Digital reprint, DFZ.

Skinner, William G. "Marketing and Social Structure in Rural China: Part I." *Journal of Asian Studies* 24.1 (1964): 3–43.

Sneath, David. *The Headless State: Aristocratic Orders, Kinship Society, and Misrepresentations of Nomadic Inner Asia.* New York: Columbia University Press, 2007.

Snyder, Gary. *The Practice of the Wild.* Berkeley, CA: Counterpoint, 1990.

Sommer, Matthew. *Sex, Law, and Society in Late Imperial China.* Stanford, CA: Stanford University Press, 2000.

Sonoda Kazuki. *Dattan hyōryūki* [Record of castaways in Tartary]. Tokyo: Heibonsha, 1991.

Soulé, Michael E., and Gary Lease. *Reinventing Nature? Responses to Postmodern Deconstruction.* Washington DC: Island Press, 1995.

Spence, Jonathan. *Emperor of China: Self Portrait of K'ang-Hsi.* New York: Vintage Books, 1988.

Struve, Lynn A. *Voices from the Ming–Qing Cataclysm: China in Tigers' Jaws.* New Haven, CT: Yale University Press, 1993.

Su Xiaokang and Perry Ling. "A Collapsing Natural Environment?" In *Restless China*, eds. Perry Link, Richard P. Madsen, and Paul G. Pickowicz. New York: Rowman & Littlefield Publishers, Inc., 2013.

Sun, E-Tu Zen. "Ch'ing Government and the Mineral Industries before 1800." *The Journal of Asian Studies* 27.4 (1968): 835–845.

Sun Laichen, "From *Baoshi* to *Feicui*: Qing–Burmese Gem Trade, c. 1644–1800." In *Chinese Circulations: Capital Commodities, and Networks in Southeast Asia*, eds. Eric Tagliacozzo and Wen-Chin Chang. Durham, NC: Duke University Press, 2011.

Sutherland, Heather. "A Sino–Indonesian Commodity Chain: The Trade in Tortoiseshell in the Late Seventeenth and Eighteenth Centuries." In *Chinese Circulations: Capital Commodities, and Networks in Southeast Asia*, eds. Eric Tagliacozzo and Wen-Chin Chang. Durham, NC: Duke University Press, 2011.

Sutō Yoshiyuki. "Shinchō ni okeru Manshū chūbō no tokushūsei ni kansuru ichi kōsatsu [An examination of the particular nature of banner garrisons in Manchuria during the Qing]." *Tōhō gakuhō* 11.1 (1940): 176–203.

Symons, Van Jay. *Ch'ing Ginseng Management: Ch'ing Monopolies in Microcosm.* Tempe: Arizona State University Center for Asian Studies, 1981.

Szonyi, Michael. *Practicing Kinship: Strategies of Descent and Lineage in Late Imperial China.* Stanford, CA: Stanford University Press, 2002.

Tamamura Jitsuzō, Imanishi Shunjū, and Satō Hisashi. *Gotai Shin bunkan yakukai* [The annotated Pentaglot Dictionary]. Kyoto: Kyōto daigaku bungakubu nairiku ajia kenkyūjo, 1966–1968.

Tan Qian. *Beiyoulu* [Record of a Journey North]. Beijing: Qinghua shuju, 1997.

Tanesaka Eiji, Fukata Shuzo, Okada Mieko, and Kinugawa Kenjiro. *"Mongoru sōgenni jiseisuru* tricholoma mongolicum *Imai* [*Tricholoma mongolicum* Imai in Mongolian grasslands (steppe)]." *Memoirs of the Faculty of Agriculture of Kinki University* 26 (1993): 33–37.

Tarasov, P. P. "Intraspecific Relations [Territoriality] in Sable and Ermine." In *Biology of Mustelids: Some Soviet Research, Volume 2.* Wellington, NZ: Science Information Service, Department of Scientific and Industrial Research, 1980.

Tegoborski, Ludwik. *Commentaries on the Productive Forces of Russia: Volume 2.* London: Longman, Brown, Green and Longmans, 1856.

Teng, Emma. *Taiwan's Imagined Geography: Chinese Colonial Travel Writing and Pictures, 1683–1895.* Cambridge, MA: Harvard University Asia Center, 2006.

Terauchi Itarō. "Kyŏngwŏn *kaesi* to Hunchun" [The Kyŏngwŏn *kaesi* and Hunchun]. *Tōhōgakū* 69 (1985): 76–90.

Thomas, Julia Adeney. *Reconfiguring Modernity: Concepts of Nature in Japanese Political Ideology.* Berkeley: University of California Press, 2001.

Thongchai Winichakul. *Siam Mapped: A History of the Geo-Body of a Nation.* Honolulu: Univeresity of Hawaii Press, 1994.

Timkovskii, Egor Fedorovich. *Travels of the Russian Mission through Mongolia to China and Residence in Pekin, in the Years 1820–1821.* London: Longman, Rees, Orme, Brown, and Green, 1827.

Tong Yonggong. *Manyuwen yu Manwen dang'an yanjiu* [Research on the Manchu language and Manchu-language archives]. Shenyang: Liaoning minzu chubanshe, 2009.

Torbert, Preston M. *The Ch'ing Imperial Household Department.* Cambridge, MA: Harvard University Press, 1977.

Tsing, Anna Lowenhaupt. "Natural Resources and Capitalist Frontiers." *Economic and Political Weekly* 38.48 (2003): 5100–5106.

Tucker, Mary Evelyn, and John Berthrong, *Confucianism and Ecology: The Interrelation of Heaven, Earth, and Humans.* Cambridge, MA: Harvard University Press, 1998.

Tulišen. *Lakcaha jecen de takūraha babe ejehe bithe / Manhan yiyulu* [Record of a Mission to the Distant Border]. Taipei: Wenshizhe chubanshe, 1983.

Tuo-tuo. *Songshi* [History of the Song]. Taipei: Dingwen shuju, 1980.

Tuttle, Gray. "Tibetan Buddhism at Wutai Shan in the Qing," *Journal of the International Association of Tibetan Studies* 6 (2011): 163–214.

Uekoetter, Frank. *The Green and the Brown: A History of Conservation in Nazi Germany.* New York: Cambridge University Press, 2006.

Uyama Tomohiko. "Research Trends in the Former Soviet Central Asian Countries." In *Research Trends in Modern Central Eurasian Studies (18th–20th Centuries),* eds. Stéphane A. Dudoignon and Komatsu Hisao. Tokyo: Toyo Bunko, 2003.

Vainshtein, Sevyan. *Nomads of South Siberia: The Pastoral Economies of Tuva.* New York: Cambridge University Press, 1980.

Veale, Elspeth. *The English Fur Trade in the Later Middle Ages*. London: London Record Society, 2003.

"A Very Important and Magnificent Imperial Pearl Court Necklace (Chao Zhu) Qing Dynasty, 18th Century." *Sotheby's Fine Chinese Ceramics and Works of Art*. 2010. Sotheby's. Retrieved on March 12, 2012, from www.sothebys .com/en/catalogues/ ecatalogue.html/2010/ fine-chinese-ceramics-works-of-art-hko323#/r=/en/ ecat.fhtml.HKo323.html+r.m=/en/ecat.lot.HKo323 .html/1813/.

Vogel, Hans Ulrich, and Günter Dux. *Concepts of Nature: A Chinese–European Cross-Cultural Perspective*. Boston: Brill, 2010.

Volkova, M.P. *Opisanie Man'chzhurskikh khisolografov Insituta vostokovedeniia AN SSSR* [Description of Manchu xylographs of the Oriental Institute of the Academia of Sciences of the USSR]. Moskow: Nauka, 1988.

Vorha, Ranbir. *Lao She and the Chinese Revolution*. Cambridge, MA: Harvard University Asia Center, 1974.

Wakeman, Frederick Jr. *The Great Enterprise: The Manchu Reconstruction of Imperial Order in Seventeenth-Century China*. Berkeley: University of California Press, 1985.

Waley-Cohen, Joanna. "The New Qing History." *Radical History Review* 88 (2003): 193–206.

Walker, Brett L. *The Conquest of Ainu Lands: Ecology and Culture in Japanese Expansion, 1590–1800*. Berkeley: University of California Press, 2001.

———. "Foreign Affairs and Frontiers in Early Modern Japan: A Historiographical Essay." *Early Modern Japan: An Interdisciplinary Journal* 10.2 (2002): 44–62.

Wang Jianzhong. *Dongbei diqu shi shenghuo shi* [History of the life of food in the Northeast]. Harbin: Heilongjiang renmin chubanshe, 2004.

Wang Lihua, ed. *Zhongguo lishishang de huanjing yu shehui* [Environment and society in Chinese history]. Beijing: SDX Joint Publishing Co., 2007.

Wang Peihuan. "Qingdai dongbei caishenye de xingshuai" [The rise and fall of the ginseng-picking business in the Qing Northeast]. *Shehui kexue zhanxian* 4 (1982): 189–192.

———. *Yige dengshang longting de minzu: Manzu shuihui yu gongting* [A nation that ascended the dragon throne: Manchu society and the court]. Shenyang: Liaoning minzu chubanshe, 2006.

Wang Xuemei and Zhai Jingyuan. "Qingdai dasheng wula de dongzhu caibu" [The collection of Manchurian pearls by the Hunter Ula in the Qing period]. *Beifan wenwu* 2 (2012): 76–80.

Wang Yeh-chien. *Land Taxation in Imperial China, 1750–1911*. Cambridge, MA: Harvard University Press, 1973.

Warren, James Francis. *The Sulu Zone, 1768–1898: The Dynamics of External Trade, Slavery, and Ethnicity in the Transformation of a Southeast Asian Maritime State*. Singapore: NUS Press, 2007.

Wei Ying. *Qingdai jingqi huitun wenti yanjiu* [Research on the problem of capital bannermen on state farms in Manchuria in the Qing period]. Harbin: Heilongjiang daxue chubanshe, 2009.

Wei Yuan, *Shengwu ji* [Record of military glories]. Daoguang edition. Digital reprint, ZJGK.

Weiner, Douglas. *Models of Nature: Ecology, Conservation, and Cultural Revolution in Soviet Russia*. Pittsburgh, PA: University of Pittsburgh Press, 2000.

Weller, Robert P. *Discovering Nature: Globalization and Environmental Culture in China and Taiwan*. New York: Cambridge University Press, 2006.

White, Richard. *"It's Your Misfortune, and None of My Own": A History of the American West*. Norman: University of Oklahoma Press, 1991.

———. *The Middle Ground: Indians, Empires, and Republics in the Great Lakes Region, 1650–1815*. New York: Cambridge University Press, 2007.

Williams, Raymond. *Keywords: A Vocabulary of Culture and Society*. New York: Oxford University Press, 2015.

Wong, Roy Bin. *China Transformed: Historical Change and the Limits of European Experience*. Ithaca: Cornell University Press, 1997.

Worster, Donald. "Transformations of the Earth: Toward an Agroecological Perspective in History." *The Journal of American History* 76.4 (1990): 1087–1106.

———. *An Unsettled Country: Changing Landscapes of the American West*. Albuquerque: University of New Mexico Press, 1994.

Wu Feng and Bao Qingde. *Mengguzu shengtai zhihuilun: Neimenggu caoyuan shengtai huifu yu chongjian yanjiu* [Discussing the ecological wisdom of the Mongol nationality: Research on the ecological restoration and revival of the Inner Mongolian steppe]. Shenyang: Liaoning minzu chubanshe, 2009.

Wu Xiqi. *Youzhengwei zhai ciji* [*Ci* poems from the studio of true taste]. Revised edition, 1808. Digital reprint, ZJGK.

Wu Zhengge. *Manzu shisu yu Qinggong yushan* [Manchu food culture and Qing court cuisine]. Shenyang: Liaoning kexue jishu chubanshe, 1988.

———. *Qianlong huangdi yushan kaoshu* [Study of the Qianlong emperor's cuisine]. Beijing: Zhongguo shipin chubanshe, 1990

Wuliyasutai zhilue [Draft Gazetteer of Uliasutai]. Taipei: Chengwen chubanshe, 1968.

Wurenqiqige. *18–20 shijichu Guihuacheng Tumete caizheng yanjiu* [Research on government finances of the Tumet of Guihua city in the 18th to early 20th centuries]. Beijing: Minzu chubanshe, 2008.

Xiuyan xianzhi [Gazetteer for Xiuyan County], ed. Hao Yupu. 1928. Digital reprint, DFZ.

Xu Ke. *Qingbai leichao* [Classified collection of Qing notes]. Beijing: Zhonghua shuju, 1984.

Xu Shuming. "Qingmo Heilongjiang yimin yu nongye kaifa" [Late Qing migrants to Heilongjiang and the opening of agriculture] *Qingshi yanjiu* 2 (1991).

Xu Yongnian. *Dumen jilue* [Guide to the Capital]. Taipei: Wenhai chubanshe, 1971.

Xuzeng xing'an huilan [Addendum to the conspectus of legal cases], comp. Bao Shuyun and Zhu Qingqi. 1840. Reprint. Taipei: Chengwen chubanshe, 1968.

Yanagasiwa Akira. "Shinchō tōchiki no kokuryūkō chiku ni okeru shominzoku no keisei saihen, katei no kenkyū" [Research on the form and process of re-organization of the various nationalities of Heilongjiang territory under Qing rule]. Research Report, Waseda University, 2007. https://dspace.wul.waseda.ac.jp/dspace/bitstream/2065/34041/1/Kakenhi_Yanagisawa.pdf.

Yang Yang. *Ming–Qing dongbeiya shuilu sichou zhi lu yu Xiayi jin yanjiu* [Research on Ainu brocade and the maritime and continental silk roads in Northeast Asia during the Ming and Qing periods]. Shenyang: Liaohai chubanshe, 2001.

———. *Mingdai dongbei jiangyu yanjiu* [Research on the territory of the north-east in the Ming]. Changchun: Jilin renmin chubanshe, 2008.

Yang Yulian. *Qingdai dongbeishi* [History of the Northeast in the Qing dynasty]. Shenyang: Liaoning jiaoyu chubanshe, 1991.

Yazan, Y. P. "Relations between the Marten (*Martes martes*), Sable (*Martes zibellina*) and Kidas (*M. martes x M. zibellina*) as predators, and the Squirrel (*Sciurus vulgaris*) as Prey." In *Biology of Mustelids: Some Soviet Research, Volume 2*, ed. C. M. King. Wellington: Science Information Service, Department of Scientific and Industrial Research, 1980.

Ye Longli. *Qidan guozhi* [Gazatteer of the Khitan state]. *27 juan.* Shanghai: Shanghai guji chubanshe, 1985.

Yongzheng shangyu neige [Edicts of the Yongzheng reign issued through the Grand Secretariat]. *Wenyuange Siku quanshu* edition. Issued in 1731 and 1741. Digital reprint, ZJGK.

Yuan Mei. *Suiyuan shidan* [The Suiyuan recipes]. Revised edition, 1796. Digital reprint, ZJGK.

Yushandan [Menu of imperial meals]. 1910. Digital reprint, ZJGK.

Yuzhi Manzhu Menggu Hanzi sanhe qieyin Qingwen jian [Imperially ordained Manchu, Mongol, Chinese trilingual dictionary for phonetic analysis], eds. Agui et al. 1780. Reprint, *Jingyin Wenyuange Siku quanshu* 234. Taipei: Taiwan shangwu yinshuguan, 1983.

Zeng Weizhi. "Songdai maopi maoyi" [Fur trade in the Song period]. MA thesis, Chinese Culture University, Taipei, 2008.

Zhang Jie. *Hanguo shiliao sanzhong yu Shengjing manzu yanjiu* [Three types of Korean historical materials and research into the Manchus of Shengjing]. Shenyang: Liaoning minzu chubanshe, 2009.

Zhang Zhengming. *Jinshang xingshuai shi* [History and rise and decline of Shanxi merchants]. Taiyuan: Shanxi guji chubanshe, 2001.

————. *Mingqing jinshang ji minsheng* [Shanxi merchants and folkways in the Ming and Qing periods]. Beijing: Renmin chubanshe, 2003.

Zhao Xiong. "Guanyu Qingdai dasheng wula dongzhu caibuye de jige wenti" [Some problems on Manchurian pearl collection by the Hunter Ula in the Qing period]. *Lishi dang'an* (1984): 79–85.

Zhao Zhen. *Qingdai xibei shengtai bianqian yanjiu* [Research on ecological change in the Northwest during the Qing]. Beijing: Renmin chubanshe, 2005.

Zhao Zhongfu. *Jinshi dongsansheng yanjiu lunwenji* [Collected essays on the study of the Three Eastern Provinces' modern history]. Taipei: Chengwen chubanshe youxian gongsi, 1999.

Zhao-lian. *Xiaoting zalu* [Miscellaneous notes from the whistling pavilion]. 10 *juan*. 1814–1826. Beijing: Zhonghua shuju, 1980.

Zhongguo jiben guji ku [Database of Chinese Classic Ancient Books]. Beijing: Beijing Airusheng shuzihua jishu yanjiu zhongxin, 2009. http://server .wenzibase.com/dblist.jsp.

Zhou Chengwang, Dong Huimin, and Zhao Jiangping. *Longjiang sanji* [Three records of the dragon river]. Harbin: Heilongjiang renmin chubanshe, 1985.

Zhou Xiang. "Qingdai maopi maoyizhong de Guangzhou yu Qiaketu" [The Qing period fur trade of Canton and Kiakhta] *Zhongshan daxue xuebao luncong* 20.3 (2000): 85–94.

————. "Yiwu yu shangwu—yi Guangzhou kouan maopi jinyun shijian wei li" [Barbarian and business affairs: The case of the embargo on the Canton fur trade]. *Zhongshan daxue xuebao* 40.2 (2000): 85–91.

Zhu Sa. *18–20 shijichu dongbu Neimenggu nongcun luohua yanjiu* [Research on eastern Inner Mongolia's agricultural villages' decline in the 18th to early 20th centuries]. Hohhot: Neimenggu renmin chubanshe, 2009.

Zucchino, David. "Smoky Mountains National Park a Hotbed for Ginseng Poaching." *Los Angeles Times*, August 10, 2013. Web. 22 February 2015. Retrieved from http://articles.latimes.com/2013/aug/10/nation/la-na-ginseng-rustlers-20130811.

INDEX